France, the United States,
and the Algerian War

France,
the United States,
and the Algerian War

Irwin M. Wall

UNIVERSITY OF CALIFORNIA PRESS
Berkeley · Los Angeles · London

University of California Press
Berkeley and Los Angeles, California

University of California Press, Ltd.
London, England

© 2001 by
The Regents of the University of California

Library of Congress Cataloging-in-Publication Data

Wall, Irwin M.
    France, the United States, and the Algerian
War / Irwin M. Wall.
        p. cm.
    Includes bibliographical references and index.
    ISBN 0-520-22534-1 (cloth : alk. paper)
    1. Algeria—History—Revolution,
    1954–1962—Diplomatic history.   2. France—
    Foreign relations—United States.   3. United
    States—Foreign relations—France.
    4. France—Foreign relations—1945–1958.
    5. France—Foreign relations—1958–1969.
    6. United States—1953–1961.   I. Title.

    DT295 .W26 2001
    965'.046—dc21   2001017326

Printed in the United States of America
08 07 06 05 04 03 02 01
10 9 8 7 6 5 4 3 2 1

For Sarah

Contents

Illustrations

Preface

I first conceived of this book as a kind of sequel to my previous one, *The United States and the Making of Postwar France, 1945–1954*. Having examined the critical American role in the foundation and early functioning of the Fourth French Republic, I became curious to see how American influence figured in the Republic's collapse in May 1958, and in the eventual predictable outcome of the Algerian War, which precipitated that collapse and brought de Gaulle to power. The State Department records at the National Archives in Washington, D.C. were the obvious focus of my concern. In the meantime, however, the volumes of the French series of Diplomatic Documents were rolling off the presses. I had worked on the materials dealing with U.S.-French relations in the Quai d'Orsay, but I had not suspected, until the appearance of those volumes, which cover all of French diplomacy, just how much the Algerian question dominated the entire functioning of France in the world from 1954 to 1962; especially surprising was the continuity the documents revealed between the international relations of the Fourth Republic and the foreign policy of de Gaulle.

Whatever hypotheses I began with, and they were vague at the outset, do not resemble the theses contained in what follows. I did not expect, when I began, to find official Washington welcoming de Gaulle to power, nor did I expect the American documents to reveal so many details about the inner workings of the Fourth Republic and its conflicts with its military and colonial bureaucracy. Chapter 4, on the

Sakiet crisis, is therefore a kind of excursus; between American sources and the French military archives at Vincennes, I believe I have been able to explain, at least better than has been done so far, the workings of the military-civilian problems that led to the Republic's collapse. As a specialist on modern France, I apologize for what international historians of the period might consider excessive detail. Again, my findings surprised me: it was not so much the bureaucracy or the military disobeying the governments of the Fourth Republic as the fact that cabinet government itself had broken down that explains the crisis of the regime. Governments were paralyzed by their own internal divisions, and ministers pursued their own policies like so many feudal barons. This in turn exasperated the British and the Americans, who found the regime dysfunctional in terms of the needs of Western security; the Americans helped to topple it when they knew the alternative was de Gaulle.

In 1990 the Fondation Charles de Gaulle sponsored a week-long conference of scholars to celebrate the centenary of the birth of the man of June 18. Assignments were given to foreign scholars, who were invited to search their national archives so as to shed light upon the international brilliance, the *rayonnement* of de Gaulle's influence around the world. Among the often impressive array of international persons invited Americans seemed the most numerous; my modest assignment was de Gaulle and Truman, which of course has little to do with what follows. Nor is the point that doing that piece got me a free trip to Paris. The point is rather that I then shared the French admiration for de Gaulle, as did, I believe, most of those who attended, although I was skeptical of the virtual absence of criticism of him that characterized both the conference itself and the "preparatory conferences" that preceded it. Indeed, following the preparatory conference at Columbia I was quoted by the *New York Times* as characterizing the proceedings as the "canonization of a Saint." But I was only lamenting the absence of discussion of the student-worker revolt of May 1968 that drove de Gaulle from power. I nevertheless believed at the time, like everyone else, that whatever his faults, the man who restored French dignity by founding the Free French in 1940 was also the man who carefully and methodically extricated France from its Algerian burden after 1958, and launched France on a resolute policy of independence geared toward the creation of a multipolar as opposed to a bipolar world.

Here again the documents surprised me. In writing this book I believe I "discovered," in the old-fashioned sense of history as a scientific record rather than fictional "emplotment," that, contrary to what most historians have believed, de Gaulle instead intended to keep Algeria French, that he never meant to disappoint the hopes of the constituencies which had brought him to power, and that the Algerian War underlay practically all his diplomatic initiatives from 1958 to 1962, which were designed to achieve that end. The major reason for the failure of de Gaulle's diplomatic initiatives from 1958 to 1962 was his inability to convince the Americans to cooperate with him; only then did he begin to think about diplomatic "independence." What was planned as a concluding chapter on how de Gaulle brought an end to the Fourth Republic's Algerian agony, therefore, became three chapters on how he escalated the war and prolonged that agony unnecessarily, ensuring that the war's end took place in the worst conditions that anyone could have imagined: amid an unprecedented outbreak of European-sponsored terrorism, followed by a chaotic withdrawal and resettlement in France of virtually all of the one million-plus settler population of Algeria, many of whose families had lived there for generations and had known no other home. If I am right, de Gaulle will join many other giants who in our estimation must be regarded as having had at least one foot made of clay.

During the writing of this book I have incurred a great many debts, which it is a pleasure to acknowledge. A number of respected colleagues, whom I am privileged to regard also as friends, read and commented on the completed manuscript: Gérard Bossuat, William Cohen, Helmut Gruber, Fred Logevall, David Schalk, and John Sweets. Other friends provided help and input along the way, in particular John Kim Munholland, Richard Kuisel, and Wayne Northcutt. Sheila Levine helped me through the review process at UC Press. The librarians and archivists who helped are too many to mention, but the interlibrary loan people of the University of California, Riverside deserve special thanks. I received financial help from several sources, all of them UC-connected, which says much for the research support that this institution provides to its faculty. In my case it is a pleasure to thank the Institute on Conflict and Cooperation at La Jolla, the Institute for German and European Studies in Berkeley, and the Research Committee of the Academic Senate of the University of California, Riverside. Everything I have done throughout my career has been in the final analysis for my wife, Sarah, and daughter, Alix, who as "the other writer in the family" has brought us no end of joy. The interpretation offered here is controversial, and the errors readers may find in the text regrettable; for both, alas, the responsibility is entirely my own.

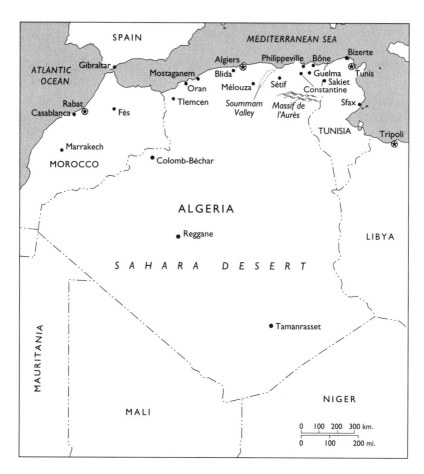

Algeria under French rule.

Introduction

The French war to keep Algeria coincided with eight years of Cold War history during which much of the world was transformed. The war began on All Saints Day, November 1, 1954, more than a year after the death of Stalin and only a few months after the Geneva agreements ending the Indochina War in June 1954. The conflict ended in March 1962, only months before the Cuban crisis of October of that year inaugurated an era of détente. During the Algerian War Britain and France invaded Egypt in an effort to hold on to the Suez Canal, while the Soviets invaded Hungary (1956), and the United States went to the brink of nuclear war with China over the islands of Quemoy and Matsu in 1959. The European Economic Community began operations in January 1959, an American U2 spy plane was downed over the USSR, disrupting a summit conference in May 1960, while the Berlin crisis, which opened in November 1958, monopolized much of the international news until it was awkwardly settled with the construction of the Berlin Wall in August 1961. This was also a period when North-South questions came to the fore, challenging the placid assumptions of politicians focused on Cold War questions at issue between East and West. The Bandung Conference of nonaligned nations met in April 1955, and fifteen new countries entered the United Nations the same year. By the Algerian War's end, the United Nations had eighty-seven member states, the majority of them Asian and African and passionately anticolonial.

The Fourth Republic came to an ignominious end in May 1958 with the coming to power of Charles de Gaulle, while in the United States two years later John F. Kennedy was elected president of the United States to succeed Dwight D. Eisenhower.

The Algerian War had an impact on, and was in turn affected by, all these changes and crises. France regarded itself during this time, and had been courteously permitted to act after the war by the United States and Great Britain, as a great power, one of the so-called big three. But the Algerian War consumed all of French energies and dominated political debate in France after 1954, with the result that in international politics France came to count for little. During the first half of the war, until 1958, French troops were withdrawn from NATO for use in Algeria while governments in Paris displayed characteristic indecision and instability. During the war's second half, from 1958 to 1962, de Gaulle made a heroic effort to reassert France's international position but found virtually every initiative blocked by the "running sore" of Algeria, until he finally recognized Algerian independence in 1962.

Six chief executives attempted to deal with France's Algerian problem in the eight years of the war: Pierre Mendès France (June 1954–February 1955), Edgar Faure (February 1955–January 1956), Guy Mollet (January 1956–May 1957), Maurice Bourgès-Maunoury (May–November 1957), Felix Gaillard (November 1957–May 1958), and Charles de Gaulle; seven, if one counts the interim attempt by Pierre Pflimlin to deal with the May 1958 crisis from the 13th to the 28th of that month. All these men pursued the same policies in Algeria in which they were more or less representative of the French political class as a whole: they meant to keep Algeria dominated by France, although all of them toyed with the idea of limited internal autonomy, the minimum necessary to satisfy the Americans and international opinion, while at the same time hoping that programs of economic development and social reform could eventually win the Muslim population over to French rule. None of these men were free to do as they wanted in Algeria and all of them pursued failed policies; it fell to Charles de Gaulle, whose policies were no more successful than his predecessors' had been, to grant Algeria what only pitifully few French people had recognized as inevitable as early as 1954—independence. The price of failure was the loss of about 25,000 French and 300,000 Muslim lives, the squandering of countless billions of francs, continual currency and financial crises in France despite ever-burgeoning national wealth, and the erosion of France's international position to the point that when de Gaulle was once again able to assert France's will in international affairs he could be safely ignored.

The current work attempts to put the Algerian War in an international context, to deal with it as a world crisis and not simply a French one. For France was severely constrained in the prosecution of the war by international realities: the Cold War, Soviet ambitions in the Middle East and North Africa, the aspirations of the Third World for independence, its own forced process of decolonization of North and Black French Africa, and the attitudes of its European allies. But first and above all stood the problem of French relations with the United States. At times American influence manifested itself in tandem with that of Great Britain. As much as France aspired to independence from American or Anglo-American dictates and freedom from their yoke, it had to recognize the reality that no policy was possible without their agreement or toleration and that no action was free from their influence. The British recognized the overwhelming importance of the Americans to their own policies after their attempt to pursue an independent policy with France and Israel during the Suez crisis; Anthony Eden was forced ignominiously to resign after that failure and Harold Macmillan firmly set England on a course of faithful second to the United States, calculating that Britain could count for more as trusted advisor to the Americans than as independent ally and occasional adversary. France took the opposite path of "independence," initiated by the premiers of the Fourth Republic but later symbolized by the policies of de Gaulle, which built upon and differed little from those of the Fourth Republic. French historians have seized upon that "independence" as a hallmark of de Gaulle's prescience and greatness while ignoring the role of his predecessors. It remained, for all that, severely limited by the international constraints of the Cold War and by American hegemony.

A second theme here is to demonstrate the links between France's turbulent internal politics and its international relations, and to gauge the influence on internal French politics exercised by external powers, in particular the United States. To be sure, the Americans no longer exercised the heavy-handed influence in French internal affairs characteristic of the period from 1947 to 1954. During that period, armed with extensive programs of financial assistance in the form of the Marshall Plan, the Military Defense and Assistance Pact of 1950, a variety of "Off-Shore" schemes to help the French balance of payments by contracting out to France the production of NATO (and French) armaments, and finally direct aid to finance the Indochina War, Washington was able to exercise considerable influence in French internal affairs. With the advice of a sophisticated and talented group of experts on French politics and society, some extraordinarily capable American ambassadors used the extensive resources of the State Department and the Economic Cooperation Administration to influence the course of French politics by direct relationships with French interest groups, the press, the trade unions, and political parties. The Central Intelligence Agency also funneled a considerable amount of money into France in an attempt to strengthen pro-American French politicians; much of this was channeled through the AFL-CIO with the intent of strengthening noncommunist trade unions in France. American ambassadors directly tried to stabilize French governments and support a "third force" center of the political spectrum against simultaneous threats posed by the Communist party and, to a lesser extent, by Charles de Gaulle, at the time regarded as a dangerous adventurer and would-be dictator. This form of intervention, both financial and political, came to an end with the government of Pierre Mendès France in 1954 and the end of the Indochina War, during which French and American policies radically diverged.

Whatever the activities from 1954 to 1962 of the CIA, whose archives remain classified, the American Embassy clearly pursued a hands-off policy in terms of relations with French political groups after 1954. While some French politicians continued to frequent the American Embassy and provide confidential information, this was usually with the intent of influencing American policy in the direction they favored; Washington listened and acted according to its own counsel, although after 1957 it relied increasingly on the British for advice on how to deal with France in particular, but also with Europe as a whole. However, Washington was always aware of the fragile nature of French coalitions and troubled by French ministerial instability, and France's Algerian problem after 1956 became increasingly an American concern, hampering Washington's relations with the Arab world, Africa, and Asia, to the extent that American support of France was perceived as the main ingredient that enabled France to carry on the Algerian struggle. Much of the war was fought with American weapons; in that the rebels fought with captured American weapons at the start this became true of both sides. But further, the Americans were painfully aware that the stability of French internal politics, and by extension the entire structure of NATO and the West, were capable of being upset by precipitate American actions with regard to Algeria, which Paris stubbornly insisted was an internal French problem. Washington was expected to do nothing other than support its French ally.

As the war wore on, this policy revealed itself to the Americans as more and more bankrupt, while every attempt to pressure the French was frustrated by the continued political chaos and paralysis of the Fourth Republic. The Fourth Republic was incapable of bringing peace to Algeria: it could neither win the war nor amass a majority that could negotiate peace while keeping at bay the extensive colonial lobby in France and the infrastructure behind it, the representatives of the settlers in Algeria themselves, and, increasingly, a more and more rebellious army. The realization grew in Washington that the policy of preserving the Fourth Republic come what may, for fear of encouraging a regime of right or left, was precisely the problem. The Fourth Republic had to be abandoned if peace was to emerge; and the alternative of abandoning it looked less and less dangerous as it became apparent that this alternative was much less likely to be a popular front government of the left including the Communists than a conservative semiauthoritarian regime under de Gaulle. And whatever the outlook for de Gaulle's likely policies in Algeria—as yet it was not apparent that he would pursue peace there by any means short of military victory—it was clear that a regime dominated by him would alone be capable of bringing a resolution to the problem by one means or another. The Fourth Republic was paralyzed because anything it did might provoke its collapse and bring de Gaulle to power. De Gaulle could act because there was no alternative to the Fifth Republic except a Communist-led government or one in which the Communists participated, both clearly unacceptable in Paris and Washington. With these facts apparent, Washington made its fateful decision to attempt to bring about an end to the war come what may. The Fourth Republic's regime was dysfunctional in terms of the needs of NATO and the foreign policy of the West. Washington would pursue its policies even at the price of bringing about its end and inaugurating a Fifth Republic.

French-American relations took on an increasingly surreal character as the Fourth Republic headed toward what seems in retrospect its inevitable demise. It has long been typical of the new diplomatic or international history to stress the importance of internal politics for international diplomacy. The interconnection was most apparent during the last years of the Fourth Republic, as the Americans became increasingly unable or unwilling to deal with the internal complexity and shifting power relationships within a faltering regime. The Fourth Republic resembled a feudal system: it had a ceremonial president, a premier whose theoretically extensive powers were never clearly defined or fully exercised, and a shifting number of ministries which fell under the domination of politically powerful ministers, frequently able to defy the premier and the cabinet as a whole, or long-term civil servants who were able to take advantage of the shifting political heads to arrogate power to themselves. Proportional representation in elections produced a multiparty system, with six major parties or political groups, befitting the hexagon. Different coalitions tended to form around divergent questions, eighteen cabinets came to power and fell during eleven years, and ministries as a result were frequently free to pursue their own policies because ministers were not around long enough to influence them. Finally, there were two executives with which to deal, the president and the premier, a situation that did not change, but rather became exacerbated, under de Gaulle.

There are four essential and overarching themes that characterize this narrative, as it seeks to place the Algerian War in its international context. The first is that Algeria was at every step of the way from 1954 to 1962 central to French diplomacy, the one problem that for the French dwarfed all others, and the problem that dominated every other for most nations, particularly the United States, in their own attempts to deal with France. Because the French political class did not believe it could abandon Algeria without inaugurating a future of decadence and decline, it therefore subordinated everything else to keeping it French. The second theme is to explain how the internal dynamics of the French regime and its shifting, impenetrable lines of authority added complexity and confusion to the practice of French diplomacy and to the diplomatic relations of others with France, especially the United States. A third is to explain how and why the Americans lost interest in and concern for the preservation of the Fourth Republic, having concluded that its continued existence and inability to extricate itself from the Algerian War were dysfunctional to the Western alliance, and how they contributed to its demise, gambling knowingly on de Gaulle.

The fourth theme functions as a motif for a lengthy coda that brings the war and this narrative to its conclusion. That is to examine how the war underlay de Gaulle's startling and unorthodox diplomatic initiatives from 1958 to 1962. In doing so, this work challenges some essential views of de Gaulle's early diplomacy and his original aims and intentions with regard to French colonialism generally and the Algerian War in particular. I will argue that de Gaulle came to power with the intention of keeping Algeria, if not French, at least under French influence and domination. Further, he carried out his spectacular diplomatic initiatives toward the Americans, the European powers, NATO, and French African colonies with this aim in mind. There was nothing new in these initiatives other than the man who carried them out and the manner he employed to do so. In its broad outlines, de Gaulle's policy was that of the Fourth Republic. And that policy was to establish the basis of France as a world power at the core of three revolving spheres of influence. First, there was the all-important Anglo-American-French imperium over the free world, according to the terms of which each power would use its resources and strength to guarantee and buttress the spheres of influence and power of the others. Second, de Gaulle intended to put France at the head of an organized system of European political cooperation—the six Common Market nations—with a Franco-German nexus at its core, and to have France represent the interests of the reorganized Europe in the councils of the big three. Third, de Gaulle meant for France to act as the core and dominant state within a French-African federation, and in doing so to provide the fulcrum for its establishment as the economic hinterland of Europe in what the French termed *Eurafrique*. The basis of this new French *Weltpolitik* was Algeria, France's bridge to the rest of Africa, the heart of *Eurafrique*, the basis of France's influence and prestige in Europe, and in turn the hinge on which France's joint hegemony as part of the big three was to be established. By 1962 de Gaulle's dreams lay in ruins, essentially because of his inability to handle the Algerian mess, which in turn compromised French relations with America, Europe, and French Africa. The irony was that France did not lose the war on the ground but in the international arena. De Gaulle's diplomatic success would have been to have the world acknowledge French Algeria, while Algeria provided the basis for a measure of French hegemony in the world. How that dream came to lie in ruins amid the collapse of French Algeria in 1962 is the conclusion to what in retrospect is a sad, if not a tragic, story.

CHAPTER ONE

The United States
and the Algerian War

The United States welcomed the collapse of the Fourth French Republic in May 1958. This is paradoxical in that an almost obsessive concern with its internal political stability had characterized the earlier postwar period of U.S.-French relations, while the Americans appear in 1958 to have played a considerable role in undermining the very stability of the regime they had done so much since 1947 to help preserve. Much had changed in the intervening period that helps explain the revised American attitude. The French economy, precarious and dependent on American assistance in the years 1947 to 1952, was now robust and growing, and the threat of the French Communist party, which the Americans believed strong enough to seize power virtually at will in 1947, was now much reduced. The French army had been built by Washington into a powerful military force, meant to be the linchpin of European defense against a Soviet invasion, but it became heavily embroiled in Algeria, and its role in Europe was on the way to being assumed by a restored German army, negotiated on the heels of the failure to construct a European Defense Community in 1954.[1] In the immediate postwar period Paris and Washington had acted as allies. The United States offered extensive military assistance to France under the auspices of NATO in 1950 and was almost fully financing the Indochina War by 1953–54, although the French goal, to preserve their crumbling empire, conflicted with the American obsession to prevent any apparent expansion of Soviet power there. In Algeria, in contrast, the conflict began in November

1954 on the heels of the humiliating French defeat at Dien Bien Phu and withdrawal of French forces from Indochina. In the absence of communism as a salient issue, American anticolonial attitudes came into play, and frustration grew with the French inability to bring a conclusion to a war that increasingly appeared to play into the hands of Soviet ambitions.

Legally annexed to France and administered by the Ministry of the Interior in Paris, Algeria nevertheless had a typical colonial economy in 1954, and was distinguished from other French colonies only by the extent of European settlement there. There were about one million settlers of European descent, French in language and culture, and 140,000 Jews enjoying French citizenship, amid eight million Muslims, themselves divided between Berbers and Arabs. Although there was considerable French settlement in neighboring Tunisia and Morocco as well, it was nowhere near the dimensions of that in Algeria, and these countries were regarded as "protectorates," administered by the Ministry of Foreign Affairs. The nationalist movements in Tunisia and Morocco were consequently better developed, and Tunisia, after considerable violence and instability, was granted its autonomy in 1954. Morocco was also in crisis, and well on its way to independence in 1955. The experience of the protectorates, together with the French defeat in Indochina, greatly stimulated the development of nationalism in Algeria.

European immigration to Algeria had virtually ceased by the 1920s, moreover, and the demographic tide had been reversed; the Muslim population was now growing much faster than the European, and created enormous pressure on the limited arable land, most of the choice parcels in the northern coastal strip having long since been expropriated by Europeans. An estimated 6,385 European cultivators possessed 87 percent of the land, while there were over 1,000,000 rural Muslims under- or unemployed.[2] To the growing rural poverty there was added the urban misery of the Arab masses who migrated to the cities, rapidly building shantytowns, which the French called *bidonvilles*, around the European-built sections of Algiers, Oran, and Constantine. Economic growth could not create jobs fast enough to keep pace with population growth, and an increasing rootless and marginal labor force at the edges of the economy made up the hard core of nationalist support.[3]

The origins of Algerian nationalism go back to the 1920s and Messali Hadj, who created the *Etoile Nord Africain* in 1926. Messali flirted with communism and Trotskyism in the interwar period, but by 1945 his movement was Muslim nationalist, and his Mouvement pour le Triomphe des libertés démocratiques spawned a splinter group that broke away in 1954, abandoning his now more moderate policies to lead violent rebellion in the form of the Front de Libération Nationale (FLN). Messali Hadj faced more moderate competition from the French-educated doctor Ferhat Abbas, whose Union démocratique du Manifeste Algérien, named for a manifesto published in 1943, began with the very moderate program of equal rights for Muslims within a French Algeria, but quickly evolved after the war into a full-fledged Muslim nationalism, advocating autonomy while working within the system for democratic rights in Algeria. World War II gave tremendous impetus to Arab nationalism in North Africa. The American invasion of November 1942, followed by American occupation of French territories there, made the "protector" itself a protectorate in the eyes of the Muslims, and French rule was consequently delegitimized. Moreover, the Americans made no secret of their anticolonial sympathies.

In fact the first shots in what became the Algerian War were fired on May 8, 1945, in Sétif, when disillusioned Muslims rioted against French rule and wantonly attacked Europeans, 103 of whom were killed in four days of disorder that spread throughout the Constantine area.[4] Brutal repression followed; the French called in a cruiser and bombarded Muslim villages from the air in order to teach the Muslims a "lesson," although the one they learned was not the one intended. The French counted 300 Muslim dead; the nationalists later claimed 45,000; historians have settled on a figure of between three and ten thousand, but either way the Muslim population was greatly alienated from French rule. De Gaulle presided over this brutal return to French colonial domination; although preoccupied at the time by the armistice and other problems, he was determined not to allow Algeria to "slip through our fingers." It was his government also that created what became the Statute of 1947, under which Algeria was officially governed until January 1958, when it was displaced by a new loi-cadre, or framework law. The statute created two electoral "colleges" of sixty persons each for Muslims and Europeans in Algeria, and gave thirty representatives to Algeria in the National Assembly in Paris. Unequal though this system was, elections through the 1950s were nevertheless manipulated to exclude nationalists and elect docile Muslim collaborators whom the French called Beni Ouis-Ouis.

American policy toward North Africa must be seen over a broad continuum during the postwar period; except for nuances, the Eisenhower-Dulles policy toward French colonialism was no more indulgent than that of Truman and Acheson. After the war the Americans concluded that preserving French hegemony in the region was the best way to guarantee North African security, but the Americans continuously advocated a liberal approach to Arab demands and the French began to blame the United States for their growing problems, suspecting Washington of wanting to replace French influence in the region with its own. During the Sétif riots of May 1945, the Governor-General's office in Algiers blamed the Americans and the British for the disorders.[5] Paris was not, however, dissuaded from carrying out its pitiable repression. Washington continually pressed the French for reforms thereafter, and virtually every subsequent French effort at reform in Tunisia and Morocco until 1954 stemmed from direct American influence. In 1952 the French deposed the Tunisian government, which was too nationalistic in their eyes, and exiled the nationalist leader Habib Bourguiba. Tunisian nationalists brought their complaints against the French to the United Nations; an American abstention on a UN resolution calling for peaceful resolution of the crisis infuriated Paris and contributed to one of the most serious Franco-American crises of the postwar period. The Americans continued informal contacts with the nationalist Istaqlal in Morocco and the Neo-Destour in Tunisia despite repeated protests by Paris. After the outbreak of the Korean War in June 1950, American pressure on the French lessened. The Americans began to finance the French war against the communists in Indochina, and the U.S. desire to place military bases in Morocco led to French demands that Washington cease its interference in North Africa as a quid pro quo.[6] John Foster Dulles consequently declined to intervene when the French deposed the nationalist Sultan of Morocco in 1953 despite the disapproval of American diplomatic personnel on the scene. But Washington continued to pressure the French to grant autonomy while at the same time trying to moderate nationalist demands for independence.

At French insistence, Algeria had been included among the areas covered by the NATO alliance in 1949, although Congress excluded the Sahara and declared that nothing in the treaty was designed to ally the United States with French colonialism.[7] The Americans were also aware that Algeria was heavily settled by over one million Europeans who dominated its economy and politics. For these reasons Washington understood that any American attempt to influence French policy in Algeria would inevitably raise charges by the French of direct interference in their internal affairs. The CIA warned as early as 1952, however, that the situation in Algeria was a potential source of problems for France and the United States because of the unrecognized demands of the indigenous Muslim majority. Washington, like Paris, was surprised by the outbreak of the rebellion in November 1954.[8] The Americans never understood, moreover, how much France's sense of identity as a great power was tied to its colonial empire; the essential "true France" was a nation surrounded by its colonial possessions that adopted its culture and its civilization. From 1880 to 1895 the French conquered a colonial empire in Africa and Asia of some 9.5 million square kilometers and fifty to fifty-five million inhabitants, the basis of the myth of one hundred million French.[9] A national consensus existed among the French political class in 1954 on the necessity of keeping Algeria French, and this was supported by a large majority of public opinion.

Neither Messali Hadj nor Ferhat Abbas was behind the terrorist outbreak of November 1, 1954, that led to full-scale rebellion by 1955, and their movements were rapidly eclipsed by the more radical leadership of Ahmed Ben Bella and Belkacem Krim. The war began with isolated terrorist incidents that the French thought they could control. Pierre Mendès France, who had just granted autonomy to Tunisia, could not go as far in the case of Algeria, needing the votes of its representatives to support his London-Paris agreements on German rearmament; he responded by allowing the French army to conduct repressive operations throughout the Aurès mountains where the rebellion occurred, establishing the pattern of displacing peasants from their villages so that the rebels could be pursued with impunity in search and destroy operations that the French called *ratissages*. There were an estimated 700 rebels at the war's beginning, with perhaps half that many weapons, but their initial dramatic success, together with the French repression, swelled their ranks. The FLN also practiced "compliance terrorism," which included the selective murders of Muslim "collaborators" whose bodies were often mutilated as signs of their humiliation, and this won it further support. The war settled into a pattern of sporadic attacks on French governmental and military installations, with rebel "actions" gradually increasing from 200 per month in April 1955, to 900 per month by October of that year, and 2,624 per month by the war's height in March 1956.[10] The war's earliest turning point, however, occurred in August 1955; on the 20th of that month, the rebels launched a massive attack on the civilian population of the area around Constantine, repeating in Philippeville what had been done in 1945 in Sétif: 123 Europeans were massacred, most of them miners, including their wives and children. The war was further escalated as the FLN carried its attacks against Eu-

Figure 1.   Bodies of riot victims covered the stadium area at Philippeville, Algeria, after the bloody battle on August 22, 1955, between nationalists and French troops. The hills and villages of Algeria took on a war aspect on August 23 as French forces launched large-scale reprisals against nationalist rebels. The bloody riots and native raids cost an estimated 1,000 lives over the weekend. (Associated Press / WIDE WORLD PHOTOS)

ropeans to isolated and defenseless outlying farms. Jacques Soustelle, the liberal governor-general put in place by Mendès France to carry out social reforms, reacted in horror, and brutal, often vigilante repression followed the Philippeville massacre, in which some 1,200 Muslims were murdered in reprisals, and Edgar Faure, the premier, responded by doubling French troops, then numbering 90,000, to 180,000 by December 1955.

The Americans reacted to all this with alarm and sympathy for the nationalists; French North Africa generally came to provide an example of Eisenhower-Dulles diplomacy that supports the contentions of American "revisionist" historians of that era. Recent works on American relations with the Third World and neutralism would seem to refute successfully earlier views according to which the Americans always saw the Kremlin as the principal instigator of global unrest and President Eisenhower "never arrived at a clear distinction between Communism and revolutionary Arab nationalism." On the contrary, H. W. Brands notes that American hostility to Nasser from 1956 to 1958 was based on the latter's policies, not the belief that he was a Soviet puppet, while Peter L. Hahn shows that the United States tried to mollify Egyptian nationalism as much as was possible in terms consistent with Western strategic imperatives. Brands asserts that the United States showed "insight and flexibility in its relationships with the Third World and a pragmatic ability to deal with neutralism on its merits." As will be seen below, this is a fair characterization of American policy in North Africa. Similarly in Lebanon, where the Americans intervened militarily in July 1958, they did not confuse indigenous nationalist and populist movements with the communists: they merely showed categorical hostility to both in preserving the interests of the ruling elite with which they had established close ties.[11]

The Americans were able to maintain satisfactory relations with the rebels, though at the risk of compromising their relations with France. Algeria was a clear case of a Third World revolution that Washington believed it could accept; it appeared to have the capability of producing a noncommunist, if not a democratic, regime, and the rebels from the outset were clearly conscious of the need not to appear to take sides in the Cold War. Consequently, the Eisenhower-Dulles policy attempted the almost impossible task of continuing constructive dialogue throughout the crisis with both parties to an intractable dispute, the French government and the rebel Algerian National Liberation Front. In March 1958, in an observation with extraordinary contemporary salience, Dulles observed to the National Security Council (NSC) that in the three world crises of most immediate concern, Indonesia, North Africa, and the Middle East, communism and the USSR were absent and there were no "Soviet plots" anywhere in evidence.[12] On the contrary, the immediate threat appeared to come from fundamentalist Islam.

Washington's policy in the case of Algeria was complicated, and its influence limited, by the chronic state of chaos that seemed to characterize internal French politics. Governmental instability in Paris allowed cabinets to come and go and policy to remain paralyzed. Cabinet division and indecision in Paris had exasperated Dulles ever since Dien Bien

Phu. In concluding their own tacit alliance with France in 1954–55, the Israelis found French authority fragmented, responsibility diffuse, and the execution of policies sporadic, inconsistent, or hesitant. The Interior and War ministries were pro-Israel, the Ministry of Foreign Affairs was not; each ministry, according to Sylvia Crosbie, was virtually a closed institution with a particular historical outlook.[13]

The same situation very quickly manifested itself in Paris during the Algerian affair. But whereas Washington had once sought to mitigate the effects of instability and division in Paris, now the Americans were content to use these developments to their advantage. The privileged nature of American-French relations characteristic of the earlier postwar period was now gone, but the American ability to gather confidential information on French affairs was not. Internal American accounts of critical political and military events during the French-Algerian War stressed the disarray of the regime: its authority was often ignored on the local level by military and diplomatic officials, and individual cabinet ministers flouted the authority of the premier. Americans were also able to observe the growing interest among French politicians in a return of de Gaulle to power as early as mid-1957, an interest that, as de Gaulle entered into contacts with them, they eventually came to share.[14]

The unstable Fourth Republic, moreover, as a result of the Algerian conflict, created serious crises in American-French diplomatic relations, which appeared at times on the brink of collapse. French leaders took their military forces away from the NATO command in order to carry on the Algerian War, and they were willing to threaten the alliance itself when they did not get the support they thought they deserved; before de Gaulle appeared on the scene they had already called into question the whole structure of postwar European politics built in response to the Cold War. The Americans feared that a Popular Front-type regime might take France out of the NATO alliance and turn it toward neutralism, if it did not orient itself toward the Soviet bloc in exchange for a benevolent Soviet attitude toward France's colonial problems. Dulles had suspected Mendès France of harboring such designs in 1954. These fears were perhaps exaggerated, but they stemmed from the constant warnings and even threats that came from the French government itself, and Washington became convinced that it would do better with a stable political order in France, even one that threatened on occasion to clash with American policies, than to continue dealing with the shifting cabinets that were increasingly tempted to play upon irrational anti-American sentiment in order to preserve themselves in power. At the same time, Algeria was certainly the catalyst in convincing the French, even before the advent of Charles de Gaulle, of the limited value of NATO for the protection of French interests.

As the Algerian rebellion escalated into a full-scale war in 1955, the Eisenhower administration's sources of information convinced it that the French could not win. The conflict concerned Washington on a number of counts. There was first the anticolonial heritage of American foreign policy: Dulles told the embassy in France that "we must face the fact that the basic U.S. attitude on colonial problems is displeasing to the French as well as to others of our allies" and therefore it was "unrealistic to expect mutual understanding and confidence [with France] in North Africa." But Washington needed France, it remained the linchpin of Washington's NATO strategy for European defense, it was expected to provide the bulk of the ground troops for NATO's "shield," and its consent and cooperation were needed for German rearmament, painfully renegotiated following France's refusal to join the European Defense Community in 1954. As early as January 1955 the American Embassy feared that France might refuse to ratify the London-Paris agreements on German rearmament and integration into NATO if politicians in Paris believed that the United States might reverse its support of the French presence in North Africa. Theodore Achilles warned that if ratification were followed by a more pro-Arab policy in North Africa "the results would be disastrous"; the French would throw every possible roadblock in the way of implementation of German rearmament. The average French person still believed that the United States wanted to subvert and replace French influence in Morocco with its own. Achilles thought "it is essential to our ultimate objectives in Europe to continue our present middle-of-the-road policy in North Africa, and not to take a line overtly or covertly against the continuance of the French presence there."[15] To one extent or another, this injunction haunted American policy in the region throughout the Algerian conflict.

Washington had bad relations with the Mendès France government (June 1954–February 1955), resenting its sudden ending of the Indochina War at Geneva in June 1954 and its rejection of the European Defense Community treaty in August. Suspected by Dulles of flirting with neutralism, if not communism, Mendès aroused little sympathy in Washington when he asked that the Americans use their influence to moderate Cairo radio's broadcasts of support for the Algerian rebels; but Washington complied, once again fearing that France would refuse to ratify the London-Paris accords on the rearmament of Germany. On

November 27, 1954, Cairo Ambassador Jefferson Caffery extracted a promise from the Egyptians to reduce their propaganda on behalf of the Algerian rebels.[16] But Washington was still relieved when Mendès France fell in February 1955 and hoped for better from his successor, Edgar Faure. Faure in fact cooperated readily with Washington, and Achilles was authorized to assure him that the United States recognized that Algeria comprised several departments of France, and supported the French presence in North Africa generally. But the State Department was internally divided on the Algerian question, with different perspectives emerging from its European and African desks; William Tyler, long regarded as an authority on France, thought the United States must respond to the aspirations of the Muslim peoples of the region, and he characterized the administration's support for France in Algeria as "politically absurd." However, Ambassador Douglas Dillon was undeterred: he was pleased with Faure's appointments at the Quai d'Orsay, where he reported that "We can now work easily and freely with three or four of the top men," and the prospects seemed promising that Washington could influence French policy along liberal lines. Faure was committed to negotiating the independence of Tunisia and Morocco, which pleased the Americans.[17]

But when Dillon met with Faure and Foreign Minister Antoine Pinay, he was confronted with a request that in view of "liberal" French policies in North Africa, the United States more actively support the French position on Algeria. Faure had to play a delicate balancing act between the conflicting demands of the Americans and the French National Assembly, which he did by granting independence to Tunisia and Morocco in exchange for the promise that he would hold firm in Algeria. Dillon protested that the United States had repeatedly expressed its support for France in North Africa, but Faure complained that the general feeling in France was quite the opposite; many believed that the United States was lending its support to those opposing France. Faure cited U.S. Labor representative Irving Brown's support for nationalist trade unions, and claimed that Caltex (oil) in Libya hired "anti-French" Moroccan and Tunisian refugees. Dillon demanded that France pursue a liberal policy in Algeria; Faure repeated that such a liberal policy was his intention.[18] This pattern was to recur again and again. France sought support and the United States parceled it out in exchange for any sign of French concessions. Not surprisingly, Dillon told Dulles on June 5, 1955, that North Africa was both France's number one problem and the number one sore spot in Franco-American relations.[19] In frustration, Dulles asked State Department North African expert Julius Holmes for the first of several policy reviews on North Africa. Holmes replied with a recommendation that American policy shift away from support of France and toward support for the Arabs, telling Dulles that "France cannot ignore the march of history as expressed by the wave of nationalism that has swept the western world."[20] Dulles rejected this recommendation as extreme; but it was to return on several occasions, eventually strong enough to force itself on the secretary of state as policy.

Thus in September 1955 Washington anticipated that Pinay would ask for American support for French North African policy if the Algerian question came up in the United Nations. The U.S. position was that "we wish to be as helpful as we can," but the extent of American assistance "will depend on how prompt and effective French actions are" in terms of carrying out reforms. The General Assembly of the world body put the Algerian question on its agenda for discussion in September 1955 over French protests. Paris argued that according to its Charter the UN was incompetent to intervene in the internal affairs of its member states; Algeria was part of France. Simultaneously the Americans pressured Edgar Faure to come through rapidly with a statute on Moroccan independence against the conservative elements in his own and allied government parties, in the hope of warding off international criticism.[21] When French delegates in the Trusteeship Council of the United Nations came under attack for their country's allegedly repressive actions in Togo and the Cameroons, they charged that the United States used the opportunity to criticize France for the lack of economic and social progress in its territories. Aligning themselves with England and Belgium, the French resolved on protesting Washington's "defection" from the side of the administering powers to the anticolonialist majority in the United Nations.[22]

While in general Washington did try to support the French position in the United Nations, friction nevertheless occurred between the two countries over tactics. The Americans could not prevent the General Assembly of the UN from placing the Algerian question on its agenda for discussion in October, which precipitated the first of several French walkouts. Under Secretary of State Robert Murphy explained to René Massigli that the United States had tried to be helpful, "but he should realize that the United States could not muster 20 Latin-American votes by merely pressing a button."[23] In November 1955 the Assembly voted not to take up Algeria after all; but the French remained bitter over what they regarded as a near-defeat in the world body, and were quick to voice recriminations in Washington. The Americans had failed to work sufficiently "in the corridors" in favor of the French position or to use their influence with countries amenable to their views. UN Ambassador Henry Cabot Lodge, in reply, accused the French of an ineffective defense of their policies and a lack of sophistication regarding UN procedures: the United States, he said in what Paris had heard from Washington as a tired refrain since 1945, "can only help those who help themselves."[24] In Algiers the American Consulate reported an explosive growth in anti-American sentiment; anti-U.S. feeling was growing among all sectors of the European population, extremists played upon known American "anti-colonial tendencies," and they alleged an American plot to displace French influence in North Africa. Governor-General Jacques Soustelle, an anthropologist whom Mendès France had appointed for his known liberalism, virtually ceased contacts with the American Consulate, and in Bône the French Secret Service blocked official consular business by "frightening off" people the consul had tried to see.[25]

Dillon very early saw North Africa as a "festering sore hidden under the surface that could break open with devastating effect for our policies in Europe."[26] The Algerian War diverted French troops and matériel away from the Rhine and NATO's defenses, at which Washington took alarm, as did the Council of the North Atlantic alliance. Initial French troop transfers from the European theater to Algeria caused trouble in NATO as early as May 1955, and although the alliance's council approved them reluctantly, Supreme Allied Commander in Europe General Alfred Gruenther complained to French Defense Minister General Pierre Koenig that France was not keeping its commitments on the Rhine.[27] None of the NATO countries regarded the Algerian insurrection as an issue in the Cold War, although support for the French position varied: Belgium and the Netherlands tended to support the French position fully, the Dutch angry over Washington's support of Indonesian independence, the Belgians concerned over the Congo. Germany did as well, Adenauer having made relations with France the linchpin of his European policy. The Italian government was less enthusiastic but equally eager to maintain good relations with France. The Scandinavian countries, however, were opposed to colonialism on ideological grounds, while Turkey and Greece put relations with Egypt and the Middle East above French considerations in Algeria. The British were torn: they had colonial problems themselves, but they also felt constrained to put alliance and European questions ahead of all others.

Again, France was a traditional rival in the Middle East, where it opposed the Baghdad Pact and favored Israel, and Britain could not afford bad relations with the Arabs. For the most part, the British tried to avoid controversy with France while urging a liberal policy in Algeria on the French government. But their policy wavered as Britain swung closer to France during the Suez episode, and then back to alignment with Washington by the time of the Sakiet crisis in 1958.[28]

NATO questions again became paramount in March 1956, when the Socialist-led government of Guy Mollet informed the NATO Council of its intention to redeploy more French forces to Algeria. Mollet declared his actions were in the interests of the alliance, and demanded approval. Algeria was covered by the Atlantic treaty and threatened by nationalists in alliance with world communism. The rebellion thus represented a threat to European security. Alexandre Parodi, the French representative at NATO, explained that there had been a necessary shift in the center of gravity of French military potential from Europe to North Africa that was designed to meet the new threat of a flank attack on the alliance from the south. Algeria represented, with England, one of "two essential platforms upon which the military readiness of the alliance rests." The analogy with the Second World War was clear: England and North Africa had been the bases from which the Allied invasions to liberate Europe had been launched. No objections were raised in the NATO Council, which, however, "took cognizance" of the transfer of French forces taken by France "in the interest of its own security" in Algeria. The Council recognized that Algeria was covered by the NATO treaty, and it understood the importance of the North African region to the security of Europe.[29] But the statement refrained from endorsing the French claim that the rebellion in Algeria was in itself a threat to NATO, and its limited wording barely won it the support of Denmark and Norway, both fearful of offering any blanket endorsement of "French colonialism."

The French promptly trumpeted this statement as a manifestation of the solidarity of the alliance and of "unquestionable political value" to France. But underneath the action was a basic divergence of views between France and NATO; French security was seen, by the Fourth Republic and later, by de Gaulle, as no longer depending on the Rhine or the Elbe, but rather running along an axis from the Mediterranean through Algiers to Brazzaville in the French Congo.[30] Moreover, Council members showed obvious irritation when they queried Parodi about the meaning of a statement by Foreign Minister Christian Pineau on

March 2 to the effect that behind the insurrection the French had the impression of "certain powers seeking to reap the heritage of France" in North Africa. Which powers did Parodi mean? The French could not continue to have it two ways, brooking no outside interference in their Algerian problem on the grounds that it was French territory, but asserting their right to the full support of their allies with the argument that the Algerian insurrection represented a front in the struggle against international communism.

Tension was building between France and NATO throughout the period of the Fourth Republic, and it culminated in the partial French withdrawal from the alliance under de Gaulle. French requests for inclusion in what Paris believed to be an Anglo-American condominium in the alliance were repeatedly rejected, French colonial policy received no support from the alliance per se, and France was sidelined in U.S. and British nuclear planning.[31] France and the United States were on a collision course, which finally helped derail the Fourth Republic. The Americans resented the French redeployment of forces because it increased pressure on themselves to maintain their heavy troop presence in Germany despite growing balance of payments difficulties. In an April 1956 meeting with General Valluy, the French representative in NATO's Standing Group, President Eisenhower criticized the French deployment, and the Standing Group agreed to it only "in an appropriately circumscribed form," meaning that they would approve the troop transfer to Algeria but not one to North Africa generally. In particular, Washington feared that the troops might be used for action against or within the borders of Tunisia or Morocco, which turned out to be the case. On May 10, 1956, Dulles complained to the National Security Council about the lack of solidarity in the NATO alliance, citing the French redeployment and the contemplated withdrawal of British forces from the Middle East. Neither had ever been fully discussed in the NATO Council, which was simply informed of faits accomplis. Dulles expressed concern in London about British force reductions on July 13, 1956; Eden replied that the danger of war had receded, that a reduction of British forces was desirable, and reappraisal of the British world position urgent.[32] Still, Dulles and British Foreign Secretary Selwyn Lloyd agreed that their nations bore the brunt of the NATO obligation: German force contributions were insufficient, while "French forces were in North Africa and there was little contributed by the others." Indeed, by the end of 1956 virtually all important French troops had been deployed to Algeria with almost nothing left for NATO.[33] General Valluy was blunt: for France to stay in North Africa was a matter of "life and death" for the French people. He specifically asked for an active show of solidarity by the alliance, that it not simply "take note" of French troop transfers as in the past. In Karachi, where Pineau conferred with Dulles and Lloyd on the occasion of a meeting of SEATO, Pineau declared that France of necessity saw all problems through the prism of Algeria; any threat to North Africa risked the existence of the regime in Paris, and any attempt to replace France with allied influence in the region "would be resented by France so bitterly that her fidelity to the alliance would be shaken."[34] Fourth Republic politicians never came to understand that their exaggeration of threats to the alliance, like their attempts to escape responsibility for irresponsible policies by blaming them on rogue civil servants or military officers, made the opposite impression in Washington from that intended.

The French army was still in large part armed by Washington; it used American weapons to fight the Algerian War, and Paris very early on began sending requests to Washington for more. This worried Washington; the State Department wrote that a French appeal for U.S. helicopters in 1956 "demonstrates the French failure to appreciate the problems created for us by the rapid deterioration of the situation in North Africa and the apparent inability of the French to formulate and apply specific imaginative programs to which the local population will rally and which other countries can reasonably support."[35] The helicopters were nevertheless provided on a priority basis. Much of French army equipment had been provided from American stocks through Military Defense and Assistance Program (MDAP) aid since 1950, and a good deal of the matériel of French manufacture was financed by American "off shore" credits. Algeria remained dependent on other types of American heavy equipment, bulldozers for road building for example, which had military uses as well, and the program of civic development undertaken by the French army as part of its pacification program in 1956 was dependent on U.S.-built heavy trucks, alone found adaptable to certain types of rural terrain.[36]

The central dilemma of American policy toward Algeria stemmed from its need to balance the alliance with France against its concern to use what it regarded as its anticolonial heritage to solidify relations with the Afro-Asian bloc in the United Nations and to prevent North Africa, sub-Saharan Africa, and Asia in general from falling under Soviet influence. France could not win; its policy, Dulles said, was characterized by "short-sightedness and lack of realism," and the only solution for Algeria lay in autonomy or independence. The longer the war continued and Algerian independence was delayed, the more the interests of world communism were served and the greater the danger of a right-wing coup in France itself; with "no early desirable solution in sight," Dulles thought, "Algiers is moving toward catastrophe." Allen Dulles told the NSC in January 1957 that the CIA had concluded that the French would have to leave Algeria. President Eisenhower, however, expressed his concern for the European population of Algeria if "the French abandoned them."[37]

The French government reacted sharply, regarding Washington's policy as "unfriendly," alleging that the U.S. Information Services (USIS) systematically supported separatism, and the American Free Trade Union Committee, under Irving Brown, unconditionally supported nationalist trade union development in Tunisia, Morocco, and Algeria. American consuls were seen by French intelligence personnel consorting with officials of the Moroccan Istaqlal, the Tunisian Neo-Destour, and the MTLD-PPA nationalists in Algeria, all of whom they allegedly encouraged. Standard Oil of New Jersey, mining companies, Coca-Cola, even American Protestant missions present in North Africa fell under French suspicion as being part of a broad effort to undermine French influence and replace it with that of Washington.[38] From the French point of view, France deserved the full support of the United States, a NATO ally, for the FLN was tied in to the international communist movement; if France abandoned Algeria the result would be communist domination of all North Africa. Further, the French were convinced that Washington contributed to a prolongation of the war because the rebels believed that the United States was on their side; Soustelle convoked Consul Clark in Algiers in August 1955, confronting him with rebel boasts gathered by French intelligence that "America was with them."[39] If the rebels realized that U.S. power was firmly behind France, they would give up their struggle. The counterpart of this argument was that the FLN believed that Washington was capable of forcing the French to grant Algeria independence. Finally, the French were obsessed with keeping the war out of the UN, and they once again counted on Washington to use its influence in the world organization in 1956 to prevent the conflict from being placed on the UN agenda.[40] When the world body decided to discuss Algeria in 1956, even if only to vote out a vague resolution calling for a just and democratic peace, Washington took the blame in Paris.

In a more charitable moment, Mollet played with words: Americans were not playing *"un double jeu"* in Algeria but *"un jeu double."* Rather than pursuing a devious double game, telling the French one thing and pursuing an entirely different policy with the Arabs, Washington was in fact hedging its bets, tactically supporting the French effort to hold on to Algeria in some kind of relationship, regarding that as the best policy outcome, but also preparing the ground for an expected French failure and an independent Algeria, in which case Washington would have to step in to save the area from communism.[41] Die-hard partisans of *Algérie française* took little comfort from this casuistry, however, and the Quai d'Orsay was a good deal more caustic than Mollet: the United States was wedded to a useless policy based on "the seduction of Arab nationalism." Nonintervention, for the Americans, meant the protection of American citizens and interests, and anticolonialism meant the zealous pursuit of American commercial rights, while the United States maintained an "open door" to nationalists hostile to France. Private American charities showed excessive zeal in their concern for the plight of Algerian refugees and other victims of the war; Algerian nationalist and "anti-imperialist" organizations were allowed to operate freely in New York, and their officials could enter and leave the United States as they wished, even when traveling on passports of convenience granted by other Arab countries. The Quai complained bitterly that the rebel propaganda apparatus in New York cultivated American and United Nations opinion, State Department diplomats maintained personal relationships with Algerian rebel leaders, American oil companies sought concessions from the Algerian rebels in anticipation of their victory, and American trade unions supported independence and sent aid to trade unions in Algeria and throughout North Africa.[42] Most of these charges were, in fact, the case.

Mollet took power in January 1956 at the head of a Republican Front that won a clear plurality in the elections on a program promising to implement liberal policies and bring peace to Algeria. Mollet planned economic reforms and the recognition of an Algerian "personality"; there could be no mention in France of independence, which few in political life at the time thought possible or desirable. The French political class adhered to a "colonial consensus" according to which the loss of empire meant French decline and eventual decadence, a consensus that was shared in mitigated form even by the Communist party.[43] Mollet promised to hold free elections, however, in a single-college voting system giving equal weight to Europeans and Muslims, and he promised the creation of new, if as yet undefined, institutions that would provide for "indissoluble ties" that bound Algeria to France yet allowed the expression of its separate personality. Mollet's visit to Algiers on February 6, 1956, was meant to replicate the dramatic voyage of Mendès France to Tunis in July 1954, when the latter had announced autonomy for Tunisia with great aplomb. Nor is it clear, although Mollet could not avoid the impression at the time, that the rioting colons who greeted him with rotten eggs and spoiled tomatoes actually achieved a radical revision of his program.

According to his biographer, Denis Lefebvre, Mollet did not fire General Catroux, his choice for governor-general, as a concession to the rioters; rather, the general, who had a reputation as a *bradeur des colonies* (colloquially, a person who sells at a discount) among the ultras for his role in the restoration of the Sultan of Morocco in 1955, quit of his own volition, and Mollet offered the post to several Socialist party stalwarts, all of whom refused, before settling on Robert Lacoste, who accepted out of party discipline.[44] Mollet gave the title of resident minister for Algeria to Lacoste instead of the traditional governor-general so as to emphasize his responsibility to and role as spokesman for the cabinet in Paris and not the settlers. But like his predecessors, and in part because of the way he came to power, Lacoste became the prisoner of the same settler groups who traditionally ran the colony. It was clear, moreover, that France had reached what many would later remember as a defining moment in the Algerian conflict in February 1956: the victory of the settlers in setting French policy in Paris on February 6, 1956, in retrospect clearly prefigured the crisis of May 1958 and the collapse of the regime.

On February 28, Mollet announced his famous three-point program, appealing to the rebels to accept a cease-fire, elections, and negotiations, in that order, and on March 8 he asked the National Assembly for plenary powers enabling him to make changes in Algeria while imposing the equivalent of martial law. The National Assembly obliged him with an overwhelming vote in favor, with the Communist party offering its support as well, and in June 1956 Mollet opened secret negotiations with the rebel leadership in a vain effort to accomplish a cease-fire while urging Lacoste to implement extensive social reforms. He also began a massive troop buildup; French forces, 200,000 strong when Mollet took power, rose to 400,000 by the end of the year.

It was in this dramatic context, while Mollet approached NATO for formal approval of French troop transfers to Algeria, that he immediately began to press Washington for a public statement of support for French policies, which presumably met Dulles's insistence on a "liberal program" as a condition of American support. But Washington confronted the same dilemma as in the past. Robert Murphy had just returned from Paris, where he noted the unhappy French attitude that placed the onus for the French predicament in Algeria and North Africa generally on the United States, a psychological phenomenon that he said resulted from the previous French failure to develop "a constructive, sound program for the area." The United States had consistently supported Paris in the UN to its own embarrassment because of the issue of colonialism, and Murphy thought that it should not do so again. Ambassador Dillon, however, argued strongly for a statement of support, ignoring Mollet's reforms but focusing on the anti-Americanism allegedly rampant in Paris; and Under Secretary of State Herber Hoover, Jr., who was never a Francophile, now concluded that the ambassador was right, the United States must act to offset the current wave of anti-Americanism. Hoover warned that the affair must be managed with caution and skill, however, because French resentment was hardly limited to the North African maelstrom: it included Indochina, an internal French posture of weakness, the loss of the Saar to Germany, the tendency to blame a benefactor, and of course the "insidious work" of the French Communist party.[45]

On February 4, 1956, before the premier's ill-fated visit to Algiers, Dulles cabled Dillon to tell Mollet that efforts to implement a liberal policy in Algeria "have the sympathy and support of the U.S. government," and the secretary of state specified that he would support a French plan to abolish the two-college voting system and negotiate a federal solution linking Algeria with France. The United States was also willing to try to pressure Egypt again into moderating its support for the rebels. But on February 6, the consulate warned that Mollet had "capitulated" to the rioting colons in Algiers, that he was watering down his peace plans, and had become a "prisoner of the right." Still, in Paris, he appeared to be pushing ahead with a liberal program, and American support now seemed all the more critical for France given the dimensions the Algerian crisis was assuming. Dulles's instinct at first was to refuse any statement of support, but the State Department warned that Paris increasingly tended to blame its predicament on insufficient backing from Washington. On March 2, just as France was approaching the NATO Council on Algeria, Dillon cabled in a virtual panic about the volume of anti-American propaganda in Paris and the spreading belief that Washington wanted to eject France from North Africa; the United States was alleged to be standing by cynically while the French risked their lives in the struggle against international communism. There was, Dillon said, "a dangerously sharp rise in anti-American sentiment because of what the French public believes our North African policy to be," and he predicted an explosion in France with serious consequences for NATO. Former President Vincent Auriol called on the Americans to "cease their intrigues," asking whether France could count on the solidarity established by the NATO pact.[46]

Dillon now insisted that a public statement of support was essential. Virtually all the French believed that Washington wanted them out of North Africa; not to counter this belief would do irreparable harm to French-American relations. Dillon noted that the British were supporting Paris—Sir Gladwyn Jebb made a declaration of support for Paris on March 6—and that even the Communist party was prepared to vote full powers to Mollet in the hope that he could bring about a settlement. U.S. Ambassador to the United Nations Henry Cabot Lodge, who also was not regarded in Washington as a Francophile, now agreed that present circumstances dictated a statement of support for the French. Dillon reported that even the Soviets had informed the Quai that they supported a continued French presence in North Africa. France's allies could do no less; not to act would risk "catastrophic damage to French-American relations."

The Soviets were in fact pursuing an active policy of détente with France's second Socialist-led government; on 13 January 1956 Molotov had told French Ambassador Dejean that as far as the USSR was concerned North Africa was a French problem. President Auriol told Molotov on March 10 that the Algerian rebellion represented a quite un-Marxist "Koranic feudalism"; it was therefore all the more surprising that public opinion in France saw the French Communist party as being in complicity with the rebellion while the future of France as a great power hung in the balance. Molotov was embarrassed; whereas the Soviets sympathized ideologically with anticolonialism and Arab nationalism, he assured Mollet that he recognized that Algeria was an internal French problem. As for the French Communists, he protested that of course the Russians played no role in the determination of their policies, but the party in any event had voted Mollet its support. Auriol warned that it was in the Soviet interest that France remain in North Africa, for if not, "it was not the Soviets who would succeed her." Mollet and Pineau led a French delegation to Moscow to pursue détente further in May, and they received a very cordial reception, although Khrushchev complained that the French demonstrated a very "feeble" voice in favor of peace in the world. Algeria did not come up for extended discussion, however, and in their final communiqué the Russians limited themselves to the pious wish that France, animated by a liberal spirit, would find the "appropriate" solution for the times and the peoples involved.[47]

Algeria was also beginning to become entangled with the growing crisis over the Suez Canal, the subject of the next chapter. Dulles came under considerable British pressure between January and March 1956 to take a harder line with Egypt's Nasser, who had accepted Soviet and Czech weapons in September 1955, and refused Eisenhower's offer to send a trusted envoy, Robert Anderson, to the Middle East in an effort to settle the Arab-Israeli question. The Americans had offered to finance the Aswan Dam, but in March 1956, under Eden's prodding, Dulles came to the conclusion that Nasser should not be allowed to work with the Russians and expect American support at the same time.[48] Perhaps there was something in French arguments that Nasser was behind the Algerian insurrection as well. Finally, Pineau told Dulles that the forthcoming Dillon statement was one of the major considerations of the French government in its decision to conclude the treaty negotiations on Tunisian independence, which took effect March 20. Without a statement of American support for France these negotiations might break down.[49]

In view of all these considerations Dulles finally authorized Dillon to make the statement in support of the French in Algeria. Lodge brought the news personally to Mollet in Paris, explaining that the statement would be made in view of the "misunderstanding" in France of the U.S. position, which had always been one of complete support for France in North Africa. Mollet, while grateful, said he had no complaint about the U.S. government's attitude; the problem was, rather, unofficial elements in the United States, the press and its "blanket anti-colonialism," and the labor movement with its support of North African unions that had created the impression that America did not support France. The United States was not well served at the consular or embassy level either, Mollet observed, or even by its businessmen in this regard. Taking the occasion to ask for eighty more helicopters and fifty low-flying reconnaissance planes, Mollet said France must have the support of NATO as well: no one knew better the strategic importance of North Africa for the defense of the free world than President Eisenhower, who had commanded the invasion there during World War II and who had been supreme commander of NATO forces in Europe. Returning to another favorite French theme, Mollet said that three-power unity among France, England, and the United Sates would make a greater impression in Cairo, the real source of the Algerian rebellion, than any other single act.[50]

Dillon made his statement on 20 March 1956 to the Anglo-American press club in Paris. The French misunderstood American policy, he said; the United States had no ambitions to replace French influence in North Africa with its own. Washington had consistently given loyal support and close cooperation to France in its policies in Morocco, Tunisia, and Algeria; it had supported France in the United Nations, and was sending a new shipment of helicopters to France. Private American citizens, the French must understand, were not controlled by their government, and their actions were of minor importance. The United States understood the unique nature of the Algerian problem and its difference from other colonial crises around the world: 1.2 million French people lived in Algeria amid eight million Muslims; the European population had been there since early in the nineteenth century and knew no other homeland. "France has our profound sympathy and support in its attempt to work out a liberal solution to this problem of coexistence," Dillon concluded. The United States supported a continued French presence in Algeria and would "stand solidly behind France in the search for a liberal and equitable solution to the problems" there.[51]

It was a carefully crafted and qualified statement that fell considerably short of an endorsement of existing French policy, but it was enough to assuage the French temporarily. Le Monde trumpeted the story, seeing in the statement a definitive end to rebel illusions of American support for their cause.[52] This would appear, from French intelligence reports, to have been the case: a National Liberation Front white paper prepared for the African-Asian group of nations at the UN interpreted the Dillon statement to mean that France had received full American and NATO support for its policy of repression in Algeria, in violation of the principles and purposes of the Charter of the United Nations.[53] The French Embassy in Washington meanwhile noted a favorable evolution of American public opinion with regard to the Algerian question, and sympathy with Washington's official statement of support: there was greater understanding in America of the plight of the European population in Algeria, and realization that the territory was an integral part of France, different from Tunisia and Morocco. The New York Times referred to Resident General Robert Lacoste as "one of France's most intelligent and capable leaders." To be sure, the embassy noted, Americans believed colonial empires to be on the eve of disappearance and they regretted that their British and French allies did not react more gracefully to the "imperatives of history." But modernized liberal British and French policies were now understood by more and more Americans to be the best antidote to Russian influence in the area. It was in the French interest to encourage this attitude.[54]

But even as he instructed Dillon regarding the speech, Acting Secretary of State Herbert Hoover, Jr. revealed the American ambiguity that ensured that no statement of support could be more than a brief palliative. "We must face the fact that the basic U.S. attitude toward colonial problems is displeasing to the French," Hoover wrote, echoing Dulles, "and it is unrealistic to hope for complete mutual understanding." Hoover instructed Dillon to tell Mollet that the speech was designed to allay French doubts and reassure the French of American understanding and sympathy. "We are anxious to be helpful to France and we hope that M. Mollet understands that we are." But Hoover also wanted Mollet to be told that "the French program is not always known to us."[55]

Dillon's statement led to a brief honeymoon, but it fell far short of the kind of support Paris felt it had a right to expect, and by the summer of 1956 Franco-American relations had once again soured. The American consul in Lyon reported that the Dillon statement was regarded in some circles as inadequate and not very convincing.[56] In Algiers, U.S. Consul Clark heard Lacoste accuse him of playing a "double game," and repeat earlier complaints that the United States was not fully supporting France. Lacoste said that U.S. officials in New York admitted off the record that the government did not internally support French policy in North Africa, despite official statements. The Dillon speech was good, but it was not enough to convince the French military that the Americans were on their side. In a French Senate debate in May, Michel Debré, later de Gaulle's first premier, lambasted the Americans as "consistently hostile" to French policy in Algeria. Debré was to continue in the same vein through the end of the war. In July, Dillon saw Mollet to complain that a majority of officials in Lacoste's office in Algiers were unfriendly to and distrustful of U.S. officials; Mollet again blamed American trade union organizer Irving Brown and other private American visitors to Algiers who, he said, frequented the region for reasons that were "unclear."[57] Meanwhile, American dispatches showed an unwillingness to believe French claims of the successful pacification of Algeria. General Charles P. Cabell, deputy director of intelligence for the CIA, candidly told the NSC that, on the contrary, French efforts to pacify Algeria had failed. The back of the rebellion had not been broken, he said, a hard core of twenty thousand rebels continued operations, and Mollet's new statute for Algeria was likely to win the assent of neither the Arab nor the European population there.

Lacoste, who was aware of American attitudes, reportedly "never missed an opportunity to make a cutting remark toward the United States."[58] He expelled American trade union organizer Irving Brown from Algeria despite the fact that Brown, whose Paris office represented the American Free Trade Union Committee, had funneled many thousands, perhaps millions, of dollars to non-Communist trade unions in France, particularly Force Ouvrière, during the early days of the Cold War; in fact he had helped engineer the split between the Force Ouvrière and the Confédération Générale du Travail (CGT). But Brown reflected the AFL's anticolonialism as well as its anticommunism, and his International Free Trade Union Committee (IFTUC) had taken to organizing Tunisian, Moroccan, and now Algerian unions, in opposition to the desires of the French.[59] Lacoste complained that the IFTUC would do better to concern itself with the plight of blacks in the American South.[60] Dillon protested, sent Lacoste documentation about labor conditions in Puerto Rico and the American South (one wonders what it could have contained), and extracted an apology.

But U.S. Consul Louis Clark remained carefully watched by the French, as was his reported staff of five consuls and two vice-consuls. All were believed to have had relations with the Algerian nationalist movements before the outbreak of the rebellion, although their current attitude was described as correct. Their caution, combined with an "equivocal" neutrality, was thought by Paris to stem uniquely from their concern for the Atlantic alliance.[61] Given all this paranoia in France, it is hardly surprising that Robert Buron recounts that some influential people were seriously thinking of a military-progressive alliance coming to power in France in the name of "political renovation," with the aim of holding Algeria. The army would take an anti-American position favoring rapprochement with the USSR, and the extreme left supposedly would accept a change of regime and a firm policy in Algeria in exchange for some social progress at home. De Gaulle would cover the whole operation. If such conspiracy theories could flourish in France in the summer and fall of 1956, this was because the Algerian question was briefly becoming entangled with and overshadowed by another serious French-American divergence in policy—over the Suez crisis.

CHAPTER TWO

The Suez Crisis

There was a direct causal connection for France between the Algerian insurrection and the Suez crisis: the Egyptian dictator, Gamal Abdel Nasser, was perceived to be at the root of the new radical brand of Arab nationalism rampant throughout the Middle East, and the principal source of support for the Algerian rebels. The conviction quickly arose in Paris that if Nasser could be toppled, the Algerian rebellion would dissipate. The French were able to find support for their dislike of Nasser in London, but Washington was much more hesitant about how to deal with him, and Western disunity over attempts to unseat the Egyptian leader during the Suez crisis became the defining development for the future structure of postwar relations between France, the "Anglo-Saxons," and Europe generally. The outline of the crisis is well known: Great Britain entered into a French scheme to entice the Israelis into invading the Egyptian Sinai, thus providing cover for an Anglo-French military invasion of the Suez Canal, ostensibly to protect the canal and keep the warring nations apart. When Washington, instead of quietly supporting the operation, condemned it publicly and forced the British to call off their participation through pressure on the pound, Great Britain was forced once again to choose between France and Washington. The British chose to realign their foreign policy with Washington, provoking the definitive break between France and the Anglo-American tandem, and the foundations of the Fench quest for *in-dépendance* that became the basis of the diplomacy of the Fourth Re-

public, and subsequently of de Gaulle. Simultaneously, France turned to
Europe and the dream of *Eurafrique* in compensation for its loss of support among the Anglo-Americans. If the Americans would no longer
prop up the French colonial empire, perhaps the Europeans in some
measure could be enticed to do so in exchange for France's willing participation in the drive for European unity. The Americans were, of
course, supporters of the Common Market at its inception. Yet the
Common Market was launched around a newly built Franco-German
partnership, the foundation of which was suspicion and fear of Washington's intentions with regard to Europe.

Nasser's plans for the Middle East were a matter of concern both in
Paris and London throughout the spring of 1956, and Mollet, whose
government manifested exceptional sympathy for Israel, also shared the
perspective of his predecessors that the Egyptian dictator was behind
the persistence of the Algerian rebellion. This belief was general among
the French political leadership, for whom the future of Algeria in 1956
depended upon checking the ambitions of the Egyptian dictator.[1] Abel
Thomas, who was director of the cabinet of Bourgès-Maunoury, interior and then defense minister in 1955–56, had direct responsibility for
Algerian affairs in 1955; in that post, which was at the center of the
flow of French intelligence on the rebellion, he concluded that "Cairo
was the source of all subversion."[2] French sympathy for Israel can be
traced back to 1954, but became active after Nasser accepted a massive
offer of Soviet arms in October 1955. The Israelis went on a shopping
expedition for arms among the Western powers, but received a warm
welcome only in Paris, which shipped some Mystères II in 1955, and
then some modernized Mystères IV in April 1956. The Israelis enjoyed
sympathy among individual ministers of the Mollet government elected
in January 1956. Christian Pineau, the foreign minister, was a veteran
of eighteen months in Buchenwald; Maurice Bourgès-Maunoury, the
defense minister, was an internal Resistance hero who developed an independent regard for the Jewish plight during the war. His ministry, led
by assistants Louis Mangin and Abel Thomas, put out the welcome mat
for the Israelis, who, with Pineau, found themselves easily able to bypass the pro-Arab sentiment evident in the Quai d'Orsay.[3] Max Lejeune,
the secretary of state for the army, was also part of the loop.

British concerns in the region were somewhat different, but the
British shared the French preoccupation with Nasser's ambitions; his
Philosophy of the Revolution was read with anxiety in London, where
there was no sympathy for his Pan-Arab, Pan-Islamic, or Pan-African

goals. There was a tendency both in Paris and London to see parallels with Hitler in Nasser's policies, and if few thought the Egyptian dictator capable on his own of implementing them, there was presumably no limit to what he could do with Soviet backing. The French escalated their rhetoric with regard to the alleged Arab threat. It was a question of the West against Islam, a war for civilization. France, in Algeria, was defending freedom against Pan-Islamic theocratic fanaticism.[4] The West faced a fusion of the Bandung Conference of anticolonial, nonaligned nations and the Soviet bloc. The British and French did not necessarily agree at first on how to meet the challenge. The British, with Washington's support, created the Baghdad Pact in 1955, a "Northern Tier" of conservative Muslim states, including Turkey, Iran, Iraq, and Pakistan, designed to provide a barrier against Soviet penetration of the Middle East. Washington declined to join but supported the scheme. The French were not pleased by this; they thought the "barrier" already breached by the Soviet presence in Egypt, and the pact only capable of further inflaming the Egyptian dictator against the West, but their own policy of arming Israel in response to Soviet weapons pouring into Egypt was hardly calculated to please Nasser either. The difference perhaps was that the French were already contemplating a military strike to bring the Egyptian dictator down, having little faith in a dubious alliance.

In March 1956, invested by the National Assembly with special powers, Mollet undertook a new global approach to the Algerian problem. On the ground the French troop buildup of draftees continued throughout the rest of the year; 190,000 were in Algeria when Mollet took power in January, and a full-strength 400,000 were in place by the end of the year. The conscripts did not do the actual fighting, which was left to elite professional units like the paratroopers and the Foreign Legion. While these units conducted mobile operations against rebel bands, the conscripts became a virtual army of occupation, charged with the protection of the European and compliant Muslim populations from FLN attacks. The country was laid out in a kind of grid, called by the French command *quadrillage,* effectively divided into military zones within which the work of pacification could be carried out. Resident General Lacoste was totally committed to his predecessor Soustelle's goal of integration, and he immediately set about trying to compensate for years of French neglect of the Muslim population. The army expanded its Section Administrative Spécialisée (SAS), originally created by Soustelle, special units trained in civilian tasks of bringing medical clinics, public

health facilities, rudimentary engineering, and education to the Muslim
village populations. Over 400 of these units were created, many of them
made up of quite selfless soldiers devoted to the welfare of the Muslims;
the counterpart of this, however, was a corresponding politicization of
the army, which became loath to abandon its successful effort in Algeria. Lacoste carried out a large-scale administrative reform, expanding
Algeria's three departments into thirteen, establishing Muslim munici-
palities, and trying to promote responsible Muslims to positions of some
authority in the new administrative structures. He also pursued a policy
of land reform.[5]

Soustelle had authorized the removal of civilian populations from
areas subject to mobile military operations and their internment in spe-
cially constructed camps, which quickly became the ugliest hallmark of
the war, excepting the torture. *Quadrillage* was initially successful but
at the cost of alienating the population subjected to it, and it probably
accounts for the decision of the rebels at their meeting in the Soummam
valley in August 1956 to undertake a campaign of terror in Algiers
against the civilian population. At Soummam the rebels further ration-
alized their system of command, settled jurisdictional disputes between
the exiles in Cairo and the military leadership in the interior, and agreed
upon a moderate-sounding nationalist-Muslim ideology for the rebellion. What became known as the Battle of Algiers opened on September
30, 1956, with coordinated attacks on popular European gathering
places in the city; bombs exploded in the Milk Bar and the Cafeteria;
three persons were killed and about fifty seriously injured, many of
them children.[6] The Europeans had opened their own terror campaign
against the Muslims in August, however, murdering over seventy Muslims in attacks on the rue de Thèbes; the French police stood by and did
nothing, in contrast to the vigorous military reaction to the Battle of Algiers, which was defeated early in 1957 by military control of the city
and the application of systematic torture.

It was against this background of rapid expansion and escalation of
the war on the ground that Mollet carried out his diplomatic efforts to
isolate and quash the source of the rebellion in Egypt. On March 11
Mollet met with Anthony Eden at Chequers. King Hussein of Jordan
had just dismissed Glubb Pasha, the British head of the Jordanian legion, and the British feared a Nasserite coup. The French foreign minister, Christian Pineau, had meanwhile made his own effort to come to an
agreement with Nasser, who assured Pineau that there was no Egyptian

training or weapons help being provided to the Algerian rebellion. Pineau appeared at first to believe this, but then concluded he was being taken for a fool. On this basis of mutual hostility to the Egyptian dictator, Mollet and Eden established a basis for understanding otherwise lacking between French and British leaders of the period, and if the meetings did reveal some divergences between them, they agreed to concentrate on their areas of agreement. Mollet returned to France with solid British backing for French Algerian policy; Eden agreed that American "elementary anticolonialism" was an obstacle to the pacification of North Africa and the Middle East and that the Egyptian dictator's Pan-Arab and Pan-Islamic policies were as great a danger to the world as Russian Pan-Slavism. Eden defended the Baghdad Pact, however, and refused to give arms to Israel as inconsistent with it; Mollet asserted that France was morally obliged to help the Jewish state even if it meant being left alone to draw upon itself all the hostility of the Arab world. But despite this disagreement, both countries coordinated their policies separately from Washington, which was accused of "playing the Nasser card" while ignoring French problems in North Africa.[7]

Despite Dillon's March 20 statement of American support for France in Algeria, the Americans were far from showing the kind of cooperative attitude available in London. Washington created an embassy in Tunisia on June 5; the French, in the process of granting Tunisia independence, wanted all American actions cleared with Paris first and their own "preeminence" in Tunisian affairs recognized, and they protested the American action as "inopportune." Dulles also informed Mollet that the Americans would negotiate their interests in Morocco directly with the sultan, and he refused French requests to join in arming Israel. Mollet asked Washington to pressure Libya and Spain not to help the Algerian rebels, and he assured Dulles that France "does not wish to engage the U.S. government in the Algerian affair and at no cost will she resume with the U.S. the policies that were followed in Indochina." But Mollet could not get satisfaction from the Americans. Things were not any better in Moscow either in the aftermath of Mollet's visit there. Khrushchev told French Ambassador Dejean in June that Moscow would support the inscription of the Algerian question on the UN agenda. Dejean warned that "France recognized its friends by their attitudes in the Algerian affair," but Khrushchev said Moscow was bound by its anticolonial ideology and "trapped" between its desires for friendship with France and with the Arab states.[8] Only London remained steadfast: the British refrained from establishing relations with Tunisia or Morocco until the French had settled matters in the two countries to their satisfaction.[9]

At no point in the Suez drama did Paris and London, on the one hand, or Washington, on the other, come near understanding or agreement on what to do about Nasser. The French, at the outset of the crisis, bluntly accused Washington of precipitating the nationalization of the canal by "abruptly" canceling American aid for the Aswan Dam project, and then abandoning its allies to face the terrible consequences. Couve de Murville cabled a week before the nationalization that Dulles's decision on Aswan was "sudden, abrupt, and brutal" and taken without consultation with Washington's allies, and he anticipated some Egyptian retaliation focused on the Suez Canal. This was something of an exaggeration. British Foreign Minister Selwyn Lloyd and Dulles had agreed in May that the Aswan Dam project should be allowed to "wither on the vine," given the Egyptian dictator's growing hostility to the West.[10] But the British also criticized Dulles's curt manner of breaking the news to the Egyptians. When, on July 27, Nasser announced the nationalization of the canal, the French ambassador to Cairo immediately warned that Paris must administer "a very clear, arresting blow" to Nasser because if he got away with this he could get away with anything. Couve de Murville assumed a relationship between the canal action and Egyptian hostility to the Jewish state, adding that Egypt would lose in any military conflict with Israel that might occur as a consequence of its action. Jean Chauvel, the French ambassador to England, cabled from London that Eden thought the nationalization a "test of strength" that Nasser must not be allowed to win. Pineau outlined the French government's position in reply: Nasser would not be given a victory, France would act to protect the shareholders in the canal and its position in Algeria. More Mystère jets were at once dispatched to Israel, and Chauvel was instructed to query the British about an eventual joint military action to deal with the situation.[11]

The British were not entirely happy about being thrust into cooperation with the French, whom they believed were widely hated in the Middle East in comparison to themselves, but the common hostility to Nasser overcame their scruples. Both agreed on the need for force to topple the Egyptian dictator, while the French said they were prepared to act independently if necessary. On July 31, Robert Murphy reported from London that Eden and Macmillan had decided "to drive Nasser out of Egypt"; they believed that military action was "necessary and inevitable," their decision was firm, and they hoped that the Americans would be with them as the French were.[12] Murphy argued against military action except as a last resort, but Chauvel told him that the United States had precipitated the crisis with its Aswan Dam decision and that "it was more important for us [France] to defeat Nasser than to win ten battles in Algeria."[13]

From the outset Washington resolved to prevent the use of force. On July 28, Hoover, Dulles, and the president agreed that the United States would discourage France and Britain from taking military action and seek a diplomatic solution to the crisis. At all costs, the canal issue must be kept separate from the Arab-Israeli crisis; Nasser was legally within his rights to nationalize the canal, and cancellation of the Aswan Dam project was simply a pretext for an action that would have been taken anyway. Nobody had a thought for the preservation of the interests of the canal company; its lease was in any case due to expire in 1968, although its directors hoped for a renewal and believed themselves solely capable of operating the canal.[14] The only option Washington could envisage was to seek the agreement of the canal's major users and Washington's NATO allies on an appropriate diplomatic response short of force. On July 31, Eisenhower told John Foster and Allen Dulles that the British attitude was "very unwise" and "out of date." Allen Dulles said the entire Arab world would unite in opposition to the West if force were used against Egypt, and Foster Dulles said the British were trying "to reverse the trend away from colonialism, and turn the clock back 50 years." Admiral Burke, on behalf of the Joint Chiefs of Staff, said the American military believed that Nasser must be "broken," but Eisenhower would have none of it: Washington could not afford to have the entire world arrayed against it.[15] The president sent an immediate message to Anthony Eden stressing the importance of diplomacy and asserting the "unwisdom [sic] even of contemplating the use of military force at this moment."

The Americans had their work cut out for them in selling this attitude in Paris. Dillon reported that Mollet was in a "highly emotional state." The challenge was like that of Korea and the 1948 Berlin crisis, the French premier asserted, and unless there was an appropriate response the entire position of the West in the Middle East and North Africa would be lost. France was now being abandoned by Washington after the United States had started the whole affair by canceling the Aswan Dam project. Ironically, Egypt, with Soviet help, had a better bomber force than France, which out of loyalty to NATO had concentrated on the production of fighter aircraft. Washington could not now leave its ally in the lurch. Nasser was like Hitler, *The Philosophy of Revolution* echoed the themes of *Mein Kampf,* and the Suez Canal was a repetition of the Munich crisis.

Mollet told Dillon that in Moscow the Soviets had offered to bring peace to Algeria on French terms if France would come "part way" to meet their views on European matters. The Russians did not ask that France abandon NATO, only that it become "semi-neutralist." Surely Dillon must see the temptation in such an offer to any French statesman. But Mollet had indignantly refused. He had been loyal to Washington. He now had the right to Washington's sympathy and understanding in return.[16] Mollet knew that Dulles had accused Mendès France of arranging such a "planetary deal" with Moscow when, allegedly in exchange for the Indochina settlement at Geneva in 1954, he allowed the National Assembly to kill the treaty establishing the European Defense Community. Mollet was also anticipating the foreign policy of de Gaulle.

On August 2, 1956, the foreign ministers of Great Britain, France, and the United States agreed in London to convene an international conference of powers to consider what to do about the Egyptian nationalization of the canal. The choice of those to attend was somewhat arbitrary: eight countries were chosen as signatories of the 1888 canal treaty, eight more for their volume of tonnage shipped through the canal yearly, and a final eight as especially dependent on the canal.[17] The ministers' intent was to establish some kind of international administration of the canal, which should not be allowed to remain in Egyptian hands, and to obtain appropriate compensation for the shareholders. If Nasser refused, they would "reconsider the matter," which the French took to mean "tacit acceptance of the necessary [i.e., military] follow-up of any eventual refusal by Nasser," but there was still almost total divergence between Britain and France on the one hand and Washington on this point. Dulles made it clear in London that the United States did not consider military action justified, and he warned against any separate operation by the British and the French that might precipitate a Soviet reaction. Even if Nasser refused any reasonable international settlement, the United States could not participate in military operations although it might support them.

Pineau told Dulles that France had 80,000 canal shareholders to protect and only a window of a few weeks in which to save North Africa and the continent as a whole for the West. France was prepared to act alone, although he had British support for an eventual military strike to recover the canal and bring Nasser down. Both powers judged the American attitude as weak and agreed that if Washington persisted they must act alone: "it was better for two to act than for three to do nothing." It would be better, of course, from the angle of an eventual Soviet involvement, to have Washington on their side, but the British observed that Washington often followed when others acted first.[18]

Eden bluntly told Dulles that prompt and forceful action was necessary or there would be disaster for the United Kingdom in the Middle East and France in North Africa. Britain expected moral support, oil supplies, and the neutralization of Moscow from the United States in the event of British-French military operations. Britain and France would take care of the Arabs if "the US would take care of the bear." Dulles refused: Washington could not back military operations against Nasser, and Murphy and Dillon delivered the same message to Pineau on August 2. Pineau retorted that Nasser could not be allowed to keep the canal, or the Sultan of Morocco and Bourguiba of Tunisia would be overwhelmed by extremists, the French would be forced to quit Algeria, and all North Africa would be lost to the West. Pineau repeated that France would act militarily, and it would do so alone if necessary. During the course of the London meeting Pineau wanted it understood that at the end of the conference of signatories "Egypt will be required to accept the proposals put to her." But Dulles refused; Washington could not tie its hands.[19]

The conference of signatories, twenty-two nations, met in London from August 16 to August 23. Eighteen of the nations, the USSR not included among them, agreed on a set of proposals for international operation of the canal, which was then put to Nasser by Australian Prime Minister Menzies on September 5. Predictably, the Egyptian dictator refused; he was quite capable of running the canal himself, in the interests of everyone, thank you. The diplomatic failure only sharpened the divergence between Washington and its two most important allies. From Cairo, French Ambassador du Chayla reported that Nasser had refused the Menzies proposal because his foreign minister had assured him that the United States would prevent any recourse to force against Egypt.[20] In both Egypt and Algeria the French now saw their opponents emboldened by the belief that they enjoyed American support. Paris moved ahead unilaterally with preparations for an eventual military action. Initial inquiries were made to Israeli Defense Minister Moshe Dayan about the possibility of an Israeli attack on Egypt, with French help, as

early as September 1. By September 28 an Israeli delegation was in
Paris, and a secret agreement on an eventual attack was concluded that
would be put to the British.[21] American observers listened uncomfort-
ably as the French Arabic-language broadcasts to the Middle East took
on vituperative anti-Nasser tones; Paris was now in a "fire-eating
mood," the country unified in its recourse to a violent policy. Washington noted that the British were divided on what to do about the crisis,
with the Labor party against any military action, but in Paris all opposition was nullified by the Algerian question. A CIA "Watch Committee" reported that the British and the French were likely to launch military action if negotiations failed; French preparations were already
being detected under General Beaufré, in the belief that "France would
have less trouble in Algeria if Nasser were removed." A National Intelligence Estimate reported French military objectives: Cairo could be
taken in a few days, but there would likely be rioting, sabotage, terror,
and a prolonged, difficult occupation in store. The Americans would be
confronted with a dilemma—either to identify with colonialism, or suffer strained relations with their allies and the opening of new opportu-
nities for the communist powers.[22]

But the State Department needed neither its watch committees nor its
intelligence estimates to know what was happening. Dulles understood
Macmillan's dilemma: Nasser must accept or be forced to accept the results of the conference of signatories. The obvious third possibility,
which was unthinkable, was that Britain accept Nasser's control of the
canal, but this would mean that the United Kingdom was finished as a
great power and that Eden would be forced to resign. Pineau, at 10
Downing Street for meetings with the British, told Dillon that military
action against Nasser was now inevitable. The Joint Chiefs themselves
shared the French perspective: if Nasser won, the West would lose the
Mideast, be forced to abandon its North African bases, and a new impetus would be given to the rebellion against the French in Algeria. On
August 28, Eden told Dulles that if the British were to meet with disaster it was better that it come as a result of action rather than inaction,
and Lloyd wrote: "As you know, it is our intention to proceed with our
[military] plans unless Nasser can be seen clearly and decisively to have
given in." Dulles told Eisenhower that British military planning appeared "irrevocable," and he repeated this to the National Security
Council the next day.[23] The French "would rather fight at the center of
the trouble—namely Egypt—than fight around the periphery of the difficulty, namely Algeria," and he (Dulles) found it "extremely difficult to

take a stand against British and French views since they would be finished as first-rate powers if they did not check Nasser." Admiral Radford, chairman of the Joint Chiefs, wanted logistical support for the British and the French, if not direct American participation in their operations. But to Eisenhower, to whom he always deferred, Dulles indicated he was of two minds; he wondered whether the use of force must not be avoided even at the cost of a Nasser victory. Eisenhower decisively tipped the balance against the use of force, and, whatever his private feelings, Dulles followed suit. The State Department informed its missions abroad that it viewed with the deepest concern British and French plans for military action against Egypt, and the United States was doing all in its power to prevent it, for the consequences would be "incalculable."[24]

Dulles had another diplomatic option up his sleeve; instead of the failed conference of powers there should now be formed a "Suez Canal Users' Association" to be made up of all those nations most dependent upon the canal for their international commerce. Dulles thought that there was still a window for action, for despite the bluster in Paris and London their military plans were not yet in readiness. Moreover, the British would not act until they had exhausted one last option, the United Nations, which had to be demonstrated to be paralyzed by the inevitable Soviet veto. Dulles did not want Suez to come before the UN, lest Washington be constrained to demonstrate its opposition to the plans of its closest allies. The French, too, disliked the notion of a naked act of colonial aggression, and were busy drawing the Israelis into the famous and devious scheme devised by General Challe of having Israel attack Egypt so that the British and French could appear not to be invading but rather carrying out a police action to keep the Israelis and Egyptians apart and the canal in operation. The British agreed to try the Users' Association idea and put the scheme to the French, who were persuaded to sign on. But Pineau and Lloyd agreed privately that Dulles was simply playing for time until the American elections. The American secretary was too fertile in ideas, and would do better to stick to just one. Any Users' Association must operate the canal and receive the dues for all shipping, and "shoot its way through" if the Egyptians refused the deal.[25]

Meantime Dillon reported the most "disturbing interview" with Pineau, as if he had not had enough of these already in Paris. The French foreign minister demanded immediate action, starting with the withholding of toll payments to the Egyptians. Washington, he warned, was leaving the British and the French no options except war. There should not be the slightest doubt that French national interests were involved and that France and the United Kingdom would resort to arms. Dillon had never seen Pineau so upset. Pineau more calmly delivered the same message personally to Dulles on September 19. There must be a solution within a month or it would be too late, and "the Soviets will have the canal." Israel would no doubt attack Egypt if the West were to weaken, Pineau offered, anticipating an Egyptian attack upon itself. And this would give the British the right to reoccupy the canal according to the terms of the Suez evacuation treaty signed only a few years earlier.[26] Pineau thus laid out for Dulles the entire scheme that would be put into operation at the end of October. It is difficult to understand Washington's later protests that it was taken by surprise by the British, French, and Israeli actions; Dulles's only real complaint was that he was left out of the specific planning.[27] Why he should have expected anything else, not being in sympathy with British and French plans, is not clear.

Ominously, French Ambassador Dejean reported that the Russians were behind Nasser, and were using Arab nationalism and anticolonialism to turn the southern flank of NATO in the Mediterranean while dislocating the Baghdad Pact. In case of a British-French attack in the Middle East Moscow would not intervene but would send war matériel and possibly "volunteers" to the Arabs. Mikoyan asked the French ambassador directly, "Do you want war? Have you not enough of it in Algeria?" And he had included a gratuitous warning: "there [in Algeria] at least you are claiming French territory; here [in Egypt] all the Arab world will turn against you." Meanwhile, in Washington, trouble was again surfacing in the United Nations. Paris wanted American help in blocking the Algerian question from coming up on the General Assembly agenda, and Ambassador Hervé Alphand told Herbert Hoover, Jr., that the French again expected Washington to exert pressure on certain governments to vote favorably. But Hoover was reserved; if the French government could announce a liberal plan in Algeria, of course, the situation would be easier, but while supporting France "in principle," Hoover could not promise a vote against UN competence on the issue or its inscription on the agenda of the world body.[28] Finally, in Morocco, French Ambassador Dubois reported the prestige of Nasser at an all-time high because of his success thus far in operating the canal and collecting dues from many of the nations using it. The danger of the appeal of Pan-Arabism was consequently increased and the threat to Algeria magnified. The French policy of "interdependence" with Tunisia and Morocco would be fatally compromised if Suez turned out badly for France; France must remain strong.[29] Besieged French leaders saw their entire world policy threatened with collapse.

The conference establishing the Suez Canal Users' Association (SCUA) met from September 19 to 21 in London, but the French, who wanted it to impound dues from all shipping through the canal, judged it meaningless when it refused to do so. Immediately thereafter the British brought the entire Suez matter to the Security Council of the United Nations. Dulles had not been consulted and thought this foolish; the French said they had been reluctantly led to agree. On September 25, Dulles told Alphand that the United States lacked the power to force its shipowners to pay tolls to SCUA rather than to the Egyptians. And what if the Egyptians then blocked the canal? Were the French prepared to pay the cost of shipping around the Cape of Good Hope? Alphand asked if Washington would be prepared to help in such an eventuality, but Dulles said this would require congressional approval. Alphand asked for American support in the Security Council, but Dulles said he could guarantee nothing, having been kept in the dark about British and French intentions. Alphand said that three-power talks were urgent; Dulles said they should have preceded bringing Suez to the UN, now the damage was done.[30] To British Ambassador Makins and Harold Macmillan, Dulles said that the United States could prevent American shippers from paying canal tolls to Egypt, but it could not force them to pay tolls to the SCUA. Moreover, if payments to Egypt were interrupted and Egypt closed the canal in retaliation, the consequences would be heaviest for Britain and France. The secretary of state did not think the plan to withhold canal dues from Nasser would work. Macmillan agreed that the British could not afford shipment around the Cape. Dulles said it was best to let the present situation continue, "although the French are violent on this subject." Macmillan was noncommittal in reaction to this, and went on to pay a courtesy call on the president, to whom he said that "he hoped devoutly that there was no question of his reelection." Eisenhower said that he "hoped that nothing drastic would happen through British action which might diminish our chances."[31]

But the drastic action the American president feared was already in preparation in Paris, where Moshe Dayan, Golda Meir, and Israeli Prime Minister David Ben-Gurion met with Defense Minister Bourgès-Maunoury and General Challe on September 30. Bourgès wanted Israel to attack Egypt first by itself and prior to the American elections; before the elections, Pineau agreed, Eisenhower would be unable to oppose the British-French action for fear of the Jewish vote, while afterward American policy would revert to its traditional reflection of the will of the American oil companies, whom the French thought to be in league with the FLN.[32] General Challe, however, thought Washington would not oppose the operation. NATO had furnished special equipment for British and French planes being sent to Cyprus, a clear sign of Washington's encouragement. Dayan said Israel needed to be sure that the UK would not act against Israel to defend Egypt. There was still no love lost between the British and the Israelis, a scant eight years since the struggle for Israeli independence. Bourgès said, on the contrary, France had no bombers, and was counting on the British to help Israel against the Egyptians. But to the Israelis the situation still gave cause for suspicion: the British apparently wanted Israel to attack Egypt and play the villain in the entire operation so that the British could appear to be entering the fray against Israel on the side of the angels. Ben-Gurion to the end distrusted what he insisted was a "British idea" to profit at the expense of Egypt while pretending that it was opposing Israeli wrongdoing. Dayan, however, went on to discuss eventual military operations against Egypt and Israel's equipment needs with French Chief of Staff General Paul Ely on October 1.

Ely liked the Israeli operational plans, and General Challe the next next day led a military group to Israel, where the French officers were in turn impressed by what they saw of the Israeli army. The Israelis could take and hold the canal, the French reported, until the French and the British were ready to strike, although they would need French assistance to neutralize Egyptian air power.[33] The French secured the promise of the British not to intervene on the Egyptian side, although the Israelis remained suspicious. On October 10 the Israelis carried out a massive antiterrorist reprisal raid against Jordan at Kalkilia, and the British continued to support Jordan. But on October 18, Mollet invited Ben-Gurion to France for the famous Sèvres meeting at the home of Bonnier de la Chapelle, whose son Fernand had assassinated Admiral Darlan in Algiers in December 1942. The talks began on October 22, with the British joining in to do the final planning, despite their obvious distaste for dealing with the Israelis. According to Dayan, Lloyd reported at the meeting that the Egyptians had in fact agreed to compromise on the SCUA plan in the United Nations, but it was too late; the UK had decided to topple Nasser anyway.[34]

Dulles continued trying to obtain a satisfactory settlement with Egypt that might avert military action. He did not know the details of British and French military planning, and particularly that it might involve Israel, although he perhaps should have guessed this from Pineau's warning that the Israelis might attack. But American intelligence estimates judged an Israeli attack on Egypt unlikely. Dulles complained to Alphand on September 27 that the United States was being "left out of the planning" by London and Paris, but he was specifically referring to the UN Security Council initiative, which Alphand dismissed casually, claiming that France was also opposed to involving the UN, but had gone along to satisfy London. Dulles remarked that it was "natural that the French should want to bring in the British on military action because in effect the French already had an Arab war on their hands and this would give them a powerful ally." Suspicion increased in Washington after the Israeli-French meeting at Sèvres, although the American leaders had no knowledge of the specifics. Dulles told Eisenhower that U.S. relations with the British and French were now bad because they did not feel Washington was backing them sufficiently and they were blaming the Americans for the lack of results. Eisenhower remarked that the United States must maintain an independent position in the crisis "until we know what they are up to." In the American National Security Council, Dulles had already laid bare all his suspicions and frustration. Relations with the French, he said on October 5, were "strained to a degree not paralleled for a very long time in the past." The French were eager to use force in Suez on the grounds that "it is vital to their war in North Africa." The United States was restraining the UK, but the French expected that "if we are allies in NATO we must be everywhere in the world." "We don't know their plans. Never in recent years had we faced a situation where we had no clear idea of the intentions of our British and French allies." Part of the problem was that Pineau and Lloyd were not "strong men who spoke for their governments." Suez could be negotiated if they were willing, and consequently the United States would be dead wrong to join in any use of force.[35]

Dulles cabled the results to Dillon, who agreed that the French were weak, frustrated, divided, and upset that they could not count on the United States outside of NATO. This was a curious conclusion. The French may have been wrong in their policy choices and angry at the lack of U.S. backing, but on few occasions in the past had they been so unified or determined in their course of action. Dillon noted ominously, however, that their only alternative in the long run to reliance on Washington was European unity, which, paradoxically, Washington favored. In fact, simultaneously with the Suez talks, the French Foreign Ministry was dropping its insistence on separating Euratom, the European Atomic Energy pool, from the creation of a Common Market; Paris would now agree to the Common Market on the condition that it accepted the harmonization of social legislation among the six countries, the abolition of duties on French agricultural products as well as industrial ones, and the inclusion of the French empire.[36] The French had been inhibited from pursuing European unity, Dillon noted, by their reliance on the United States in the past; if they were now turning toward it, it was from frustration with Washington and hostility to its policies. In any case, the United States should not buy pro-U.S. sentiment by blindly supporting French policies in North Africa.[37]

Dulles confronted Pineau and Lloyd at the United Nations on October 5. Was there real purpose in going to the UN to find a peaceful settlement of Suez, or did the British and French simply intend to "clear the way for stronger measures"? President Eisenhower, Dulles warned, believed that war would drive the area into the hands of the USSR. Lloyd accepted responsibility for the approach to the UN, but the Users' Association had revealed its inadequacy. The British faced a ten-day limit, Lloyd warned, after which they "must decide what to do next." Pineau insisted that the time had come for action. Dulles interjected that war would be a disaster, but Pineau warned that the existence of NATO was at stake. To be sure, he would never abandon the alliance so long as he was foreign minister, but French public opinion was aroused, and the destruction of the Atlantic alliance would be the greatest victory the Soviets could obtain in the Cold War. Not only the canal but the fate of the Middle East, and Algeria, Morocco, and Tunisia was involved as well. Egypt must be made to accept the terms of the London conference of signatories, meaning international control of the canal, or catastrophe would follow.[38]

Dulles informed Eisenhower immediately that Pineau and Lloyd both believed that only force could maintain their nations' prestige. Dulles had argued that force would drive the area into the arms of the USSR, but he had been unheard. Egyptian Foreign Minister Mahmoud Fawzi meanwhile had indicated that he was ready to negotiate an agreement with the Suez Canal Users' Association. But Dillon cabled further disturbing news from Paris: the French wanted international control of the canal or they would use force. A pretext was necessary, but a provocation could easily be arranged via the Arab-Israeli conflict. The French believed that the United States was letting them down and Suez had indeed given renewed impetus to the idea of European unity in France, but a neutralist Europe. French confidence in NATO was impaired. The United States would view with concern a Europe headed by leftists like Aneuran Bevan, Pietro Nenni, and Daniel Mayer, but that was where the French were heading if let down by the United States in Suez or Algeria.[39]

The British initiative in the United Nations was designed to fail but almost achieved success despite itself. The Security Council had little difficulty reaching agreement on hardly exceptionable principles of operating the canal. They included free transit of the canal for everyone, respect for Egyptian sovereignty, insulation of the canal from politics, negotiations on the amount and attribution of tolls, and measures for arbitration of differences. Egypt appeared to want to compromise with the UN and the Users' Association, and Lloyd and Fawzi appeared to be moving toward an agreement; Eisenhower, indeed, latched on to the Egyptian agreement with delight, rather prematurely announcing on October 13 that "the crisis is behind us."[40] But Pineau, acting as president of the UN Security Council, insisted on the terms of the eighteen-nation accord or nothing, blocking a compromise. The British forced a vote, which, as anticipated, was blocked by a Soviet veto, the Egyptians believing this to be an infringement on their sovereignty.[41] Dulles believed that this was what the British and French had wanted all along, but he thought negotiations were not dead for all that, and Dag Hammerskjöld believed the outlook for agreement was still favorable. But this implied a will to compromise, which was now lacking. Lloyd wrote Dulles a letter on October 15 detailing his grievances: this was, he said, "a testing time for Anglo-American relations," and warned that this divergence between the Americans and the British would have the most serious repercussions in Great Britain.[42] But Dulles replied that both he and Eisenhower had separately announced that the Americans had never entertained the idea of "shooting their way through" the canal on their own terms. Lloyd reacted in anger, and Pineau, for his part, professed to be "double-crossed" by Washington's attitude.

With all possibility of compromise now excluded, the French, British, and Israelis went ahead with their planning. At this point Dillon was told of the impending Israeli military strike by Jacques Chaban-Delmas, who led him to believe, however, that it would occur a few days after the American election. Was this a subterfuge to disarm Washington, since the action was already set for the end of October? In fact the British had insisted on action prior to the American elections, calculating that it would be impossible for the administration during the campaign to do anything about the crisis. Dillon believed the Israelis had gotten word that Eisenhower was planning a new and dramatic peace appeal on the day after the elections, and that this precipitated their strike, which dragged the British and the French in with them. This version of what occurred was also later propagated by Christian Pineau.[43] The CIA was able to confirm the imminence of a military action in late October from the Israeli military buildup and the concentration of British forces on Cyprus, both seen through U2 airplane reconnaissance. When Dillon took up Israeli preparations with the Quai, Secretary-General Louis Joxe assured him that nothing was taking place; but the Quai itself and Joxe were bypassed during the planning in Paris.[44] The Israelis were dependent on French pilots and air power to defend their skies and destroy the Egyptian air force on the ground before they could invade the Sinai peninsula.[45] French air force squadrons were flown to Israel during the week preceding the Israeli action and painted over with Israeli markings to mask their participation in the early stages of the operation. All this required careful coordination and later proved to Washington's satisfaction that the action was a joint French-British-Israeli enterprise from its inception. Yet Eisenhower persisted in believing almost to the last that somehow the British were not really involved, and that the Israelis were responsible.

It was hardly a coincidence that while the Israelis were meeting with the British and French at Sèvres, on October 22–24, 1956, French intelligence engineered the arrest of five leaders of the FLN, including Ahmed Ben Bella and Mohammed Khider, by forcing down a Moroccan plane carrying the Algerian rebel leaders from Morocco to Tunisia. A week earlier, acting on intelligence apparently supplied by the Israelis, the French navy intercepted a Yugoslav ship, the *Athos,* in international waters; it was bound for Morocco with a cargo of weapons destined for the Algerian rebels.[46] The French now had incontrovertible proof, as if they needed it, of what they had long known, that Egypt was actively assisting the Algerian rebels. Furthermore, the war in Algeria had once again taken an ugly turn. On September 30 the terrorist campaign began in Algiers with explosions at the Milk Bar and the Cafeteria; after that, terrorist incidents in the city occurred on an average of four times daily.[47] The ship interception and arrests, moreover, were meant to scuttle continuing secret talks between the French and the leaders of the insurrection on terms for a cease-fire. Mohammed Khider, who had participated in three of four rebel meetings with the French in Rome and Cairo, was in the plane and captured with Ben Bella.[48] Clearly, with the relative success of the military *quadrillage*, the decision for military action in Egypt now taken, and the expectation that Nasser would be toppled, many in Paris and Algiers no longer thought it necessary or desirable to negotiate with the Algerian rebels, who were the objects of revulsion for their terrorist tactics, and who, it was expected, would shortly be defeated. The head of the rebellion could be lopped off through the arrests; its roots would be destroyed once Nasser was gone.

The arrests of the rebel leaders marked a turning point in French policy and a fundamental break, along with Suez, in the development of French-American and French-British relations. There were two reasons for this: with Ben Bella in jail, his release became a rebel demand overshadowing the question of actual cease-fire negotiations; but even more seriously, the circumstances of his capture raised the most serious doubts about the stability and functioning of the Fourth Republic, leading to the development in Washington and then NATO of serious reservations about the regime's future usefulness and France's place in the North Atlantic alliance. The airplane carrying Ahmed Ben Bella was en route from Casablanca to Tunis, where a conference was to bring together Sultan Mohammed V, President Bourguiba of Tunisia, and the Algerian nationalist leader to discuss plans for a future North African federation. Both Mohammed V and Bourguiba were rival candidates to head up such a federation, which they saw as a vehicle for their own ambitions as well as a covering scheme through which Algeria might receive its independence from France and maintain some form of association with the French community. Most important, the moderating influence of Tunisia and Morocco on the more radical tendencies of the Algerian rebels would be manifest. The idea was also attractive to Washington, where it appeared to be a useful device for the construction of an independent and anticommunist Maghreb. Ben Bella and his retinue first flew to Rabat, where they were initially received by the sultan, much to the annoyance of the French, who warned him in advance to be "prudent" with the Algerians lest French opinion take offense at his actions. The sultan was not dissuaded by this, however; he was seeking to upstage Bourguiba in a kind of competition to be the mediator in the Algerian War, he believed he could influence the rebels to be more flexible in the secret negotiations then in process between the French and the FLN, and he may well have relished this show of independence of the French. Perhaps more than any of these motives, however, the monarch was attracted by the idea of a North African federation of the Maghreb in association with France that would, he hoped, be headed by himself.[49]

The sultan was convinced by the French warnings not to fly together with the Algerian leader to Tunis in the same plane. But he still regarded Ben Bella as under his protection while in a Moroccan aircraft; moreover, the plane was forcibly diverted to Oran, Algeria, while over international air space. The French pilot, who was under contract to Air Morocco, was then ordered by General Frandon, the air commander for Algeria, to proceed to Algiers. Lacoste was away at the time; his secretary-general, Pierre Chaussade, was approached by two military figures on behalf of General Frandon, who noted that this was a unique opportunity to strike a permanent blow against the rebels. Chaussade in Lacoste's absence secured approval for the action from Max Lejeune, who was secretary-general of the army. Neither Chaussade nor Lejeune tried to reach the premier, Mollet, who was deliberately confronted with a fait accompli.[50] Clearly, they had reason to believe Mollet would refuse to agree to the operation or they would have consulted him. Nor did Lacoste, who approved the arrests upon his return to Algiers, try to reach Mollet either. It became clear in Washington that the arrests were a rogue operation, which was to become all too characteristic of the Fourth Republic's modus operandi.

Washington was informed separately by both Habib Bourguiba of Tunisia and the Sultan of Morocco, and the FLN also appealed directly to President Eisenhower for Ben Bella's release. Mohammed V was particularly incensed, and regarded his honor as having been personally compromised. To the French chargé, Lalouette, he complained that the operation was beyond his comprehension. Everything he was doing was in the spirit of helping France through its predicament; it was his understanding that the French government favored his efforts to pressure the rebels in favor of conciliation; and the Algerians had left for Tunis under his engagement of honor as their safe-conduct.[51] Lalouette said the embassy had no foreknowledge of plans for the downing of the plane, but he had warned the Moroccans against mixing in the Algerian problem. The sultan had been receiving mixed signals from Paris, another indication of the political disarray there.

Personally offended, Mohammed V broke off diplomatic relations with Paris to protest the French action. Paris requested that the United

States step in to help reestablish ties, but on this occasion Washington refused, "since it would inevitably involve the U.S. in the whole Algerian question" and France had always taken exception to American involvement in that issue in the past.[52] The French breach with Tunisia over the arrests turned out to be not easily reparable either. Tunisian Ambassador Mongi Slim called on Robert Murphy in Washington in the company of Habib Bourguiba, Jr., to protest the Ben Bella arrest, warning that there could be no resumption of normal relations with France until the rebel leaders had been released. Tunisia was now prepared, moreover, to support the Arab states in their efforts to have the Algerian issue brought before the Security Council of the United Nations. Slim reminded Murphy that Tunisia had demanded that French troops evacuate the country ever since it had received its independence from France, and he demanded to know Washington's position. Murphy was unable to answer and could only remind the Tunisian of French sensitivity to intrusions into their internal affairs, "of which they consider Algeria to be one."[53] In fact, Paris expressed its appreciation that Washington did not intervene in the capture of the rebel leaders, "since this would have been deeply resented in France."[54]

Washington had been aware of and encouraged by the secret talks between Paris and the rebels. American sources confirmed that four of the six leading rebel chiefs in exile in Cairo wanted an agreement with Paris on terms for a cease-fire, and that the sultan was working with the rebel leaders in an attempt to get them to abandon their insistence on French recognition of their right to independence as a precondition for entering talks.[55] The French government had been secretly in contact with the rebel leadership from April through October 1956 about terms for a cease-fire, and informal meetings were held between two Socialist party functionaries and representatives of the FLN about the possibility of entering formal negotiations. Pierre Commin and Pierre Herbaut met with Mohammed Yazid and Ahmed Francis in Belgrade in July 1956 and again in Rome in September; on September 22, they returned to Belgrade and agreed tentatively that France might recognize Algeria's right of self-determination, not independence, in exchange for an agreement to a cease-fire and negotiations. Neither negotiating team could necessarily have carried these terms with their respective leaders in Paris or Cairo, but negotiations had not been broken off until they were derailed by the downing of the Moroccan plane and the arrest of Ben Bella.[56] Yazid, back at his regular United Nations post in New York in October when the plane was downed, told the Afro-Asian bloc representatives to the UN that the rebels had safe-conduct guarantees from Paris, and their security had been assured by the French government in view of the negotiations in progress.[57] The French had violated their own word in making the arrests.

Bourguiba meanwhile told the American Embassy in Tunis that he had talked directly to Alain Savary, French minister for Tunisian and Moroccan affairs, who condemned the arrests as a "shocking and un-precedented act of piracy" by his own government. Savary was shortly to resign in protest, further proof of the growing political disarray in Paris. The sultan joined Bourguiba in immediately requesting that the Americans intervene to secure the release of the rebel leaders. Washington strongly disapproved of the arrests; Dulles, reporting on the matter to Eisenhower amid concerns over the Suez crisis, "expressed great concern lest the British and the French commit suicide by getting deeply involved in colonial controversies in an attempt to impose their rule by force in the Middle East and Africa. The President indicated that he fully shared my concern in this respect."[58] At the Quai, bitter officials, bypassed during the crisis, sniped at their own government: Jean Daridan, echoing Savary, condemned the operation to William Tyler as "an act of folly," and asked the Americans to try to intervene with his government to secure the release of the rebel leaders.

The British were similarly worried about the breakdown of cabinet government in France. Lloyd complained to the American ambassador that he deplored the necessity of cooperating with France because "Among other things, he believed the French are politically inept and may be counted on to make major political blunders, such as the arrest of the five Algerian leaders."[59] But the Americans reluctantly concluded that they had no "legal right" to intervene, and the British, at the very moment deeply involved in planning the invasion of Egypt with France and Israel, were not about to do so either.[60] The British decision was particularly regrettable, because the French government was itself divided over the possibility of releasing the rebel leaders, Mollet apparently having been initially favorable to doing so; the British in particular at this point might have tipped the balance. Washington was impeded from forming a clear policy by the clouds of uncertainty that surrounded the captures. Mollet privately told the Americans that he had been kept in the dark but, once the arrests were accomplished, he had no choice but to go along. Publicly, however, the French leader covered for and defended the arrests, taking personal responsibility for them. Mollet angrily put Tunis and Rabat on notice that the Algerian problem was an internal affair of the French, France was still juridically responsible for Moroccan aviation, and the French military were within their rights to order down a French pilot and plane carrying French citizens wanted by French justice.[61]

But Alain Savary, following his resignation, confirmed for the Americans what he had told the Tunisians and Washington already knew: the affair was prearranged by French intelligence and the military five days in advance and undertaken to torpedo the Algerian negotiations. But Savary added more: several members of the Mollet cabinet, he said, had been informed; there had been considerable discussion, and several ministers favored the scheme, while Premier Guy Mollet and Savary, among others, had been opposed. Mollet at the conclusion of the discussions gave specific instructions that the operation not be carried out. Washington had every reason to suppose Savary's version worthy of credence, because he was a direct witness to the events he described. Moreover, Mollet was informed of the arrest while at a dinner with General Alfred Gruenther, the commander of NATO, where the French premier appeared visibly shaken upon receiving news of the arrests. Gruenther understood from Mollet's demeanor that the premier's authority had been specifically contravened; he was embarrassed in front of the Americans, showing that the collapse of political authority in France had already progressed much further than anyone yet imagined.[62]

The arrests were followed by widespread allegations that among Ben Bella's papers were documents from American oil companies about expected leases and exploration once Algeria became independent, demonstrating American support for the Algerian insurrection. Washington was aware within days of the arrests, however, that study of the documents revealed that "involvement of any US individuals or concerns were very minor," contrary to sensational reports in the French press.[63] The French government could easily have confirmed the existence of such documents if it had them by publishing them, or it should have issued a denial of the allegations, as Washington demanded. It did neither, despite the fact that the government knew the allegations to be false. According to the American Embassy, which persisted in trying to obtain a denial from Mollet, the premier had found the allegations to be false after first telling the American ambassador that they were authentic; Lacoste had passed them on to newspaper people without checking. After the Matignon found the stories to be false, Mollet wanted to issue a denial, but when the source was revealed as Lacoste it became politically impossible for him to do so. Matthew Looram observed that "Lacoste must really have Mollet cowed if the Government is so reluctant to take a public stand on the matter." The hypocrisy of the French was all the more glaring in that while they did nothing to squelch rumors of the oil companies' collusion with the nationalists, they did everything themselves to get the same companies interested and involved in the exploitation of the Sahara. In fact, an official from the Bureau de Recherche du Petrole was traveling around the United States trying to interest American companies in Algerian exploration.[64] The French inability to deny what they knew to be false reinforced Washington's image of a French government in disarray, its ministers, in this case those responsible for national defense and Algeria, conducting policies independently of the prime minister, who did not have the power to prevent them from doing so. Pineau was in the habit of complaining to the Americans that France would negotiate with the Muslim population once it could settle upon "*interlocuteurs valables*," or valid authorities, with whom to deal in confidence. The Americans discovered, however, that it was rather they who lacked "*interlocuteurs valables*" with whom to deal in Paris.

If Washington was disturbed by the Ben Bella kidnaping, it was infuriated to see French aircraft and pilots participate in the initial stages of the Israeli attack on Egypt a week later.[65] Although the French strongly insisted that the Suez operation was aimed entirely at the preservation of Western interests in the canal zone and the containment of Arab nationalism, it was clear that the French were seeking a solution to their Algerian dilemma. Dulles became extremely irritated at the lies the British and French now told him; while his intelligence reported evidence in the Israeli attack of an impending three-power war on Egypt, Paris and London denied all knowledge of what the Israelis were doing.[66] The Israeli parachute drops at the Mitla Pass came on the late afternoon of October 29; by the next day Ariel Sharon's forces were penetrating the Sinai desert in order to hook up with the parachutists. On October 30, Dulles told Eisenhower that Israeli-French-British complicity was now apparent. It was not really a question of the Suez Canal alone for any of the three, moreover: the Israelis were worried about their security, the British were concerned about their position in the Persian Gulf, and the French believed they were protecting their position in Algeria. The British and French, as privately agreed at Sèvres, followed the attack with an ultimatum to Egypt (and ostensibly to Israel) that Dulles termed as "crude and brutal as anything he had ever seen." It put

Egypt on the same plane as the aggressor, Israel, and demanded that Egypt agree to the occupation of its territory in the canal zone to boot, while the Israelis stopped their forces ten miles short of the canal. This was as utterly unacceptable in Washington as it was in Cairo; Dulles told Alphand that this was "the blackest day which had occurred in many years in the relations between England, France, and the United States."[67] To the British, he said "We are facing the destruction of our trust in each other."[68]

Washington quickly forced a cease-fire upon the British, which the French had no choice but to observe as well, and it eventually obtained an Israeli withdrawal from the Sinai desert. The coincidence of the operation with the U.S. election particularly angered President Eisenhower. Dillon had been assured in Paris that no military operations would take place until after the American elections, if at all. Dulles declared that "the United States must now exercise leadership, and cease walking a tightrope between British and French relations and the friendship and understanding of the newly independent countries escaped from colonialism."[69] The United States had known the French were planning the use of force from the beginning; it was a French plan to which the British had acquiesced. The secretary thought the French-Israeli connection especially noxious. But all the NATO powers, with the exception of the Dutch and the Portuguese, were against the British-French action, which must mark the "death knell" of British and French colonialism, their governments having acted both "contrary to our advice and principle."[70]

An American resolution in favor of an immediate cease-fire was easily carried in the UN General Assembly on November 2; Under Secretary of State Hoover received the thanks of the Arab countries for Washington's strong position. Guiringaud, the French delegate, told Lodge that France was furious at being treated the same as Nasser, the guilty party, and warned of very serious consequences for French-American relations. But the ponderous British military machine was still in process, preventing the actual landings until November 5, while the Israelis sat poised a few miles from the canal, having scored an impressive triumph over the Egyptians on the ground. In the meantime the Soviets warned the British and the French to desist, and on November 5, as the British and French paratroops landed near Port Said, Bulganin and Khrushchev threatened to rain nuclear missiles on Paris and London if they did not do so. The French panicked and demanded an American response to the Soviet threats. Alphand delivered a message to

President Eisenhower while Mollet convoked Dillon in Paris and demanded a clear warning to Moscow that the United States would defend its allies, in the interest of avoiding any Soviet "miscalculation." Dillon told Mollet he assumed that in the event of a nuclear attack NATO would come into play and the United States would stand with France.[71] Mollet demanded confirmation of this from Washington, however, which Dillon was unable to obtain. To the amazement of the French, the Americans refused Alphand's entreaties delivered personally in Washington as well. It would not be an exaggeration to see here the origins of the French disillusionment with the NATO alliance. Murphy told Alphand that the only way to restore the situation was for the British and French to accept a cease-fire. Alphand insisted that Soviet nuclear threats against Paris and London were a different issue than Suez: they involved NATO and direct aggression against an American ally. But the French government was undercut by the British; Murphy had already been informed of the British cease-fire, which obviated the Soviet threat and the need for any U.S. action.[72]

The French and Americans traded angry charges at one another in the aftermath of the cease-fire and the accompanying misunderstandings. Alphand saw the sinister guiding hand of the U.S. State Department behind American press reports equating the French-British operation in Suez with the Soviet repression in Hungary. Murphy denied this, but said the State Department could not prevent others from making that connection; besides, had not Pineau been spreading "fantastic" stories to the effect that Nasser had wanted to resign, but was dissuaded from doing so by the American ambassador in Egypt? Alphand insisted that direct Soviet intervention in Suez must be recognized by the administration as bringing NATO into play. Murphy refused to agree that any such Soviet intervention had been intended. Alphand said he had also heard that the United States intended to take the leadership of the Bandung powers against colonialism; Murphy condemned this as a wild rumor.

The Quai d'Orsay wrote Suez off as a major disaster; none of the French objectives in the operation had been attained. The only exception was the successful destruction of the newly built Egyptian air force on the ground. Nasser had gained prestige, the USSR escaped opprobrium for its repression in Hungary, and big-three relations had been harmed. The French position in Algeria was weakened rather than strengthened by the crisis, Israel remained endangered, and the canal was closed. The United States had forced France into a thankless impasse and had failed to support it in its most difficult moment. Washington had abandoned the French in Indochina and declined to support them in North Africa, and now the Americans colluded with Moscow and the Arabs against France. France had no choice but to doubt seriously professions of American solidarity and friendship: "They chose to cause us to fail" at Suez. The worst was that French security depended on the American alliance for all that. France must bring Washington around to its views, which was impossible, or adopt the American perspective, which was clearly unacceptable. Yet there appeared to be no other options. A unified and independently strong Europe would provide such an option, but this was still in the future while the Russian danger was immediate. For France, North Africa remained the key to most of the problems with its allies; an Algerian solution was essential to the restoration of big-three unity.[73]

More broadly, the American reaction to the Suez operation was seen in Paris as a humiliating betrayal "beyond all reason." The Americans pursued pro-Arab policies while "calling to order" their independent allies, a golden opportunity to demonstrate to the Arabs their freedom from "encumbering allies" while winning a place for American oil companies in the Middle East as well. The State Department, Paris concluded, was now hopelessly pro-Arab. In fact the trio of under and assistant secretaries Robert Murphy, Livingston Merchant, and Herbert Hoover, Jr., joined by Henry Cabot Lodge at the UN, constituted a group of short-tempered policymakers who had little sympathy for Paris's peculiarities and who advocated letting the French take American policy as it was or leave it and go their own way. The anti-French group easily overcame Dulles's reputed pro-French sympathies, and the secretary's emergency operation for abdominal pains at the height of the crisis left them in control at the State Department. Eisenhower himself, of all the American foreign policy leaders, was best able to imagine himself in the French position. But he was as capable of expressing total exasperation with them as sympathy, apparently depending on his mood and the issue at hand.[74] Christian Herter, Dulles's second in command and ultimate successor, would seem to have shared anti-French feelings as well. Despite Dulles's long history of association with France, moreover, he had no really close relationships with the current flock of French politicians and remained out of circulation during the immediate aftermath of Suez owing to his operation, which disclosed cancer, the malady that eventually was to kill him in 1959. [75]

Reports reached Paris in January 1957 that the American-supported Free Trade Union Committee had extended a loan of forty million francs to the Moroccan, Tunisian, and Algerian unions in order to help them to form an international league of Arab trade unions based in Cairo.[76] This seemed the last straw: the Quai noted nervously that responsible "patriotic" newspapers in France attacked the Americans "with all the fervor of the PCF [French Communist Party]" while rumors continued to circulate of the alleged deal between Ben Bella and the American oil companies that was discovered in the Algerian leader's papers at the time of his arrest. Suspicion grew in France that the American aim was to oust France entirely from North Africa in the hope of replacing French interests and influence there with American hegemony.[77] In Algiers, reports flowed in of feelings of betrayal among the French residents and encouragement felt by the rebels following the Suez failure. Mollet himself believed that Nasser's popularity was now much greater in North Africa, where the situation was bound to deteriorate further.[78]

The result of all this has been described as an "orgy of anti-Americanism" in France and the emergence of "national Molletism." To Dillon, Mollet professed dismay at the anti-American feeling in France, which he said the government was trying to play down. But the premier's reassurance was combined with a threat. A statement of support from President Eisenhower was imperative, for "France's membership in NATO is no longer by any means assured."[79] From Paris, Dillon counseled that Mollet's threat be taken seriously. Embassy informants said that "comprehension and sympathy for US policies are zero" in the habitually pro-American Socialist party. Paul Devinat, a pro-American politician, said the situation was "deteriorating with a rapidity which he, as a political veteran, would not have believed possible." Attempts to defend U.S. policy were met with demonstrations that had forced him to leave the speaker's platform; a "national wall" of anti-Americanism was being created in France, there was even talk of the return of de Gaulle, the growth of Poujadism, a coup d'état by "any plausible general, even General Juin," although "de Gaulle could return easily if he wished."[80] General Juin, recently retired, in fact joined with General Weygand, a pillar of the prewar French army, in a personal appeal to President Eisenhower: France was losing faith in the Atlantic alliance as a result of the American position. The American failure to respond to the Soviet nuclear threats against Britain and France showed Washington's apparent willingness to throw North Africa and the southern flank of NATO into the hands of the Russians. The two generals posed as representatives of the military tradition that assured the continuity of the

French state as against the passing instability of French governments by faction and party. They were yet another example for Washington of the existing breakdown of normal civil-military relations.[81]

Dillon concluded that French stability was threatened; he thought the choice of Juin as the maker of a coup unlikely, "since Juin's I.Q. and reputation for political acumen are widely recognized as low," and he advised Eisenhower to reply curtly to the Juin-Weygand letter, which the president did. But de Gaulle was more serious than the antiquated generals, a "hardy perennial now again in bloom," while the army was "according to our sources thoroughly fed up with the Fourth Republic"; its leaders thought the results of Suez had "proved the failure of the parliamentary regime in France." The French state of mind had been "abnormal since 1940," adjustment to the second or third rank as a world power remained a trauma "the explosive character of which was not fully understood in the U.S. or elsewhere." The French were angry over the American failure to counter the Soviet nuclear threat of November 5 and infuriated that the United States refused to ship oil to its allies. Both the French and their leaders, Dillon thought, are "not in a logical frame of mind, and present anti-NATO talk seriously concerns us." The French were capable of quitting the UN and NATO and "retiring into neutralistic isolation."

How serious a possibility did Washington think the return of de Gaulle was? It is interesting that at moments in the history of the Fourth Republic during which the stability of the regime appeared to be in question and de Gaulle's return a possibility, the American records show evidence of subtle contacts with and reassurances from the general. One such flurry of indirect contacts occurred in December 1956, another in April-May 1958. On December 19, 1956, Alain Savary told Dillon that he had talked with de Gaulle and found him "extremely liberal" on North Africa and especially Algeria, where he was "much more understanding of reality than Lacoste." De Gaulle would accept a loose federation within which French ties to Algeria could be maintained; he was "authoritarian but not conservative" (Dillon no doubt would have preferred it the other way around) and was capable of forming an alliance with the Mendès France group and with the Socialist left in order to come to power. Debré told Dillon that he had met with de Gaulle and found him "for the first time since 1952...believing that there was a possibility of his return to power." This was not completely accurate: the general had thought the aftermath of Dien Bien Phu in 1954 an opportunity as well. But no matter, France could not survive the loss of Algeria, which would cause it to turn to de Gaulle, or to communism. And from the office of the French president Dillon learned that if Mollet fell President René Coty would call upon Pleven, Pflimlin, or de Gaulle as possible successors: "I was surprised that Ganeval [Coty's spokesman] talked openly about the possibility of a serious enough crisis to warrant Coty's calling on de Gaulle, which could only mean the eclipse, at least temporarily, of the Fourth Republic as it has been known since the war."[82]

Meanwhile, in the NSC, Allen Dulles expressed concern about the "acute rise in anti-Americanism in France in recent days," and Eisenhower complained to John Foster Dulles that French filling stations were refusing to sell gas to American tourists and that Paris taxis turned down American fares. Dulles observed that "they double-crossed us and now are trying to put the blame on us." The British and French would get no American oil until they fully complied with UN resolutions. Mollet was able to ride the anti-American wave of opinion to almost unprecedented heights of personal popularity. The problems in Algeria, he claimed, were the fault of a flagging national will, the corrupt influence of a certain defeatist press, and "powerful foreign economic interests taking action there against us."[83] Mollet accelerated work on the French atomic bomb, sought improved relations with the USSR, and intensified efforts at European unity culminating in the Treaty of Rome.

Was Suez responsible for French acceptance of the Common Market? Pierre Guillen, in a colloquium on the unity of Europe in 1987, asserted that Mollet turned to the pursuit of European unity as a compensation for his humiliation over Suez, only to be rebuked there by Christian Pineau, who insisted that Mollet and he had taken the decision earlier, before the eruption of the Suez crisis.[84] Pineau had the better of the argument. The French decision to accept the Common Market was the consequence of an internal debate of several years standing in which the main protagonists were officials in the Ministry of Finance, who wanted French industry exposed to European competition as a means of forcing increased productivity, and those at the Quai d'Orsay, who clung to traditional ideas of French protection.[85] Mollet and Pineau, to be sure, had always in principle been "Europeans." But Mollet, as premier, was not initially clear about what kind of Europe he wished to see. The intergovernmental committee established at Messina in June 1955 published its conclusions in April 1956, advocating the creation of an all-European agency for atomic energy, Euratom, and a customs union or Common Market. Mollet followed Jean Monnet in preferring a sectoral approach to European integration as politically more feasible than a Common Market; the French strongly favored Euratom in the hope that it would finance the construction of an isotope separation plant at Pierrelatte, essential for the French atomic program. Mollet was further hesitant about entering a European union without Great Britain; in fact, in a moment of desperation, at the height of the Suez crisis, he suggested to London an economic union between Britain and France and their empires, reminiscent of Churchill and de Gaulle's short-lived project put forward during the Battle of France in 1940. The British, however, despite military cooperation with Paris during Suez, rejected the Common Market in favor of a European Free Trade Association from which agriculture and a common external tariff would be excluded.

Algeria and the French empire were the linchpin, however, that tipped the scales in France toward acceptance of the Common Market. Traditionally, France had monopolized trade with its empire and regarded it as the basis of its claims to be a world power, harboring assumptions about autarchy inherited from the 1930s. But from the inception of the Algerian rebellion in 1954 the conviction grew that the industrialization and economic and social development of Algeria and the empire provided the only alternatives capable of winning indigenous populations away from the idea of independence.[86] Mendès France was determined to set such a program in motion for Algeria, and the process of fashioning what was later to become de Gaulle's Plan of Constantine was already in preparation in the Ministry of Finance by 1956 under Mollet.[87] The enormous financial needs of the plan revealed glaringly the inability of France to provide the capital necessary for economic and developmental schemes in Algeria or the French Union. How much better would it be to draw France's European partners into the development of the French Union as a source of capital? Paris could then become the vortex of a unified Europe and a federated Africa linked in a common network of trade and political and cultural relations expressed through the increasingly popular notion in France of *Eurafrique*. France at the head of *Eurafrique* could realize its claims to be a world power and take its seat alongside the Anglo-Americans. By the summer of 1956 the idea of *Eurafrique* had caught on with important segments of French opinion and was being advocated by several pressure groups.[88]

There was finally the question of the French atomic bomb. France had been a center for nuclear research since before the war; its postwar efforts were initially oriented toward peaceful uses, but the possibility of weapons development was always there. Mendès France was primarily responsible for the decision to go ahead with nuclear weapons research, taken in late 1954. It was confirmed under Faure in 1955, and Mollet, who was ambiguous on the issue when he came to power, was initially obliged to continue the policy because it was the will of the National Assembly. In the spring of 1956, Mollet did agree to a moratorium on any French nuclear explosion for five years, but that was cosmetic only, since the French would not be ready to explode a weapon until about 1961 in any case. By 1956 it was also becoming apparent that the American attitude on the nuclear defense of Europe was changing; the "New Look" policy of Eisenhower when he took office, which featured reliance on "massive retaliation" in the case of any Soviet attack, even by conventional forces, was giving way to a theory advocating a more graduated response, and consequently pressure on the European allies to build up their conventional forces in Europe.[89] All this caused increased nervousness in Europe over American intentions with regard to their willingness to use nuclear weapons in defense of Europe, and by 1956–57 all the major European nations were becoming interested in their own atomic forces. Suez finally confirmed for Mollet the direction in which France was already heading, but the French decision to build the bomb, like the desire to create *Eurafrique,* further made apparent the consequent strains on the French budget, and pushed strongly in the direction of united European policies. The decision was consequently made in Paris, between July and October 1956, to accept the linkage of Euratom and the Common Market, on condition that the French Union be included along with French agriculture.

The same concerns inspired the German chancellor, Konrad Adenauer, creating the paradox that despite American support for European integration, the impetus for the break in the impasse in Common Market negotiations in 1956 came out of anti-American animus rather than the reverse. In fact, American policy on Europe was circumspect with regard to the Common Market, precisely from the fear that any too overt a support of the project might work against it.[90] Adenauer, in Paris to conclude negotiations for the Treaty of Rome on November 6, expressed contempt for the American policy at Suez; the United States had abandoned the leadership of NATO, he said, after causing the crisis itself by canceling the Aswan Dam project. In Washington, Adenauer had asked whether, if the United States were directly attacked itself, it would have the nerve to start a nuclear war, and had never gotten a satisfactory answer. Even less did the German chancellor believe that the Americans would undertake a nuclear response on Europe's behalf. The Americans had never really known war; only one in thirty or fifty soldiers in their army had ever seen combat.[91] This was de Gaulle's question two years later, which he answered by continuing the nuclear program he inherited from Mollet and Mendès France and taking France out of NATO's integrated command. Suez prompted Adenauer to agree to escape clauses demanded by Paris as the price of France's entry into the Common Market, and he promised German participation in a joint investment plan for French Africa. The way was now clear for the European community's construction.

By the time he received the notices of French interest in a return of de Gaulle to power, Dillon thought the crisis had receded. In the Paris embassy counselor Charles W. Yost agreed: thanks to "hopeful US actions," Mollet would not fall, and the anti-American rhetoric was cooling down. Yost also thought the reports of French army dissatisfaction with the Republic exaggerated, but the embassy consensus refused to yield on this point. Events, of course, were to prove it was right. However, the coming tests of U.S. friendship, Yost agreed, would be over Algeria: "we must face the possibility that we cannot satisfy the French in which event new and furious outbursts against us may occur."[92] Meanwhile Mollet put a new spin on his European policy, arguing in Gaullist style that a united Europe would provide a counterweight to any U.S.-USSR division of the world as at Yalta, "in which we would be the first to bear the costs."[93] Pineau declared that "It is more than ever indispensable before the Soviet menace and the American indifference that Europe construct itself." Mollet resolved that U.S. hostility to the French nuclear program would not deter France. The nation was independent, would develop its own nuclear weapons, give itself confidence against the threat of Soviet invasion, and thereby strengthen itself and the North Atlantic community.[94]

Dillon feared "lasting damage to the Western alliance" unless the United States solved Europe's oil shortage, ceased favoring Nasser, and met with its allies.[95] Both Hungary and Suez appeared to have intensified the pursuit of European integration in Germany as well, where Adenauer and the government saw a united Europe as the only way Germany might have influence in the future.[96] Suez, however, produced precisely the opposite effect in Great Britain, where Eden was eventually forced to resign, although many British officials were equally furious at Dulles and Eisenhower's policies. The British government had never enjoyed a consensus on Suez; Hugh Gaitskell had led the Labor party in vocal opposition, which was covertly supported by the Americans. The British concluded that they must remain junior partners of the Americans and dissociate themselves from the French, since "the Americans could abide the French as little as could the Arabs."[97] Whitehall was motivated out of concern for sterling and loyalty to the Commonwealth, which it had neglected to consult prior to Suez and which was hostile to the operation.

France, however, enjoyed an internal consensus, since Suez had always been about Algeria, on which the political class agreed. Mollet was buoyed by the wave of anticommunism that swept the country in the aftermath of the Soviet invasion of Hungary. The long-run consequence of Suez was that France turned toward its policy of "independence," which under de Gaulle meant eventual withdrawal from NATO's integrated command. Dillon noted that French opinion was enraged by its humiliation at American hands and consequently "scapegoated" the United States and the United Nations for what had been a French act of folly. The result was particularly alarming, for France was capable, if provoked enough, of quitting the United Nations and NATO, going neutral, and seeking a separate deal with Moscow that would enable it to hold on to Algeria. The specter of a "planetary deal" remained a constant threat underlying French policy. The Americans had best manage to cooperate with France, Dillon warned, "or we may get a French government here whose potential for damage to western security would be infinitely greater than that of Nasser."[98]

CHAPTER THREE

The Degeneration of the Regime

One can hardly speak of an erosion in Franco-American relations during 1957, since at the end of 1956 the two countries appeared already to be on as bad terms as they had ever been. As the year wore on, one issue after another seemed to prevent them from coming to agreement. Algeria remained the principal irritant: the United States was embarrassed by its alliance with France in the United Nations, where increasingly strident anticolonialist voices were being heard, and the situation was made more acute by the location of the world body in New York, where "observer" delegates from the National Liberation Front carried on their activities with impunity and infuriated the French no end. The French use of torture in Algeria became a popular cause in the United States, helping to alienate American opinion and the press. It also became an irritant in French relations with Great Britain. Disagreements about Algeria spilled over into Tunisia and Morocco; Washington managed to affront Paris with every step it took toward establishing its own relations with them. But elsewhere French-American ties displayed the same frictions. Washington would not, could not, accept the existence of an independent French nuclear program and sought to impede its development, while suspicion of France grew as the Franco-German partnership blossomed almost to the point of nuclear weapons collaboration. In the midst of all this the French managed yet another of their balance of payments crises, this amid unprecedented economic growth and prosperity. Almost as if by reflex the Americans rushed in with an aid package, while increasingly rumblings were heard about the dysfunction of the French system, and American officials in Paris began once again to examine the de Gaulle option.

Meanwhile Washington, now joined by the British, found itself embroiled in a controversy over arms for Tunisia, necessary to keep that country in the Western camp, but bitterly opposed by Paris so long as Tunisia appeared to be assisting the Algerian rebels. The denouement of that crisis marked the reemergence of the British-American "special relationship" and the corresponding demotion of France from membership in a putative "big three" alongside the Anglo-Saxons. By year's end the Americans were almost ready to give up on the Fourth Republic, which could not control its military and bureaucracy, provide a stable, durable government, or put its economic affairs in order. But it still required another major confrontation to push Washington over the edge. The French suitably provided that early in 1958 with the Sakiet affair, the complexity of which requires study on its own—the subject of the following chapter.

Washington's UN tactics on the Algerian question were to remain a source of disagreement with the French for the duration of the war. The French victory in the "Battle of Algiers" during the winter of 1956–57 comforted the French leadership after the Suez disaster, but opened up the question of the use of torture to counter the threat of terrorism. Some 120 actual FLN gunmen in the city managed over 100 individual terrorist attacks in January 1957 alone, and a general strike was set for January 28, the day the General Assembly of the United Nations took up the Algerian question. Muslim demonstrators were called into the streets in an effort to get the UN to take a stronger interest in the Algerian situation. In response, Lacoste called in the elite paratroops under General Massu, who entered the Casbah, routinely applied torture in order to break the terrorist infrastructure, and forced open Algerian shops in an effort to break the strike.[1] In effect, the French won a double victory, defeating the strike and stopping the terror, while preventing the UN from going beyond its anodyne resolution of the year before. But if the Battle of Algiers was won by the torture, the war may have been lost.[2] The use of torture opened up the rift between French intellectuals, who broadened their critique into general opposition to a colonialist war, and the government and military, increasingly driven to blaming the opposition for the war's continuation. Mollet was forced to establish a committee on the "rights of man" to examine the torture issue, while his and succeeding governments cracked down on the press by seizures of newspapers carrying offensive articles before they could be sold. Torture, censorship, and the establishment of a military government in Algiers became the hallmarks of an ostensibly Socialist government.

The strike and demonstrations were successful in catching the United Nations' attention, and the Americans thought France wrong to challenge the world organization's competence to deal with the Algerian question: France should submit the "facts" on Algeria and argue its case. The French should be "made to understand" that the United States could not support a resolution against UN competence; if it did, its influence would be diminished and its ability to secure a "moderate" resolution on Algeria later would be compromised. Such behavior would endanger U.S. policy in the Middle East and constitute "gratuitous American approval of ritualistic French colonial attitudes."[3] The General Assembly voted out an innocuous resolution expressing its hopes for a peaceful, democratic, and just solution in Algeria in conformity with the UN charter; but the Americans could not guarantee the French the same outcome in the future in the absence of a liberal program in Algeria, which the French promised to undertake in a forthcoming loi-cadre, or framework law for the territory, a promise on which they were never able to deliver.

Meanwhile neither the saturation of the Algerian countryside with French troops nor the defeat of terrorism in Algiers promised a conclusion of the war any time soon. The war was like the proverbial hydra; to cut off one head was to see it pop up somewhere else. Now that Tunisia and Morocco were independent states, there was no way to prevent the rebel armies from taking sanctuary there and establishing bases from which to carry out their raids into Algeria. The frontiers of Algeria became the latest theaters of bitter warfare. The situation was worse on the Tunisian than on the Moroccan border, but it led to a deterioration in relations with both countries. The French initially responded in the summer of 1957 with the "Morice line," named for the hawkish war minister, a barrier of barbed wire and electrified fence and other obstacles designed to seal off the Tunisian frontier, but the rebels became adept at crossing it, and in the winter of 1957–58 the war remained concentrated on the Tunisian border.[4] Morice turned the entire question of frontier control over to the French army in the fall of 1957. Pressure grew within France for authorizing more and more punitive raids against Tunisia, which was accused of becoming a cobelligerent of the FLN, and these raids in turn led to an internationalization of the war.

Washington was distressed by France's problems with Tunisia and Morocco, neither of which could help but be caught up in the Algerian War, to which they may well have owed their own independence. The Americans had played an approving and encouraging role behind the scenes as France negotiated their independence, and it came to regard them as bastions of pro-Western anticommunist political stability in a dangerous and unstable Third World.[5] The Tunisian president, Habib Bourguiba, in particular was valued in Washington as a moderate nationalist and anticommunist, and Tunisia regarded potentially as a model nation in Africa for how underdeveloped countries might achieve economic benefits through alliance with the West. Sultan Mohammed V of Morocco was similarly thought a paragon of moderation and good sense, if less attractive as a model because of the feudal monarchy under which his country lived. The French also had reason to regard Bourguiba favorably, especially when they compared him to his radical opposition within the Tunisian Independence party, the Neo-Destour. The opposition was headed by the charismatic demagogue Salah ben Youssef, who fought the conventions signed in 1955 and openly supported the Algerian rebels. Bourguiba, by contrast, was judged by the French to have acted with "total loyalty in his dealings with Paris," and thereby also served the "real interests" of Tunisia.[6] But by its pursuit of continued hegemony in North Africa, the French government seemed to Washington to be driving the two countries and their moderate leaders into the arms of Nasser and the Soviet Union.

In effect, what the French had in mind for their two former protectorates was a thinly disguised form of neocolonialism, euphemistically termed "interdependence."[7] There remained after decolonization between two and three hundred thousand French residents in both countries who controlled the best lands, continued to receive French economic subsidies, enjoyed extraterritoriality, and had their security assured by French troops who roamed the two countries at will. These internal security arrangements the French called "military interdependence," and the same unequal relationship also characterized future desired relations in terms of foreign affairs and economic and cultural relations with Tunisia and Morocco. France conducted the foreign policies of the two countries pending establishment of their own diplomatic representation abroad, and refused to relinquish full control until the Tunisians and Moroccans negotiated diplomatic conventions granting it a "preeminent" position in their foreign relations. Both were expected to "concert" their policies with France on subjects of mutual interest through regular consultations. France also expected to monopolize economic aid to the two countries, which remained in the franc zone, and maintain its cultural influence through its control of higher education.

Tunisia received its independence from France on March 20, 1956, in circumstances which soon degenerated into bitter recriminations. Bourguiba chafed under the French preconditions, regarding them as a form of neocolonialism inconsistent with full sovereignty; without bothering to negotiate a diplomatic convention with France, he requested all countries that had consulates in Tunisia to upgrade their representation to embassies.[8] The French government responded with a warning to most governments with which it had relations that the opening of an embassy in Tunisia before it came to an understanding with France would be regarded by Paris as an "unfriendly act." The Arab nations were not intimidated by this, however, and to forestall their being the first to act in the Tunisian capital Washington also ignored the French warning and announced that it was upgrading its consulate to an embassy with the appointment of a chargé d'affaires or an ambassador soon to follow. Paris immediately protested and succeeded in getting Washington to delay appointing an ambassador until a Franco-Tunisian agreement was eventually signed, but from their inception French-Tunisian relations were off to a rocky start, with Washington inevitably becoming the unwitting or unwilling intermediary.[9]

The Sultan of Morocco had a different concern; he nullified the accords permitting American bases in Morocco that the French had negotiated with Washington in 1950, forcing Washington to renegotiate its rights, which turned out to be a long and arduous process that culminated in the bases being dismantled in the early 1960s. France, however, insisted that it had granted the Americans rights to the bases and therefore remained sovereign; any negotiations of their fate must be tripartite, including France, the United States, and Morocco, as must any extension of economic or military aid by Washington to Morocco. The sultan would have none of this, however, and would only deal with Washington directly. After long and arduous negotiations with both Paris and Rabat, Washington agreed to the sultan's demands and excluded Paris from its talks with Morocco over the future of the bases.[10]

While the French credited the Americans for their "comprehension" of French policies in North Africa, they had a long list of desiderata that Washington appeared to be dilatory or recalcitrant about observing, quite aside from its embassy in Tunisia. Paris wanted recognition from

Washington of its "preeminence" in the region and a promise that there
would be no attempt by the Americans to substitute their own for
French influence in the internal affairs of the two states. The Americans
were to refrain from giving military assistance, subordinate their economic aid to prior arrangement and consultation with France, take no
cultural initiatives without prior French agreement, restrain the activities of the AFL, influence Spain to cease its interference in French-
Moroccan affairs, back Morocco in its claim to Tangiers against Spain,
and pressure Libya to control the transit of arms through its territory to
Algeria.[11] In none of this did Paris ask the opinion of the Moroccans
and Tunisians themselves, who tended to regard recognition by and private dealings with Washington and the United Nations as the symbolic
consecration of their independence.

Nor was Washington particularly pleased by the Mollet government's rapidly developing friendship with Israel. Dulles's annoyance
with the unnecessary problems and the hindrance to American policy
that the Jewish state represented is well documented, and his attitude
was widely shared in the State Department. Robert McBride rather
snidely reported to the State Department on the alarming solidity of
French support for Israel: the policy had the support of all parties from
the Communist to the otherwise anti-Semitic Poujadist; no criticism of
Israel was heard anywhere in the country, the left saw "Buchenwald
with trees and cows" in the Jewish state, and the right a check to Pan-
Arabism. The French expressed some discomfort with the fact that
France had become "Israel's only loyal friend," and they wanted the
Americans also to back the Jewish state. But their policy perturbed the
Americans. The Quai d'Orsay was bypassed because its career diplomats were pro-Arab, while the Interior and Defense ministries harbored
the Israeli sympathizers who did the planning with Mollet himself, although the foreign minister personally, Pineau, was also "in the loop."
McBride saw little logic, order, or "sense of international realities" in
the policy, but concluded that France would defend Israel whenever and
wherever it believed it necessary to do so.[12] All this added to the growing American conviction that the Fourth Republic was not a worthy
consultation partner on the Middle East, "since we are unsure of French
motives in the area."[13]

It was hardly surprising, then, that the American policy review of
France for 1957 presented a grim picture of French-American relations.
The French judged their friends by their attitudes on Algeria, they had
totally lost confidence in the UN, and Morocco and Tunisia looked to

the United States to protect them from French pressure. The French continued to make demands that Washington could not meet. Even after the Suez fiasco they still wanted a voice in Middle East policy and membership in a reconstituted "big three," while they seethed with resentment over Washington's shutoff of oil during the Suez crisis until they had withdrawn their forces from Egypt. The embassy thought further shocks in Paris like these from Washington could well cause a crisis of the regime. The review recommended that the United States support France in the UN while pressuring for a liberal settlement in Algeria and play honest broker between France and Morocco and Tunisia without giving rise to a suspicion that the United States wished to replace France in its privileged relations with the two countries. The United States should consult France on the Middle East, agree to tripartite talks with Paris and London, allow oil to flow freely to Paris, and continue to give France residual forms of economic and military aid. All this was capped with a prophetic warning: U.S. policy "can very largely determine," the embassy claimed, whether France acquires a government "totally indigestible in the NATO system and obliging us to revise our entire European strategy."[14] French internal politics seemed from Washington's vanatage point, in a way reminiscent of the period from 1947 to 1954, to be dependent on American policy. This could be read two ways, however. The embassy advised a greater effort in Washington to accommodate the French, but it was also inviting the conclusion that the Fourth Republic and its ill-defined system of political responsibility was already "totally indigestible in the NATO system." For the moment, Washington stuck with the first interpretation, preferring the evil at hand to the one it knew not of.

As Suez stimulated the rethinking of American policy, it did the same for the French, convincing politicians and the public alike that the NATO alliance was of much less use to France than had previously been thought. The weakness of NATO's system of an integrated military command, against which de Gaulle had warned, was apparent. Paris had put its forces under the command of the British, who under American pressure had ordered a halt in operations before the Suez Canal had been secured. In NATO's system of integrated command France's European forces served under an American general. Moreover, France had only one major command post in NATO other than its key post in Central Europe, whereas the Americans had seven and the British five. De Gaulle's negative experience with an integrated command dated from the Second World War, and he resolved to eliminate it if he ever re-

turned to power; the politicians of the Fourth Republic were now coming to the same conclusion. The issue was never the NATO alliance itself, but Suez created a consensus in France around rejection of the pact
in its current form. When combined with the realization that the Soviets had apparently achieved nuclear parity with the United States, it led
a great many French politicians to agree with the general that "The
United States will not fight for us." The Americans in turn had less reason to fear an eventual de Gaulle government since French participation
in the alliance as it existed was anyway now in question.[15]

The unreliability of NATO made the acquisition of an independent
French nuclear deterrent appear to be a matter of greater urgency in
Paris. In French negotiations with Benelux, Germany, and Italy over the
establishment of the Common Market and Euratom, the French made it
clear that they would never renounce the right independently to produce their own nuclear weapons. From American accounts it would appear that very early in his administration Mollet had already decided
definitively to go ahead with a nuclear weapons program.[16] Dillon reported in February 1956 that the French already had the capability to
produce nuclear weapons, and he warned that if Washington tried to
pressure Paris to renounce the right to manufacture them there would
be a "storm" of anti-American protest in France. In December 1956 the
State Department advised Dulles that the French would explode a
weapon within the next four years.[17] Meanwhile, in the NATO Council, Pineau asked that the alliance be "redefined" so as to be worldwide
in geographical scope, a demand that de Gaulle would later formulate
as a sine qua non for French participation.[18] France, based on its projected nuclear capability, wanted recognition as a world power on the
same level as Great Britain.

In February 1957, the Quai said France must demand from its allies
recognition of its "vocation" to be a fourth nuclear power. The United
States should understand the reasons that compelled France to acquire
nuclear arms and help it in doing so.[19] But there was no such understanding in Washington. In 1956, when the administration realized that
the French were depending upon Euratom for help with their nuclear
program in the form of a European-financed uranium-enrichment
plant, Eisenhower lowered the price of uranium sales to Euratom for
peaceful purposes by executive order, thus removing the financial in-
centive for France's partners to contribute to the cost of the project. In
a striking reversal of objectives, the United States now favored the
Common Market over Euratom, which earlier had seemed more attrac-

tive to it as a step toward unity and a means of controlling European nuclear developments. Washington now began to pursue a more tempered policy toward European integration. It had previously feared that the EEC customs union of the six might adopt a prohibitive external tariff discriminatory toward American agriculture, but it now decided that the supranationality of the EEC constituted a better step toward real integration than the British-sponsored Free Trade Association, which was devoid of any real unifying characteristics. However, while favoring the continental model in economics, Washington limited its nuclear weapons collaboration to the British, thereby helping ensure British isolation from the continent.[20]

American opposition to the French nuclear program stemmed from fear of nuclear proliferation, the instability of the Fourth Republic, and the concern lest Germany too demand the right to build nuclear weapons. The head of the Atomic Energy Commission, Admiral Strauss, further regarded France, with its large Communist party, as a sieve for the leaking of classified information. As a way of stemming European desires for nuclear weapons, Washington offered to share its own arsenal with its allies in NATO. Nuclear strategy was in any case being rethought in Washington in the 1950s. As part of the "New Look," top American strategists concluded that "massive retaliation" as an automatic response to a Soviet invasion must be abandoned in view of the Russian acquisition of nuclear parity. The Americans were aware, however, that as they sought to de-emphasize nuclear weapons themselves, they increased the appetite for such weapons on the part of their NATO allies. Eisenhower himself regarded it as inevitable that the NATO countries would acquire nuclear weapons; the British were already well on their way to the bomb, Adenauer frequently expressed the desire of the Germans to possess such weapons, and the French atomic energy establishment was clearly capable of and on its way to developing them.[21] But his resigned attitude ran counter to that of the Washington foreign policy establishment.

During the Dulles-Mollet talks at the Matignon on May 6, 1957, Pineau expressed interest in American suggestions that "integrated nuclear equipment for NATO" might be deployed in Europe, which would include Germany; when Chairman of the Joint Chiefs Radford came to Paris a month later, he told General Ely that the establishment of nuclear storage depots in Europe under NATO's integrated command was already under study. Washington wanted to stockpile nuclear weapons on European soil in case of need in a nuclear war, and it eventually came up with the so-called double key idea of sharing with its allies both the weapons and the decision as to the circumstances in which they might be used. Washington offered to equip its allies with nuclear weapons and to train their armies in their use, in exchange for which the allies would abandon the quest for their own deterrents. Dulles counted on this roundabout approach because he did not believe that any overt attempt to discourage the French, much less the rest of Europe, would work. Another tactic was to combat French and British plans to reduce their conventional force contribution to NATO.[22]

The one bright spot in French policy for Washington in 1957 was Mollet's avid desire to construct Europe. But the Europeans were not pursuing unity out of an idealistic transnationalism or the realization that the nation-state was obsolete, but paradoxically, to strengthen their individual nation-states, which in the postwar era had assumed greater roles in the lives of their citizens than at any previous point in history. As Alan Milward has argued, Europeans sought to accomplish in an international framework only what they could not accomplish by themselves. The French wanted to use Euratom as a means of securing cheaper enriched uranium for their nuclear weapons program, and they insisted that their African territories be included in the Common Market to help them retain their imperial influence and role. As the summer of 1956 wore on, Common Market negotiations became bogged down over French demands that their overseas territories and their heavily subsidized and protected agricultural sector be fully included. Behind French concerns was the growing popularity of the "Eurafrican" idea, the key to which was Algeria, the foundation of France's "African vocation." Algeria made France an African power and hegemonic in North Africa, and helped make French influence in sub-Saharan Africa dominant. Reciprocally, the weight of its African possessions made France the preponderant Common Market country rather than simply one of the three largest. The British, who were hostile to the Common Market, understood that in Mollet's mind the EEC offered a solution to the Algerian problem.[23] The overall French design for the reestablishment of France as a world power thus becomes clear in Mollet's policies, which also became those of de Gaulle. Paris would be the capital of the French Union, the center of the new Europe, and the spokesman for *Eurafrique* in the councils of the big three.

It is common for historians to praise Mollet as a founder of Europe, builder of France as a nuclear power, and progenitor of the decolonization of Black Africa, while criticizing the apparent contradiction of his repressive Algerian policies as well as the Suez episode.[24] But there was no contradiction between these policies in Mollet's mind. In creating the institutions of a rudimentary self-government in Black Africa, Mollet saw himself as bringing these countries into a closer, eventual federal relationship, based on consent, with France. His Algerian policy was predicated on the same assumptions. The French presence there was regarded as progressive and modernizing as against an indigenous culture of obscurantist Islam and retrograde nationalism. The rebellion exposed France's relative neglect of Algeria during the early years of postwar reconstruction. But now, with the French economic takeoff under way, it became possible to envisage extensive plans for economic reform and investment there which would bring about modernization, alleviate the extensive unemployment, educate the population, and win its Muslim people over to France. Social reform would be a substitute for political autonomy. Lacoste carried out a policy of agrarian reform, industrialization, and the facilitating of Algerian emigré labor to France, while attempting to harmonize social legislation in Algeria and metropolitan France so as to bring immediate help to the unemployed, European or Muslim. He also favored "Algerianizing" Algeria through the projected loi-cadre. Meanwhile, what was to become de Gaulle's much more ambitious Plan of Constantine for the industrialization of Algeria was already in preparation under Mollet in the Fourth Republic's ponderous bureaucracy.[25] Neither the construction of Europe nor the building of a French nuclear deterrent was conceived of or understood in Paris as a substitute for a moribund colonialism, as several historians have argued. On the contrary, both were meant to provide the means of maintaining France's Eurafrican hegemony.

European negotiations became stalled in October 1956 over French demands, but obstacles were overcome at the height of the Suez crisis, on November 6, 1956. Adenauer was in Paris at the moment of the British halt in canal operations, which he deeply resented. Mollet and the German chancellor came to an easy mutual understanding; both rejected Washington's unilateral behavior in the Suez crisis, and Adenauer expressed his mistrust that when the chips were down the Americans would fight for Europe. Mollet read to Adenauer the menacing note from Bulganin of the day before, in which the Soviet leader had threatened to rain down missiles and nuclear warheads on London and Paris, and the French leader recounted his frustration and failure to get a commitment from Dillon with regard to a firm NATO response to the threats. Against this backdrop the two men agreed on the urgent necessity to "make Europe." But more, between them they adumbrated co-operation in the manufacture of weapons and joint procedures for nuclear research. The French would provide the means for Germany to acquire nuclear-weapons access as part of a common European defense, while German rocket scientists toiled in the manufacture of missiles symbolically situated at the Algerian launching site of Colomb-Béchar. A protocol was signed at the Sahara missile site in January 1957 between German Defense Minister Franz-Josef Strauss and French Defense Minister Maurice Bourgès-Maunoury; the two countries would cooperate closely on military matters and seek to coordinate their scientific and technical research programs. There was no mention of nuclear collaboration as yet in the official documents, but both these men were responsible for nuclear research in their respective nations and it is difficult to imagine that there was no informal discussion between them.[26] Adenauer and Mollet met again in February 1957 to discuss nuclear weapons research; in the interim, in December 1956, the NATO Council decided that any "localized" Soviet attacks in Europe should first be met by conventional, nonnuclear responses, feeding Adenauer's apparent paranoia about the unreliability of the American nuclear deterrent in the defense of Europe. All this came to a culmination in November 1957 when Strauss and the new Gaullist French Minister of Defense Jacques Chaban-Delmas both expressed hostility to the American "double-key" initiative as dangerous because the Americans would retain the last word on the use of nuclear weapons stockpiled on European soil. Plans were laid for the joint German-French production of nuclear weapons, to begin with common financing of an isotope separation plant at Pierrelatte, exactly what France had wanted from Euratom. The Italians were brought into the agreements, and on November 25 a tripartite nuclear weapons agreement was signed; the Americans were not told of it. On April 8, 1958, an accord was reached on the isotope separation plant: payments were to be 45 percent by France, 45 percent by Germany, and 10 percent by Italy, but little more could be accomplished before de Gaulle came to power, and he quickly broke off the arrangements in favor of France going it alone.[27] It was hardly coincidental from the French standpoint that the conclusion of the November agreement came a week after the confrontation with Washington over the Tunisian arms crisis.

When Mollet came to Washington in February 1957 and laid before Eisenhower the terms of the recently concluded Treaty of Rome, the American president waxed enthusiastic about this being one of the best days of the postwar era. The French hoped to use the construction of Europe to win their way back into Washington's good graces after Suez. But the Americans were already fearful that the cause of European integration itself might become fused with the nuclear question in France into a kind of vague aspiration for a kind of European neutralism, fears that would have been magnified had they known of the developing Franco-German agreements. Guy Mollet's speech of November 27, 1957, to the Socialist party congress was disturbing enough: Mollet asked rhetorically, without the construction of a united Europe, what means would France have "to prevent the installation of a dialogue between the USSR and the US, a dialogue that would risk ending up in a division of the world, or in a war in which we would be the first to bear the costs"? The Paris embassy meanwhile nervously noted a Mendèsiste and rightist thesis of a "New Yalta Agreement" gaining ground in France; Mollet seemed "to envisage Europe as a counter-weight to both the U.S. and the USSR."[28] Paris always understood Yalta to mean a deal between the superpowers at the expense of the rest. While European unification remained the basis of American policy, the initial steps toward the making of the Common Market were taken as a means of countering American influence.

Although broad geopolitical concerns and fears of a French lapse into neutralism provided the backdrop to the making of American policy toward France, short-term, immediate problems often seemed of even greater import. One of the dilemmas presented in Washington by the Algerian War was what to do about the presence of the rebels. From the outset, Washington maintained an uneasy and unofficial relationship with them, and it would not cut off its unofficial contacts with the Algerian rebel leadership despite recurrent French protests. Even the brutal FLN massacre of 300 residents of the Muslim village of Melouza, who were accused of harboring supporters of Messali Hadj, did not change this policy. The Americans received representatives of the Algerian nationalist organizations "from time to time," but the French were always advised. The State Department regarded the policy as "useful" and continued it despite French protests, which came in a constant stream. The problem was compounded because the FLN planned to open an office in Washington as well as the one in New York, where it operated in conjunction with the United Nations; the Americans had advised the rebels to restrict themselves to New York, but if they chose to open one in Washington the State Department determined that it could not legally stop them.[29] In their Washington talks the rebels sounded a reassuring message: communism held no attraction for them, nor would an independent Algeria be drawn into the orbit of radical Egyptian Pan-Arabism. North Africa was historically separate and distinct from Egypt, and a North African federation that included Tunisia, Morocco, Spanish Morocco, and Algeria could act as a bridge between the West and the Middle East. But first, France must recognize Algeria's right to an independent national existence, extend an amnesty to all those struggling for independence, and recognize an Algerian provisional government headed by the FLN. Only under these conditions would the Algerian rebels consent to free elections and move toward the construction of a federation of the Maghreb.

State Department officials found Abbas's idea of a North African federation appealing but noted the "impasse" between Algerian demands and the French formula of a cease-fire, elections, and then negotiations with a newly elected Algerian leadership. The rebels feared that in the event of a cease-fire they would not be able to restart the war if negotiations failed, and they did not trust the French to conduct honest elections. The Americans gently tried to pressure Abbas to accept "more gradual formulas" in the FLN quest for independence. But Abbas responded to this pressure rather sharply. He insisted upon more American comprehension of the Algerian side and accused Washington of attempting to "rescue Mollet." The Americans replied that they had no intention of taking sides in the Algerian conflict or of trying to mediate, but sought only compromise. Such unofficial assurances to the rebels were in conflict with the official policy in support of Paris, and they made their way to Paris where they were not appreciated. The French government consequently intensified its pressure on Washington to cease its contacts with the Algerian leadership. But despite repeated protests from Paris, which became more intense once de Gaulle came to power, Washington continued its unofficial contacts.[30]

The FLN mission in New York, moreover, put out a continuous barrage of pamphlets and press releases, organized public meetings, and was quite effective in mobilizing American opinion in favor of the cause of Algerian independence. The rebels played on American anticolonialism and evoked outrage by their accounts of the French use of torture in the war. They reveled in dubious analogies between their struggle and the American war of independence. In New York the FLN was particularly active in the United Nations and won over international opinion in favor of its cause, infuriating the French. French military intelligence maintained a complete collection of FLN documents submitted to the

United Nations, and noted with particular concern those that focused on the European settler and Jewish questions in Algeria, to which American opinion was regarded as being particularly sensitive. While promising the European minority full rights in an independent Algeria, the FLN claimed that only 21 percent of the European population was actually French; the rest of the European population was "racially different from that of France." Moreover, while comprising one-eleventh of the total Algerian population, the Europeans were favored 17 to 1 in the distribution of land; 25,000 Europeans had 1,540,650 hectares of arable land, whereas 532,000 Muslim farmers had to make do with 2,593,410 hectares. Moreover, the best land in Algeria was used for the production of wine, which Muslims did not drink. Europeans enjoyed a monopoly of industry, commerce, administration, and education in Algeria; the rebels offered them integration with equality in a new and independent Algeria but not colonial privileges.[31]

The FLN paid particular attention to the Jews, whom it believed to be influential in the media and with the American government. It presented Algerian Jews as classic victims of colonialist policies of divide and rule; anti-Semitism had persisted among the colon population since the Vichy era, but among the Muslims there was only "profound comprehension" of the concerns of their Jewish neighbors, whose 140,000 strong were among Algeria's earliest inhabitants. Independence would bring an end to all discrimination in Algeria; Algerian Jews were said to have demonstrated their solidarity with the FLN and were equally regarded as "sons of our country."[32]

Equally disturbing to French authorities was the propaganda of the Mouvement National Algérien (MNA), the nationalist group headed by Messali Hadj, from which the FLN had broken away. The MNA published a report of "French Crimes" in Algeria, calling upon the United States to intervene: had not United Nations Ambassador Lodge already called for an end to all actions in Algeria hampering an eventual ceasefire? Yet the French continued their "war of extermination." But the greatest blow to Paris's pretensions came from dissident French opinion. The Americans reported on the campaign against the war in Paris; *Time* magazine featured the works of Pierre-Henri Simon, who indicted the French authorities for torture, as well as Jean-Jacques Servan-Schreiber's *Lieutenant in Algeria,* which was condemned by Mollet's successor, Prime Minister Bourgès-Maunoury, for demoralizing the French army. "All reports in the French and American press testify to the complete collapse and bankruptcy of Mr. Mollet's policy in Algeria," French army intelligence complained. The MNA presented documentation directly to President Eisenhower of an "Algerian Nuremberg"; pictures of corpses had captions asking whether they were Jews in Nazi Germany or Hungarians after the Soviet invasion; in actuality French intelligence identified them as victims of an "alleged" French massacre in Philippeville, where in fact FLN rebels had massacred French colons. The MNA asked the mediation of President Eisenhower to end the war.[33]

On April 1, 1957, Douglas Dillon left his post as American ambassador to France to take up the post of under secretary of state in Washington; his replacement was Amory Houghton. Houghton was a politically prominent Republican and an executive of Corning Glass; he had no particular qualifications for so demanding a job as the Paris embassy and he showed a limited comprehension of the political circumstances in the country while he was there. Dulles briefed Houghton on the Algerian question: "there was no solution to the problem other than independence and the longer the French resisted the inevitable the worse the situation and the final result would be." Meanwhile the French balance of payments situation spiraled downward; there initially seemed to be little the United States could do about this given the outlook for congressional appropriations, and Dulles hoped responsible people in France realized that the United States would not be able to "bail them out" as it had done so many times in the past. Dulles was afraid Mollet would fall before the EEC or Euratom were ratified; if these treaties failed, the United States would be displeased. As a final word of advice, Dulles suggested that Jean Monnet should not be made an "habitué" of the embassy, since he was seen in France as too pro-European and pro-American.[34]

Dulles and Houghton met with Mollet and Pineau at the prime minister's residence on May 6, 1957. They addressed the question of deploying American nuclear weapons in Europe under the so-called double-key system and the question of stockpiling weapons in France. Pineau spoke up in favor of "integrated nuclear equipment for NATO," but made no mention of French initiatives toward nuclear cooperation with Germany. But the conversation inevitably got around to Algeria, which was draining away the conventional French contribution to NATO. Mollet said that militarily the situation was improving there, but politically it was not. The rebels were divided, feared a ceasefire, and were under the influence of young hotheaded radicals who preferred to fight rather than work. The French government had no choice but to persevere in its policies: elections, following a cease-fire, would be held to produce *interlocuteurs valables* among the Algerian population, but there could be no prior political discussions with the FLN. Mollet went on to insist that the major objective in the Middle East, even after Suez, must be to get rid of Nasser, whose book he had read ten times; its thesis of Pan-Arabism was as dangerous as Hitler's Pan-Germanism.[35]

Mollet said nothing to make the Americans regret his fall, which occurred weeks later, and during the ensuing crisis the embassy picked up signals that growing interest in a return to power of de Gaulle was becoming manifest in the French political class. American officials now undertook to explore these currents with interest. Dillon, while ambassador, had long since dropped the proscription against any contact between the American Embassy and General de Gaulle, who was already on record with the Americans as a kind of "liberal" on Algeria, whatever front he presented to his supporters. On May 2, 1956, de Gaulle had met with Theodore Achilles, an embassy official, and frankly offered the view that it was far too late for a policy of assimilation to be successful in Algeria. The best to be hoped for, de Gaulle said, was an Algerian state in some kind of loose federation with France, failing which Algeria would become independent. Thus in 1956, de Gaulle said that he rejected "integration," the program of the military rebels and colons who brought him to power in May 1958. The general thought France would have to negotiate protection of the civil rights of the European community in Algeria, but he nevertheless coldly anticipated that in the event of independence most of the settlers would leave. De Gaulle confided similar thoughts to several other French politicians and associates during this period. Alain Savary, who resigned from the Mollet government after the Ben Bella arrest, talked with de Gaulle in December 1956 and reported to Washington that he was "extremely liberal on North Africa and especially on Algeria, much more understanding of reality than Lacoste." Savary thought that the Socialist minority, who were against Mollet's Algerian policy of repression, and even Mendès France were considering seeking common ground with de Gaulle.

But Washington got contrary signals from Michel Debré, a radical partisan of *Algérie Française* known to be close to the general: Debré found de Gaulle "for the first time since 1952... believing that there was a possibility of his return to power," and he added that France could not survive the loss of Algeria without turning to de Gaulle or else to communism.[36] That the anti-American Debré took the time to bring messages to the embassy was in itself astonishing; but on balance the

Americans preferred to believe that de Gaulle intended to end the Algerian conflict, on the basis of self-determination if necessary, despite the studied ambiguity of his public posture which enabled those supporting him to believe the contrary. Gaullist Roger Frey again told embassy officials in June 1957 that de Gaulle was prepared to grant "autonomy virtually approaching independence" to Algeria, and that he was the only French politician capable of implementing such a solution.[37] British Ambassador Gladwyn Jebb visited General de Gaulle in February 1957, and his report, transmitted to Washington, noted that there was much talk of the general returning to power, but the ambassador thought that eventuality "unlikely," since neither de Gaulle's thoughts nor his actions seemed to lead in that direction.[38] Jebb heard further about the general from Gaston Palewski and René Massigli, who agreed that de Gaulle's views on Algeria were more reasonable than those of the Mollet government in that de Gaulle favored a North African federation encompassing Algeria and permitting French penetration of the Sahara, in line with what he had told Jebb privately the previous February.[39] But Jebb thought the country uninterested in de Gaulle's return, which he could not foresee except in case of a very serious crisis in Algeria.

After Mollet's fall, Bourgès-Maunoury formed a short-lived government that was overthrown in October. In October 1957, with France again in a lengthy, seemingly unresolvable cabinet crisis, Allen Dulles raised the question of de Gaulle's return in the National Security Council, but he doubted that the general would accept the position of premier in France without extensive decree powers, which the National Assembly was unlikely to grant him. Jebb noted that a crisis of the regime was possible, in which case de Gaulle was now prepared to pick up power that would be "lying in the gutter." But Dulles warned that de Gaulle's assurances to the Americans about his intentions in Algeria should not be taken at face value. Whatever the general said to the Americans did not jibe with the position of his followers; in a meeting of the Social Republican party, Debré called for a government of "national salvation" behind de Gaulle that would keep Algeria French "at any cost." The embassy observed that "this ill-assorted [Gaullist] party has nothing in common except a wish to see a French triumph in Algeria," unless it was hostility to the United States. There was a tirade against Dulles, the Eisenhower doctrine was described as American imperialism in the Middle East, and suspicions were voiced that after agreeing to the "neutralization" of Europe, the United States and the USSR would go on to partition the world.[40]

Washington received many reports that French intransigence was the primary obstacle to an Algerian peace. The Moroccan dissident Mehdi Ben Barka saw Robert Murphy in April following consultations with the rebel leadership in Tunis, reporting that the Algerian military leaders were ready to accept the Mollet plan of a cease-fire, elections, and negotiations if Lacoste's brutal "pacification" effort in Algeria were first halted. French reports of alleged rebel intransigence were manufactured by Paris only as an excuse for continuing repression. The Sultan of Morocco wanted to mediate and the governments of Morocco and Tunisia were in agreement; the only obstacle was the continuing French "pacification" effort, which made FLN acceptance of the Mollet plan equivalent to capitulation.[41] Herter concluded that it was most important that the Lacoste campaign be halted, and he ordered that efforts be made to impress the French along these lines: the Algerians were dropping their demand for independence, the attitude of FLN leaders appeared accommodating, and the Moroccans wanted to help achieve a peaceful solution. But after Mollet fell in May 1957, Houghton discovered that the successor cabinet of Bourgès-Maunoury, "while firmly and predominately pro-European, is also for a continued pacification effort in Algeria, along Lacoste lines." In fact the new government promised little "give" on the Algerian question generally.[42]

It was against this backdrop of perceived rebel accommodation and French intransigence that on July 1, 1957, Senator John F. Kennedy made his widely publicized speech criticizing Washington's support for France in the Algerian War. Kennedy urged American and/or United Nations intervention in the conflict in favor of a negotiated peace on the basis of autonomy or independence for Algeria. There was an immediate, angry reaction to the speech in Paris, and Alphand registered French concern by calling on Dulles to repudiate Kennedy's views. The French ambassador wanted the secretary to block Senate passage of a resolution offered by Kennedy. Dulles said he would try, but made light of it, insisting that the French need not worry since in any case such a resolution could not be binding on the administration. It is by no means clear that Dulles cared to block the Kennedy resolution; rather, the administration may well have been privately pleased by Kennedy's remarks as both a warning to the French about the evolution of American opinion and a not inaccurate reflection of what Washington would have

liked its policy to be had it felt free to act in accordance with its incli-
nations.[43]

Perhaps the Kennedy speech had its intended effect: France made a
brief attempt to coordinate its policy with that of the United States in
the United Nations and to meet American insistence that it show
progress on the internal political evolution of Algeria. Louis Joxe told
the State Department that France wanted to cooperate and avoid the
impression that it wished to leave the UN; it would abandon any attempt to oppose Algeria's inscription on the agenda of the General Assembly, although it had "no solution to offer" beyond the continuation
of its present policies. These did include a more liberal *loi-cadre* in Algeria. Francis Wilcox, assistant secretary for international organization
affairs, thought any show of progress in Algeria by France might be sufficient to forestall extreme action in the UN. But one wonders if the
Kennedy incident did not create a nest egg of rebellion in Paris as well.
J.Y. Goeau-Brissonnière, at the premier's office, undertook further
soundings of the rebels for Bourgès-Maunoury in July 1957, but he ran
into the same obstacle that had been present during the secret negotiations in 1956; the FLN insisted on prior recognition by France of its
right to independence before it would enter negotiations. During their
conversation the FLN trade union leader Abdelaziz Rachid told Goeau
that time was working in favor of the rebellion and, citing the Kennedy
declaration, Rachid allegedly remarked that "The United States will not
abandon us." Goeau experienced a moment of doubt: had not Dulles
also brought France to Dien Bien Phu? "History is in danger of repeating itself."[44]

On July 7, 1957, Dulles ordered a démarche to Pineau about an impending resolution in the French National Assembly in favor of recognizing Communist China. Houghton warned Pineau of the negative effect the resolution's passage would have in Washington, but now it was
Pineau's turn to play games. Paralleling Dulles's observation to Alphand
on the Kennedy resolution, Pineau told Houghton not to worry because
its passage was aimed at him, Pineau, and it would not be binding on
the French administration. The Foreign Affairs Committee of the Assembly eventually postponed consideration.[45] The French were not so
subtly retaliating on Washington, pressing the sensitive recognition for
Red China button in proportion as they were made to feel the heat on
Algeria. But at the same time the French remained aware of Washington's insistence that they appear to be applying a liberal program in Algeria, whatever that might mean. On September 5, Alphand called in

Washington with the news that the new *loi-cadre,* or framework law, had been formulated. The law was ostensibly designed to establish a genuinely liberal political regime in Algeria capable of winning the adherence of the Muslims to French rule, while assuaging international opinion and winning Washington's full support for French policy. An elaborate system of territorial assemblies was to be created in which Muslims would enjoy political representation; most cities with Muslim majorities would be turned over to municipal councils representing the inhabitants; and nationally there would be a single assembly created in which Muslims would enjoy equal rights under the principle of one person, one vote. The Americans initially hoped that the framework law's passage would indeed inaugurate a liberal regime in Algeria capable of creating a situation all could live with.

Disillusionment was quick, however. When the *loi-cadre* was published, Washington immediately noted its inadequacy and concluded that it did not enjoy much hope of passage anyway. In fact the National Assembly did reject it, and overthrew the Bourgès-Maunoury government in the process in September. Most troubling of all was the preamble to the projected law, which repeated that Algeria must remain an integral part of France; this tended to destroy whatever effect the actual legislation, once implemented, might have. The British were even more caustic; the Foreign Office deplored the project as a demonstration of the powers of "a few wealthy men who have failed to learn any of the lessons of post World War II history," characterizing it as typical of a "short-sighted, narrow, vicious, nationalism." Soustelle now was allegedly acting under the orders of de Gaulle to provoke a crisis of the regime that would bring the general to power.[46] The framework law, rather than solving anything, thus became yet another bone of contention between Washington and London and Paris. Yet no matter what its provisions, for the French it permanently bore the stigma of having been devised in response to American pressure. Bourgès-Maunoury's successor, Felix Gaillard, finally secured its passage in an adulterated form in January 1958, but it was never fully implemented.[47]

Later in 1957 the French troubled Europe's equilibrium yet again with one of their notorious balance of payments crises. Dulles had seen it coming in May and contemplated using the French situation to force an end to the Algerian War, but Secretary of the Treasury George M. Humphrey noted that financially "the French are just going down the drain" and insisted that an emergency package of aid would again have to be put together for them after all by the end of the year. From a financial perspective, France continued to be "the sick man of Europe," and the inability of its governments to master its budgetary problems was yet another reason for the frequent expressions of contempt in Washington for the Fourth Republic. The British also deplored the regime's apparent inability to tax its population or to cut the enormous military expenditures and subsidies earmarked for Algeria.[48] For Jacob Kaplan, who then worked in the European Payments Union, "Neither the political nor the economic results of such a system [the Fourth Republic] were acceptable to France or its allies."[49] Joxe confirmed to Robert Murphy that Algeria was the cause of the financial crisis: it cost Paris one billion francs per day.[50] The Mollet government, while initiating a French old-age pension system and extending the period of paid vacations for workers, had increased military spending by 25 percent and brought the deficit from 650 billion francs to one trillion. When the Bourgès government fell in October 1957, Houghton reported that the emptiness of the treasury was the reason. But France had a booming economy and full employment, so nobody understood the basis for the crisis, which affected only the nation's foreign exchange balance and its unbalanced budget. The French economy was rock solid.

Economically, the Algerian War made hardly a blip: economic growth remained constant as France moved into a consumer economy of asssembly-line production in the midst of thirty years of spectacular, uninterrupted growth. From 1950 to 1962, France enjoyed a growth rate of 4.6 percent per year. This was somewhat slower than Germany's but much higher than Britain's, and from 1962 to 1970 French growth averaged 5.8 percent, still among the highest rates in the world. Investment, at 18.3 percent of the GDP in 1947, grew to 21.6 percent in 1956. Clearly the budget deficit in Paris was an arm of expansionist economics; the war was not permitted to interfere with internal investment, burgeoning consumer demand, or the French drive for economic modernization, which continued unabated.[51] Real wages were permitted to grow 6.3 percent per year from 1950 to 1955, a total of 41 percent, and then somewhat more slowly, 4.3 percent per annum to 1959. Consumption gained 5 percent in 1953, 5 percent in 1954, 6 percent in 1955, 5.5 percent in 1956, and 5 percent again in 1957. This was achieved, moreover, despite the dispatch of 450,000 men to Algeria amid a serious labor shortage in France, and declining levels of American aid.

The Americans had paid 80 percent of the cost of the Indochina War in 1954, and pumped over one billion dollars (428 billion francs) into the French economy, in effect allowing the French to export the war's cost to cover their balance of payments deficit. In 1955, American aid declined precipitously to 122 billion francs; in 1956 it was 102 billion, in 1957 only 50 billion, and in 1958 a scant 22 million dollars, or less than 8 billion francs.[52] The French budget deficit correspondingly grew to 970 billion francs in 1956 and 974 billion in 1957, while the balance of payments deficit went from $835 million to $1.4 billion in the same two years.

By continuing high rates of consumption and internal investment in the face of the war effort, the French chose to live beyond their means and to import far beyond their capacity to export, and they appeared deliberately to have created a situation from which they could only be extricated by means of U.S. aid.[53] And so once again they went to the Americans for help. Inevitably, the French balance of payments crisis of 1957 became bound up in Washington with broader issues of relations with France. In October the question of bailing out the French came before the National Security Council in Washington. The NSC proposed that existing grant aid to France be continued through 1958 but be reconsidered if the French failed to redeploy their forces from Algeria to NATO. Dulles, who had earlier said he would not bail out the French from their economic difficulties, now objected, saying that he needed flexibility on this question given France's "transcendent importance" to Western security: he was now seeking the right to store and deploy American nuclear weapons in France and apparently feared the effect on these negotiations of any threat to curtail American aid. The NSC then proposed that aid be reviewed but that the policy be to condition it on future redeployment of French forces from Algeria to Europe; this policy would be followed but unstated. Believing it was better that Paris surmise rather than hear explicitly the American message, Dulles professed himself satisfied.[54]

In the meantime the Gaillard government, which took power in October 1957, initiated a financial stabilization policy designed to bring the deficit down to 700 billion francs, and promises were made to Washington to that effect. But French negotiators still informed the European Payments Union (EPU) that the country would need at least $500 million in emergency aid. Washington was now confronted with a serious dilemma. To fail to come to the assistance of Paris would be to repudiate a time-honored postwar pattern of such short-term assistance in the face of recurrent French budget deficits and balance of payments crises. The machinery of the EPU and the IMF, moreover, had been created for helping with just such short-term crises. Failure to help would have a negative impact on NATO, European financial stability, and French-American relations generally. On the other hand, to help Paris over its crisis might involve Washington in a more obvious way in supporting French policies in Algeria. Perhaps this was the French intent— to force the Americans, when push came to shove, to back them in their Algerian policies in deeds if not in words. British Ambassador Jebb did not trust Gaillard, who at age 38 was the youngest premier the French had had since the nineteenth century. Despite his brilliant oratory, Jebb thought him glib and insincere, with an opportunism "reminiscent of an old-style radical politician."[55] The dilemma hung over the NSC, which wanted seriously to inhibit prosecution of the war by making aid conditional on the return of French forces to the NATO shield. But Dulles, in the end, shrank from this option.[56]

In the end, Washington helped put together a financial aid package amounting to about $650 million in order to stabilize the franc in late January 1958. The credit was disguised as such, and advertised instead as a first-time application of innovative economic methods. It tied together funds from the EPU, the IMF, and various U.S. aid agencies in a single coordinated package, designed to have the maximum impact on French and foreign opinion and to underline the close cooperation of these three sources of credit. It did that and stands as one of the success stories of the EPU, which played a critical, if often ill-understood, role in creating the institutional basis for the future development of European integration. But in pursuing the international package, Washington was also involving the EPU and the IMF willy-nilly in the image of Europe as imperialist in its policies. Paris received some $600 million: $88 million came from the Export-Import Bank in Washington, $131 million from the IMF, and $250 million from the EPU; U.S. direct Treasury participation was $186 million.

The aid package brought an immediate protest from the Saudi ambassador in Washington, who accused the Americans of helping the French in Algeria. Not at all, he was told; the package was for the purpose of stabilizing the French balance of payments and was "not related to the Algerian situation." It was said to involve postponements of loan installments and purchases of U.S. agricultural surplus, and Washington pretended that it provided no new money to the French. The United States, the Saudis were assured, would continue to press for a fair and equitable solution to the Algerian problem.[57] Meanwhile continued pressure was put on the French to redeploy their forces to NATO, and the NSC only reluctantly continued military grant aid to France in October 1957 on the condition that it be reviewed by the end of 1958 if France had not by then done so.[58] Dulles and NATO Secretary General Paul-Henri Spaak commiserated together on October 24, 1957, that a once-projected French contribution of fourteen divisions to NATO as well as twelve German divisions in fact to date amounted to five German divisions and four French, and these were under strength. Spaak deplored the fact that the French continued to be short because of their war in Algeria.[59] But despite the aid, French policy in Algeria remained unchanged, and in fact the war was escalated.

The aid package was concluded shortly before the eruption of the final, most serious crisis in Franco-American relations during the Fourth Republic, the bombardment of the Tunisian village of Sakiet in February 1958, which finally caused Washington to abandon its support of the regime. It is clear in retrospect that had the crisis erupted earlier the aid package might never have been negotiated, with incalculable consequences for the continued prosecution of the war. But the aid package was immediately preceded by yet another Franco-American crisis, this one over American arms aid to Tunisia. In May 1957 France had suspended economic assistance to Tunisia in an attempt to punish it for Algerian rebel raids operating from "sanctuaries" within its territory. Paris insisted that Washington do likewise and also withhold economic aid to Morocco, which since the Ben Bella arrest had refused to reestablish diplomatic relations with France. Washington put together a modest aid package totaling $3 million for Tunisia in March 1957; Bourguiba accepted it, but he was disappointed at the small amount and accused Washington of seeking to placate Paris.[60] The State Department deplored the French suspension of economic aid to both countries and it was embarrassed by Tunisian requests that it step in to substitute for the French; Dulles warned Alphand that if France failed to help Tunisia the United States would have to act lest "Communism triumph" in the country. Houghton put it rather more curtly: the United States simply could not allow Tunisia to go bankrupt.[61] Morocco eventually accepted a French offer to establish a joint committee of inquiry into the circumstances of the downing of the plane carrying the Algerians, and it resumed ties with France. But rather than being pleased, the State Department saw the Moroccan action as capitulation to economic pressure by Paris, while "Algeria continues as the mortgage hanging over Morocco and French-Moroccan relations."[62]

The same, of course, was true of Tunisia, where the French continued to insist stubbornly that aid could be resumed only when the Tunisians

stopped helping the Algerian rebels. When Alphand carried out this representation in Washington, Herter told him bluntly that French troops
must cease chasing Algerian rebels into Tunisian territory, and that the
United States would extend economic aid to Tunis.[63] This led in turn to
French charges that Washington aimed to supplant France's influence
and "leading role" in North Africa.[64] Washington tried to hold off on a
full-fledged aid program to Tunisia, allowing $2 million to enter the
country in the form of aid to children in July, but in September 1957
Bourguiba added an arms request to his persistent pressure for economic aid, and he threatened to turn to the Soviet bloc for assistance if
he did not get his way.[65]

By the terms of an exchange of letters in June 1956, France was to be
the sole arms supplier to Tunisia. France did initially supply light
weapons sufficient for a small force of 2,243 men, the nucleus of an
eventual Tunisian army. Further requests by Tunisia for arms were
stalled in Paris, however, and on February 7, 1957, France informed Tunisia that no further requests would be honored until Tunisia gave sufficient guarantees against their being diverted to the Algerian rebels. In
frustration, Bourguiba turned elsewhere in a search for weapons, initially directing requests for purchases to Belgium, Turkey, West Germany, Switzerland, and Italy. Each of these nations was pressured in
turn by the Quai d'Orsay into denying the Tunisian requests. In May
1957 the Tunisian government approached Washington, which entered
into laborious negotiations that still had not come to a conclusion in
September, when Bourguiba lost patience and declared to the Americans that the situation had become urgent. Border incidents showed
that Tunisia must have the weapons to control its territory; ammunition
supplies had been exhausted; and all alternative efforts at finding supplies among Western nations had turned up empty.

American Consul G. Lewis Jones pleaded the Tunisian case to the
State Department: the Americans had been postponing the issue, Paris
consistently refused to help, and the Tunisian government urgently
needed weapons for an additional 4,000 troops. Tunisia's pro-West orientation was in jeopardy, despite the obvious preferences of Bourguiba,
because of what appeared to be an arms embargo. Arms supply had become a symbol of the West's continuing interest in Tunisia, which faced
strangulation by France.[66] Dulles pleaded for time, asking Jones to explain the "delicacy" of the American position to Tunisia while Washington studied its request. The French meanwhile protested that Bourguiba's demand for arms was absurd, since the country was threatened

by nobody; Bourguiba would do better to concentrate on ending his own aid to the Algerian rebels. But Jones warned that Bourguiba had been ready to seek arms from Egypt and the Soviet Union and turn toward neutralism until Dulles intervened.[67] To complicate matters, Cairo offered a gift of small arms to Tunisia, which Bourguiba, in an ostensible act of brotherly gratitude, felt obliged to accept, despite his loathing for the Egyptian dictator.[68]

Meanwhile border incidents between Tunisia and Algeria increased in volume, and on October 5, 1957, Habib Bourguiba, Jr., the Tunisian president's son, formally requested United States intervention in Paris to stop French incursions across the frontier. Washington now concluded that "From the facts available it is difficult to escape the impression that the French army has taken matters in its own hands in border areas during the present government crisis." In fact the Defense Ministry had approved a policy of stepped-up military actions on Tunisian territory the month before, but Washington was kept in the dark about the changed policy. The effect, however, was the same; while Washington tried to work on the Tunisian arms problem in a way that would minimize the effect on France, the French army created pressure in the opposite direction.[69] It was not clear, moreover, that everyone in the French administration, or even the premier, was aware of the army's authorization to step up its retaliatory policy across the Tunisian frontier. The Tunisians believed the French army was acting on its own, and even the French chargé, Armand Bénard, told Washington he feared that "freewheeling military or intelligence operations were taking place on the frontiers without his [Bénard's] knowledge."[70] Once again the French government had revealed to its major ally its incapacity to conduct its internal affairs in a rational and legally ordered way.

Coordinating its policy with London, which also had received Tunisian arms requests, Washington informed the French of its intention to provide light arms to Tunisia if Paris did not act first. The British agreed that delay was no longer possible; in fact they thought delivery by air unavoidable if only to get in ahead of the Egyptians.[71] The French now promised that they would deliver arms to Tunis after all: they were aware of the danger that the Tunisians might turn east, they wanted to preserve their monopoly as the unique Tunisian source of supply, and they were responsive to Bourguiba's arguments that without weapons he could hardly be expected to control his frontiers as the French were demanding of him. But as Gaillard formed his government, he prevaricated, refusing to act in the face of charges from the political right that the Tunisian dictator would allow the weapons to slip into the hands of the rebels. Turning to Washington, the premier insisted that it fulfill several conditions on its aid before he would agree.

Paris wanted all the serial numbers of the weapons to be delivered registered with the French government so that the weapons could be traced if found in rebel hands, and it stipulated that Washington supply the Tunisian army only, not the national guard or the militia. It was not clear to the Americans how or why the Tunisians could or should be prevented from allocating their weapons internally as they wished. Nor were the Americans pleased at the idea of giving Paris the serial numbers of the weapons delivered. Perhaps Washington was unconcerned about a potential delivery to the Algerians; more likely, the Americans were unwilling to be seen as compromising Tunisian sovereignty. Washington had promised Bourguiba a decision by the end of October; when the French still did nothing, paralyzed by yet another cabinet crisis in Paris, the Americans prepared to act. Dulles warned Paris on November 5 against a further prolongation of the Tunisian arms stalemate lest it force a total change in American policy toward North Africa. The key to continued French influence in Morocco and Tunisia was "French willingness to treat both countries as independent partners and carry out military and economic programs in accordance with this principle."[72] France protested further, however, stubbornly insisting on its hegemony over Tunisian foreign policy and showing no signs of willingness to supply arms of its own. Washington delayed until November 12, allowing time for Gaillard to form his government, but it would not accept the cabinet crisis in Paris, now over a month old, as an excuse for French inaction. When Gaillard finally won investiture from the Assembly on November 5, France had been without a government since Bourgès-Maunoury's fall on September 30, and for fifty-eight out of one hundred sixty-nine days since the fall of Mollet.[73] With an Egyptian shipment of light weapons imminent, and with the agreement of London, Washington told the Tunisians of its willingness to provide 500 rifles on November 12.[74] The British agreed to a somewhat larger delivery.

The size of the shipments was meant to be symbolic, but the comedy continued; on November 6 Gaillard again asked for a delay; he needed time to convince his colleagues of the necessity of aiding Bourguiba, but if the British and Americans acted it would become impossible for him to do so.[75] The State Department believed that further delay would be worse rather than better; but the British now tried to hold off further. Gaillard warned Jebb that the decision would harm British-French relations; he expected as much from the Americans, but it would be a real blow to have the British associated with them.[76] This was enough to give the British grounds to hold off, but Washington was committed to the November 12 date. On November 11 Dulles appealed to Lloyd for joint action, as the likelihood of being attacked either by French public opinion or the government was much less if both the British and the Americans acted together.[77]

Gaillard warned that the British-American action constituted a threat to Atlantic solidarity, and threatened that France might torpedo the forthcoming December meeting of the NATO Council. Alphand said that if France was not supported on the Tunisian question the NATO meeting in December would be consigned to "irremediable failure."[78] The *loi-cadre* would be jeopardized, and the government might fall. On November 11, Dulles made a last-ditch appeal to Gaillard, to which the British added their own. Gaillard first said that he would, then that he would not, and finally that he could not. Having been rejected in his previous attempt to place conditions on the arms sales, the French premier tried a new tack: Paris would not arm Tunisia unless Bourguiba agreed to reject the impending shipment from Egypt; it was intolerable, Gaillard said, for Western arms deliveries to be followed by Eastern ones, lest the West be trapped in a situation of continuous blackmail.[79] The British dutifully carried Gaillard's request to Bourguiba, but the latter flatly rejected it, and on November 14 Eisenhower personally supported Tunisia and rejected Gaillard's last argument. Confiding to his diary his frustration with "French stupidity and refusal to face facts as they exist," he calmly wrote Gaillard that he was confident that French-American differences in NATO would be discussed "in friendship and mutual understanding," notwithstanding the differences between them over Tunisian arms. The president could not agree that Tunisia, as an independent country, should be constrained to accept any one country as the sole supplier of its arms.[80] The arms were delivered on November 14.

A chorus of protest arose in the Paris press. France had been betrayed by its allies, whose arms would be used to kill French soldiers. The Americans and British had given France an "ultimatum" prompted by their crass desire to safeguard their Middle East oil interests; it was an "odious" blow to the Atlantic alliance.[81] Gaillard was bitter in the National Assembly, declaring that Algeria was formally covered by NATO and the threat there involved the entire Atlantic community, yet the United States and United Kingdom were assisting a country that in turn was helping the rebels. France wanted to strengthen the alliance, Gaillard insisted, and it would seek resolution of the matter at the forth-coming NATO Council meeting in December. If it failed, however, its faith in NATO would be undermined, and Gaillard warned that he would turn to parliament to find a new outcome "in the French national interest."[82] To Macmillan, Gaillard said that Tunisian aid to the rebels was the central factor in the continued ability of the Algerian rebels to carry on the war; if it ceased, the military aspects of France's Algerian problem would soon be over. The British were aggravating the problem for France by augmenting the arms pool available to the rebels. Macmillan cabled Gaillard's claim to Washington, but he also assured the Americans that there was no commitment on the British part to give in to French policies; he had made it clear to Gaillard that Britain expected France to work for a progressive and liberal solution of the Algerian question to be achieved as soon as possible. But Macmillan was having second thoughts; Ambassador Jebb reported from Paris embarrassing cries of "Et tu Brute" toward the British; the halcyon days of cooperation with Paris after Suez were over. Ugly chauvinism and nationalistic pride were on the rise in Paris, with calls for France to leave NATO and go it alone. Macmillan was impressed, and wrote in his diary that the Tunisian arms deal had been a "serious error," as neither he nor Foreign Secretary Lloyd had fully realized the true situation in France.[83]

Ever since Anthony Eden's resignation following the Suez crisis, Prime Minister Harold Macmillan had been assiduously courting and ingratiating himself with the Americans. His cooperation during the Tunisian arms crisis consecrated the success of his efforts; the special relationship, all the more precious to the two English-speaking nations for its assumed but undocumented nature, had been restored. The special relationship throughout the immediate postwar years had uneasily coexisted with participation in a council of the big three that included France. This grouping had also been informal, although the French had always sought to institutionalize it in some fashion. The Algerian War and the Suez crisis in turn ruptured the assumed mutual interests behind the councils of the big three and the special relationship between Britain and the United States. Now that British-American bilateral ties had been restored, could the big three exist again too? Dulles was horrified at the thought. On November 19, not a week after the denouement of the Tunisian arms crisis, Dulles informed London that he was averse to any further tripartite meetings that included France. He did not want to give the world the impression that France, "with ourselves," was in a

different category as "one of the three great powers in the Free World."
France had been demoted. The British, for all their satisfaction with the
restoration of their bilateral relationship with Washington, knew that
this would not make their tasks any easier. From Paris came the report
that the French suspected that they had ceased to count as one of the big
three, and suspected a plot to impose an Anglo-U.S. directorate on the
alliance. "Our ganging up," wrote Sir G. Young from the British Embassy to Sir F. Hoyer Millar, "can bring into being an authoritarian
regime with neutralist tendencies in France: We should not underesti-
mate the nuisance value of an affronted France."[84]

All this prompted Gaillard once again to request a statement by President Eisenhower recognizing the French "special position" in North
Africa.[85] When Dulles came to Paris in December for the NATO Council meeting, he found himself closeted with Pineau and Gaillard, who
pressured him "by all means short of open force to extract a declaration
conceding a French sphere of influence in North Africa and a French
veto over American arms deliveries to Tunisia." Dulles refused.[86] Washington had demonstrated its lack of patience with the French and its
willingness to act notwithstanding the constant barrage of threats coming from their leaders. And try as they might, whether under Gaillard,
Pflimlin, or de Gaulle, the French would not again win admission to the
councils of the big three.

In this context it is perhaps worth pausing over a CIA estimate that
provoked a policy debate and apparently influenced Washington's
thinking during late 1957 and early 1958. The agency thought there
was an "even chance" that Algeria would achieve autonomy within
eighteen months with the possibility of independence. It was likely that
the European population would violently protest, even rebel against,
such a solution, but their only prospect of success was if the army sided
with such a rebellion, and the agency, noting the army's long tradition
of loyalty to the Republic, thought it would not do so. This, however,
was completely at variance with opinion within the State Department,
which criticized the report. Its officials in Algeria had warned as early
as January 1957 that although the army was not yet in revolt against
the regime, such a tendency was crystallizing within its ranks, and that
any attempt by a French government to take steps leading to the "abandonment" of Algeria might well lead to an army seizure of power. But
the CIA insisted that the French government was capable of implementing a solution granting independence to Algeria. Business interests increasingly saw the futility of the war, which consumed 25 percent of

France's military budget, while the military budget in turn accounted for 7.6 percent of the GNP. There was no immediate prospect of the regime being overthrown, said the CIA, because the extreme right wing lacked both a leader and a program. As for de Gaulle, his actions "have not been those of a man who is interested in taking control of France."[87] The CIA momentarily had the last word. But by spring 1958, the State Department's more pessimistic views came to prevail.

The persistence of doubts among France's most important allies about the stability of the regime and the capacity of its government both to make decisions and to see that they were carried out augured ill for the future of NATO, quite apart from continued French threats to cause a crisis in the alliance. As it turned out, the French bluff was called successfully, and the December 1957 NATO meeting was untroubled by the Tunisian arms crisis or unsatisfied French demands for recognition of their hegemony in North Africa or reestablishment of the councils of the big three. But the French seemed intent on demonstrating yet again, in a final and most dramatic way, that the internal functioning of their institutions and policies must involve their allies in sufficiently disturbing and dramatic a fashion as to force them indeed to conclude that the regime in Paris was "indigestible to NATO" as it was. This became apparent during the Sakiet crisis, which brought about the fall of the Republic, and revealed that the Republic's collapse was, paradoxically, a condition for the settlement of the Algerian War.

CHAPTER FOUR

The United States, Great Britain, and the Sakiet Crisis

The French bombardment of the Tunisian border village of Sakiet Sidi Youssef on February 8, 1958, marked the turning point of the Algerian War, leading from a politics of military escalation, to Anglo-American intervention, to a government crisis that rapidly evolved into a crisis of regime, and the coming to power of Charles de Gaulle. The Anglo-American intervention was the decisive element in this series of events, and thus arguably the most important development in turning around French policy in the Algerian War. De Gaulle's intentions with regard to Algeria when he came to power remain the subject of debate and will be discussed later; what is important here is that he settled the crisis of Sakiet along the lines of the suggested Anglo-American settlement at the conclusion of their good offices mission, restoring French relations with Tunisia. He also satisfied the British and the Americans, and hence France's NATO partners, that he would bring the Algerian crisis to a conclusion, and then eventually did so. To the extent that the Anglo-American intervention brought about this chain of events, which of course could not be precisely foreseen, it must be considered a significant success for American foreign policy, and perhaps one of the most important of the postwar era.

The intervention originated with two firmly held convictions that grew in the mind of the American secretary of state, John Foster Dulles. The first was that chaos prevailed in the decision-making apparatus of the Fourth Republic; the regime was dysfunctional from the standpoint of maintaining France's place in the Western alliance, and no longer necessarily merited the support the Americans had lavished upon it since its inception in 1947. The nightmare scenario Dulles envisaged was clear: French policy was bound to embroil Algeria's neighbors in the unwinnable struggle, in the first instance Tunisia, but then Morocco and Libya. Soon France would find itself fighting the whole of North Africa, supported by Nasser's Egypt and other Arab states, and they would be armed and financed by the Soviet Union and international communism.[1] The second belief was that France would soon weary of the expanded struggle, a popular front government would then come to power, and it would liquidate the war and withdraw France from the NATO alliance while losing all of North Africa to communism. For Dulles, defeatist regimes in France had liquidated wars twice in recent memory, in 1940 and in 1954, a pattern that would occur again unless something were done.

With the relative success of the French tactic of *quadrillage,* the saturation of Algeria proper with a virtual army of occupation, the focus of the war shifted to the Tunisian border. For a long time preceding Sakiet the French army had been focusing on Tunisia as the source of military raids against French forces in Algeria; Tunisian territory was a sanctuary from which the Algerian National Liberation Army (ALN) could mount raids into Algeria with impunity. French military intelligence reported that the Tunisian government in September 1957 had abandoned a strip of its territory along forty kilometers of the frontier with Algeria, in the extreme south of the country, to the ALN, which had chosen the village of Sakiet for the installation of training camps, the storage of arms and supplies, and as a launching base for raids into Algeria designed to draw French troops to the frontier.[2] Clashes on Tunisian territory between French troops in pursuit of Algerian rebels and Tunisian forces occurred as early as June 1957, and the Tunisians immediately lodged complaints in both Paris and Washington, which was requested to use its influence in Paris to get the French to stop their incursions. The State Department could do little but ask both sides to exercise restraint, which satisfied neither.[3] Following a frontier incident on August 26, the French government, urged by Lacoste, took a firmer hand with the Tunisians: a protest note was sent September 6, 1957, warning that Tunisia would be held responsible for the neutrality of its territory. If rebel actions continued, French forces would be forced to take whatever actions were necessary to assure their security. The Tunisian government was further accused of tolerating the presence of the Algerians and facilitating their training.[4]

But the Quai was trying to negotiate a modus vivendi with the Tunisians, understanding that a politics of confrontation with Bourguiba might drive him into the arms of Nasser. The French informed the United States and the UN of their protest, but officials at the Quai were clearly unhappy with their instructions, which originated with Lacoste: they told Washington that the resident general was a "law unto himself" in Algeria who refused to collaborate with the Foreign Ministry or the Office of Tunisian and Moroccan Affairs and would not permit policy in Algeria to be formulated by the Inter-Ministerial Committee of the Cabinet on North Africa, which was specifically charged with that function.[5] The Fourth Republic consequently was unable to formulate a coherent policy toward Tunisia. Washington once again was invited to deduce that the government in Paris was powerless to control its bureaucracy and that ministers ruled their departments irrespective of government policy like so many feudal satraps. What the French hoped to gain by helping to create this picture is not entirely clear. Could they have thought this a means of excusing or obscuring otherwise deliberate and indefensible policies, or were they inviting Washington to intervene and restore order in Paris? What is clear is that Washington could have found none of these explanations reassuring.

The French were aware that the Tunisians were incapable of controlling their territory, and they knew that Bourguiba could not risk action against the Algerians, who enjoyed the natural sympathy of his population. Bourguiba reportedly requested the rebels on several occasions to cease their attacks from Tunisian territory but to no avail.[6] In frustration he blamed the French for denying him arms to control his frontiers, and tried to mediate the war, asking that France first accept the rebel condition that the talks lead to independence, or at least "self-determination." He joined the Sultan of Morocco in offering his good offices in November 1957, warned that France could only lose further influence in North Africa by prolonging the struggle, and held out the prospect of a North African federation encompassing Algeria, Tunisia, and Morocco that would naturally fall under strong French influence. But behind this rhetoric, which resonated strongly in Washington, the French saw only untrammeled personal ambition: Bourguiba sought to influence the United States and the European countries against France while offering himself to the Americans as the "man of destiny" capa-

ble of settling the Algerian problem. He had sent his son to Washington to lobby in the belief that the United States had the power to force
France to accept Algerian independence, and he repeatedly urged the
Americans to use all means of pressure at their disposal to this effect.[7]
Meanwhile the Tunisian leader rejected French protests; no less than
twenty-three protests were lodged in Tunis between July 1, 1957, and
February 10, 1958, in reference to eighty-four incidents of military
skirmishes involving Algerian forces using Tunisian territory as a sanctuary, all without effect.[8]

In January 1957, French intelligence sources had estimated that there
were 5,000 rebels in Tunisia, with 2,500 stationed at Sakiet Sidi
Youssef, a small town located only 1.5 kilometers from the French Algerian frontier.[9] By December 1957 the French army put this figure at
6,000 ALN fighters, with Sakiet as their "principal center of resupply
and distribution." Bourguiba was concerned about the possible reverberations for his relations with France and in February 1957 demanded
of the FLN that rebel troops be redeployed to Algeria, returning only to
regroup and resupply as a result of actual conflict with French forces
initiated on Algerian territory.[10]

In March 1957, Bourguiba and his prime minister, Bahi Ladgham,
met with Belkacem Krim and Omar Ouamrane, rebel leaders, and expressed their anger at the "occupation" of the west and north of Tunisia by the ALN; Bourguiba reportedly threatened to evacuate the Algerians, assisted if necessary by the French. He was squeezed between
rebel pressure and French assertion of the *"droit de poursuite,"* the alleged right of a nation faced with internal war to pursue enemy forces
into the territory of any nation that gives them sanctuary. The Quai was
aware that no such right existed in any existing international convention, but the only alternative was to accuse Tunisia of aggression against
France and assert the right of self-defense according to the Charter of
the UN, but the world organization was hostile to French policy in Algeria and unlikely to find for the French.[11] Detailed maps of rebel "im-
plantations" on Tunisian soil meanwhile accumulated in French military dossiers, with their strongest base consistently identified as being at
Sakiet. By September 1957 the Algerians, aided by Tunis, allegedly had
begun systematic infiltration across the frontier, with the intention of
provoking a French response so as to influence the UN General Assembly debate scheduled to begin in the fall.[12] In November and December
1957 confrontations between rebel forces based in Tunisia and the
French army occurred regularly, with the rebels systematically striking

from ambush and then fleeing back across the frontier.[13] On January 3, 1958, American Ambassador Lewis Jones reported a new French raid on a Tunisian village, denied by the French military and played down by the Tunisians: "the timing," Jones reported, "seems almost calculated to frustrate efforts by [Ambassador] Gorse and Bourguiba to establish a favorable climate for Franco-Tunisian negotiations."[14] The military was using the situation on the frontier to undermine the Quai's efforts at accommodation with Tunisia.

On January 11, 1958, three hundred rebels, allegedly encamped in an abandoned lead mine outside of Sakiet, participated in an ambush of a French detachment of fifty soldiers on the Algerian side of the border in the immediate vicinity of the village, killing fourteen, wounding two, and taking four more prisoner. Of the dead, twelve were reported to have been brutally murdered and their bodies mutilated.[15] Tunisian authorities were now fearful, according to French reports, "that a French military action might cause heavy losses and prove the co-belligerence of Tunisia" in the Algerian War, and rebel forces were ordered to abstain from operations for a period of four days after January 17, 1958. France demanded that Tunisia obtain the release of the prisoners and broke off negotiations pending their return. Paris knew that the Tunisian government, fearing French reprisals, was trying to get the Algerians to return the prisoners; the Americans believed the Tunisians powerless to force the rebels' hand, however.[16] Washington also remained skeptical of French charges that Tunisia harbored extensive rebel bases. Jones reported that a British Embassy counselor, who was an experienced truce observer and Arabic speaker, found no signs of FLN activity on a visit to Sakiet. A French Embassy official, moreover, privately admitted to the Americans that the French military were deliberately putting out an exaggerated picture of FLN bases in Tunisia, whereas the reality was that there were 5,000 rebel combatants in the country who were constantly on the move.[17]

Dulles intervened personally after the ambush in an effort to get Franco-Tunisian negotiations off dead center. But the Tunisians rejected French charges of responsibility for the prisoners and professed ignorance of their alleged presence on Tunisian soil while demanding a full French troop withdrawal from Tunisian territory. Bourguiba embarrassed Washington by offering to turn over the French naval base of Bizerte to Washington and NATO once the French were gone. The Tunisians knew that the suggestion, if entertained by Washington, would infuriate the French. The French continued to insist that the

United States recognize the primacy of French influence in North African affairs, which Washington refused to do.[18]

Premier Gaillard, in the meantime, sent a personal envoy, General Buchalet, to Tunisia in an effort to restart Franco-Tunisian negotiations and warn Bourguiba of his obligations as a neutral, but Bourguiba pretended irritation and announced that he would negotiate only with a civilian.[19] Gaillard in turn claimed to be insulted by Bourguiba's refusal to accept his envoy. The Americans thought Gaillard had sent a general to intimidate Bourguiba and they admired the latter's courage in refusing to receive him. But either way, Franco-Tunisian relations deteriorated further and it was clear that one more incident would provoke a major crisis from which there might be no recourse.[20]

The tiny Tunisian village of Sakiet now became a French obsession. Increased rebel concentrations were noted in an abandoned mine there, while the village itself was allegedly used for rest, recreation, and resupply.[21] On February 7, 1958, the eve of the bombardment, French military intelligence reported that "Sakiet has become an Algerian town"; most of the civilian population had fled, with only a few Tunisian families remaining in the village, and most Tunisian-run stores had been closed or taken over by Algerians.[22] Tunisia was the logical and necessary entrepôt for arms delivered to the Algerian rebellion from abroad, and for the last eight months had become "the principal logistical base of the Algerian rebellion." Cairo was the supplier of rebel arms, Tunis their distributor, and Sakiet their central destination.[23]

French airplanes regularly carried out surveillance of the border at Sakiet, and it appears that the very plane that took the excellent aerial surveillance photos extant today in the archives at Vincennes was the one forced down by antiaircraft fire coming from the vicinity of the village and the immediate cause of the bombardment, or *"riposte,"* of February 8, 1958. The bombardment of Sakiet is often taken as the most flagrant case of an independent military run amok and a civilian regime unable to control its military. Ironically, although the French government for its own purposes disseminated that view at the time, this does not appear to have been the case. From the standpoint of the military, the attack was within the framework of the standing orders of the army that had been in effect since September 1957, when the French government placed its first of many protests with the Tunisian authorities. Note the text of the following "Personal Instruction" issued to the commander of the eastern zone of Constantine, signed by General Loth, commander of the army corps of Constantine:

In the event of a generalized attack by the ensemble of FLN elements stationed in Tunisia, our response on rebel bases would be capable of provoking serious incidents in TUNISIA and requiring our intervention with a view to
reestablishing our control on a part of Tunisian territory, notably the regions
of Tunis, Bizerte, and Sousse.... The mission of General Commandant of the
Army Corps of Constantine is essentially:

  1) the destruction of rebel bands and their bases as far as the TABARKA-
THALA lateral and the control of the part of Tunisian territory included between this lateral and the frontier which falls under our command.... In consequence I have the intention of:

- preventing any aggression by means of an increased effort in aerial and
  land-based search for intelligence notably along the frontier strip and,...
- to block immediately any rebel attack using to the maximum artillery fire
  and aviation upon the request of troops in contact.
- to counter-attack with the elements of intervention with a view to destroying the rebel bands and their military bases situated between the
  frontier and the TABARKA-THALA line after having crushed them under fire
  of air power and assured the control of this portion of Tunisian territory.[24]

In a subsequent version of these orders issued on September 18,
1957, General Loth inserted an underlined paragraph specifying that
any operation going beyond the classic right of pursuit and including
use of heavy air power needed to have his specific authorization. Ever
alert to the broader implications of what he might be called upon to do,
Loth wrote to his commanding officer in Algiers, General Salan, that
the operations envisaged, although justified by the necessities of a war
of internal subversion, "would make us guilty of what is classified as aggression, this at a time when our cause in the United Nations appears to
present itself under favorable auspices: we must not forget, in addition,
the extent to which our military capability is vulnerable to an attack
carried out by a third power, disposing, for example, of significant air
power; this is a risk that I am, however, unable to evaluate"[25] The third
power, presumably the Soviets, was not otherwise identified, but General Loth was clearly throwing the issue of possible foreign policy consequences of such a raid back upon Algerian Commander Salan and
the government. But Salan wrote Minister of Defense Jacques Chaban-
Delmas that he preferred rapid one-time blows to long-term raids across
the frontier that might last several days and be costly in casualties, and
specified that "of course such operations would only be launched upon
your [direct] orders."[26] Chaban-Delmas should have brought the question of confirming these orders to the rest of the cabinet. There is no
record of whether he did.

These orders were further clarified, as if they needed to be, in response to the January 11, 1958, raid in which the French soldiers were taken captive. On January 19 General Loth wrote, in implementing a plan to assure the security and protection of French troops stationed in Tunisia, that "General Salan has just given me carte blanche to react brutally in TUNISIA in case of new frontier incidents...well within the framework of pursuit.... He has specified equally that the means used must be calculated in a manner so as to inflict upon the enemy an unquestioned and bloody defeat." General Loth in turn delegated authority to local commanders to initiate any such action, with the provision that he be informed ahead of time so as to be able to provide "heavy aerial means proportionate to the lesson we want to give the enemy"[27] Whatever the responsibility of the French government as a whole in the Sakiet raid, the military archives at Vincennes would seem to confirm that such operations were implied in orders that made their way right up the chain of command from the battlefield to the office of the defense minister; and this is the precise information which the Americans and the British were privately given.[28] British Consul R. F. G. Sarrel reported from Algiers on February 11 that the secretary general of the resident's office had assured his American colleague that the order for the Sakiet raid came not from Resident Lacoste but directly from Paris. "He did not dissent when asked if this meant Chaban Delmas." It was clear to Washington and London that the French hoped that a serious escalation of military means used in Tunisia and the infliction of serious damage there might serve to convince the Tunisians to take action once and for all to limit Algerian operations from their territory.

But the Sakiet raid appeared also to be an overt demonstration of French unwillingness to heed Washington; Dulles made a personal appeal to Paris and Tunis on February 1, 1958, a week before the bombardment, for a resumption of talks to prevent a "dangerous crisis" in Franco-Tunisian relations, and he specifically asked that the French keep border incidents to a minimum. Fearing that the French military was capable of acting on its own, Dulles warned that actions by local military authorities would have "unpredictable repercussions." Needless to say, Dulles also counseled moderation to the Tunisians.[29] On February 4, Houghton conveyed the substance of Dulles's message to Pineau, who admitted that the Tunisian government was not in control of its territory and assured Houghton that the French government had taken the firm decision not to carry out any general military operations across the Tunisian border. He could not, however, rule out local actions in exercise of the right of *riposte* to particular instances of aggression. On the other hand, the French government wanted acceptable international means of controlling the frontier, and would act with "prudence." Did Pineau's caveat about "local actions" justify or warn against the Sakiet raid? Could the Sakiet raid be described as "prudent," even given the caveat? Clearly, the answer is no to both questions. Pineau was sincere in his promises; he was just unaware of what Chaban-Delmas was planning.

While Dulles was being reassured, British Ambassador Jebb reported the French to be saying that if Bourguiba continued giving aid and comfort to the rebels he must be prepared to suffer the consequences; indeed, on February 3, Lacoste remarked that the hypothetical shooting down of a French plane from Tunisian territory "might unfortunately lead to consequences that the Quai would be the first to deplore," another remarkable revelation of the bureaucratic wars in France. Lacoste knew that the Quai would disapprove of the raid so he bypassed it along with the rest of the government. Jebb, five days prior to the Sakiet attack, thought bombardment had "seemed probable for some time," and he thought Pineau had made it "clear to us and explicit to Dulles" that the French military might be ready to intervene on a major scale, even going so far as the reoccupation of Tunisia.[30] But whether or not Dulles understood the import of what he was being told, one can still understand his fury once he learned of the Sakiet bombardment; only two days earlier, on February 6, 1958, he conveyed what he believed to be a favorable French response to his démarche to the Tunisian government. Pineau, he reported, had given him firm assurances that the French government had no aggressive designs on Tunisia, desired to reopen negotiations, and would minimize border friction.[31] Both the American secretary of state and the French foreign minister could not have been made to look more foolish by the Sakiet raid.

When Premier Gaillard later assured Washington that he had not known of the operation, which was unauthorized, American and British diplomatic personnel were already in possession of accounts attributing the attack to its prior approval by Chaban-Delmas, if not by the cabinet as a whole. It is difficult to see how General Loth's standing orders, in effect since July 1957, could have been kept a secret from the minister of defense, if not from the cabinet. The orders envisaged, moreover, the use of B 26 bombers and other sophisticated aircraft, raising obvious questions as to whether American restrictions permitted such use in Algeria and whether such escalation of means hitherto used might provoke an international crisis.[32] The Sakiet action, often taken to be the most flagrant example of military disobedience under the Fourth Republic, ironically was within the context of French government authorized action, as General Jouhaud, commander of the French air force in Algeria, always later maintained. British Consul Sarrell, echoing American reports that the order for the Sakiet operation came from Defense Minister Chaban-Delmas, attributed his information to Algiers Prefect Paul Teitgen, a seemingly unimpeachable source.

Sarrell further reported that Chaban-Delmas was systematically rotating Gaullist officers into Algiers, presumably with the express intent of channeling any eventual trouble that might arise there toward support of de Gaulle. In fact, within the Gaillard government, Chaban-Delmas, by his own later admission, actively pursued the return of de Gaulle to power, which Premier Gaillard did not object to so long as the defense minister acted legally. This even included visits to Algiers, during which Chaban, in his own words, "vilified the regime, the system, indeed the Fourth Republic" which he had sworn to serve.[33] The journal *L'Express,* which carried out its own inquiry, came to the same conclusion: Chaban-Delmas bore personal responsibility for Sakiet, and Gaillard was not informed until after the raid had taken place. A clipping from *L'Express* is conserved in the military archives at Vincennes as well as in the archives in Washington. It concluded that "In fact, the government had left the choice and responsibility to Messieurs Lacoste and Chaban Delmas, who delegated their authority in turn to the military. The government was solidly responsible [for the Sakiet raid] a priori."[34] The operation had been planned by General Jouhaud and submitted to General Ely, who, having obtained the oral accord of Chaban-Delmas, agreed to a first-time use of heavy air power. Little wonder, then, that after the raid, General Ely and Defense Minister Chaban-Delmas both warned Gaillard that if the army were disavowed, "it would be impossible to respond to the reactions that would be produced." Gaillard, having no choice, covered the raid.[35]

Assuming Gaillard's ignorance of or opposition to the operation, it appears likely that the Gaullists, in the person of Chaban-Delmas, triggered Sakiet in order to trap the premier and perhaps undermine the regime.[36] Although in testimony before the National Assembly, Gaillard later included Chaban-Delmas as one of those who did not have prior knowledge of the raid, the Americans, correctly as it turned out, settled on the account in *L'Express* as confirmed by their own sources. But whether the military was indeed running amok in Algeria, or individual cabinet ministers were acting without the authorization of the premier and the government, or indeed whether Gaillard knew all along of the raid and was lying to Washington, the outlook was equally dispiriting from the American point of view. There was nobody in authority with whom one could reliably negotiate in Paris.

Sakiet threatened the destruction of American hopes to make of Tunisia an example of successful capitalist development and a point of attraction for the rest of the developing countries; with it also went dreams for the construction of a united Maghreb consisting of Tunisia, Morocco, Libya, and Algeria, linked to the West and a counterpoint to the radical expansionist nationalism of Gamal Abdel Nasser. Nor should the strategic importance of North Africa be forgotten; Tunisia had been the jumping-off point for the reconquest of continental Europe from Hitler's armies during World War II, and might become that again in the event of a Soviet invasion and occupation of Europe. The United States maintained air force bases in Morocco, where, since 1953, nuclear weapons had been stockpiled and could be rapidly launched against the eventual Soviet aggressor.

It was hardly surprising, then, that the Sakiet bombardment on 8 February 1958 provoked one of the harshest exchanges of words between France and the United States in the whole of the postwar period. Dulles warned Alphand that he feared the incident would cause "a major disaster for us all." The situation in Algeria was out of control and going from bad to worse, and now threatened to provoke a war involving all of North Africa. France had used American equipment against innocent civilians and involved the United States in the conflict. This could not be allowed to continue. France's efforts at reform in Algeria, such as the new statute (*loi-cadre*) were "feeble," Dulles said, and French claims of the successful military pacification of Algeria were patently false. Alphand protested that the aim of the raid was to deal with the source of rebel antiaircraft fire, and he warned that if the United States went against France the consequences would be unpredictable and certainly play into the hands of neutralists. Dulles shrank back from too extreme a confrontation. The Americans had never tried to "prescribe a solution" in Algeria, he said, but he repeated his belief that current French policies would lead to the loss of all of North Africa to communism. Alphand in turn insisted, on the contrary, that if France abandoned Algeria the result would be chaos and the victory of communism.[37]

Alphand was shaken by Dulles's remarks, as was Pineau, and the French ambassador returned to the State Department two days later with instructions to express his "surprise" at the vehemence of the American reaction. If the secretary's remarks became known, he told Assistant Secretary of State Charles Burke Elbrick, "there would be very serious repercussions on French-United States relations." The raid, he said, was caused by rebel provocation, and France was "shocked" by Dulles's strong words. Elbrick curtly replied that he hoped the secretary's remarks would remain confidential, but that world opinion was equally shocked at France, and that the universal condemnation of France among the nations of the world could hardly be in its interest or that of the West.[38] Elbrick appeared to be inviting Alphand to make public Dulles's tongue-lashing. The Americans had everything to gain if he did so.

The French military initially appeared pleased by the results of the raid. An agent present in the village on February 8 reported Tunisian customs and police headquarters destroyed, an old school entirely gone, with victims estimated by Tunisians at about a hundred innocent civilians, among whom, however, they were in reality counting military personnel. More important, the rebel base in the abandoned mine outside of town was totally destroyed and few of the rebels stationed there had escaped.[39] The French Military Command in Algiers confirmed the importance of the objectives attained: antiaircraft emplacements and the mine, used as an encampment for 500 to 600 men, had been destroyed and 100 rebels killed. All available information justified this military action.[40] In the UN the French argued that Sakiet was a training center of long usage, harboring 500 to 700 rebels, antiaircraft emplacements, and an extensive Tunisian military and civilian presence that was mobilized in the service of the rebellion. Tunisia had become a cobelligerent against France and must accept the consequences. To Washington the French sought to justify their use of American equipment. The bombardment had involved 25 planes, including 11 B 26 bombers, 6 Corsair fighter-bombers, and 8 Mistral fighters. The B 26s had been separately purchased by France in the United States and were not part of military aid, while the Corsairs, which were received under the aid program, were no longer assigned to NATO but were under French command. The Mistrals were of French manufacture. Only military targets had been hit, 80 percent of these had been destroyed, but nine-tenths of the village was intact.[41]

The French military equally affected to be mystified by the response to the raid, and Loth warned the government that disavowal by those higher up would put the army in a dangerous situation.[42] General

Jouhaud wrote Salan in turn, citing specific orders and "instructions for their application," noting that he had approved the attack in the context of these orders; he deplored the loss of civilian lives, but the installation of antiaircraft emplacements among a civilian population was a deliberate provocation demanding a response. No international legislation authorized a nation to shoot at the planes of a neighboring nation, even if they strayed across the frontier.[43] General Salan, in a letter to Chaban-Delmas, assumed full responsibility for the raid: "In execution of orders that I had given for response to anti-aircraft fire and aerial fire, and which I have since confirmed, an action of legitimate defense has been unleashed against armaments and known rebel military installations at Sakiet Sidi Youssef." Salan specified that "This action was in the framework of received orders," an authorized reply by air power to antiaircraft fire, and was not a "local initiative." The military means used were justified: the Corsairs had taken out the antiaircraft installations and the B 26s had destroyed the mine that served as a rebel encampment.[44]

However, the Military Command was prepared for the worst: the International Red Cross was in the vicinity of the village in strength during the strike distributing assistance to refugees, and two of their trucks had been destroyed. "The testimony of their delegates is not doubted by world opinion, and one must expect full exploitation of the incident on the international level." This the Tunisians undertook immediately: Bourguiba demanded the immediate, total evacuation of all French military forces from Tunisia, and Tunisian authorities forbade commercial dealers from supplying French bases and civilian personnel, which threatened to put the French in a "humiliating" position. Even the base at Bizerte was now in question.[45]

Whether or not Sakiet was authorized, it was a blunder, and it is all the more remarkable to discover that French military intelligence saw it that way, fearing the consequences as "incalculable." The damage to France was at once tactical, diplomatic, and moral. As one minister said, "one has taken a sledgehammer to crush a fly"; one plane could have silenced the antiaircraft installation at Sakiet, there was no need for B 26 bombers. Gaillard was embarrassed and forced to cover for the army, the Americans now felt obliged to take international action, and a severe malaise was apparent in the army, which was increasingly susceptible to the propaganda of M. Le Pen, then a loyal follower of the rightist anti-tax demagogue Pierre Poujade, who accused the Communists and Mendèsistes of always blaming France. Interestingly, French intelligence thought "it remains no less true that no minister had been informed prior to the operation," but it is difficult to sustain this conclusion given the army's standing orders. In justification of what French intelligence seemed to blame on military disobedience, officers observed that it was difficult to tell soldiers not to react when attacked. For deeper causes, military intelligence cited a "general downgrading of Public Service," and recruitment of officers from among modest families of insufficient means to educate their sons beyond the lycée.[46]

The report was right in one respect at least. The bombardment prompted Dulles to seek radical means of liquidating the French crisis with Tunisia. His initial suspicion was that the raid was premeditated and had been planned by the French government since the January 11 incident in which French soldiers had been taken captive; the bellicose National Assembly debates that had ensued were a kind of warning. But having given the Tunisian government worthless French assurances, American diplomacy was the real victim in all this. Dulles ordered an approach to Pineau and a demand for a full explanation. Jones reported the further disquieting news that American equipment had destroyed three-quarters of the town and killed one hundred persons and wounded seventy-five more because the attack was carried out on market day. Jones hoped the State Department would devise an appropriate response to what was, at the least, a shocking lack of the "prudence" promised by Pineau through Dulles to Bourguiba.[47]

State Department officials told Alphand that whatever France's legal justification for the attack, it was a public relations disaster. France needed a spectacular gesture such as reconstruction of the village and indemnification of the victims to reverse world opinion. Publicly, Dulles was more restrained in his reaction. In his press conference, however, he noted that the Algerian crisis had now been internationalized to the point of involving Tunisia and Morocco, and he said the United States would not exclude taking action itself to "improve the situation."[48] Dulles would not justify the incident in terms of "hot pursuit" and privately vented his fury. He demanded to know where responsibility for the raid lay, but, more seriously, it was clear that France did not have the capacity to deal with the Algerian problem. Unfortunately, there were no clear answers to be got from the French. Algiers Consul Clark's investigation for Dulles confirmed the above account. Lacoste and possibly other competent government ministers had approved the retaliatory policy. There had been much talk of "dealing a heavy blow" and pursuing rebel bands into Tunisian territory. Air attack was the chosen modus operandi to avoid a lengthy ground raid that might be costly in casualties and give the impression of an invasion at the same time. Clark was told by Lacoste's chef du cabinet, Pierre Chaussade, that Lacoste had in fact been against the air bombardment, although, like the others, he had covered for it. It had been authorized in Paris, however, and Chaussade implied that responsibility lay with the minister of defense, Chaban-Delmas. General Quénard said the same. So had Paul Teitgen, prefect of police in Algiers, who also told this to British Consul Sarrell. To be sure, the truth might never be known. But Clark's conclusions were that the government had authorized a vigorous response and that the army's selection of the scale and means used was within the letter, if not the spirit, of its orders.[49] At the Foreign Ministry in Paris Louis Joxe refused the excuse that it had been a local initiative: Lacoste would be recalled, he promised Washington, and there would be an investigation.

At a luncheon on February 10, 1958, Houghton found Gaillard distressed, seemingly at a loss for what to do. He admitted the action had been a mistake, but claimed that it was "taken without authority and not on orders from Paris or the government." The premier could not now admit publicly that the action had been a blunder for fear of the consequences to army morale, but he promised Houghton that if he found a "grievous error" he would not cover it up. He would investigate, and he hoped in the meantime that President Eisenhower and Dulles would refrain from further comment. Dulles's comments to Alphand had been distressing: French policy sought to prevent communism, not to effect its spread.[50]

Dulles seized upon the idea of a French "military excess" as a way out of the crisis, counseling moderation on Tunisian Ambassador Mongi Slim pending the investigation in Paris. The French government was weak and unable to control events, Dulles explained; the military had taken advantage and forced its hand. The French government should not be held responsible. Slim could hardly take comfort in this explanation; if true, it was all the more necessary that the French remove all their potentially disobedient troops from Tunisia. The Tunisian government would lodge a formal complaint with the United Nations, where it expected American support. Dulles could not be completely satisfied with his own explanation either. Gaillard, in the French National Assembly, took a hard line, covering for the military and arguing that the attack had been justified by Algerian rebel provocation from across the border. Houghton was disappointed; in contrast to what the prime minister had told the ambassador earlier, he would now neither admit error nor express regrets. Houghton explained that the cabinet had decided against sanctioning the military in view of the consequences to army morale. The government had authorized a *riposte* but not specifically one on the scale of Sakiet. That the military had gone too far was the general government opinion, which Pineau, Gaillard, and even Lacoste would express privately but not publicly. The French politicians, Houghton said bluntly, feared their military.[51]

There is some doubt about the original suggestion of the good offices mission; the impression in London and Washington seemed to be that the idea was proposed by Tunisia, but it appeared there first in the form of a rumor. Pineau grasped at it, asking the Americans to request of the Tunisians that they permit the provisioning of French troops in Tunisia; their situation, under virtual blockade by Tunsian forces, was becoming increasingly critical and the French army was threatening to provoke a new crisis and supply the troops by force. Bourguiba appealed to the Americans in turn on February 12, asking Washington to obtain from Paris the complete evacuation of French troops from his country and the conversion of Bizerte from a French naval base to a Western NATO base, "free of colonialism." Only the Americans could clean up the ugly situation created by the French military, Bourguiba told Lewis Jones; because Washington helped France militarily and financially, it alone could make its voice heard and prevent France from spoiling its chance to retain its North African interests. Bourguiba was aware of his importance to the Americans: "If I am swept out, you won't have much left in North Africa," Bourguiba told Jones. "I can count on you, you can count on me."

Under Secretary of State Christian Herter told Alphand on February 13, 1958, that Tunisia would accept American mediation in the crisis and asked for the French reaction; Alphand did not refuse, but replied that he could not respond to an as yet unformulated request.[52] There was good reason for Washington to grasp at the good offices idea, for if Tunisia took the Sakiet affair to the UN the United States would be placed in an impossible dilemma. To preserve its credibility in the world organization and its coveted relations with the African and Asian bloc, Washington would have to vote against France, with full knowledge that such a vote might rupture the Western alliance. Herter warned the French that Washington could do little to help the French either to supply their troops in Tunisia or to prevent the closing of French consulates there; nor could the Americans prevent the expulsion of French nation-

als from Tunisia, given "the intransigent position of the French government." France must make conciliatory gestures to Tunisia—express regret for the raid, offer to indemnify the victims, and withdraw its troops
from all bases on Tunisian territory other than Bizerte. This was the
only way to avert the loss of Bizerte to the West and possible communist domination of the African continent. Herter stressed that "We have
made no offer of mediation." But clearly the Americans were already
mediating.[53] Elbrick informed Alphand officially on February 17 that
the United States was willing to extend its good offices to Tunisia and
France; Alphand phoned the next day to say that the French government accepted, on condition that the mission be confined to good offices only, and not be construed as mediation.[54] The difference might
appear to have been hairsplitting, but the French hoped that the Americans would facilitate Franco-Tunisian negotiations and carry proposals
from one side to the other, and not make proposals of their own.

In the meantime, the use of American weapons in the Sakiet raid became an issue in Washington. Dulles was asked about it at his press conference, and Senator Hubert Humphrey made a speech strongly critical
of Paris for the use of American planes assigned to NATO. Noting that
Tunisia lay outside the NATO zone of defense, Humphrey demanded
that the administration obtain the return of the French weapons. Alphand reported all this back to Paris, where the Ministry of Foreign Affairs instructed him to tread gingerly on the issue: it now turned out that
both the Corsairs and the B 26s had been sent to France under the title
of military assistance for NATO use after all. The U.S. Military Assistance and Advisory Group (MAAG) and the American military attaché
were aware of their use in Algeria, however, and had not raised objections. In view of the comprehensive attitude of MAAG it was best not
to mention in Washington that the military group was aware of the use
of its equipment; on the other hand, Alphand was authorized to say that
the American military attaché knew and had chosen to say nothing.[55] It
was not only the French bureaucracy that could be caught hiding its
role from those in authority over it.

But if Sakiet posed a dilemma to Washington it also offered an opportunity. Indeed, in a private comment to Saudi officials the Americans
suggested that it "might turn out to be a blessing in disguise."[56] It
prompted the American secretary of state to adopt as policy a suggestion emanating from Special Assistant Julius C. Holmes at the Africa
desk that Washington "serve notice that we propose to do what we can
to save the North African litoral in the name of Western security."

Washington now for the first time felt enabled to entertain the idea of playing an activist role in an attempt to settle the Algerian War. Holmes proposed a high-level démarche to Paris to bring home to the French the immediate necessity of accepting a cease-fire in Algeria and negotiations with the FLN at an international conference in which Tunisia, Morocco, Libya, the United States, and Great Britain would participate, the aim being eventual self-determination for Algeria. The French should be told that if they refused to adopt this policy, then the United States would cease its support of France in the UN and adopt an active policy of political support for and economic and military aid to Tunisia and Morocco, clearly with the intent of substituting its own influence for the existing French role in these countries, thereby saving them for the West.[57] The implication was that the United States would do the same for an independent Algeria.

As the British quickly perceived with alarm, Washington finally proposed to "grasp the nettle" of the North African problem, ostensibly one of Franco-Tunisian relations, but insoluble without reference to its real cause, French policy in Algeria.[58] What was further remarkable in this suggestion, but unsaid, was that the previous caution in approaching Paris, based on the fragility of its government, would no longer prevail. The French were now vulnerable: Alphand cabled in despair that the Sakiet raid "has neither been understood or regarded as admissible" in the United States. Irritation was particularly evident in Congress, and Dillon said that the use of arms provided under the Military Defense Assistance Program (MDAP) was difficult to excuse. Sakiet had become a symbol that had gone far beyond its origins, fatally harming the French cause.[59] The Fourth Republic had always been supported in Washington owing to the fear that what might succeed it—de Gaulle or a popular front government—would be worse. But the chaos in Paris revealed that the Fourth Republic itself had become dysfunctional. The Americans were prepared to act as they saw necessary and let the chips fall where they may, although they suspected strongly they would fall on de Gaulle.

The Americans regarded British support for this new policy initiative as crucial. The Americans understood that the British were less resented in Paris than themselves, and they often deferred to British advice in dealing with European affairs. NATO was much more likely to respond affirmatively to an Anglo-American initiative than to a purely American one, and Washington feared being regarded as exercising hegemony alone over an unwilling Atlantic community. London had by no means gone as far as Washington had in expressing its reservations about the Algerian War; true, the rapid British capitulation to Washington after Suez had been regarded almost as a betrayal in Paris, and it was compounded when London joined Washington in sending a token arms shipment to Tunisia in November 1957. Still, London remained very much the privileged interlocutor between Paris and Washington, and the British ambassador, Sir Gladwyn Jebb, had much better relations with his French colleagues than his American counterpart, Amory Houghton, had.

From the first indication they got of American plans, the British tried to moderate Washington's design without dissociating themselves from American policy. Robert Murphy, chosen with Harold Beeley to carry out the good offices mission, informed his colleague of the new American activist policy on March 12, 1958. Beeley reacted with alarm; he thought that the British government might associate itself with parts of the American initiative, but not with the aim of supplanting French influence in North Africa, which would have "incalculable consequences in France." The British Embassy in Tunis, informed of Murphy's proposal, said flatly that Britain could not be associated; there was "no point in trying to save North Africa for the free world by means which would at least risk the loss of France." Beeley was instructed to warn Murphy that the United States would be undertaking a commitment in North Africa "the limit of which could not be foreseen."[60]

British Ambassador Jebb, in London, immediately cabled his own objections and "extreme suspicion" of Dulles's intent. If it were "French surrender and retreat," he wrote, "I imagine that we, for our part, would in no circumstances agree to associate ourselves with such a proposal," the effect of which would be the breakup of NATO and the loss of North Africa to the West. "In the long run some form of Algerian independence is no doubt inevitable," Jebb continued, but pressure on France "will have a fatal effect. ... As seen from here it is not a question of the West fighting the whole of Araby 'from Morocco to the Persian Gulf' (as Mr. Dulles imagines) if we do not compel the French to surrender to the FLN." Prime Minister Macmillan agreed. He thought such an approach might become necessary at a later time, but it would be a mistake to rush into it now for fear of a "violent French reaction spoiling any prospect of our being able to influence French North Africa policy thereafter."[61] But W. Hayter in the Foreign Office dissented: "French policy in Algeria is an albatross tied round the neck of western policy on the Middle East as a whole, almost as disagreeable as that represented by our obligations toward Israel," he wrote, and French intransigence was certain to lead to FLN control, which would be "disastrous for us."[62] With a great many misgivings, the British were to be dragged into associating themselves with some attenuated form of the new American policy.

The motives for British restraint are apparent in a Foreign Office minute of February 24, 1958: the United States could afford strained relations with France, Great Britain could not. The French-Tunisian crisis could not be more awkward in terms of European economic affairs. The European Community was an accomplished fact, with tariff reductions to begin on January 1, 1959, and it was vital that the British have it associated with their own projected "Free Trade Area" (FTA) by then or British goods faced exclusion from the continent. The year 1958 might be a turning point in European relations for the British, "and we are in French hands to a most uncomfortable degree." It was vital not to alienate sensible French opinion. On the other hand, Britain could not appear to be more pro-French than the Americans, or it would find itself in serious trouble in the Middle East, jeopardizing its oil supplies, as serious a matter as the FTA. Britain must "steer a middle course between the French and the Arabs on both of whom we are dependent."[63]

The British also had to steer a middle course between the French and the Americans on the issue of free trade. This was one subject on which Washington had deeply questioned the British point of view; the United States favored Euratom and the EEC and regretted the "unrealistic" attitude of the British, who, torn between the Commonwealth and Europe, were trying to "immobilize the whole development" of the Common Market, with which they refused to be associated. On the other hand, cooperation with Britain on France's Algerian policy may have caused the Americans to see the situation in a new light. On February 20, 1958, Dulles sent a message to all European posts stressing that the United States had "a continuing deep sympathetic interest in the progress of negotiations seeking multilateral association between the Six and the remainder of the OEEC." Although the most important initiative toward European unity was the Common Market, 25 percent of its trade was with the remaining eleven members of OEEC; the interdependence of the European economies therefore made imperative new arrangements to associate OEEC and EEC in a Free Trade Association.[64] This was essentially the British position. The French, for their part, tried to minimize their differences with Washington on the issue; Robert Schuman, newly elected president of the Council of Europe, assured Dulles that the EEC would not be discriminatory and that France wanted an agreement with Great Britain with whom "We are condemned to live together."[65] Fortified by American support on the Free Trade Association, the British assumed the role of advisor and counselor on French-Algerian affairs to the State Department during the Sakiet crisis, ever trying to moderate between the French and the Americans.

Meanwhile Alphand angrily protested in Washington that not only had Bourguiba cut off French troops in Tunisia from food supplies, he had also expelled French residents from Tunisia and closed five French consulates in the country. But Herter offered little solace: he would not pressure the Tunisians in view of the intransigence Paris was showing, and he warned that the situation was explosive. If it went to the Security Council of the UN, the United States would be obliged to take a position against France "which will have a very adverse effect on US-French relations." He again insisted that France express regrets to Tunisia, offer compensation to the bombing victims, and withdraw its troops from all bases in the country except Bizerte. Failure to do so risked open hostilities with the entire Muslim bloc of nations followed by communist domination of the Middle East and Africa. Herter questioned the legal basis of French troops in Tunisia and deplored the hard line expressed by Gaillard in his February 12 speech to the National Assembly. Alphand was further told that French use of American MDAP equipment in the Sakiet raid had been a violation of the terms under which France received those weapons.[66] In Tunis, Jones would not ask on behalf of France that Tunisia allow supplies to French troops, cease its expulsions of French citizens, or reopen French consulates. These actions were the "sovereign rights of the Tunisians"; in no way could they justify French retaliation.[67]

The British and Americans were thus in effect already acting as intermediaries between France and Tunisia, and Washington was leaning strongly toward the Tunisian position, when Herter formally suggested the creation of a "good offices" team to settle the dispute between Tunisia and France. Pineau had no choice but to accept; he, no less than Washington, wished to avoid condemnation by France's allies in the UN. Tunisia and France accepted Washington's offer of good offices, France with the proviso that Algeria not be included, the United States with the understanding that Tunisia would postpone any approach to the UN. Herter reserved the right for the Americans to "make affirmative suggestions" toward a settlement, although Paris rejected any suggestion of mediation or arbitration.[68] The choice of Robert Murphy as the American member of the good offices team was in itself a warning to Paris; he was notorious among Gaullists and the left for his alleged pro-Vichy sympathies during his mission to North Africa in World War II, and he was not appreciated by the Socialists either for his role during the Suez crisis.[69] He had supported General Giraud against de Gaulle and was equally disliked by the Gaullists, the military, and the left. Michel Debré regarded him as "generally contemptuous of our country." General Ely thought the army likely to reject any solution suggested by Murphy. As for the Socialists, Murphy himself may be cited as witness: "Nobody can be more ruthless in playing power politics or more intellectually insolent than the French Socialists, once they believe their ox has been gored."[70] It is probably safe to assume the feeling was mutual.

It was at once clear, moreover, where Murphy's sympathies lay. Alphand tried to set the limits of the French acceptance of the mission: the officers were to facilitate negotiations, not make suggestions, and Algeria must be excluded from the discussions. Murphy countered that Tunisia had been within its rights to order French troops out of the country and close French consulates. Why did France need five air bases in Tunisia that had no NATO role, he asked? Did France consider Tunisia an independent country or a protectorate?[71] Dulles warned both sides against any hardening of attitudes that might complicate the good offices mission and he again asked Paris for a unilateral "gesture," such as the regrouping of forces in Tunisia, to show its good will.[72] Gaillard agreed to regroup French forces in Tunisia, but insisted that Bizerte and five airfields in the south of the country must be reserved for French use to control Algerian arms traffic in the country.[73] Murphy would not pressure the Tunisians, however; France must make concessions. Upon arrival in Tunisia, Murphy told Beeley that the good offices must begin with a discussion of Algeria, because it was no use pretending that the current Tunisian crisis could be separated from the Algerian War. This was in direct violation of the terms under which Paris had agreed to American intervention. The FLN also placed high hopes in Murphy; during a general discussion between Murphy and Bourguiba on February 26, the FLN leaders Belkacim Krim and Mahmoud Cherif were reported as standing by for consultations, having flown to Tunis for the occasion. Murphy managed to avoid any direct contact with them, but the American Embassy in Tunisia remained authorized to carry on conversations with the FLN, and the rebels wanted to be heard. Increased American involvement in the Algerian problem could only help put needed pressure on the French to end the war. When Krim and Cherif asked to meet Murphy they were refused; Consul Blake told Ahmed Boumenjel that Algeria could not be discussed as part of the good offices mission without French agreement, and Murphy needed to avoid open contacts with the FLN for fear of jeopardizing his mission. Boumenjel promised that the FLN would avoid any steps that could jeopardize the good offices mission or embarrass Murphy.[74]

After meeting with Bourguiba, Murphy sent to Washington his "considered opinion" that a French agreement to evacuate all military personnel from Tunisia, with the exception of those in Bizerte, was a condition for the resumption of bilateral French-Tunisian negotiations. The French troop presence was inconsistent with Tunisian sovereignty.[75] Murphy put this bluntly to Gaillard and Joxe in Paris on March 3: only if France withdrew from the rest of the country could it hope to keep Bizerte. Gaillard said the southern airfields were equally important to France; the crux of the problem was Tunisian aid to the FLN. If France withdrew from North Africa, Tunisia and Morocco would be lost to the West. Algeria was covered by NATO and NATO should rally behind France. Murphy asked whether Gaillard had any solution to offer in Algeria other than repression. He got no satisfactory answer: "they [the French] appear to believe that without military victory there is no political solution," he reported. Murphy asked the French premier bluntly whether France wanted to reconquer Tunisia; Gaillard admitted this was a possibility. Bourguiba was a sick man, Gaillard offered, mentally unstable, who had temper tantrums and was dependent on drugs. Murphy was unimpressed, cabling to Washington that the French government was the prisoner of its domestic political situation and "simply incapable of clean cut, bold, decision even if convinced of its wisdom." He now feared that an independent approach based on the lines of the interventionist policy earlier planned would cause the French government to fall and a government of the extraparliamentary right to come to power that would jeopardize the building of Europe and the Atlantic community. Houghton meanwhile cabled from Paris repeating earlier concerns that the French military, if they believed the abandonment of Algeria to be in the offing, would undertake a coup. Personally he thought it unlikely, but he could not rule it out.[76]

But Eisenhower and Dulles were not to be deterred; they were prepared to risk the government's collapse and even a crisis of the regime: "we consider, the President concurs, you [Murphy] should weave into your talks with Gaillard at psychological time of your choosing the US concern about the disastrous consequences of French policy in Algeria

and our suggestions as to cease-fire and conference along the lines of
Holmes's memorandum of February 20." Dulles added that "We are
aware of the possible political repercussions in France but see no alternative given the short time at our disposal."[77] Dulles tried another tack,
approaching Alphand as a "friend": surely he must recognize that it
was not possible for France to resolve the Algerian problem by force
alone. The secretary feared that the war would be extended to encompass all of North Africa with the active support of Nasser, and that
France would eventually abandon the area as it had done in Indochina.
France should search for a political solution while there was still time.
Alphand protested that Algeria could not be compared to Indochina.
But Dulles insisted; he wanted France to remain in North Africa, but he
warned that had the recent American aid package not been voted prior
to the Sakiet bombardment, it would never have been accorded to
France in the first place.[78]

In Tunisia on March 12, Murphy secured the agreement of the
Tunisian government to neutral observers staffing the airfields in the
south of the country that the French had thus far refused to surrender.
The observers could certify to French satisfaction that the bases were
not being used to help the rebels, but the French could not be allowed
to use them against the rebels either. Bourguiba still preferred that the
French leave Bizerte also, but he was willing to postpone discussion of
the naval base for later. The resupply of French troops was already
under way; the consulates might or might not be reopened, but the expulsions of French citizens had ceased, and their return would be examined on a case-by-case basis. In exchange for all this, Murphy told
Bourguiba confidentially that a "helpful" contribution by the United
States toward an Algerian settlement might be possible. This hint did a
great deal to make the Tunisian leader more malleable.[79] Murphy now
thought he had cleared the obstacles in the way of an agreement. On
March 15, 1958, Murphy and Beeley returned to Paris with the text of
their proposed agreement on the basis of which France and Tunisia
were to resume bilateral negotiations. The agreement provided for neutral observers to have access to the southern airfields evacuated by
French forces; for all French military personnel outside the Bizerte
perimeter to be withdrawn from Tunisia as soon as possible; for Tunisia
to give "sympathetic consideration" to the reopening of French consulates when normal relations were reestablished; and for Tunisia to review individually each case of expelled French citizens desiring to return
to Tunisia. In a second phase, Tunisia and France would negotiate a

more lasting status for the base at Bizerte on the basis of recognition of Tunisian sovereignty. One crucial French demand was absent, however, to which Bouguiba would not agree: Gaillard demanded international control on both sides of the Tunisian-Algerian frontier to prevent further incursions of the kind that had led to the Sakiet crisis. Bourguiba rejected this demand flatly: neutral observers would constitute an infringement upon Tunisian sovereignty, compromise Tunisia's support for the Algerian rebels, ensure continuation of the war, and explicitly recognize French sovereignty in Algeria; they would also harm the goal of cooperation and unity of the Maghreb.[80] Bourguiba also thought the Algerians would respond by declaring themselves a provisional government, which would necessarily entail recognition by Tunisia and the end of relations with France. He could not consent to any concessions that might appear to harm the FLN in order to obtain a withdrawal of the French army from his soil or he would be accused of treason in the Arab world.

Obtaining the agreement had involved a good deal of haggling in the Tunisian capital. Beeley complained that his conversation with Ladgham, the Tunisian prime minister, ran into Algeria at every turn. Tunisia could not cease its aid to the Algerian rebels, nor could it accept neutral controls on its frontiers. The French had proposed the establishment of a western Mediterranean pact against communism; this was impossible at present, and the blockade of French forces in Tunisia could only be lifted in order to facilitate their departure. Ladgham returned to the idea of the British and Americans taking over Bizerte from the French; Beeley immediately said that Her Majesty's Government could not consider it, but Murphy remained ominously silent. Beeley concluded that agreement was impossible and the Foreign Office agreed that Bourguiba was being unreasonable; he must be told that the French would never accept an agreement without frontier controls, and he must agree to normalize the situation regarding French troops and accept international observers on the southern airfields. But this was to reason without Murphy, who clearly took the Tunisian side. After a "tussle with Murphy and the US ambassador," Beeley had to settle for an agreement that he knew was "obviously unsatisfactory from the French point of view." Without the frontier observers the French would never go along, he thought.[81] Beeley was right in the short run, wrong in the larger perspective. The agreement was accepted by the Fifth Republic under de Gaulle. Beeley apparently did not know that Murphy, to secure Bourguiba's agreement, had confidentially assured him that an

American "helpful contribution toward an Algerian settlement" might be possible.[82]

The agreement was presented to Gaillard on March 18. The British were pessimistic: "Gaillard will either have to contemplate a crisis which, at this particular moment might be long and fraught with dangers for the regime, or accept what for him might be the lesser evil and dig his toes in as regards the report of the Good Officers." Gaillard opted to do the latter, asking that the good officers return to Tunis to get Bourguiba to agree to frontier controls. He also wanted an end to pressures on the Bizerte base, immediate action on the return of French citizens expelled from Tunisia, and the reopening of French consulates. Murphy and Beeley refused; it was quite useless, they said, all arguments with Bourguiba had been exhausted. If France did not accept, the next step would have to be the United Nations.[83] Gaillard warned that more important than the agreement was whether the Anglo-Saxons were saying that Bourguiba's present attitude was justified. It would be deplorable if the French were to be presented with a Tunisian proposal that the British and the Americans were pressing them to accept. As a member of the UN, Tunisia could not allow its territory to be used as a base for military operations against another member state. If Bourguiba would accept neutral observers on his airfields, why not on the frontiers? But Jebb told Gaillard that logic was not the issue. Murphy finally agreed to make one last appeal to Bourguiba, but only through Ambassador Jones; Murphy would not return to Tunisia, anticipating that he would come back empty-handed. Jones was instructed to approach Bourguiba again on the matter of frontier controls. The Tunisian president turned Jones down flat; he had made all concessions possible, any more would only serve Cairo's charge that he was betraying the FLN. Bourguiba would not commit "political suicide," or the entire free world would be the loser.[84]

Gaillard and Pineau, confronted with Bourguiba's latest refusal, now informed Murphy that negotiations had hit a "grave impasse." Murphy pressed strongly for acceptance of the agreement as it was, but the French ministers explained that it was "politically impossible," the government would fall.[85] The good offices mission had failed. But the Americans were already preparing their ultimate effort to break the logjam by overcoming French resistance. Dulles could not allow the dispute to reach the UN, and he regarded the situation in North Africa as explosive: it was imperative to preserve the moderate regimes there. The Tunisian idea of a Maghreb federation including

Libya and Morocco could provide the framework for an Algerian solution. The State Department was ready to say it would view this with
favor; it attached extreme importance to a peaceful evolution of the
Algerian situation. To achieve this the Americans must undertake independent initiatives toward the nations of the region, bypassing
Paris, in accordance with the Holmes memorandum. Murphy must
explain to Beeley that contemplated American aid to Morocco and
Tunisia was not meant as an "ultimatum to the French," but would be
designed to keep these countries aligned with the West; it was not
"punitive," but there was a need for action if France was unable to
modify its Algerian policy. "We would hope to persuade the French to
modify their policy and call for a cease-fire and a conference of interested states on the North African crisis," Dulles continued, but if this
failed further independent action by the Americans and British was
necessary.[86]

Murphy put Dulles's ideas to Beeley: it was better to plunge ahead
with assistance to Morocco and Tunisia now, which might force an evolution of the French attitude on Algeria; if the French did not bend, "we
would naturally try our best to avoid an open break with France," but
the policy must go ahead anyway.[87] A special high-level envoy would be
sent to Paris to force acceptance of a cease-fire and an international conference, failing which Washington would proceed to assist Morocco
and Tunisia financially and militarily. "It was hoped Her Majesty's Government would view these measures sympathetically, since British support would be vital."[88]

Dulles was also now seriously concerned about the internal evolution
of the FLN. When Ahmed Boumanjel first met with State Department
officials Looram and Blake in Tunisia, the Algerian told the Americans
that the FLN was under pressure to seek help from the Eastern bloc and
would soon form a government in exile. The FLN wished for the success
of the Murphy mission, however, and was eager to do its part. It was favorable to the idea of a Maghreb union, and would join an international
conference with the Tunisian, Moroccan, and French governments if the
United States and Great Britain were involved. In the meantime the governments of Morocco and Tunisia were authorized to speak for the
FLN. There were no secret talks under way with the French, Boumanjel
said, and he personally doubted that de Gaulle's accession to power in
France would help matters; the best hope was for the United States to
persuade a government of the center-left to change its policy. Looram
and Blake stressed the FLN's moderation and the ease and relaxed na-

ture of the conversation.[89] The moderates must be kept in power, for a radical group was waiting on the fringe.

Dulles now believed he had reliable information that the FLN would accept a cease-fire within the framework he had outlined: it would keep its weapons and its positions, while France agreed to discuss the future of Algeria in a conference of North African states in which the FLN was included. Tunisia and Morocco had called for French recognition of Algerian "sovereignty" rather than independence in their mediation proposal of November 1957; if France was now prepared to accept this formulation, Dulles thought the FLN would do so too.[90] *L'Express* meanwhile got word of the new U.S. policy toward the Algerian War: the Americans would press Paris to understand that its *loi-cadre* was insufficient, and persuade the FLN to change its attitude enough so that Paris could be brought to deal with it. The American consul in Tunisia, Blake, had many contacts with the FLN, and the U.S. policy, according to *L'Express,* had reached a point of no turning back.[91]

Dulles now asked Murphy whether a personal letter from President Eisenhower to Premier Gaillard could break the logjam in Paris. Murphy said yes, but it should be held as a last resort. Dulles, however, feared further deterioration of the situation resulting from a failure of the good offices mission, with war breaking out all over North Africa. Under British pressure to avoid such intervention, Murphy again returned to Tunisia, but Bourguiba was adamant, he would not commit political suicide. The risk of a popular front in France with Communist support was worth it if it brought an end to the Algerian War. The sooner France faced a major political crisis the better. Even chaos would be preferable to the present situation if it forced a change in France's Algerian policy, the Tunisian president said.[92]

Jones cabled Dulles that the Tunisian offer was the best that could be got; the good faith and prestige of the United States and the United Kingdom were on the line, and "I think we have earned the special right, even responsibility, to tell the Government of France to take what it can get from the Government of Tunisia while it is still available." Breakdown was imminent; it was time for the United States to implement its new policy in North Africa. Faced with failure of the good offices mission, Dulles and Eisenhower agreed and resolved on the personal letter to Gaillard. A draft was in British hands by April 5. Beeley was horrified. The letter preached too much, dealt with both Algeria and Tunisia, and was hardly written in terms that were likely to convince Paris. The draft text asked that France "show comprehension of the practical limits on the Tunisian government. Sentimental ties unite the Tunisian and Algerian people who seek an opportunity for self-government and self-determination. Is this not only consistent with French interests, but also a way to promote them?"[93] French influence, the draft said, must be freely accepted by Muslim peoples, it could not be imposed on North Africa, including Algeria, or the cohesion of the entire Atlantic community would be undermined. All the freedoms of the West were specifically threatened by events taking place in the Algerian departments of France; the decisions of France in dealing with its problem, therefore, involved everyone.

Clearly the British could not block the message, they could only modify its terms. The Foreign Office was frustrated; one would have thought, based on their wartime experience, that the Americans would have realized how sensitive the French were to lecturing of this kind. "The Americans want nothing out of the French and can afford to lecture them. We want a great deal from them." The end of plans for a Free Trade Association, the permanent division of Western Europe, even the end of NATO seemed to loom in London as possible disastrous consequences of Washington's ill-considered actions.[94] Murphy and Houghton in Paris thought the message "skillfully drafted," but reported Beeley's many objections and warned Washington that the British would not be associated with the letter as presently written; Dulles replied that he would change it, but a letter along the lines of the draft must be given Gaillard if the good offices mission failed; the timing would be up to Murphy.[95]

Unaware of American plans, Gaillard and Pineau on April 9 confronted Murphy directly: what would happen if France, rather than Tunisia, took the Sakiet matter to the Security Council of the United Nations? But the Americans could see no improvement in this course of action. Murphy said "he was not in a position to promise the support of the United States in any recourse to the Security Council." This implied that the American government no longer supported French policy in Algeria, if indeed it ever really had. Gaillard warned that if France and the United States parted company in the Security Council of the United Nations, France would regard this as betrayal and it would cause a crisis in the Western alliance.[96] In desperation Gaillard turned to Beeley; the latter refrained from supporting Murphy completely, but he made it clear that the British position was that France must control its own frontiers and expect nothing from the Tunisians; if not, and the matter went to the Security Council of the United Nations, the British position, too, would at the least remain "reserved."[97]

Jebb protested angrily from Paris that delivery of the president's letter "would probably destroy the chance (which still exists) that the
French may accept the good officers' proposals without damaging conditions."[98] But Jebb was told that the British position was determined
by Prime Minister Macmillan personally; Paris must be warned against
recourse to the UN because the British attitude there would be dictated
by concern over its position in the Arab world.[99] Meanwhile the French
Embassy in Washington cabled back similar warnings: if Sakiet were
permitted to come before the Security Council, the Americans would be
unable to oppose a resolution explicitly condemning the French bombardment, and the debate would greatly harm French-American relations. Alphand advised that Paris postpone the question of frontier controls and focus on the positive aspects of the good offices agreement.[100]

In the end the British managed to pressure Dulles into deleting the
most damaging passages from the final draft of the letter to Gaillard;
gone were any mention of self-determination in Algeria or any reference
to events in the "Algerian departments of France." Instead Paris was
simply asked to accept that there existed "practical limits on the Tunisian government which inescapably lead the people of Tunisia to sympathize with the aspirations of the Moslem nationalist elements in Algeria." Murphy wanted the message delivered to Gaillard on April 11, just
before the French cabinet was to meet on the good offices proposal.
Dulles agreed, noting that "We have eliminated reference to Algerian independence [in the letter] to reflect our conclusion which coincides with
that of the UK that it is better that this be implicit rather than explicit."[101] In view of the text, which London no longer found objec-
tionable, Beeley was authorized to inform the French that if they accepted the good offices agreement, Britain would support France if it
pressed for border controls with Tunisia in the United Nations, as well
as in its efforts to keep the Algerian question off the UN agenda. With
British objections satisfied, Washington could now go ahead with the
letter.

In the last analysis it was not the text of the message but rather the
fact of its delivery at all that rankled in Paris. Murphy gave the
amended letter to Gaillard on April 11; the premier read it and immediately asked once again whether the United States would support
France in its quest for border controls if the matter came before the UN
Security Council. Murphy said he preferred to avoid a UN debate.
Pineau said he thought the Eisenhower message "very vague," and
complained that it "gave no indication of what the Americans thought

the French should actually do with respect to North Africa generally, still less of what the Americans would do" after France accepted the good offices agreement. Gaillard and Pineau both cited the failure of previous efforts to negotiate a cease-fire with the FLN and complained that the impediment to negotiations was not the a priori FLN demand for independence but the "brutal determination of the FLN leadership to control elections and seize political power in Algeria leading to a 'bloody anarchy.'" This would lead to the massacre of thousands of loyal Muslims and the betrayal of 1.2 million French nationals. Murphy said the French military policy in Algeria was no solution either, and sealing the Tunisian border would not help the situation. The French leaders could only reply that there were "serious misunderstandings on the part of the US government regarding the practical features of the Algerian situation."[102] Worth noting was the shift in the conversation from the Tunisian border question to the Algerian War; the French understood the Eisenhower letter to mean that Washington favored independence as a solution in Algeria.

Gaillard pressed Murphy again on the UN, but he offered only further vague replies; the United States would "presumably" support France in the Security Council, but it could not give a commitment since the actual content of a resolution could not be foreseen. As to what the Americans would do in Algeria, they were prepared to "confer with the French government urgently and intimately on the Algerian question" if the latter so desired.[103] The letter convinced the French leaders that they had no choice but to accept the good offices mission on Murphy's terms. But Gaillard thrashed about for a way to mitigate what he knew would be a fiercely hostile reaction in the National Assembly. On April 13, Pineau told Murphy that he had no criticism of the "substance" of the message, and the next day Joxe asked whether the Americans would agree to its publication in order to stem criticism in France of alleged U.S. pressure on the government. Houghton called Washington to check and quickly relayed Washington's agreement, only to be told that the French had decided not to publish it after all because of "certain dangerous sentences." The word was that Lacoste feared the effect the letter's publication might have in Algiers.[104] Alphand instead was instructed to ask Dulles for a public statement that the United States had no designs on North African oil, and did not wish to replace France in North Africa, where the French had "leading interests" that Washington recognized. Dulles could only ask whether Alphand was serious; the French were again asking for recognition of their "preeminence" in the region, which they knew Washington could not give. Alphand warned that a French cabinet crisis the next day would be serious indeed and could only be prevented by such a statement; Dulles admitted that a crisis would be serious, but he would make no such statement.[105] He was prepared to see the government fall.

On April 13, the French cabinet, after eleven hours of debate, approved the good offices memorandum of March 15 and submitted it to the National Assembly. On April 14, at 2:00 A.M. and after eleven hours of debate, the National Assembly rejected the agreement, thereby overthrowing the Gaillard government. Pineau told Murphy and Beeley that the government had been overthrown not because it had accepted the good offices agreement but because of the Eisenhower letter, which was thought to have determined the cabinet decision. The implication was that the government would have accepted the agreement in the absence of the Eisenhower letter, but that can never be known. Rumors of the existence of the letter, even parts of its text, had been everywhere in the press meanwhile, according to the French leaked deliberately by Washington, and it was now clear to everyone that the Americans were pursuing a new activist policy with regard to the Algerian War and French relations with Tunisia and Morocco. That and the letter's existence, whatever its content, were enough to cause the collapse of the government in Paris.[106]

Was the letter to Gaillard a mistake? German Foreign Minister von Brentano certainly thought so; he told Livingston Merchant that the French were sensitive to this type of warning from even the best of friends. Merchant replied that when one sees a friend committing suicide, "one does all to prevent it even at the risk of people reading the mail." Dulles remarked that all the pros and cons of the letter had been thoroughly discussed, it was sent on the strong recommendation of Murphy and the embassy, and although the British had not liked the idea from the beginning, even they admitted that without it Gaillard would never have accepted the recommendations of the good offices mission. The letter probably had adverse effects in the National Assembly, but the Americans had even agreed to publish it to dissipate all the misinformation French politicians were disseminating about it. It was Paris in the end that had refused its publication. As for the Germans, Dulles observed that they had refused to use their own influence on the French even when they thought Paris was wrong—they wanted too much to be liked.[107]

Not all of Washington's NATO allies were pleased either. Foreign Minister Joseph Luns of the Netherlands told Douglas Dillon in Paris that developments in France were dangerous to world peace: the Algerian leaders were "murderous cutthroats with whom it was impossible to deal." Pineau had told his colleagues in the West European Union of an FLN plot allegedly uncovered in Brussels to assassinate the French president, prime minister, defense and foreign ministers, and the Belgian foreign minister had confirmed this story for Luns. The Dutch were opposed to Algerian independence, which they regarded as a threat to the NATO alliance. Luns expressed his contempt for the leadership in the developing world generally and insisted to Dulles that Washington support the maintenance of French influence in North Africa.[108]

Murphy offered more advice from Tunis on April 17, declaring that France should negotiate directly with the FLN. Murphy's statement would have caused the government to fall had it not already done so. His remark, reported in *The New York Times* with indications of a fundamental policy change on Algeria in Washington, nevertheless caused an uproar in Paris, and it brought an immediate démarche from Alphand, who demanded a correction by Dulles or there would be "incalculable consequences." Houghton was summoned by Pineau to explain the remarks, which were bound to have a "serious effect on French-American relations; the US should not shut its eyes because 'it is the Atlantic Pact which is at stake.' "[109] Pineau never seemed to realize that he might be in danger of crying wolf once too often. Acting Secretary of State Christian Herter insisted to Alphand that Murphy's remarks, which were the basis of the story, had been misinterpreted; the United States had always favored a negotiated solution to the Algerian War, but Washington had no specific view on the form negotiations might take. Alphand replied that France would not accept an internationalization of the war, to which Herter replied that internationalization had already occurred anyway. Despite consistent support for France in the past, Herter noted, the United States had always made clear its "doubts and preoccupations" over French policies. Alphand and Herter finally agreed that Dulles would say that "It has always been the hope of the United States Government and still is that France itself will be able to work out a solution." There was no change in U.S. policy, Herter assured Alphand.[110] Herter cabled the embassy in Paris that the "Acting Secretary had informed the French Ambassador this morning that press speculation to the effect that there has been a change of US policy with respect to Algeria is without foundation." But it was clear to everyone that Washington's policy had changed.

The overthrow of Gaillard of course led directly to the insurrection in Algiers, the collapse of the Fourth Republic, and the coming to power of Charles de Gaulle. The extent to which these events represented an "anti-American revolt on the part of the French, as they desperately grappled for a national solution [in Algeria] rather than one imposed by the Western superpower," cannot precisely be determined.[111] Nor can it be argued that the Americans foresaw exactly the development of events of such historic proportions. What is clear is that the American mood was impatient; Washington wanted an end to the war, whatever the internal political consequences in France. Noting that the French took the line that they were fighting for the West in Algeria and therefore deserved the full support of NATO, American Consul Clark in Algiers suggested that NATO in turn demand from the French a formula for the war's end. The alliance could not underwrite a policy leading to the war's extension; on the contrary, NATO should offer international guarantees of self-determination for Algeria as a means of forcing the war's end.[112] There was no question of Washington ever adopting or NATO agreeing to so extreme a policy. But as the Americans and British correctly surmised when Gaillard was overthrown, any successor government would face the same dilemma: the only alternative to acceptance of the terms of the good offices mission was recourse to the UN, where France was very likely to be condemned at least in the General Assembly and left without the support of its allies. De Gaulle, to be sure, had been opposed to the good offices, preferring direct talks between France and Tunisia. He told Ambassador Jebb on March 24, 1958, that he objected in principle to what appeared too near to direct interference in French affairs. "The Arabs in any case were highly excitable characters and it was not good that they should be given an undue sense of their own importance." If they thought the Anglo-Saxons were on their side, things would only become more complicated.[113]

But once in power de Gaulle's sense of statecraft dictated that he assure France's allies that France would fulfill all its contractual obligations. On June 5, 1958, de Gaulle's foreign minister, Maurice Couve de Murville, told Ambassador Jebb that France wanted direct negotiations with the Tunisians and that "the present government, like the last, were entirely prepared to carry out in all its details the recommendations of the Good Officers." On June 17 Joxe called Jebb with the happy news that France and Tunisia had come to an agreement; he conveyed the thanks of Couve de Murville for British help during the good offices mission and satisfaction that the mission's report was the basis of the agreement. Convey to Mr. Beeley, Joxe said, Couve de Murville's congratulations for the "masterly conduct of the negotiations."[114] Although Dulles and Eisenhower took note of the French-Tunisian agreement with pleasure, observing that "in effect" it implemented the terms of the good offices mission, no similar French congratulations to Robert Murphy appear in the American archives.[115] But the success of the American diplomatic initiative, in which the British were at every stage reluctant, even unwilling participants, was no less palpable. De Gaulle brought about the solution in Tunisia for which Washington had been hoping when it gambled on his return to power. It remained to be seen whether he could or wished to bring about a solution in Algeria.

CHAPTER FIVE

The Fall of the Republic and the Coming of de Gaulle

In April 1961, when de Gaulle faced rebellion in the French army in Algiers, he received a message from President Kennedy stating that the United States would provide all necessary assistance and support for the French government that might be needed to deal with the insurgency. Kennedy may have been seeking a foreign policy success in the aftermath of the Bay of Pigs fiasco, but he should have guessed that de Gaulle would consider it beneath his dignity to accept assistance. The most interesting aspect of the Kennedy offer, however, is its contrast with the absence of any comparable Eisenhower message to the French government during the May 13, 1958 crisis, when it might have been appreciated. American policy when the Fourth Republic faced collapse was studiously to stay out of French affairs and to behave as circumspectly as could be, so correctly, as it were, that the French offered their appreciation for the way in which the Americans handled themselves. Contrast this in turn with Dulles's promise to the Tunisians and Moroccans during the May 1958 crisis that in the event of any aggression by the French army in Algiers against them, the United States would react "as at Suez." The Americans would do nothing to further destabilize the regime in Paris, but they did nothing to protect it either. The equanimity with which the Americans watched the collapse of the Fourth French Republic remains a glaring reflection of a policy based upon disillusionment with a dysfunctional regime.

By April 1958, as the final death agony of the Republic began, the French were as thoroughly disgusted by their American allies as the Americans were with them. Paris persisted in its belief that the rebels were sustained by their hope of eventually getting American support, a conviction strengthened by Murphy's call for direct French-FLN negotiations following Gaillard's fall. French intelligence reported copiously on the FLN's views of Washington and its policies. The Americans, the FLN believed, did not want to leave France alone sitting on top of the resources of the Sahara; and Washington wanted to limit Egyptian influence in North Africa and prevent Soviet intervention on behalf of the Algerian rebellion. Sakiet had "opened the eyes of the American people," according to the rebels, and the FLN representative was received more warmly thereafter and listened to attentively in Washington. FLN propaganda stressed the possibilities for U.S. investment in Algerian oil after independence and the creation of a North African barrier to communism, which the rebels said was in their own interest as well.[1]

The Service de Documentation Extérieure et de Contre-Espionnage (SDECE) reported that Algerian nationalist groups abroad thought the United States wanted an Algerian settlement as soon as possible in order to hasten the formation of a "Greater Maghreb" that could act as a bulwark against Nasser. The FLN was awaiting American press reaction to the forthcoming Tangiers Conference of North African states in June 1958, but it was convinced that Washington would support Algerian independence in the context of a North African federation. France would be forced to take American advice or risk losing its economic aid and being accused of pillaging NATO supplies for use in Algeria. The Americans allegedly understood that so long as they aided France the Arabs would accuse them of morally assisting a war of oppression; the FLN further reported that the Americans were enlisting the support of the Vatican and Italian circles of opinion to support Algerian independence and to help them achieve the concept of a greater Maghreb.[2]

All this may have been wishful thinking on the FLN's part, or exaggerated French fears concerning rebel policies. It is clear that all sorts of things were believed about the depths of American perfidy in the France of April-May 1958. But from the opening of the last cabinet crisis of the Fourth Republic, American policy became judiciously circumspect. Paul Devinat, who worked in the premier's office, told Houghton he hoped that the good offices mission could be kept "on ice" in the normal interim between governments; he was sure that the next government would accept the accord with Tunisia, for there was no other choice. The anti-American feeling in the National Assembly had been "stupid and un-justified," and everyone understood that if Bourguiba had accepted international control of his frontiers he would have been assassinated by his own people. Gaillard had fallen because the delivery of the Eisenhower letter had been "inopportune," but its contents were unexceptionable. The crisis would be long, but Devinat hoped for the eventual success of a new Mollet government with a resumption of the good offices mission.[3]

The administration's report to Congress on the French situation in April 1958, however, was far less sanguine. Algeria was a difficult, "extremely complex and potentially explosive situation," in that the FLN would settle for nothing less than complete independence, which no French government could grant and survive. In effect, the regime was trapped, stalemated, in a situation that one way or another needed resolution. The *loi-cadre* that was finally passed by the National Assembly was not nearly enough to satisfy the insurgents: "We have made known to the French government our preoccupations with regard to an indefinite continuation and extension of the Algerian conflict." It was hoped that whatever new government was formed would accept the good offices compromise over which Gaillard had allegedly been overthrown, but the reality was that the outgoing premier had been suspected of being soft on Algeria. This crisis, more than any other, opened the possibility of a turn toward de Gaulle, which the administration now contemplated with mixed feelings: "He would reportedly follow a liberal policy on North Africa, but his policies on NATO and East-West relations would be unpredictable. He would oppose European integration."[4] But in the context of 1958, a liberal policy in North Africa seemed by far the more important issue.

As the crisis became prolonged, Washington's determination to insist upon a conclusion to the war was compounded by worry about the outcome of the breakdown of political authority in France. The combination of political instability, collapsing authority, and military rebellion proved enough for the Americans to have done with the Fourth Republic and to take their chances on de Gaulle. The seemingly endless cabinet crisis had internal roots. Sakiet, despite everything, had a salutary effect. A large number of French politicians had apparently decided that it was time to negotiate with the rebels. This was clear from the failure of several hard-liners to form a government because of opposition from within their own parties. Thus, Georges Bidault, known to be a proponent of a military solution, was opposed in his efforts to form a government by his own MRP (Christian Democrats), and Jacques Soustelle, who had similarly uncompromising views, ran into the opposition of his own Gaullist party. The Socialists took the lead in demanding the removal of Lacoste, one of their own, from Algeria. And the Radical party reacted with hostility when their uncompromising colleague, André Morice, proposed to join a Pleven government as minister of defense.

Both René Pleven, who narrowly failed to form a government on May 6, and Pierre Pflimlin, who succeeded on May 13, were known to be advocates of a more or less liberal solution, and they were prepared to carry discussions with the rebels beyond the question of a cease-fire to the conditions of a political settlement, thus satisfying a basic rebel demand. It was to take de Gaulle over three more years of drawn-out war to come to a similar position. In trying to form his aborted government, Pleven asked the State Department to use its contacts with the FLN to discuss terms of a cease-fire. Did Washington think the FLN could be split, separating its moderates from the hard-liners? Rather than protest American contacts with the rebels, Pleven now proposed to make use of them. The French army understood this, thus its unprecedented step of writing President René Coty on May 9 that it would accept only a government committed to a French Algeria.[5] The letter was delivered by Chief of Staff General Ely and signed by Generals Jouhaud and Allard. But behind it were a number of influential civilians, all of them Gaullist: Jacques Soustelle, Michel Debré, Jacques Foccart, and the representative in Algiers of Chaban-Delmas, Léon Delbecque. Military insurrection and its inevitable Gaullist outcome were in the making even before Pflimlin formed his ill-fated government.

Washington was kept closely informed of the progress of French cabinet negotiations by Guy Mollet, who was himself a candidate for premier. He claimed now to favor a cease-fire on compromise terms and said he hoped to work closely with Washington if his bid were successful. On May 1 Mollet told the embassy that his party would support, but not participate in, a Pleven government; for Mollet's part, he hoped Pleven would get rid of Lacoste. Others in the Socialist party, Mollet said, also felt that Lacoste must go but were not courageous enough to say so. U.S. officials warned Mollet of American concern at the continuing lack of a solution in Algeria: "present methods do not appear to be bringing results and...there was growing fear in the US that the end result of the present course would be disastrous." The only recourse was opening negotiations between the interested parties. Mollet replied in guarded terms: even the

Soviets had attacked the good offices mission as American interference in French internal affairs and claimed to favor a "French" solution to the Algerian problem. French nationalist rhetoric was working against the Americans, who could be effective only by means of private pressure on the parties for a cease-fire. For Washington to pressure France publicly under present circumstances, Mollet thought, would be catastrophic and possibly lead to a blowup of NATO.[6]

Washington was encouraged by the formation of the Pflimlin government on May 13, 1958, but guarded as to its prospects. There was foreboding over the building tension in Algeria stemming from hints that Pflimlin would seek contacts with the FLN to negotiate a cease-fire. His investiture speech, moreover, was disappointing; he demanded that Atlantic solidarity be extended to North Africa, declared that France would never abandon Algeria, and insisted that the Tunisian frontier must be sealed. A cease-fire and elections could only take place, Pflimlin said, under the recently passed *loi-cadre* for Algeria, which Washington thought inadequate. The Radical Mendèsistes were said to be having second thoughts about participating in Pflimlin's government as a consequence, and *L'Humanité* was seized by government police censors the day of the government's formation. Meanwhile the FLN decided to execute three French soldiers held captive in what looked like a deliberate bid to make the new premier's task more difficult.[7] This act, in effect, provided the stimulus to the army insurrection in Algiers on May 13. On the other hand, the American Embassy was informed that the CFTC and FO, non-Communist unions, would cooperate with the government on wage and price stabilization, but their precondition was its willingness to negotiate directly with the rebels.

There were reasons for hope: Pierre Pflimlin was regarded as an outstanding MRP leader, honest, courageous, a man of liberal ideas, matched by few in the public esteem he enjoyed. He had blocked Bidault's investiture over the Algerian question, wanted good relations with Tunisia and Morocco, and was prepared to withdraw French troops from the two countries, and just might pursue liberal ideas in Algeria with his typical "Teutonic tenacity." His cabinet was described as a good one; it would have been better with Pinay and Schuman in it, but it contained several first-rate individuals most of whom had liberal views on North Africa. Pleven at Foreign Affairs was solid on NATO and a good friend of the United States, although this had hurt him in the past. Edgar Faure, however, was "an unscrupulous and brilliant opportunist," who was not reliable on East-West issues and favored recognition of Red

China, but he too favored negotiations with the Algerian rebels. Even Maurice Faure, who was known to be close to de Gaulle, had come out recently in favor of changing French North African policy.[8]

But Washington's hopes for Pflimlin foundered on the insurrection that broke out in Algiers on the very day of his government's formation. It seemed to the French that a "gag order" took effect in Washington. U.S. officials were now clearly under orders from the highest levels not to comment on French affairs. Alphand surmised from this that the Americans regarded the return of de Gaulle as a remedy for French instability even though they remained fearful that he might harm the Atlantic alliance. For months preceding the crisis, Washington had been in regular contact with the general. On March 20 he had again met with British Ambassador Jebb, who found him having no great desire to come to power and unlikely to take part in any effort to overthrow the regime. If he came to power, Jebb thought, he would favor appeasing the USSR, which might break up the alliance system as it was. Opposed to the Anglo-American good offices mission, de Gaulle was sanguine about Algeria; an association of Tunisia, Morocco, Algeria, and the Sahara would come about in time, he told Jebb, and provide a framework for Algerian independence under the influence of France. Jebb thought de Gaulle would be better able to bring this off than anyone else, but there was an obstacle: his sense of honor would block negotiations with the FLN except as a result of a French military victory, which was nowhere in sight. The general saw no rapid end to the war either; unrealistically, he hoped that eventually the rebels would become reasonable, understanding that they could not govern Algeria by themselves, at which point negotiations with them would become possible. The length of the struggle would depend on the extent to which the FLN thought it was supported by "outside powers," by which the general clearly meant the Americans and perhaps even the British. De Gaulle did think that French policy must change, and the *loi-cadre* was a step in the right direction. Posing to himself the question that most interested Jebb, de Gaulle said that the present regime was incapable of achieving a solution; but at age 67, could he, de Gaulle, establish a new political order? "I tell you Mr Ambassador that all the chances are that before this regime collapses de Gaulle will be dead."[9]

While the Americans hedged their bets as to the outcome of the May 13 crisis, the British saw it as having been orchestrated by the general from its inception with the intention of bringing him to power, with the senior ministers in the Pflimlin government directly implicated. On

Figure 2.   An estimated 40,000 persons jammed the forum in front of
Government House, Algiers, on May 16, 1958, displaying French flags
and signs that read "French Algeria," "De Gaulle to power," and "Long
Live Salan and the Army." Gen. Raoul Salan was the French military
commander in Algeria. (Associated Press / WIDE WORLD PHOTOS)

May 14, Pleven told Jebb that he regretted that the events in Algiers had
not occurred just a bit earlier, just before Pflimlin had formed his government. Had that happened, President Coty might have called on de
Gaulle directly, whereas now it was too late. But Jebb gained the impression that the present government existed only to find a way to bring
de Gaulle to power. Michel Poniatowski, who was close to Pflimlin
throughout the crisis, has recently confirmed what London so cleverly
perceived: Pflimlin's government was basically a holding operation until
de Gaulle came to power, and throughout the crisis the premier and de
Gaulle did their best to negotiate a peaceful transition.[10] Not without
some bumps, to be sure. No sooner had the crowds in Algiers called out
"Vive de Gaulle" on May 15 than the general announced that he was

ready to assume the powers of the Republic. This was a bit premature
for Pflimlin, who told General Billotte that he would make way for de
Gaulle when the time was ripe, not before. Jebb thought de Gaulle himself could cause a new crisis, following which Coty would invite him to
the Elysée; if Pflimlin tried to block the general, calling upon Communist support in the streets, then the army would put de Gaulle in power
by force. Remarkably, Pleven gave Jebb a thoroughly accurate version
of the Gaullist scenario. Consul Sarrell, meanwhile, confirmed this picture from Algiers. Power there was solidly in army hands. The de Gaulle
pronouncement had come as a relief to the military, because he alone
could enable them to establish the legality of their position. The May 13
events "were deliberately engineered as part of a Gaullist plot whereby
the Algerian action would bring de Gaulle to power in France." The
local ringleader was Léon Delbecque, the former chef du cabinet of
Jacques Chaban-Delmas, who had arrived in Algiers, sent by the Gaullist
defense minister, a few days previously.[11] To the extent that Washington
understood this, its circumspect policy becomes more undertstandable.

Washington and London consulted throughout the crisis. The immediate American fear was Dulles's nightmare scenario: the French army,
now free of Paris's orders, might invade Tunisia or Morocco, precipitating a generalized struggle for North Africa involving the Soviets on
the side of the Arabs. Dulles warned Paris of the possible repercussions
if Tunisia or Morocco became involved; it must at all costs exercise discipline over its troops in these two countries. The United States, for its
part, would urge calm and restraint upon the governments of Morocco
and Tunisia. In Tunis, Washington got some reassurance: General Gambiez had informed President Coty that he and all of his senior command
pledged loyalty to the government in Paris. But on the same day, de
Gaulle announced that he was at the service of the nation, as in 1940.[12]
Washington saw his star "shining brighter," as all the politicians were
beating a path to his door in Paris, while Hubert Beuve-Marie, the editor of the prestigious Le Monde, called on him to step in and to save
France. Houghton thought that Pflimlin still had some chance of success
in surviving the crisis, but in the event that he could not do so the return
of de Gaulle was likely. At any rate, the Americans were not now about
to help Pflimlin.

It was of course General Salan, upon whom Pflimlin had just conferred full powers in Algeria, who on May 15 cried "Vive de Gaulle" in
Algiers to the plaudits of the crowd. The fox had indeed been put in
charge of the chickens. Jean Lecanuet, Pflimlin's chef du cabinet, briefed

the Americans on the crisis. The government could not judge the depth of what was obviously a Gaullist plot under way, but the military coup in Algiers had been based on the expectation that the Assembly would refuse its confidence to Pflimlin, whom Soustelle had promised to bring down. Pflimlin enjoyed a solid majority, however, and the generals were disappointed. Pflimlin would face down the insurgency, Lecanuet said. The country was calm, and the labor movement and the great majority of the people supported the government. Pflimlin planned to widen his political base to include Mollet and Pinay, while refusing to return La-coste to Algeria as the army and the settlers wanted. The government was playing down the de Gaulle statement and it hoped the Americans would influence their press to do the same, for any publicity abroad only fueled the flames in Paris.[13] American analysts feared that de Gaulle would worsen the right-left cleavage in France, accelerate a trend to-ward a popular front, and, in tacit alliance with the generals in rebel-lion, create disorder in the streets. Dulles, however, in a summary report to London on May 16, judged Pflimlin's determination and position firm, and concluded that it was still unlikely that de Gaulle would come to power.

On May 16, Dulles promised the worried Tunisian and Moroccan am-bassadors in Washington that the United States would react to any action by France or the French army that was contrary to the UN Charter ex-actly "as at Suez."[14] This was short of a promise of military intervention, however. Meanwhile Paris asked Washington to intervene with the Tunisians to assure the supply of French troops still in the country. Jean Daridan did not believe French troops in Algeria would invade either country, but he did warn of the dangers stemming from the present mili-tary "psychology."[15] The Tunisians thought otherwise, however; General Gambiez, loyal as he was, did not necessarily control his subordinates, and Tunis could be occupied within twelve to sixteen hours of an order to do so. Bourguiba wanted positive American action in his support—a show of force by the Sixth Fleet, and paratroops if necessary.[16]

In Morocco the Americans thought the government and the French forces stationed there were both acting with "admirable moderation and astuteness." But a clash between French forces and Algerian rebels on the border caused a Moroccan request to know what the United States would do if the situation "gets out of French hands." Dulles now said the United States would stand by its obligations under the UN Charter; on a question of principle the United States would react.[17] He did not say how; but if he now meant action beyond that at Suez, then the Americans were contemplating the use of major force against the troops of one of their closest allies who were armed with their own weapons. No more glaring example could be given of the dysfunction of the regime in Paris. Authority needed to be reestablished in Paris and Algiers, and the Americans now, like many French politicians, looked to de Gaulle to do it.

De Gaulle had a large part in encouraging the evolution of a positive American attitude toward his return. While in opposition he had showered assurances upon the Americans and Britons he saw of his liberal intentions with regard to Algeria. Now, during the course of the May events, the American Embassy began to receive a continuous stream of assurances about de Gaulle's views on a broad range of subjects from a number of sources. The difficulty was how to interpret these messages, because all the "emissaries," although reportedly close to the general, appeared to be self-appointed. But several had impeccable credentials and the overwhelming tenor of what they delivered was the same. None differed seriously from the first such message delivered to the Americans as early as May 16 by the Gaullist Senator Edmond Michelet: the only choice now available to France was between de Gaulle and a communist-dominated popular front. Only de Gaulle could control the army, and he was pro-US and pro-NATO, prepared to come to power legally, and would carry out a liberal policy in North Africa.

Colonel Henri Tournet, who was described as part of the general's "entourage," got in touch with a wartime acquaintance of his, Colonel Sternberg, now in France as part of the U.S. Military Assistance Advisory Group, to "make clear to [the Americans] where de Gaulle stood" in view of the "certainty" that he would come to power. Tournet called several times at the embassy, assuring its officials that General de Gaulle wished "informal contact" with Washington to be maintained through him, Tournet. De Gaulle was disturbed by American suspicions of him as a fascist: the general was not a Franco and wanted only an American-style strong presidency for France. He was not anti-American, anti-German, or anti-NATO, Tournet said, and he would grant autonomy to Algeria, hoping for the creation of a French Commonwealth in North Africa. On May 21 Tournet specified that de Gaulle would seek to reform NATO only by asking that a greater role be given France in the determination of its policies, but he would remain within the alliance. The general favored European economic integration and would permit the Common Market to take effect as scheduled in 1959. And while de Gaulle would seek Algerian association with France, he would accept independence if it could not be achieved. All this, of course, in the long run turned out to be true. Dulles queried Paris on how to take this information; Dillon replied that Tournet was "close to [Jacques] Foccart," who was part of de Gaulle's entourage, and that his message appeared a "sincere appraisal" of de Gaulle's attitude, if "made palatable for us."[18]

Unlike the British, Dulles continued to believe that Pflimlin could hold on to power, but the American Embassy was bombarded with contrary messages indicating the likelihood of a Gaullist outcome. An apparent emissary from Jacques Chaban-Delmas reiterated the choice that was presumably open: de Gaulle or a popular front government including the Communists. Most curious was the information volunteered to the Americans by Michel Debré. A senator, Debré was a close confidant of the general and had long carried on an acerbic campaign for de Gaulle's return to power. He was later to serve as the first premier of the Fifth Republic. Debré specifically requested that an embassy officer see him so that he might explain that de Gaulle was not involved with the conspirators in Algiers. But de Gaulle saw no reason to disavow the actions of the military, however illegal, because the Pflimlin government had not done so either. Debré bluntly warned that de Gaulle must come to power within ten days or there would be civil war in France. Once in power, de Gaulle would appoint a government of individual personalities, not of parties, and propose a new constitution, and he would insist on the reform but not the rupture of NATO; de Gaulle would challenge only the alliance's integrated command. Debré pretended to have no knowledge of planned paratroop landings in Paris, although they "could not be ruled out." Debré in fact was himself designated to give the signal for paratroop landings in Paris, code-named "Operation Resurrection," should the general judge that such landings were necessary. The military were prepared to move on Paris in the event of a Communist coup, if civil war threatened, or if the National Assembly refused to give a majority to de Gaulle. Dillon observed that he did not know how much of what he had been told came from Debré and how much from de Gaulle, but it squared with information he was receiving from other Gaullists.[19]

The embassy was further reassured by de Gaulle's press conference of May 19, during which he remarked, to the amusement of the crowd, that at the age of 68 he was not about to embark upon a new career as a dictator. De Gaulle had been forceful and showed himself in complete command, and he did not now speak or act like a fascist. He had supported the army and set himself up as the only arbiter in the crisis, but he had insisted on his republican background.[20] Dulles meanwhile queried Paris about Pflimlin's remaining prospects: could he hold on? What was the likelihood of a de Gaulle return and would it be done legally? Was a popular front including the Communist party possible? Would the party attempt a general strike or play the democratic game? Or would nationalist hysteria triumph, leading to a Franco-style solution?[21] Even in this extreme case, Dulles did not raise any question of an American intervention in the crisis. The embassy got differing signals from the Elysée, which favored de Gaulle, and the Matignon, where Jean Lecanuet still insisted that Pflimlin would face down the rebellion. The premier counted on a majority of the National Assembly voting for a constitutional reform bill that would create a strong executive; once that happened, the army rebels and colons would give up their struggle. But this appeared to be wishful thinking.

The Americans were acutely aware that French politicians were showing a distinct lack of resolve in opposing de Gaulle. Pinay, whom Pflimlin had hoped to bring into the government, and who had once told Washington off bluntly as premier, was now behaving like a "frightened little man." Mollet, who boldly questioned de Gaulle about his democratic intentions, was now reported to be trying to torpedo Pflimlin and form a broader coalition including himself. Robert Burin wrote that Pflimlin's principal collaborators were counting on the American Sixth Fleet, currently off the coast of Lebanon, to forestall the possibility of a coup launched from North Africa.[22] But if so, they were hoping in vain. The Tunisians and Moroccans and the government in Paris all placed their hopes in the American Sixth Fleet. The North Africans had assurances of American protection, however, while the government in Paris had none. As late as May 20, Dillon still thought Pflimlin might hang on to power. Pflimlin was tough on respect for legality, but conciliatory toward the military in Algiers, and he continued the fiction of the government having given Salan legal authority, hoping to compromise with the army. French governments had "an infinite capacity for compromise and manoeuver," Dillon wrote, and Pflimlin just might pull it off.

But if he did, could Washington work with him, or depend upon the word of any other government in France? This question remained unasked. But Dillon did conclude that too much depended on de Gaulle and the army; the army was loyal to itself but not necessarily to the government or the National Assembly, and many politicians now believed that only de Gaulle could preserve unity. The embassy now concluded that de Gaulle had decided in February that the regime had reached a point of no return and would turn to him. Various plots had led to the revolt in Algiers based on de Gaulle's understood commitment to make himself available, although the embassy did not think de Gaulle himself was directly involved in the plots; he was much too proud to risk his reputation in this way. If he came to power it would most likely be by the resignation of Pflimlin and a call from Coty following abdication of the deputies. However, failing this option, Washington understood that a military coup was not impossible. Opposition to de Gaulle appeared to be firming up, but Pinay, on whose popularity the government had banked, was "reduced to jelly" trying to straddle both sides. Mollet, the regime's other possible strong man, was negotiating with de Gaulle. A popular front was unlikely even though the PCF was seeking to pose as the party of legality and respectability.[23]

Alphand, in Washington, confirmed Dillon's analysis, and he thanked Dulles and the State Department for its "moderating influence": the French government "greatly appreciated the fact that the American Government had shown great circumspection in not commenting publicly on the French crisis." It was not clear whether Alphand was now speaking for Pflimlin or in anticipation of de Gaulle, but the Americans' circumspection clearly worked in the interest of the latter rather than the existing government in Paris. Alphand offered little hope, nor did he appear to believe it desirable, that Pflimlin would hold on to power, while there was clear American relief at de Gaulle's statement that he would not take power by force. Pflimlin was still hoping that constitutional revision of the Fourth Republic would solve the crisis, allowing him to impose an eventual federal-type solution on Algeria to settle the war and the crisis in French civil-military relations. Dulles told Alphand that he had urged moderation on Tunisia and Morocco; he did not mention that he had done the same with the Algerian rebels, and he remarked that he thought it "amusing" that Jacques Soustelle, in Algiers and acting like a head of state, had just asked for American support. Alphand said that France was still calm and that the population supported Pflimlin, and he thought the fraternization between the army, the colons, and Muslims in Algeria a favorable sign. Dulles disagreed on this last point, finding the alleged fraternization "artificial." Alphand said finally that if de Gaulle did come to power, NATO would be safe but de Gaulle would certainly be opposed to European integration. Dulles agreed, remembering his own long conversation with de Gaulle in 1947. It appeared that both men were already assuming de Gaulle's return.[24]

Indeed, President Coty's spokesman told the Americans that a wave of public opinion in favor of de Gaulle was "sweeping the country" and that the French president now feared an airlift of paratroops descending on Paris if the National Assembly failed to give full powers to de Gaulle. Coty was counting on de Gaulle to act legally but would himself step aside in favor of de Gaulle in order to avoid civil war.[25] On 22 May 1958, Allen Dulles told the NSC that the CIA and the State Department had both now concluded that de Gaulle would soon come to power, the conclusion the British had come to much earlier. The major fear remaining was that French troops elsewhere in North Africa, if uncontrolled, might plunge the entire region into war.[26] In Paris, Houghton still thought the standoff between Algiers and Paris was working in favor of Pflimlin. But nobody mentioned coming to his assistance. Meanwhile signs of political erosion in France increased. On May 22 an embassy officer visited the Independent party and found it a "hotbed of Gaullism." Houghton reported that the Gaullists had hinted to the embassy that they were in contact with Abbas, head of the FLN, in Switzerland, who was sympathetic to de Gaulle. Yazid in New York had also reportedly said that de Gaulle could solve the Algerian problem.[27]

Washington had its own direct pipeline to the rebels in Tunis, where the Algerian rebel leadership regularly talked to American diplomats accredited to the Bourguiba government. During the Sakiet crisis the rebels made known their approval of Washington's role, applauding the idea of American good offices to achieve a negotiated solution. Ahmed Boumanjel tried to see Murphy; failing that he tried to convince embassy officials that the time had come for the Americans to force Paris to settle the Algerian conflict. Washington thought the rebels "on their best behavior" during the May 13 crisis. They would have nothing to do with the Soviets and had turned down a large offer of Czech arms. They were optimistic about the role of Washington and amenable to American requests that they postpone declaring themselves a provisional government, but they thought the chances of getting a negotiated peace would improve if Washington would cease arming the French. The rebels themselves were in need of ammunition for the American-made weapons they had captured from the French and were hopeful of getting more through Tunisia. Was this a hint asking for more? Had Washington been aware all along that by arming Tunis it was arming the rebels? The CIA maintained its own contacts with the rebel

leadership, and these were distinctly friendly, and they expanded
after de Gaulle came to power.[28] The FLN sent ambiguous signals
about de Gaulle; from Tunis, the Americans got the impression that the
rebel leadership thought he might be a "prisoner of the right" once in
power, making a peace agreement more difficult. But the Gaullists told
Houghton that they were in secret contact with Abbas, who was sympathetic to de Gaulle, and in New York the FLN representative to the
UN, Mohammed Yazid, told Henry Cabot Lodge that de Gaulle was the
most likely of all French leaders to provide a solution to the war.[29]

Dulles felt confident enough of the American relationship with the
rebels to send them a warning: they would be "well-advised" not to
complicate the crisis by any action that might involve Tunisia or Morocco in a war with France. The United States would do all it could to
restrain the French government and the governments of Tunisia and
Morocco. The FLN reply was immediate; Boumanjel called on Jones to
assure him that the FLN would cause no provocation and in fact would
withdraw its forces from the border to avoid any incidents. The rebels
would refrain from setting up a provisional government as well; their
aim was to "win the West" rather than to invite Soviet support. These
assurances were contradicted by French military reports, however,
which detailed twelve rebel actions against frontier posts in the three
nights from May 20 to 23, 1958, including an attack from Sakiet, causing one death, the wounding of several French soldiers, and the loss of
four French vehicles. These incidents were allegedly a consequence of a
May 16 rebel order to intensify internal actions following the May 13
events in Algiers in order to provoke the rebellious French army into an
intervention in Tunisia and thus to deepen the international crisis.[30] A
few days later, Boumanjel returned with some advice for Dulles: the
United States should make its opposition to General Salan clear and
warn him that it was prepared to act in the event of a paratroop drop
on Paris.[31] The rebels were now inviting Washington to save Pflimlin by
use of military force, something Pflimlin had not asked for himself. But
the rebels sought to reassure the Americans as the likely outcome of the
crisis became clear. On May 26, Mohammed Yazid lunched with an
American UN delegate in New York. Although he did fear that de
Gaulle in power might become a "prisoner of the right," Yazid said he
believed the general at heart to be a liberal. As far as an Algerian settlement was concerned, a form of a French Commonwealth of Nations
was possible, or something else: "there were many variations of independence." The FLN hoped to cooperate with Tunisia and Morocco,

for "we are all part of one North Africa." And it would wait until the French crisis was over before proceeding to form a provisional government.[32]

To exercise restraint on the French army, the Americans realized they could not get results in Paris; they needed direct contact with French army leaders in Algiers. The Algiers authority was in fact seeking such contact, and on 18 May Dulles authorized discreet talks with "self-constituted authorities [in Algiers] for practical purposes." These were to be at the staff level only and were to be kept to a minimum to "avoid the impression of recognition" of the Algiers rebellion by Washington. But Dulles hardly needed to be so careful; the French Foreign Ministry announced that U.S. contacts with the Algiers authorities were perfectly appropriate since it was maintaining the fiction that General Salan was the duly constituted agent of the French government. And Salan himself wasted no time in initiating contact with the Americans, calling in Consul Frederick Lyon to apologize formally for the sacking of the USIS office in Algiers and to assure him that the military had no intention of crossing Algerian borders. Tunisia and Morocco had nothing to fear from the French army; the Muslims had rallied to French rule in Algeria and the back of the rebellion had been broken. Salan affably invited the American consul to call on him at any time. He referred to the "great national movement" in Algeria showing its unambiguous will to stay in the French Republic, but added, in the style of a head of state, that the loyalty of France to its allies was indisputable, and the friendly relations of France and the United States "intangible."[33] In fact, Dulles noted, the "self-constituted authorities" in Algiers were openly bidding for American support. The military rebels wanted British and NATO support as well. General Massu assured Consul Sarrell that "we are not revolutionaries, and wish only for French unity." Delbecque, on behalf of Salan, issued a general invitation to the Consular Corps in Algiers, which designated the Italian consul, as doyen, to pay a call on Salan. Spain, Greece, and Sweden apparently joined in this initiative; the British and the Americans did not.[34]

Given State Department concerns over Tunisia and Morocco, Pflimlin's foreign minister, René Pleven, insisted that he had taken precautions to avoid incidents on the Algerian frontiers. Pleven sent Salan a message on May 22 asking that Salan publicly declare that the Algiers command would "avoid all provocation" in protecting Algeria's frontiers.[35] But the message was without effect; on May 24 Lecanuet reported that the government had given up on trying to maintain relations

with Algiers and now placed all its hopes on achieving constitutional reforms in Paris. If a large margin in the National Assembly gave the
regime a strengthened executive, Algiers would surrender. But the moderates in the National Assembly were fearful of reform and Mendès
France was now opposed to it as well; he was reported to be dealing simultaneously with de Gaulle and the Communists.

The next day Corsica fell to the Algiers paratroopers, and Pflimlin
warned that civil war might follow this illegal seizure of power. But renewed trouble on the Tunisian frontier threatened to eclipse Corsica;
despite the assurances given the Americans, French troops once again
struck across the Tunisian border in alleged pursuit of Algerian rebels at
Remada. The government in Paris once again "covered," or authorized
after the fact, the military action. Poniatowski, who was on Pflimlin's
staff, told the embassy that Pflimlin was more worried by French army
actions in Tunisia than by those in Corsica. French troops were highly
excited, and if Tunisian forces opposed them he feared that French
forces in Algiers would invade Tunisia after all. Pflimlin had demonstrated that Algiers flouted his orders, and Poniatowski now frankly
admitted that the government was powerless; the regime was threatened
and the military were seeking to impose their will on France. Without
reform at the last minute the regime would fall.[36]

On 25 May, Jacques Soustelle called on U.S. Consul Lyon to assure
him that he was doing everything possible to avoid tension with Tunisia. The Americans remained suspicious, however, and the Tunisians
worried. In Washington, Mongi Slim suggested that if the Sixth Fleet
were nearer it might induce the French rebels to avoid adventures: to
what extent could Tunisia count on American support and protection?
Did Murphy know Salan's intentions? Murphy replied that "we are not
in the general's confidence, he does not tell us about his intentions, nor
does Soustelle or Massu." The Americans could not admit to dealing
with the Algiers authorities out of regard for the position of Pflimlin;
the military were now really acting without the authority of the Paris
government and it would embarrass the French to have to admit this
publicly, although Pflimlin had done so privately.[37]

But Murphy may well have declined to pass on Salan's assurances to
the Tunisians because he believed them worthless. Soustelle, for example, warned Lyon that the Socialist interior minister, Jules Moch, had
passed the word to the Communists to organize in small groups and was
preparing to arm them in the event of a paratroop landing in Paris. Lyon
saw through this rather obvious attempt to curry favor in Washington,

but he forwarded the report to the Paris embassy, which brought it to the attention of the Elysée. Lecanuet formally denied that Moch was arming the Communists: there was "not a single rifle."[38] On May 30, British Ambassador Jebb received a message from General Billotte, who claimed to be speaking for de Gaulle: a reported threat given to Cyrus Sulzberger that de Gaulle would "leave NATO and wreck the Common Market" was not true but rather somebody's idea of a bad joke.[39]

On May 27, Lecanuet told the embassy that an official MRP representative, Maurice Schumann, had been sent to de Gaulle with Coty's and Pflimlin's approval to ask him to condemn the takeover in Corsica. De Gaulle had said he disapproved of it, along with Algiers "excesses," but he would condemn nothing. The weakness of the regime was responsible for what the army had done. On broader issues he had refused comment on the future of EEC and Euratom when he came to power, but promised that he would not break up the Atlantic alliance. De Gaulle expected a call to appear before parliament within days. He would ask the deputies for a two-year investiture in power, and then for parliament to go into recess while he drafted a new constitution. The rule of the political parties must cease. Lecanuet said members of the MRP were depressed by what they heard, but it was clear that de Gaulle would be in power within a week.[40] In the event, the general compromised on six months in power without parliament being in session.

The cool and careful noninterventionist position of the Americans during the crisis shows that exasperation with the Fourth Republic was deep in Washington and that opposition to de Gaulle had considerably mellowed. It had always been the Democrats in Washington who were most hostile to de Gaulle. Dulles had met with him in 1948 when it was assumed that the general would make a bid for power, leading to speculation in Europe even then that Washington was not entirely opposed to him. The American military had also favored him. The reassurances from de Gaulle's many self-appointed spokesmen certainly had their intended calming effect on Washington during the May 1958 crisis. On May 19 a long embassy analysis of a prospective de Gaulle government showed the effectiveness of the assurances and informal contacts between de Gaulle and the Americans. The analysis concluded that the general was likely to adopt a liberal policy in Algeria, keep France in NATO while attempting to reform the alliance, pursue détente with the USSR, and slow but not halt the process of European integration. De Gaulle would put into effect a presidential system of government and carry out progressive economic and social policies, which was to the good, but his temperament would make American relations with him difficult, and internally there remained the danger that he would create a popular front against himself. Dulles echoed this analysis faithfully in the NSC. He doubted that de Gaulle would take any anti-U.S. actions once in power but feared that the general was not a good European.[41]

Tournet once again called at the embassy on May 27. He said Foccart had authorized further communication on the general's behalf; de Gaulle would seek legal investiture by parliament and invite Socialist participation in his government, and he now had assurance that Pflimlin would resign peacefully. De Gaulle did not want a putsch, but if a National Assembly majority could not be obtained then paratroop drops on Paris might be inevitable. De Gaulle deplored the Corsican coup but felt unable to condemn it. Tournet hoped that the United States would take a benevolent position toward de Gaulle and avoid the appearance of any hostility. Tournet confirmed exactly what the Americans had been told about Maurice Schumann's mission to de Gaulle. The New York Times and Washington Post already were complaining of de Gaulle being imposed on France by the armed forces; the embassy should not do the same. Tournet was told that the United States would not take sides in French internal politics.[42] Whether Tournet was or was not speaking for the general, his information was entirely accurate, and his advice on target. And the American noninterventionist posture was undoubtedly meant as reassurance, through him back to de Gaulle.

C. Burke Elbrick wrote Acting Secretary of State Herter on May 27 that de Gaulle must be given a chance to succeed. Any pressure on him would backfire and threaten NATO. The United States must be discreet on the Algerian question; Africa was Europe's "hinterland," close European-African relations were natural, and the United States wanted to maintain Western, that is, French influence in North Africa, although "we do not believe this can be done by military means." The United States should give greater deference to French views on NATO, continue military assistance, and take up the matter of IRBMs with de Gaulle personally. Pressure in favor of European integration would be counterproductive. De Gaulle was solid on East-West relations, and the British were better positioned to dissuade him from any "precipitate" action in the direction of Moscow, although not with regard to Beijing. Personal diplomacy from here on in would be best, and de Gaulle should be invited to visit the United States as soon as practicable.[43]

Still another American analysis of de Gaulle focused on the line Washington should take with regard to France's European partners, and it too expressed optimism. De Gaulle's coming to power must not change American support for European integration. France needed NATO and could only draw strength from it, and its hopes of retaining its influence in Africa depended on its relationship to Europe as a whole. Internal forces in France favored European integration, the Coal and Steel Community was an international obligation that could not be broken, nor could France "go it alone"; it needed the five other Common Market countries and the United States and the United Kingdom. American policy should consequently remain calm but firm, making it clear that France was expected to fulfill its treaty obligations, and the United States should push ahead with its own commitments while avoiding for now any new ones. De Gaulle's exact intentions with regard to NATO were unknown, but it was unwise to assume he would not honor treaty obligations; the American line must be to assume that no question arose concerning French participation in NATO consequent upon his coming to power. Juin and the other generals all supported NATO, and the bulk of French forces were no longer committed to it in any case, being tied up in Algeria. Indeed, only if de Gaulle solved the Algerian question was the return of French forces to NATO likely.[44]

All this analysis was almost exactly on target, and it explains the alacrity with which the Americans accepted de Gaulle's return. But no one thought they would have an easy time with him. When, for instance, Cecil Lyon recommended that U.S. officers whom de Gaulle had known and befriended during the war be sent to Paris, he was told that "nobody who ever served with de Gaulle is a friend [of his]."[45] Even less did the British contemplate winning de Gaulle's friendship. A Foreign Office minute of June 2, 1958, worried that under de Gaulle the French were more likely to "insist upon being taken by us and the Americans into our complete confidence and treated on an equal footing as regards a military atomic programme and political consultations generally; they would expect support for French policies in general, but more particularly North Africa; they will be in financial difficulties and look to us, and more especially the Americans, for help."[46] Jebb felt that since the French were going to build their bomb anyway, Britain might as well help them, but from Washington Sir Harold Caccia reported that help to France would imperil the Anglo-U.S. bilateral arrangement; thus, once again, the British were to be forced to choose Washington over Paris, with the inevitable results for Anglo-French relations. The French would ask for tripartite consultations; again the Americans were opposed, and "We should not pressure the Americans to admit the French since that would only lead to weakening our own relationship with them." On Algeria the outlook was better: there was room for a liberal solution there still, and "every indication is that the general is moving as astutely there as on internal politics." But on the bomb, "nothing that we can do will satisfy him," and with regard to tripartite consultations, "the U.S. will not bend...and we should not be sorry. We should concentrate on our own relations with Paris, and let them handle their own with the U.S." The prime minister should try for a personal relationship with de Gaulle that had failed with Adenauer, "because it is contrary to nature to treat Germans as one's best friends." Unfortunately it was contrary to de Gaulle's nature to treat anyone as his best friend.

Pflimlin resigned on May 28; the next day, Coty called upon de Gaulle, who appeared before the National Assembly on June 1 and was voted into power by 329 votes to 224 against. Actually, it was not Macmillan whom de Gaulle knew best but Eisenhower, who was probably the one Anglo-Saxon of whom the French leader thought most highly. Eisenhower wasted no time in trading on this relationship by sending a personal message to de Gaulle, his "friend" from the war years. The American president expressed his satisfaction that the crisis in France had been resolved and his hopes for future relations of intimacy and friendship between the two governments. Alphand thought that such a declaration by an American president on the outcome of a French government crisis was indeed exceptional. But the relief in Washington that de Gaulle had come to power legally was palpable.[47] Dulles was exuberant with Alphand, remarking "Everything turned out extremely well," an expression that he repeated several times. Even the outlook for European integration was suddenly thought to be better with authority restored in Paris rather than the shifting coalitions of before; among the leaders of the High Authority of the European Coal and Steel Community (ECSC), Euratom, and the EEC, "hopes exceeded fears"; in the experience of the High Authority, "virtually all French governments have been difficult, when not downright uncooperative, most importantly because they are weak, and partly because they are made up of Frenchmen." The hope now was that "an effective French government, even under a leader with his [de Gaulle's] past predilections, might prove advantageous."[48]

The American press followed suit. As early as June 6, the French Embassy noticed a press change with regard to France beyond what one could have hoped; everyone in America now seemed to be behind de Gaulle. Alphand singled out articles by Marguerite Higgins in the *New*

York Herald Tribune and Dana Schmidt of the *New York Times* as reflecting, through unofficial channels, the administration's delight at having a strong French government with which to deal. Even after some months had passed, Alphand reported that the press remained "*dithyrambique*" with regard to de Gaulle and that even American intellectuals were now supporting him. The Americans had rediscovered the France they admired and loved, and France suddenly outstripped even Germany in American admiration. The American euphoria with de Gaulle continued into 1959, when *Time* made him its "man of the year." As Pierre Melandri points out, paradoxically, the Fourth Republic had a "structural" anti-Americanism owing to its weakness, dependence, and obsession with American recognition of its standing as a great power. The Fifth Republic eliminated this attitude, which the Americans termed an "inferiority complex," and consequently won greater respect in American opinion.[49] This view was curiously confirmed by some of the disillusioned French military themselves. General André Dulac, for example, condemned the stupidity of the colons, who brought de Gaulle to power in the belief that he would save them, while it was the Fourth Republic that could never have abandoned Algeria; de Gaulle, paradoxically, enjoyed the power and the prestige to do so, and did.[50]

This further explains, perhaps, American inaction during the May 1958 crisis. A rather extraordinary conversation occurred between a Soviet Embassy counselor, Rogov, and an unnamed American Embassy official in Paris. Rogov said that the Soviets genuinely feared the outbreak of civil war in France, and he "asked why we did not intervene... once the possibility of paratroop landings arose we had every right to do something. Why did General Lauris Norstad [U.S. NATO commander] not simply tell Algiers he would not tolerate landings? When told we could not do this he [Rogov] commented then we have not organized things well." As they demonstrated in Hungary two years earlier, the Soviets had indeed organized things better for themselves in their part of Europe. But the Russians never thought they had come out badly with de Gaulle. Jebb reported that a Soviet Embassy official had told the Americans that things might not be too bad if de Gaulle came to power; there was no advantage in violent Communist party resistance to de Gaulle, and the time was not yet ripe for a popular front.[51] But Washington had long since lost faith in the capacity of the Fourth Republic to solve pressing French problems and had every reason to suppose, based on confidential remarks from the general to several Americans, that de Gaulle could reestablish lines of authority in France and eventually bring a conclusion to the Algerian War on the basis of autonomy, if not eventual independence. To be sure, de Gaulle was likely to present inconveniences, perhaps even obstacles, to American diplomacy in terms of the structure of NATO and the building of Europe; but it was clear that he would keep France firmly anchored in the West and eventually relieve it, and Washington, of the diplomatic burden of a colonial struggle that was anathema to the Third World.

In September 1959, Eisenhower visited France to hear de Gaulle tell him that Algeria would soon be offered self-determination. Eisenhower's comment on the visit in his memoir provides a fitting conclusion: "For at least two years before he became his country's president I had often remarked to Secretary Dulles and others interested in the future of that nation that only General de Gaulle's accession to power could save France."[52]

CHAPTER SIX

The United States, Algeria, and de Gaulle's Diplomacy

.

At the moment of the Fourth Republic's demise on May 26, 1958, Minister of Foreign Affairs Pleven instructed Ambassador Hervé Alphand to inform Washington that France now had the capability to produce nuclear weapons and would in the near future do so. France expected important results from this fact: not autonomy in defense, said Pleven, but close ties to the Anglo-Saxons, who already possessed such weapons, and revision of the McMahon Act, which prohibited the United States from sharing nuclear defense information with other countries.[1] One may marvel at the timing of Pleven's request, literally under the shadow of "Operation Resurrection," the paratroop drop on Paris that threatened if the National Assembly refused de Gaulle's bid for power. But no greater example could be found of the absolute continuity between the foreign policies of the Fourth and Fifth Republics, both of which revolved around two central issues, nuclear weapons and Algeria. These in turn were the two issues that determined the nature of France's ultimate relationship with NATO.

Algeria was a central issue in the relationship between France and NATO, and it played a critical role in the eventual French withdrawal from NATO's command, a process begun by de Gaulle in 1959 with the Mediterranean fleet and concluded in 1966 with the removal of NATO headquarters and all associated military bases from France. This point would appear to have been missed by most of the literature dealing with de Gaulle's foreign policy. Several points bear making in this connection, however. Algeria was a critical cause of the French break with NATO, but not the only one—it shared place with the American-French conflict over the construction of an independent French nuclear deterrent. Both the Bourgès-Maunoury and Gaillard governments continued the development of a French nuclear capability, and in April 1958 Gaillard decided definitively on the date of the first nuclear explosion early in 1960 and chose the test site in the Sahara.[2] Had the United States, at an early stage, acceded to repeated French requests for help with the construction of the French atomic bomb and weapons delivery systems, other questions at issue between the two countries might more easily have been resolved.[3] On the other hand, the quest for a French deterrent seems to have been spurred, almost at every stage of its early development, by events connected with the Algerian War. Algeria, moreover, played a role in American opposition to a French deterrent, responsible as it was for political instability in Paris; and it similarly helped make unacceptable de Gaulle's famous proposals for a coordinating mechanism of the three great Western powers, the United States, United Kingdom, and France, to act as a kind of directing committee within NATO to deal with world problems. De Gaulle made this proposal in simultaneous letters to Prime Minister Macmillan and President Eisenhower in September 1958, and its theme underlay the agendas of Western diplomacy for the duration of the Berlin crisis and beyond. The continuing French effort to hold on in Algeria underlay de Gaulle's famous memorandum of September 1958 in the first place. The French policy, pursued by the Fourth and Fifth Republics, was succinctly stated in a memorandum by G. de Wailly of the Foreign Affairs Ministry on April 16, 1958, six weeks before de Gaulle came to power: "Our objective must be the formation of a Eurafrican sphere ["*fuseau*"] centered on the Mediterranean, tied by common interests, equally accepted by the two blocs, East and West, and free from both of them."[4] Algeria was meant to be the linchpin of this sphere of influence, for which France would speak in the councils of the big three alongside the "Anglo-Saxons."

The Fourth Republic had given Washington no reason to regret its demise, and the Americans had known what they were doing when they pressured Gaillard into accepting the conclusions of the good offices mission in the face of almost certain repudiation by the National Assembly. The gamble paid off with the accession to power of de Gaulle; he was clearly the only person with sufficient authority to deal with the crisis of the regime, and he did so. It is doubtful that the mystery of de Gaulle's intentions concerning Algeria can ever be clearly resolved, and it is most probable that he did not know himself how he would solve the problem. But in the short run his policy was that of the army, the Algerian settlers, and the Fourth Republic that had brought him to power: to keep Algeria French by means of military victory. De Gaulle included Algeria as part of metropolitan France in the constitutional referendum on the Fifth Republic held in September 1958, and in the legislative elections that followed, on the basis of a single college, one person, one vote. Alfred Grosser is no doubt correct in stating that the model de Gaulle preferred for Algeria was prefigured in the abortive French Community of African States he created in the constitution of September 1958, which offered limited autonomy within a federal community, with powers of foreign policy, defense, and finance to be held by the president of the community flanked by consultative bodies that included African representation but in which the French were preponderant.[5] Algeria was to be the linchpin of this Paris-dominated structure.

I will return to the question of de Gaulle's alleged motivation in chapter 7. The problem for historians in determining his intentions has been to pay too much attention to what he said he intended to do before he came to power and too little to what he did once he had it. The point here is not what de Gaulle did in Algeria proper, although that is important. It is how Algeria figured in the total picture of Gaullist diplomacy in 1958 and 1959. With that focus in mind, it becomes clear that de Gaulle's earliest actions were of a piece, oriented toward the single, fixed goal of keeping Algeria French. Only in September 1959 did he modify this aim, conceding self-determination in principle and setting for himself the goal of achieving a close association between Algeria and France. There was thus every reason for army leaders such as General Edmond Jouhaud, later one of the insurgents in April 1961, to advocate de Gaulle's return to power in May 1958. General de Gaulle led advocates of *Algérie française* to believe that he too was an advocate of their cause and he adamantly refused to condemn their insurgency against the Fourth Republic.[6] Once in power, he named the leader of the insurrection, General Salan, delegate general of the government in Algeria and commander in chief of the army, with full civil and military powers, exactly as Pflimlin had done, and General Massu, similarly involved in the May 1958 events, prefect of Algiers.[7] De Gaulle's words, the famous "*Je vous ai compris,*" spoken from the balcony of the Governor-General's palace in Algiers on June 4, 1958, and then the single utterance of "*Vive l'Algérie française*" at Mostaganem a few days later, were meant seriously. After the latter statement de Gaulle explained to Jouhaud that if he had not said the word "integration," this was because the crowds wanted to force it on him. What did it mean? "That Algeria is French? Is it useful or necessary to say this, since it is a fact?"

De Gaulle's words, moreover, were followed by acts, and his earliest ones, as Pierre Miquel shows, were in the spirit of integration, the policy of Jacques Soustelle, Robert Lacoste, and the army which brought him to power. It seemed quite impossible in May 1958 for anyone to believe that France would actually leave Algeria: the air force was constructing a runway of 2,500 meters in the Sahara, intensified production of oil was taking place there, a pipeline was under construction to Tunis and Tripoli, and a nuclear test site was under construction at Colomb-Béchar. De Gaulle continued all these projects, and confirmed the army in power in Algeria. All Algeria voted together with France, on the basis of equality, Muslim and French, male and female, in the referendum on the new constitution of the Fifth Republic on September 28, and in the elections for the new National Assembly that followed. It was the army's mission to get out the Muslim vote and parry the efforts of the FLN to prevent it, thus demonstrating Muslim support for France and de Gaulle in Algeria.[8] The elections were the ultimate act of integration, which the FLN fully understood in its attempt to boycott them.

The Challe plan, initiated by General Maurice Challe in 1959, constituted the most ambitious military effort yet to turn the tide of the war in favor of France. Its intent was ruthlessly to destroy the FLN on the ground and yield a victory that would enable France to carry out an Algerian settlement on its own terms. The previous French strategy had been to respond to FLN attacks wherever they might occur; the dispersion of French forces throughout the country prevented a sufficient concentration of force ever to administer to the rebels a truly punishing blow. Challe concentrated operations in one sector at a time, going resolutely on the offensive, pinning down the rebels and then bringing up a concentration of mobile reserves with the aim of methodically destroying insurgent forces, before going on to the next sector with the same tactics. This policy, supported by the significant number of American helicopters recently imported, was successful in that it administered crushing blows to rebel units from which they could not easily recover, and also improved the "kill ratio." Sectors were methodically and definitively pacified, and more rebels died for each loss of a French soldier than before, but these tactics nevertheless increased the loss of life on both sides. Large numbers of Muslims were recruited into fighting for the French, with no intent of abandoning them to their cruel fate in an independent Algeria. The corollary of Challe's brutal military offensive was the continued "regrouping" of the population with the aim of cutting them off from the rebels and causing the rebels to be asphyxiated for lack of the food and shelter they commonly obtained from the local population. Evacuated areas could then become "free fire zones" in which entire villages and even fields and crops could be destroyed as the army pursued rebel bands. Napalm was freely used. An approximation of the American "strategic hamlet" program later adopted in the Vietnam War, this policy was cruel beyond anything the French had previously attempted in the war:

> By July 1959 over one million Muslim villagers had been transferred to "regroupment camps," which varied from resembling the fortified villages of the Middle Ages to the concentration camps of a more recent past. In the latter conditions were nothing short of scandalous. Hunger first, and cold secondly, were the enemies. At one camp just outside Constantine inmates were found eating grass in the field, and in the overcrowded, tented encampments for nomads of the south infants were often found dead of cold in the mornings. Tuberculosis and other ailments raged.[9]

By these methods the country was, in a measure, pacified, but at enormous cost both in human suffering and to France's reputation in the world. That such draconian measures would have been attempted with any other aim than a victory that enabled France freely to exercise its will afterward staggers the imagination. Not for nothing does Benjamin Stora pose as one of the key unanswered questions of the war why Challe's brutal military success of 1959 and 1960 still led to Algerian independence in 1962.[10] Hopefully, the focus here on the war's international dimension will provide an answer to that question.

The Challe plan was combined with the Plan of Constantine, which committed France to the expenditure of billions of francs for Algerian modernization and economic development, in itself further evidence of de Gaulle's determination to keep Algeria French.[11] The fruit of several years of planning going back to Mendès France and Mollet, the Plan of Constantine combined social reform with industrialization and modernization designed to transform Algeria by developing and urbanizing it. On the one hand, Muslims were to be co-opted into the French administration of the territory while social benefits and wages were equalized with those of the mainland and 250,000 hectares of land were redistributed to the peasants. On the other hand, a huge petrochemical complex was planned, making use of the oil of the Sahara, plus a steel mill, with 400,000 industrial jobs to be created in four years. Education was to be expanded to encompass two-thirds of the Muslim population, and housing was to be built for one million persons. The plan was administered by a "Superior Council" of forty-three persons, twenty-eight of whom came from Algeria and fifteen from metropolitan France; of the twenty-eight, fourteen were European and fourteen Muslim. The aim of the plan was clearly to achieve the total symbiosis of the Algerian and French economies.[12]

The Challe plan was not implemented until early 1959; the Plan of Constantine in the meanwhile could be attributed to de Gaulle's expected "liberal" program for Algeria. Even those most suspicious of de Gaulle in the American State Department tended to be hopeful on the score of the French Union. The most dangerous possibility, the Americans thought, was the phantom of a "planetary deal": de Gaulle would turn to Moscow and seek assurance of noninterference in North Africa and a cessation of Egyptian and Russian aid to the Algerian rebels in exchange for close bilateral relations with France and recognition of Red China. But this was regarded as unlikely. According to an internal State Department memorandum, it was agreed that "there is reason to hope de Gaulle will move toward a liberal, although possibly paternalistic policy both with regard to normalizing relations with Tunisia and Morocco and to solving the Algerian issue." The federal system for the French Union was encouraging to Black Africa and might help with Algeria. "Without in any sense appearing to abandon Tunisia and Morocco, we believe that at least at the outset, we should avoid interjecting ourselves in North African issues." Otherwise de Gaulle might become suspicious and be diverted from pursuing a liberal policy in Algeria. Washington was encouraged to see that de Gaulle wanted close relations with Germany and applauded his efforts to put the French economy on a sound basis so as to avoid having to ask for financial assistance.[13] De Gaulle's minister of foreign affairs, Maurice Couve de Murville, was also a known quantity in Washington from his years as ambassador there.

The noted liberal French sociologist, philosopher, and columnist Raymond Aron was received in Washington by Under Secretary of State Herter, Allen Dulles, the head of the CIA, and Frank Jandrey of the State Department's European desk. Aron was hardly reassuring. If the struggle continued, he warned, the outcome might be fascism, which would take the paradoxical form of France being conquered by Algeria through its oversized army now stationed there. To avoid this outcome a solution was necessary and to achieve it Aron insisted that the United States pursue an active policy; it must pressure Tunisia and Morocco to bring the rebels to accept less than full independence for Algeria. Aron criticized American policy as giving lip service in support of France while remaining skeptical about its chances of success, in effect, open agreement but secret disagreement, the result of which had been to make any solution more difficult. The fence-sitting must end, Aron said: the Americans must go one way or the other. And since de Gaulle would not ask for American help or advice, it was for Washington to specify what kind of solution would receive its approbation.[14]

De Gaulle's first moves in power were encouraging. He sent a personal message to Sultan Mohammed V of Morocco, flattering the latter as a *"compagnon de la libération"*; Mohammed immediately informed Washington of his pleasure at this gesture.[15] De Gaulle reopened negotiations with Tunisia, promised French troop withdrawal within four months, and agreed to negotiate a change in the status of Bizerte. De Gaulle was in effect resuming the negotiations with Tunisia that were begun by Pleven on May 24, aiming at a settlement on the basis of the good offices agreement which had occasioned the overthrow of Gaillard.[16] Washington cooperated by dissuading Bourguiba from bringing his complaint to the UN. In exchange for its promise to withdraw its troops from Tunisia, France got three concessions: the end of the good offices mission and adjournment of the Security Council's consideration of the Sakiet crisis, continued maintenance of French forces in Bizerte, and the end of Tunisian obstruction of the free movement of French forces still in the country.[17] De Gaulle also cleverly managed to divide both the Moroccans and the Tunisians from the FLN.

A State Department position paper on Tunisia noted with satisfaction improved French-Tunisian ties. Washington regarded Bourguiba as a valuable asset to the West, and thought him useful in keeping the FLN from falling under Egyptian influence.[18] The paper laid out the fundamentals of an independent American policy toward North Africa in the absence of French cooperation. In Morocco, the United States had negotiated its base rights independently of Paris, owing to the stubborn insistence of the sultan; it had also increased its economic aid to compensate for French reductions. Failing French deliveries of arms to Tunisia, the Americans stood ready to step in once again as they had already done in the past. Most important was Algeria; the position of the United States was still to help maintain French interests there, and rumors that the United States sought to replace the French were simply false. Any liberal and realistic policy that de Gaulle might implement to avert an almost certain disaster there would have American support.[19] Dulles exulted at de Gaulle's coming to terms with Tunisia, concluding that "there was more hope for the future of France than had been visible for a long time." President Eisenhower agreed.

Washington was further encouraged by reports from Algiers that secret contacts between de Gaulle and the Algerian rebels existed, and from Tunis, that FLN leaders would accept less than full independence if de Gaulle was willing to negotiate with them.[20] De Gaulle maintained close relations with a moderate Muslim, Abderrahmane Farès, through whom he was able to communicate with Ferhat Abbas, shortly to become the nominal head of the Algerian provisional government. British Consul Sarrell in Algiers and Ambassador Jebb in Paris both reported possible contacts with the FLN in Cairo through the presence there of General Catroux.[21] Jebb thought de Gaulle's promise of equality for Algerian Muslims within a new French constitution meant that he would force integration down the throats of the colons, but his policy was a mystery and would remain so until he could restore the French government's authority over its army. The British government concluded that the two main problems de Gaulle faced were Algeria and finances; if he could solve them, he would be doing an inestimable service to the Atlantic alliance. Britain must give all help possible in both areas, lest he fail and a popular front develop. Most important, the British thought, it would be a mistake to press him now on NATO, Europe, or Algeria, since "we do not know his policy." Indeed no one but the general's closest entourage were thought to know exactly what he had in mind as to Algeria's ultimate destiny.[22] Jebb was mistaken on that point: not even his closest entourage knew, nor is it certain that the general himself knew.

De Gaulle met with Macmillan on June 29. After treating the prime minister to his views of the USSR, which the general characterized as old imperial Russia with a communist facade, de Gaulle explained that, unlike Tunisia and Morocco, which were states with which one could deal, Algeria had never been a state, but was rather "a heap of dust." De Gaulle would first hold elections there, establish who were viable interlocutors for the Muslim population, and negotiate with them, without prejudice as to the territory's future. All possibilities, he said—integration, separation, "dominion status," or anything else—remained open. Macmillan clarified that de Gaulle meant not separate Algerian elections but rather balloting there in conjunction with mainland

France, which de Gaulle said was correct. This, however, was integration after all. So did Jacques Soustelle, now de Gaulle's minister of information, inform Jebb. Soustelle thought only two policies possible in
Algeria—integration with France, or independence, which meant disin-
tegration and anarchy. All intermediate possibilities, he thought, must
be rejected since they would lead to independence anyway.[23]

After Dulles listened to de Gaulle carefully on his first meeting with
him on July 5, 1958, he realized that his earlier optimism might have
been ill-placed. To be sure, the talks were friendly, and that caused Dulles
to term them a success.[24] But everything de Gaulle would later propose
was articulated by the general at that first meeting: France must be a nuclear power, France must play a world role and participate in the directing councils of the alliance alongside the "Anglo-Saxons" (Dulles already referred to this demand as being for a "directorate"), and France
must have its hegemony recognized in a combined "Eurafrica." Dulles
also got a taste of the general's philosophy. The present division of Germany "did not bother him," while communism was unreal; underneath
the ideological veneer of the Soviet bloc lay the eternal reality of Tsarist
Russia. NATO as presently constituted was unsatisfactory to France,
because it did not extend to the areas of the world in which France's
vital interests were at stake. The two statesmen also discussed the crisis
in Lebanon, where a Nasserite coup seemed a real possibility, and where
Eisenhower was shortly to land the marines. De Gaulle insisted that
France must be consulted and included in any plans for an intervention
under the terms of the Eisenhower doctrine. Dulles brushed this aside,
noting that France would be a liability because of its difficulties in Algeria and ties to Israel.

Perhaps the most serious issue was the nuclear one. Taking up where
Pflimlin had left off, de Gaulle considered France already to be a nuclear
power and expected American assistance with the further development
of its weapons systems. Dulles promised that the United States would
use its nuclear weapons to defend Europe and make them available to
its allies; it would even train the French in their use through NATO in
the planned "double key" system for their shared use. But this policy
was designed to prevent the Europeans from building their own nuclear
weapons, and Dulles warned de Gaulle against the waste involved in the
creation of an independent French deterrent. Dulles then indicated that
the doctrine of "massive retaliation" needed to be rethought, which de
Gaulle in turn took to mean that the American promise to defend Europe with nuclear weapons if overrun by the Soviets was built on sand.

The disagreement between the two men was almost total, although they maintained an atmosphere of congeniality throughout the meeting.[25] Recounting the conversation immediately afterward, Dulles noted that de Gaulle's proposals would enlarge NATO's responsibilities to encompass North Africa and the Mideast and raise the danger of creating a "triumvirate" to dominate the alliance. Both of these demands were to be in de Gaulle's September memorandum on the reorganization of NATO, and Dulles already judged them to be unacceptable.[26] De Gaulle discussed Algeria briefly and separately in a private conversation with Dulles after lunch. He would move one step at a time, de Gaulle said; the age of colonialism was over, but he had to go slowly if there was to be genuine progress toward self-government, and he spoke of a ten-year interim period following pacification after which a new order for Algeria could be envisaged.[27] Was this an indication of the general's true future intentions? It is difficult to say but unlikely; de Gaulle was in the habit of saying too many contrary things to too many people, and it is not safe to take any of his statements as being a true indication of what he might do.

American-French relations began once again to deteriorate quickly over North Africa, confirming Dulles's pessimism. Tunisia requested that Bizerte be made a NATO base; de Gaulle insisted it would remain a French preserve. France wanted exclusive responsibility for the arming of Tunisia, and Dulles agreed, but Bourguiba refused; he could not accept French arms so long as France was at war with his brother Arabs in Algeria, and France had no choice but to acquiesce once again to the Americans and British equipping two Tunisian battalions.[28] Swallowing this was perhaps made easier by French intelligence reports that Bourguiba was furious with the FLN for its alleged participation in an attempt on his life, as well as its reproaches for his efforts to prevent total war in the Maghreb and settlement of the Sakiet crisis.[29] But the French always fell back on blaming Washington for their difficulties: in a "moment of candor," French Ambassador to Tunisia Georges Gorse told Jones that the reason the Tunisians would not come to terms with France was that "you have made the Tunisians too confident that your government will help and support them."[30]

A further irritant between Paris and Washington was the free rein enjoyed by Algerian FLN representatives in the United States to carry on political activities, be received at the State Department, curry favor with American public opinion, and unofficially lobby in favor of their cause in the United Nations.[31] Privately generated American aid to Algerian refugees, and the open sympathy for the rebels manifest in American public opinion also hurt; the Foreign Ministry calculated the financial aid thus far at $3.3 million, which, it informed the State Department, the French public regarded as tantamount to directly aiding the FLN. Moreover, France claimed to have exclusive jurisdiction over the Algerian refugees in Tunisia, all of whom were technically French citizens.[32] At a meeting on Algeria held in New York's New School and sponsored by the Carnegie Endowment for International Peace and the American Committee on Africa, *New York Times* correspondent Michael James, City College Professor Hans Kohn, and FLN representative Mohammed Yazid shared a podium. French agents squirmed as they listened to Kohn portray the FLN as freedom fighters, inspired by French example, and ready to negotiate without preconditions. He detailed the history of the secret negotiations under way in 1956 that had been sabotaged by the French military authorities who had kidnaped Ben Bella and four of his colleagues "at the moment when, with the agreement of Premier Mollet, Morocco and Tunisia were engaged in efforts to bring the two sides together." Kohn further condemned NATO for alleged military aid accorded France and American support for French colonialism.[33]

De Gaulle initiated a new activism on the question of Washington's contacts with the FLN, and Alphand was instructed to protest in the strongest terms. French intelligence shadowed the Algerians in New York, carefully monitoring and reporting their every move. Ahmed Francis was reported to be constantly going to public meetings while Chanderli worked the corridors at the United Nations; Yazid meanwhile carefully cultivated the Afro-Asian bloc.[34] FLN leaders continued to be received at their request at the State Department. Alphand demanded that all this be stopped. Washington replied that it was constitutionally unable to do anything about FLN propaganda activities in the United States, even if it had been willing. As for the FLN delegates being received in the State Department, it was department policy to receive all sorts of groups freely, and its contacts with the FLN, of which Paris was informed, had assisted the French in the past. In fact Washington valued its contacts with the FLN and thought they could work in the French interest if France were sincere about wanting negotiations for a cease-fire with the rebels.

In October 1958 de Gaulle made his first gesture to Algeria by offering the rebels a "peace of the brave" if they would agree to a cease-fire. Washington's reaction was positive, and William Porter of State's

African desk approached Abdelkhader Chanderli and Yazid to express the department's wish that the FLN respond constructively.[35] This was all the more reason for the Americans to insist that they could not restrict the activities of the FLN in the United States. The argument given the French was based on constitutional reasons, and indeed to attempt restrictions would have been to brook trouble with American liberals. But a March 1959 memorandum of the Algiers consulate noted the usefulness of these contacts, which were habitually reported to the French both before and after they took place, and which amounted to informal negotiations. In the short run, French pressure prevailed, however, and Yazid was given a message not to come for the time being. The same sorts of problems plagued France's relations with its other NATO allies, whom the French expected would follow the American lead on the issue. The Foreign Affairs and Interior ministries of the Federal Republic of Germany conferred on the issue of FLN activity in Germany following French protests. Paris got little satisfaction because Bonn did not want to violate the right of political exile nor alienate international opinion. The Germans thought it better to "deal with these people" than to throw them into the arms of Nasser.[36] FLN representative missions were also active in Great Britain, Italy, and Switzerland; the Quai d'Orsay protested in all these countries, but the results were not satisfactory in any of them.[37] Washington was hedging its bets in the belief that the FLN would one day rule Algeria, and the others followed suit. Couve de Murville instructed Alphand to note French government unhappiness: "You are to emphasize that the French government places the greatest importance on receiving satisfaction on this question." The FLN was at war with France, and the United States was an ally; the American government's attitude could only be characterized as shocking.[38]

On September 17, 1958, de Gaulle sent his famous memorandum to Eisenhower and Macmillan proposing the establishment of a three-power directing organism within NATO. By far the most important of de Gaulle's initiatives, it demanded a role for France in an informal arrangement, commonly referred to as a "directorate," of the three great powers to coordinate the policies of the so-called free world. The memorandum is usually interpreted as the basis for de Gaulle's claim to foreign policy independence, and the broader concerns behind it must not be forgotten. Its immediate cause may have been the Quemoy-Matsu crisis, during which, on September 4, Dulles warned that the United States would respond to any Chinese invasion of the islands with force. A world crisis thus loomed in which France might be involved militarily but in the outcome of which it had no influence.[39] De Gaulle was also enraged by the American invasion of Lebanon in July, along with the British, from which the French, despite their historic interests there, had been excluded. But a basic motive underlying the de Gaulle initiative was the Algerian War and France's continued hegemony over French Africa. There is great irony here, for the effort to keep Algeria was at once the motivation for the memorandum and the reason the "Anglo-Saxons" rejected it. This point appears to have been missed by most of the literature dealing with de Gaulle's foreign policy.[40]

This is not to downplay the importance of other critical questions at issue between France and the United States which also lay at the root of the failure of the 1958 initiative. The conflict over the French program to construct an independent nuclear deterrent was basic; instead of the much-coveted cooperation the French got only hostility from Washington on this question. Although President Eisenhower himself often appeared an unwilling participant in the rejection of French policy, he could not overcome the opposition in Congress, the State Department, and the all-powerful Atomic Energy Commission. Washington had also been unhappy with French nonparticipation in NATO since the Algerian War began.[41] De Gaulle's repeated demand that he be "consulted" on world problems, at least on the level of the British, also posed problems in Washington because the French and Americans appeared to attribute different meanings to the term. The Americans thought consultation meant just that, the sharing of information and perhaps the modification of some policies on the basis of received advice, but in the case of disagreement they would go ahead anyway. The French interpreted it to mean discussion before policy was determined with the aim of coming to agreement on a common policy. The Americans thought this meant that the French wanted a veto power over all allied nuclear policy, which was clearly unacceptable to them.[42]

The message was a terse 500-plus words, and contained only one brief but specific reference to North Africa that criticized NATO as being insufficient to meet the Middle Eastern and North African concerns of its members. But on September 18 the FLN declared itself an Algerian provisional government; the French response was immediate, and on September 20, 1958, Couve de Murville sent a message to all French diplomatic representatives abroad instructing them to warn their host governments that recognition of the newly formed Algerian provisional government in Cairo would be construed as an unfriendly act in Paris and interference in French internal affairs. Thus France undertook two major diplomatic initiatives in three days, with Washington's decision to arm Tunisia looming and its continued refusal to restrict the activities of FLN representatives in the United States part of the background as well. It would be an error to assume that these initiatives were not related; de Gaulle clearly meant his three-power "directorate," as it popularly came to be called, to associate the United States, Britain, and NATO in support of French designs in Algeria. As Alphand later explained, the three-power organism would, in addressing itself to world issues, adopt the policy of "the power that was the most involved in this or that zone. In North Africa, for example, the common position [of the three] 'would have to be the position of France.'"[43] And the policy of France was to suppress the Algerian rebellion, pure and simple.

De Gaulle's proposal was to involve two years of desultory discussions among the United States, Great Britain, and France that ended in recrimination under the Kennedy administration in 1961. The negotiations were revealing about the policy concerns of de Gaulle, however. C. Burke Elbrick noted that none of de Gaulle's proposals were new: Bidault had called for an institutionalized form of tripartism in 1948 in his proposal of a "High Atlantic Council for Peace," and so had other French politicians since.[44] De Gaulle's claim was different only in that it was based on his perception of increased French prestige owing to the country's newfound stability and ability to act. But in Washington and London French affairs still appeared unstable and chaotic, and the demand seemed impossible to meet. State thought such an organism, if it even came into existence, could not be institutionalized but must remain informal. NATO could not establish a directorate of three excluding the rest as second-class allies; sharp negative reactions swiftly came from Spaak, Adenauer, and the Italians, all of whom got word of the proposal, which threatened to break up the alliance in its present form. On the other hand, the United States and Britain could not afford to alienate de Gaulle, and exploratory talks were accepted.[45] The German and Italian ambassadors were informed, and they agreed that the talks were a necessary measure in order to enable the French to save face, but their purpose was to be directed toward convincing the French of the danger in their proposals. Macmillan told Adenauer that there was a special British-American relationship that was understood by NATO, but this "should not and could not be institutionalized to include France."[46] Dulles, for his part, told British Ambassador Caccia that the special relationship must be preserved: "It would be impossible to work as intimately on a tripartite basis as we two are now doing bilaterally."[47]

NATO Secretary General Paul-Henri Spaak told Dulles on September 27 that the de Gaulle proposal would spell the end of the alliance; Dulles assured Spaak that the proposal was wholly unacceptable to the United States, although for the time being the French would be told that the matter needed further study.[48] The Americans were further disturbed when early in October they were shown an internal French memorandum according to which de Gaulle, following the end of the Algerian War, would not redeploy French forces to NATO, but rather create a mobile strike force for use anywhere in the world.[49] In a letter to de Gaulle of October 20, Eisenhower stated that the United States could not participate in any arrangement that gave other NATO allies the impression that major decisions were being made without them, and he noted that very serious problems would be raised by any projected extension of the geographical area covered by the NATO alliance. Eisenhower clearly had in mind North Africa, where he feared the French wanted to use the alliance to back their war in Algeria.

Prime Minister Macmillan's simultaneous reply to de Gaulle was somewhat different; he agreed that NATO as presently constituted did not meet the interests of members with concerns outside NATO's zone. Britain, like France, had its own imperial legacy, and was reluctant to take too strong a stand lest its position in its own areas of influence, Cyprus or Southern Rhodesia, for example, come under scrutiny and attack as well. More seriously, Britain desperately needed French cooperation in its plans to associate the Common Market with the projected Free Trade Association, thus preventing the establishment of a tight internal European trading bloc that would exclude British products. London's fears of a split in the West between adherents of the EEC and the FTA tended toward the apocalyptic, but it was vital not to alienate Paris, for "we are in French hands to a most uncomfortable degree."[50] On the other hand, neither could the British dissociate themselves from Washington, nor appear less pro-Arab than Washington with regard to Algeria. Dulles in fact warned Macmillan against any "deal" with the French that would trade off Paris's agreement on trade in exchange for a tripartite arrangement in NATO.[51] The Middle East also remained the source of Britain's oil supplies, and Whitehall felt equally dependent on the goodwill of the Arabs. Macmillan fell back on problems of a procedural order with the de Gaulle proposals: how would tripartism work?

Would it be in addition to or a substitute for NATO's present directing organs or other regional alliances in the world?[52]

State noted that the American military would never accept de Gaulle's notion of tripartite planning, it was impossible to satisfy French requests for nuclear cooperation, and any tripartite organization would be resented by other NATO allies. The best tactic was to find a counterproposal sufficiently impressive to keep de Gaulle in NATO, and meanwhile to agree to informal talks while seeking "clarifications" and raising problems with the French initiative. In other words, stall. But Dulles was unhappy with this suggestion; he feared that even informal and secret tripartite talks would destroy NATO. Macmillan insisted, however, and Dulles reluctantly agreed. The secretary told Alphand that informal and secret tripartite talks could begin in December.[53]

By no means everyone in the State Department thought de Gaulle so far off the mark in his proposals, however. Gerard C. Smith advised Dulles that rather than being interpreted as a threat of noncooperation with NATO, de Gaulle's proposals should be taken as a challenge to improve the alliance. France wanted a tripartite organization of the United States, the United Kingdom, and France to take joint political decisions concerning world security and the deployment and use of nuclear weapons. This was not unreasonable and the United States should at least acknowledge the basis for "a measure of tripartism" in the alliance, even if it could not legally accept a de jure change setting up a directorate. France could reasonably expect a role in NATO nuclear planning as it became a nuclear power, and it deserved recognition of its special importance with respect to the EEC and the West European Union. There was in fact an "inner core" of free world nations that bore exceptional responsibilities. Not only France but also Germany, Italy, and Japan would one day have to be brought into a special relationship with Britain and the United States recognizing their exceptional importance.[54]

If these recommendations remained ignored, it was largely because Washington's policy toward de Gaulle remained conditioned by the Algerian question that had brought him to power. De Gaulle's initial steps could not be peremptorily rejected, however, and preliminary talks based on the tripartite proposal were agreed to. The Americans also did not want to disrupt the constitutional referendum of September 28, 1958, in France and the associated elections, especially the election of Algerian deputies, which might be "significant steps in France's determination to work out a liberal solution." To be sure, it would all take time, but there had been "amazing progress" in political stabilization in France, and de

Gaulle alone "has a capability for solving France's number one problem which no other postwar government ever had." The Americans let their hopes run away with them, believing that de Gaulle had already initiated "indirect and confidential talks" with the FLN; Dulles told Alphand that he saw "glimmerings of a possible solution to the Algerian problem as a result of recent developments," and he commented that de Gaulle was facing the crisis with "vision and courage."[55] De Gaulle had offered the rebels a cease-fire and negotiations and he was seeking reputable Muslim deputies as a result of the elections with whom he could deal. In view of an impending favorable evolution of the Algerian question, therefore, Washington thought it was advisable to agree to exploratory talks on the September 18 memorandum, even if it was "quite doubtful" that the Americans could satisfy de Gaulle's overall aspirations.[56]

The discussions began in Washington on December 3, 1958. One can see clearly the French purpose in these discussions in the formal instructions sent by Couve de Murville to Ambassador Alphand, who was chosen as the French representative; Alphand was to "educate" the British and Americans about French concerns. France wanted a unified world strategy, including military planning, by the three Western powers, as opposed to existing NATO plans that were developed by the Americans alone and for Europe only.[57] There must be a reorganization of NATO's military command in the Mediterranean to take into account French interests in the defense of North Africa. De Gaulle demanded a national and not an integrated defense for political reasons; France's problems with its military, he said, stemmed in part from the army's insufficient consciousness of its role as the defender of France owing to the subordination of its operations to NATO. The Fourth Republic's inability to control its army was thus blamed on NATO's integrated command. As a first step, France would reorganize its Mediterranean naval command and withdraw its fleet from NATO.

Before the tripartite talks convened, on November 27, 1958, the Soviets issued their famous note demanding the internationalization and demilitarization of Berlin under the control of the German Democratic Republic. This would necessitate recognition of the GDR, which the allies firmly refused. The ensuing Berlin crisis dragged on until its culmination in the building of the wall in August 1961, and it paradoxically necessitated continued meetings of the three Western occupying powers to coordinate their response to the Soviets. The British and Americans were thus drawn, willy-nilly, into a rough re-creation of the postwar meetings of the late 1940s and a demonstration of the worldwide policy coordination de Gaulle appeared to have in mind. De Gaulle took a firm anti-Soviet line on the Berlin crisis that reassured Washington of his underlying loyalty to the West, but his rigid support of Adenauer separated him further from London and Washington. The British in particular wanted a more supple approach to Moscow based on negotiations.[58] Almost equally significant, in November 1958 British-French talks aimed at resolving the crisis between the Common Market and the British plan for a Free Trade Association broke down over French demands that the British accept a common agricultural policy and a joint external tariff, which London flatly refused to do. According to Couve de Murville, "We now arrived at the most critical stage in Franco-British relations since June 1940."[59]

The tripartite talks began against this troubled background. Alphand tried to explain de Gaulle's memo in a few basic points. NATO was no longer adequate to meet the needs of France, now like Britain and the United States a nuclear power with worldwide interests. Consequently the three Western powers must meet periodically to take common decisions on policy all over the world on the basis of equality, as they were already doing on Berlin. NATO military planning in the Mediterranean must be revised to take into account the primary French role on behalf of the alliance in the defense of North Africa.[60] What Alphand perforce left unsaid was against whom the reorganized Mediterranean command was to be directed. For London and Washington the enemy was communist, and perhaps Nasser-type subversion of the type that had led to the intervention in Lebanon in July 1958; for Paris it was the FLN, now claiming to be a provisional government of an independent Algeria.

That difference became clear in the fourth annual UN debate over Algeria, which reached its finale in December 1958. In 1957 France had got out of the UN debate in a satisfactory way when the Assembly simply expressed its desire for a peaceful and just solution based on the principles of the UN charter. De Gaulle's tactic in 1958 was to boycott the formal proceedings but work behind the scenes to influence France's friends in the hope of achieving an outcome similar to that of the year before. At bottom de Gaulle regarded the UN, much as he did NATO, as an American-run organization. When a compromise resolution calling for negotiations between the "two parties" in the dispute was tabled, the Americans looked on with seeming indifference, but the French reacted in fury because the reference to two parties implicitly placed the rebel "provisional government" on a par with the government of France. Washington, however, remained silent in the debate over the compromise and revealed its intentions to nobody before abstaining. Because the United States voted near last in alphabetical order, other delegations could not be influenced by the Americans in casting their own votes. The resolution came within a single vote of achieving the two-thirds majority needed for adoption, which the FLN regarded as a moral victory—all the more so when American delegates fraternized with them openly at a reception given in their honor by the Tunisian delegation.[61]

Washington explained that it had opposed an immoderate Arab-Asian resolution calling for Algerian independence that failed. The compromise reported out by the General Assembly contained nothing implying recognition of the Algerian provisional government and it was impossible for the Americans to oppose it, thus the decision to abstain. This was kept confidential in order not to encourage a shift by other delegations in favor of the resolution, and it was the decisive factor in the resolution's failure. Abstention did not mean approval. The American position was complicated by France's refusal to participate in the debates or appear in the plenary session, and a negative vote on the final resolution would have hurt American relations with the African and Arab states. America's Moroccan bases were also a consideration, but a negative vote might have been considered a vote against the right of the Algerian people to self-determination, a position that it was simply impossible for the Americans to take.[62]

Assistant Secretary for Europe Livingston Merchant was already upset over the "manifest deterioration" of American relations with France that he had observed during a visit to Paris in November, and he feared a "major blow-up." The UN debate, the activities of the FLN in the United States, the "Moroccanization" of U.S. bases in that country, the arming of Tunisia by Washington, the failure to back France in its ostracism of Guinea, which refused to join the revamped French Union, the questioning of France's administration of its trusteeship in the Cameroons—all these were already an "impressive list," even without disagreements over the September 17 memorandum, divergences over the Common Market, and the nuclear question. Merchant thought more positive American support for France in the UN essential; blocking membership for Guinea and progress on giving France a nuclear submarine, which Washington had promised but Congress was resisting, would also help. De Gaulle was described as having indulged in a "diatribe" against the United States in September on both Algeria and Guinea, and the French UN delegation thought it a "scandal" that

American delegates did not walk out of a Moroccan reception when the FLN entered. Such treatment of the French, Merchant warned, might have been normal under the Fourth Republic but would not be tolerated under the Fifth.[63] But Merchant's counsel did not prevail. Herter revealingly wrote to Dulles at the Paris Embassy in December that "It does seem that our friend should cease insisting upon attempting to control the whole world, of course with partners, even before he has gotten France itself in good order."[64]

Dulles came to Paris in December 1958 for a meeting of the NATO Council and met again with de Gaulle. The meeting was overshadowed by the Berlin crisis, and de Gaulle had just concluded successful negotiations with Adenauer whom he regarded as the key to his ambitions for the construction of a new French-led Europe. De Gaulle thus had a new mission, motivated by his concern to satisfy his new European partner— to pressure Washington into the firmest possible rejection of the Soviet demands on Berlin, even at the risk of war. De Gaulle told Dulles that there had been no connection between his September memorandum and the Soviet note, but the impending Berlin crisis had clearly revealed the inadequacy of coordination among the big three that the memorandum was designed to remedy. He repeated his complaints about the lack of American support for France: the American position on Algeria at the UN was "unclear" and the refusal to cooperate in the rejection of Guinea from the world body unsatisfactory. Both revealed the alliance's inadequacy; it no longer corresponded to the existing threat in the world from beyond Europe. The alliance must cover the Middle East and North Africa, at the least, but also sub-Saharan Africa. France, de Gaulle said, had just created a magnificent structure for the free world in the form of the French Community, now formally part of the constitution of the Fifth Republic, yet everyone's attention was focused on tiny Guinea's refusal to join it. Equally important, France was undertaking an immense operation, politically and economically, in the form of the Plan of Constantine, to transform Algeria with its vast natural resources into a state that would be associated with the West. If France abandoned Algeria, communism and anarchy would result.[65] Free elections had been held there in conjunction with the recent elections in France; independence must not now be brandished as a banner against the West. Independence might come one day to Algeria, but in cooperation with the West, not against it.

De Gaulle went on to lay out with elegant simplicity his conception of how the three-power direction of the alliance would work. The three must coordinate their policies throughout the world. As it was, France could be involved in a nuclear war growing out of events in the Pacific in which it was not involved; this was unacceptable. If the United States, Britain, and France had the same policies with regard to Tunisia and Morocco as in the Pacific, for example, those countries would remain stable and securely in the Western orbit instead of tending toward anarchy as they now were doing. Implied here but not said was that the Algerian rebellion would quickly fold up as well. There must be a common policy of the three major powers on Bizerte as well as on arming Tunisia, and that policy must be that of France. Similarly, the common policy in Latin America would be that of the Americans, the common policy in India that of the British, and so on.

De Gaulle was characteristically polite with Dulles, but the British found Premier Michel Debré "bitterly critical" of Washington, particularly respecting the UN vote. Debré spoke of the "unacceptability of an alliance in which France's main ally not only failed to support her in her Algerian policy but actually tripped her up." The British Embassy remarked on Debré's "rather hysterical" anti-Americanism and general malaise, which troubled Washington as well. In 1957, American Embassy officer Charles W. Yost warned that Debré was a "violent nationalist," with a longtime penchant for raising outcries along anti-American, anti-European, and anti–European integration lines.[66] Livingston Merchant called him a "faithful, ardent follower of the general, highly brilliant, nervous, emotional." Debré was believed to reflect the views of the general more accurately than anyone else. He opposed European integration, wanted a world role for NATO, and demanded 100 percent American backing for French policies in Algeria. "The US would undoubtedly have a difficult time dealing with such a nationalistic and highly mercurial Premier."[67]

As Debré assumed a personal role as irritant and gadfly in Franco-American relations, he did much to harm whatever chances de Gaulle might otherwise have had to gain American cooperation. His more rabid hard-line anti-Americanism and forceful unwillingness to compromise on Algeria stood in contrast to de Gaulle's greater display of courtesy toward the Americans generally, as well as to the general's perceived greater flexibility on Algeria. Debré thus reintroduced the disturbing sense of divided authority in France characteristic of the Fourth Republic that de Gaulle was supposed to have banished. Routine periodic visits by an American Embassy officer to French sub-Saharan Africa, hardly noticed by the French in the past, suddenly brought complaints of unauthorized "political contacts" for nefarious purposes. For Matthew Looram it was simply a matter of "this is the type of thing we can expect from now on from Debré." With regard to FLN officials in the United States, American officials noted nervously the "extreme seriousness de Gaulle and Debré attach to this question," but it was Debré who mentioned it two or three times a week.[68]

The British nervously noted that there was no apparent evolution in French Algerian policy since de Gaulle had come to power. Jebb minuted Macmillan on 23 September 1958 that the de Gaulle policy was the same "triptych" of Mollet: a cease-fire, elections, and then negotiations with those elected. The new projected Algerian statute placed Algeria in a French ensemble that precluded independence. Military pacification and economic investment were joint policies, both designed to win over the Muslim population to France, in effect the stick and the carrot. Jebb saw no grounds for optimism.[69] In early 1959 the Foreign Office found that things were no better. The general's policy still seemed predicated on total victory in Algeria and the imposition of French terms. Worldwide cooperation with France therefore meant accepting an Algerian policy that "is leading towards a major disaster for France and the West in North Africa." A. Michael Palliser in the British Embassy in Paris advocated pressing the French harder on Algeria even at the price of greater cooperation between the two countries and British association with the Common Market. The Algerian "cancer" was poisoning the French system and the cohesion of the Atlantic alliance. The Foreign Office agreed: "we do not really approve of France's North Africa policy and such support as we give is merely that of a good ally." But nobody was willing to pressure the French; there simply was no conceivable solution for Algeria in sight at the moment and London had none to offer. Not knowing what to do, the Foreign Office did nothing.[70]

But the French demonstrated in short order that a policy of doing nothing would not suffice. In 1959 the tripartite talks got down to serious business. The Far East was discussed on February 5, and Africa from April 16 through April 21. In March, France withdrew its fleet from the NATO integrated Mediterranean command. Couve de Murville declared that the task of the French fleet was the defense of France's North African shores and to guarantee transit between North Africa and metropolitan France. "It is not admissible that this task be a part British and part American responsibility, when in addition several other political problems are at issue with our allies, and their policy with regard to Algeria...is not at all similar to our own." French demands could be reduced to three basic issues, according to Couve de Murville: tripartite cooperation on world strategy, tripartite decisions on the use of nuclear weapons, and the reshaping of naval organization in the western Mediterranean, the last a veiled way of saying that France must be supported by the alliance in Algeria.[71] Couve de Murville refused suggestions that these might be separable or that any one or two were more fundamental than the others.

Herter told Alphand that Eisenhower was visibly upset by the withdrawal of the French fleet, especially given the Berlin crisis in response to which the unity of the allies appeared to him all the more necessary for psychological reasons. Alphand replied by deploring that "we cannot unfortunately testify to a perfect identity of views between us on the policy to follow in Algeria." He complained again about the American abstention in the UN the previous December and the "inadmissible" nature of the relations between American diplomats and FLN representatives in New York, implying that de Gaulle had been motivated by anger over these questions. There followed a bewildering variety of further explanations from Paris: de Gaulle was angry at the UN vote, or upset over the Algerian election results, or he needed to show the partisans of integration that France would not abandon Algeria. The decision had little but symbolic significance in any case since France would still cooperate in NATO.[72] But all the explanations boiled down to one. The action on the fleet was not so much about the "independence" of France as it was about Algeria. Alphand returned to this point again and again with American officials.

The State Department understood de Gaulle's "fixation with Algeria" and his rage at the U.S. abstention in the UN but concluded that there was little that could be done. Nor should the rebels necessarily be kept out of the United States: "it is clear we would not accept any comments from the French on the application of U.S. laws."[73] De Gaulle told Houghton that consequently France had to look after its North African interests alone, since these were no longer a NATO responsibility. Debré added that Algeria was "fundamental": the French fleet looked after vital Western interests but the fleet could not be shared with NATO unless the Algerian problem were shared as well. France must either be supported or it must keep separate. De Gaulle repeated it once again: the fleet was a matter of vital importance to French Algerian policy. Since there was no common policy for French North Africa in NATO, and since NATO refused to cover North Africa, "we have a problem to discuss in Washington." This was a distinct charge of bad faith, since Algeria was legally covered by the terms of the NATO treaty as signed in 1949. Eisenhower was all the more annoyed, feeling that the crisis could have been avoided had the French fleet earlier been granted equality with the British and American fleets in the Mediterranean within the confines of the alliance.

On March 19, in a personal letter to de Gaulle, Eisenhower limited himself to noting the "unfortunate psychological and political repercussions" of the French decision, which risked creating the impression of division within the Atlantic alliance. He agreed that there should be equality for the French fleet in the Mediterranean. On March 22, the United States notified France that it was ready to discuss Africa in the tripartite talks in Washington.[74] Jebb reported, however, that Debré was firmly in control of France's Algerian policy, and there could be no question of negotiations with the FLN, nor could French sovereignty in Algeria be questioned by anyone.

The Quai sent further instructions for the Washington talks: France wanted a Eurafrican zone of defense centered on the Mediterranean and North Africa. NATO was insufficient to meet this challenge, which had to be taken up by the big three. The same principles should apply in North Africa as elsewhere; one of the great powers must be responsible for security in the name of the others, with which it would consult regularly. "But the government is especially emphatic that these principles be applied in a region of the world in which French responsibilities are predominant." The directing role of France in the western Mediterranean, the Maghreb, and Black Africa must be recognized by its allies and the military commands in these regions consigned to French authorities.[75] Joxe was faithful to these points when the talks finally took place: Algeria was one of the "*pièces maîtresses*" of the French presence in Africa, and no bilateral negotiations were possible there since it was under French sovereignty. France recognized the independence of Tunisia and Morocco but must be exclusively responsible for their defense and maintain bases there, in particular Bizerte, and the Sahara was a "French creation." There must be a united military approach by the West to Africa, a solid structure of defense stretching from the western Mediterranean to the Congo in which the primary responsibility would be that of France. This would require the reorganization of NATO and the construction of new forms of military cooperation among the big three and France's NATO allies.[76]

These were not forthcoming from France's partners. Rather than be involved in France's North African problems, the Americans suggested to the British a combined effort to "circumvent French demands for military approval of their views, policies, or strategic plans for Africa."[77] Merchant wrote Dulles that the tripartite talks were "useful," but they could not be formalized as the French wished. The French could be supported in efforts to keep Guinea from going communist, and FLN members would not be received in the department for the present, but they could not be deported or denied visas. The United States preferred that the French give arms aid to Morocco and Tunisia, but if they failed to do so the United States would continue to arm them itself. The United States would sell France enriched uranium fuel, but it needed a decision on storage rights on French territory for nuclear weapons. The latter was the most important for Washington because nine air force squadrons stationed in France for NATO were of limited usefulness without the stockpiling of nuclear weapons there.[78]

De Gaulle sought to prod his partners further. He categorically refused to stockpile American nuclear weapons in France failing a French veto on the terms and conditions under which they could be used. Herter told Debré that he was disturbed; without stockpiling, the nine USAF squadrons stationed in France would be moved elsewhere. Debré replied that de Gaulle's answer must be seen in the context of a solution to three problems in the alliance: the September 18 memorandum regarding tripartite consultations; the lack of support for France and its interests in the Mediterranean, Algeria, and Africa; and progress in atomic cooperation. Amplifying the second point, Debré said that France had as much of a future in the Mediterranean and North Africa as in Europe; it must square its responsibilities in both areas in conjunction with the United States. The events of May 1958, Debré said, had been caused in part by the lack of understanding of France's Algerian policy on the part of its allies, and "the lack of a Western policy for Algeria." Perhaps France had never adequately explained how important the Mediterranean and Africa were to it; if that was the case, Debré was doing so now. French support for the alliance depended on the alliance's support for France in the Mediterranean and Africa, because "Algeria is as vital to France as anything in Europe."[79]

Herter reported to Eisenhower this "unpleasant" meeting with Debré. Herter thought the French could perhaps be satisfied on the tripartite talks, although not on nuclear aid; but Debré also wanted the acceptance of his Algerian policy, stating that Algeria was as important to the security of France as was an adequate solution to the Berlin crisis. Eisenhower lamented that his hands were tied on nuclear cooperation, and that the French persisted in regarding Algeria as part of France. Could the alliance be sustained in the face of these difficulties? Of course it was no help that de Gaulle had a "messiah complex," picturing himself as a cross between Joan of Arc and Napoleon. Roosevelt had made the same observation. But Herter said that French commitments in Algeria were simply "infeasible" for the alliance to take on. Eisenhower expressed his understanding of why the French regarded Algeria as part of France, and drew a parallel to a situation in which Alaska or Hawaii, now states, sought independence from the United States. But he did not imply that the United States should support France in Algeria.[80]

As long as de Gaulle showed solidarity with Washington on core Western issues, especially Berlin, Washington was reluctant to press him on Algeria. France's hard line on Berlin was self-interested but important; somehow it must be got across to the French that sabotage of NATO helped neither their national objectives nor the U.S.-French relationship. There was irony in de Gaulle's willingness to fight over Berlin, moreover, when few French troops were deployed in Germany because of Algeria. But de Gaulle was solid on East-West relations; he recognized U.S. primacy in the Far East, and the United States granted his dominant interests in North Africa. But did it? "De Gaulle knows that if we wanted to, we could give him far greater satisfaction than we have to date in meeting his requests." If the United States gave him "real partnership" status in world policies and military strategy, perhaps other problems would be more easily solved. But the United States and United Kingdom could not grant the tripartite arrangement he wanted, and legislative authority was lacking to give him nuclear aid. It was doubtful that the president could get it even if he pushed hard, but he would not do so in any case. The United States would not compromise its security to the extent of granting tripartite control of its nuclear strategy. As for Anglo-American recognition of the French preeminent role in Africa, "We cannot give him this and maintain our own interests in North Africa."[81]

On March 30, 1959, Merchant told Alphand that contacts with the Algerian rebels would cease for now, but this did not preclude "chance encounters." Alphand professed to be gratified.[82] But this gesture was hardly enough. The issue culminated in a furious letter by Debré to Herter in which he again complained that "our alliance does not extend to North Africa." Debré was angered by a report of Jones's flattering attention to Bourguiba and private confidences to him about American differences with France. American arms and financial aid were replacing France in Tunis, Debré said, and embassy officials openly carried on relations with representatives of the FLN there. Jones openly displayed his anticolonialist prejudice while professing a desire for a Franco-Tunisian entente, and he wanted France to understand that Tunisian aid to the FLN was "inevitable." Jones had made it clear that while claiming not to want to substitute themselves for France in Tunisia the Americans were in fact doing so. On Algeria it was clear that the United States believed the FLN had to be part of any solution, which meant independence; Washington's chief concern was encouraging FLN moderation and anticommunism, not a settlement of the question on French terms. The Americans should understand, Debré wrote, that "in behaving in this way, they bring indirectly moral encouragement to the rebellion, and that their attitude could definitely lead to prolonging the war in Algeria."[83]

Debré warned Washington that American ties to the Algerian rebels "will separate us from one another." The Americans should not be "seduced by young nationalisms," Debré lectured, at the price of abandoning its allies and opening the way to communism. The issue in Algeria was liberty versus Marxist enslavement for the Algerian people. It was inconceivable for France not to be supported on this issue.[84] France, despite Berlin, would continue to make Algeria the main item of American and NATO concern. The State Department was astonished that so small a matter as FLN activities in the United States could become the critical issue in U.S.-French relations. The French seemed really to believe that the rebellion was on its last legs and only kept alive by such trivial examples of foreign support.[85] State now divided on what to do: the European desk wanted to accommodate the French, but the African desk refused. Three Algerian youth leaders were requesting a trip to the United States that would "maintain western ties with North African youth movements." These leaders were not Communists, and Moroccans and Tunisians might not come to the United States if the Algerians did not. Senators Fulbright, Kennedy, and Humphrey rallied to their cause, and the youth leaders were admitted.[86] But French protests were increasingly vociferous. In May 1959, obviously peeved at the failure of the tripartite talks to produce anything, Debré brought the Algerian visits to the attention of Dulles; the two had "an extremely difficult and disturbing conversation," and Debré appeared to link the issue to American requests that France consent to nuclear stockpiling on its territory. The Americans regarded this as an "implicit blackmail threat" and communicated their concerns to London. Debré had lost all sense of proportion on the issue; State thought the terms of his letter to Houghton "unfortunate" and noted that he was "highly and continually exercised by the activities of the FLN in New York." Every time that Chanderli had a letter in *The New York Times,* the French Embassy got a tough instruction from the Quai to protest. Verbal replies apparently did not "sink in" with Debré; a full letter would be necessary amplifying American policy.[87] Reports of private Debré conversations with his subordinates came to the embassy as well: Debré was said to believe that had the Americans not granted visas to Yazid and the Algerian youth leaders, the FLN might have collapsed. Twice in ten minutes he said the Americans had "even hoisted the Algerian flag over Carnegie Hall." There were three perils to Europe, Debré claimed, the Kremlin, the Arabs, and "our American friends." Of course this did not stop Debré from welcoming American investment in France; his government was the most favorable toward American investment in fact since the war.[88]

De Gaulle wrote to Eisenhower on May 25, 1959. His purpose, he said, was to explain certain French defense measures and to reaffirm the French commitment to the North Atlantic Treaty Organization. His intent was clearly to resolve the questions of the Mediterranean fleet and nuclear stockpiling. The problem, de Gaulle said, was that the Atlantic alliance had no policy beyond Europe, whereas the threat to world security was more "Oriental or African." France would therefore set up an independent command for the Mediterranean and Black Africa. On nuclear weapons de Gaulle noted that "America intends to keep her secrets vis-à-vis France...France reserves for herself the total decision to use or not to use the nuclear weapons which she has." The alliance automatically exposed France to immediate and total destruction, and France "obviously cannot entirely entrust her life or death to any other state whatsoever, even the most friendly." Until France could participate in decisions on nuclear matters, it would reject any storage of nuclear weapons on its territory unless it could exercise direct control over their use. The letter invited President Eisenhower to come to Paris for further discussions.[89]

But it was clear that even threats carried out were not sufficient to shake the Americans out of their North African policies. Despite further French protests, Algerians continued to come to the United States on visas issued by other Arab countries. Paris professed not to understand, but the Americans took the position that a passport, by whomever issued, in due and legal form, had to be honored. Paris did what it could to honor Washington's request to prevent the screening of *Hiroshima Mon Amour* in Japan, but Washington would not do anything about the FLN in New York.[90] On June 30, the French were informed that the United States expected a request from Morocco to purchase arms, which it would fulfill. On July 14, Paris protested the contemplated sale of another American shipment of rifles to Tunisia: the Tunisians needed no more than 3,000 but Washington planned to ship 8,000. But had not Paris agreed once in principle that Tunisia needed a 20,000-man army? This was the U.S. view, it was reasonable, and anyway it was a political decision: the United States did not wish to displease Bourguiba.[91]

The United States remained torn between its need for France in Europe and its criticism of France in Africa. On July 10, 1959, Merchant, at the European desk, complained to Herter that it was of no use to mollify the Africans and Asians over Algeria, because this only hurt relations with France, which was more important. Moreover, it was now clear that de Gaulle alone was capable of obtaining peace in Algeria, and it was essential that the Americans not do anything that might impede his efforts in that direction. The Algerian question in France was not a matter of government policy but one of survival because even de Gaulle could not maintain his position without a firm stand on Algeria. France must at the least be supported in the United Nations. But from the State Department's African desk Assistant Secretary Joseph Satterthwaite replied that "we cannot bind ourselves to defend the French," and Eisenhower decided the issue for the moment by stating that "we cannot support colonialism...we will not gain strength for the west by letting the French and the Germans walk on us."[92]

In August 1959 the American Embassy mentioned to the Foreign Ministry its unhappiness with the content of two Debré speeches during which he had again demanded full American support for France's Algerian policy, and referred to France as "crushed between two great powers," presumably the United States and the USSR. In Washington French officials said "the last straw" for Debré was the American sale of arms to Morocco, but Paris was equally exercised about Tunisia and instructed its embassy to warn the Americans "solemnly" of the political and psychological effects on French opinion, which would not understand "that the concerns of its government were not taken into consideration nor its proposals accepted" in Washington.[93] Lodge also reported that the UN situation was "grim," the outlook being for a repeat of the previous year, with a reference in the resolution to Algerian independence this time likely. In Paris, Gérard Amanrich told American

Embassy officer Cecil Lyon that Debré felt this issue emotionally and that de Gaulle agreed with him; both were finding opposition to their Algerian policy everywhere, in the American and the French press alike, and they felt that they were misunderstood. Lyon said this was perhaps because the policy was not clear: "if they could ever indicate in due course Algeria's right to self-determination this would help a great deal." Lyon remarked on the American difficulty with France at a time when France was again strong, but added diplomatically that "I would rather have a strong France, with difficulties, than the France of before." Amanrich professed surprise; not all the allies agreed. Suddenly he hinted that there might indeed be an Algerian plan in Paris after all, but de Gaulle wanted first to tell Eisenhower himself.[94]

General Norstad in fact noted to Eisenhower his hopes that de Gaulle in August 1959 was toying with a statement endorsing a fundamental change of policy in Algeria. De Gaulle planned to go to the people and win them away from a "peace by force" to a liberal solution. Norstad, like Lyon, clearly had word of de Gaulle's coming statement endorsing self-determination on September 16, and they advised Eisenhower to emphasize that the United States supported the rule of law, negotiations, and not the use of force to settle the Algerian problem. Eisenhower said the French must be made to understand the "depth" of American anticolonial sentiment.[95] Was de Gaulle's statement indeed made with Washington and the United Nations in mind? French decisions on Algeria were to have a way of occurring in the autumns of 1958, 1959, and 1960 as the UN General Assembly session loomed. In 1958 it was the offer of a "Peace of the Brave," in 1959 the offer of self-determination for Algeria, and in 1960 the decision to negotiate exclusively with the FLN. But behind each of these turnings there was also evident American exasperation and pressure, combined with an apparent willingness in Washington to carry out Paris's worst fears: abandon it to its devices in Algeria while stepping in to "save" Tunisia and Morocco for the West by replacing France in those countries as it had done in Vietnam. Under these conditions, de Gaulle understood, there was no hope of France holding on to Algeria either. France simply did not have the strength.

A lengthy discussion of American policy toward Algeria occurred in the National Security Council on August 18, 1959. President Eisenhower's visit to Paris in response to de Gaulle's invitation had been scheduled for early September. The NSC was split over Algeria; the Joint Chiefs' position was to throw support to France in an effort to save the alliance, in short to "get off the dime." If the United States backed and encouraged de Gaulle the issue might be resolved. But Eisenhower could not accept this. How could the United States support France and not damage its interests? Its history was anticolonial and France was colonialist; such a policy would "cut ourselves from our moorings, it was an adventurous idea." The French had already given independence to Tunisia and Morocco and they had no justification for withholding it from Algeria. Dillon said the United States would support an "equitable solution" in Algeria, but Eisenhower countered that that meant *not* supporting de Gaulle. The United States had sent arms to Tunisia because "we can't give France a blackmail power over our relations with independent nations." Dillon noted that the United States did not know the French position on Algeria or even whether France had a position. Algeria could not be treated separately or traded for support on other issues, even Berlin; support for France on Algeria would sacrifice important U.S. interests around the world. Eisenhower then demonstrated his grasp of de Gaulle's intent: the French president had refused to stockpile nuclear weapons and withdrawn his naval forces from NATO "to force us to support his views" in Algeria. But the United States would not be blackmailed "by de Gaulle or anyone else."[96]

At the same time, de Gaulle opened up for discussion in his own cabinet the possibility of offering self-determination to Algeria. This spectacular turn in French policy in September 1959 appears the direct consequence of de Gaulle's failure thus far to enlist the Americans in support of his Algerian policy. He would make a last-ditch effort to win American approval and blunt the hostility of the UN. The step was also taken in recognition of the failure of French efforts to isolate the Gouvernement Provisoire de la République Algérienne (GPRA), which was gaining the diplomatic recognition of more and more countries around the world. The French military were encouraged to understand the statement as motivated by foreign policy considerations. In August the general went to Algeria and met with top military officers, telling them that all the peoples of the earth were in the process of liberating themselves. "We must not, therefore, act in Algeria except for Algeria and with Algeria in such a way that the world understands it."[97] De Gaulle still refused to deal with the FLN or GPRA, however, and he authorized General Challe to tell the army it was still fighting for *Algérie française.*[98]

But with regard to the Americans France had made its best effort thus far and failed. From the moment of de Gaulle's seizure of power he had understood that the continued fate of empire in the postwar world

depended first on reform and second on the United States. Like his predecessors, he believed that a France aligned with Britain and the United
States in a three-power directorate entrusted with the fate of the "free
world" would be a France positioned to maintain its hegemony in the
Mediterranean and Africa. Such a France would be able to keep Algeria
French and thus remain the preeminent African power. But without
Washington this grandiose dream could not be realized. In de Gaulle's
eyes Washington had a great deal to gain from such an arrangement. A
fully cooperating France and Britain, their former colonies firmly behind them in federal arrangements, and the three nuclear powers with
shared military strategies and commitments of mutual support around
the world, would be impregnable to the communist or any other threat.
In its effort to achieve a similar concept, the Fourth Republic had often
enough warned Washington that it was willing to abandon the Atlantic
alliance if not satisfied. But it never could achieve sufficient internal stability and bureaucratic control to be taken seriously in Washington or
London. De Gaulle thought he had solved these problems. He had restored the power of the French state, achieved internal financial and political stability, constructed a new federal structure in French Africa,
and begun to build a new Algeria firmly tied to France. The measures of
his seriousness lay in the Challe plan to destroy the rebels and the Plan
of Constantine to bring Algeria economically up to the level of France,
to demonstrate that France was and would remain, in every sense, an
African power. Finally, through reason, in the three-power talks, and
through threats, in the almost hysterical pleadings and warnings of
Debré, de Gaulle had sought to rally Washington, London, and the rest
of Europe behind him. He had forced a rethinking in Washington. But
he had nonetheless failed. President Eisenhower would not share his
strategic vision and consequently neither would the British. Lurking behind the refusal of both was the danger that if the war was excessively
prolonged, the Americans would actively intervene to end it.[99]

This realization lay behind the famous turning point of September
16, 1959, in which de Gaulle announced that he would offer the Algerians a choice—genuine self-determination, in the form of integration;
association with France in a federal arrangement; or independence,
which he termed "secession." It was clear from de Gaulle's rhetoric
which choice he hoped and expected the Algerians to make, and he still
meant to resist the FLN's claim to hegemony in Algeria, where he
wanted to achieve "as French" a solution as possible. De Gaulle's
change in policy, if it was that, was not yet sufficient: he would need to

recognize the FLN's provisional government if he genuinely wanted to end the war. Even after recognizing Algeria's right to self-determination, he meant to continue his futile search for more moderate nationalists amenable to his Eurafrican vision. But absent American support he recognized that he could not achieve his "grand design." The rest of his diplomatic career would be devoted to demonstrating that in the absence of French cooperation, neither could Washington or London achieve theirs.

Eisenhower met with de Gaulle in Paris on September 2. De Gaulle announced that France and Germany had reconciled their differences and he was seeking "ever closer action between the two countries," and France would go ahead with European economic unity and political cooperation. Eisenhower expressed his pleasure. In Africa de Gaulle said he was implementing self-determination and had begun to do so in the community. Guinea alone had chosen independence, presumably because Sekou Touré was a communist. Eisenhower doubted this and said the Guinean leader would come to Washington in October. In Algeria de Gaulle recalled France's presence for 130 years and the population of Europeans in excess of one million; it was a complex problem, as if the United States had "40 million Indians in California." Algeria had never been a state like Tunisia and Morocco, but de Gaulle had now decided that it "should have the right to decide its own future." When the rebellion was over, the Algerians would be offered the choice between being "100% French, [having] a certain autonomy, or complete independence." De Gaulle would announce this within two weeks, but he would not recognize the FLN, a group which existed through terror and which wanted to lead the country to "totalitarian communism." Algeria was an internal problem which could not be discussed in the UN, and de Gaulle hoped the United States would not repeat its abstention of the previous year; he emphasized how important he regarded this issue for the future of French-U.S. relations.

Eisenhower said France should present its case in the UN. If France was to move toward self-determination in Algeria, the United States would react with the greatest sympathy. He wanted to go with France, but he cited the American "anti-colonial tradition" and opposition to the use of force to solve problems. The president was happy, however, at last to hear of a "courageous and realistic" French program for Algeria. But de Gaulle now drew for Eisenhower the consequences of the program he had just outlined. De Gaulle favored NATO, but its military integration took away the feeling of responsibility for their own defense of its members, and its European focus ignored French concerns in the Mediterranean and North Africa. Eisenhower said he thought any nation's forces standing alone, even those of Washington, were insufficient to meet the communist threat. De Gaulle said the Anglo-American nuclear monopoly could commit France to nuclear war without France being consulted; Eisenhower countered that the United States would never act without consultation except in the case of a surprise attack on itself. Eisenhower would be happy to study world strategy jointly with de Gaulle and Macmillan, but he could not institutionalize this against the rest of NATO. Would de Gaulle like a direct phone line to the White House? De Gaulle did not reply. He said that France would build thermonuclear weapons after it had advanced sufficiently in its atomic program. Eisenhower made no objection, but only regretted that he could not help the French nuclear program. U.S. legislation opposing the disclosure of nuclear information was a mistake which ran "counter to common sense," but France could only get assistance after expending a great deal of money and time and after itself detonating nuclear weapons. He regretted this but could not get round it. De Gaulle remarked simply that he was not asking for anything.[100]

With French Prime Minister Debré and the foreign ministers present in the afternoon, the talks took on a sharper edge. Debré warned that if there were divergent policies in the UN over Algeria between the United States and France "there would be a serious break" in relations. Herter said that when the French program for Algeria was known, perhaps the American dilemma in the UN would be easier. Eisenhower asked for an indication of the French program in its specifics, perhaps for inclusion in a joint statement by the two countries, but de Gaulle refused. Eisenhower then noted the U.S. commitment to NATO: six divisions in Europe, which had never been reduced because of the desire to contribute to European solidarity but also "because French forces had unfortunately been withdrawn from NATO for Algeria. Therefore the questions of NATO and Algeria were linked." Debré agreed, of course; this was the French argument, that Algeria and the Mediterranean were part of the European security concept. Each drew separate conclusions from this rare moment of agreement, however. Later, in the presence only of his interpreter, Vernon Walters, Eisenhower observed to de Gaulle that it would be helpful if provocative French criticism of the United States over Algeria could be avoided. De Gaulle said he did not control the press. Eisenhower said he was not referring to the press, clearly implying that he meant Debré. De Gaulle smiled, nodded, and said "I understand, I'll bear in mind what you have said."[101] The next day de Gaulle observed that France had once been great and wealthy; it was no longer so, and this was difficult for it to bear. If strident voices were occasionally raised, he hoped the president would understand. Was this a hint that de Gaulle was powerless to control Debré, whose presence as premier was a necessity to assuage the French Algeria lobby and the army? Eisenhower assured de Gaulle that no bitter public words would ever come from his own administration. Despite de Gaulle's attempt to paint his regime as the restorer of order and stability to France, he was unable to give the same assurances in return. Far from demonstrating any new French stability, the offer of self-determination was to lead to a revolt of the army in Algeria against de Gaulle the following January.

Eisenhower wrote Macmillan that he thought the talks had gone well. U.S. support for France's Algerian policy, however, had still appeared to be uppermost in de Gaulle's mind. Eisenhower had told de Gaulle that he hoped the French would make such support possible, and de Gaulle replied that he would make a statement on Algeria that he was confident the United States and United Kingdom could support. The American Embassy in Paris rated the visit an "unqualified success," and a "personal triumph" for the president. De Gaulle had been gracious and relaxed (even if Debré had not been). But the American attitude following de Gaulle's statement on Algeria would be the real test of American intentions.[102]

CHAPTER SEVEN

De Gaulle Reconsidered

In the period between his coming to power in May 1958 and his concession of the principle of self-determination in Algeria in September 1959, de Gaulle attempted to enlist the cooperation of the United States, Britain, and NATO in a policy designed to keep Algeria for France, in exchange for which France would collaborate in a British-American-French triumvirate to guide the policy of NATO and police the rest of the so-called free world. It is not at all clear, moreover, as this chapter will attempt to demonstrate, that de Gaulle fully abandoned that policy in September 1959. Although granting the principle of self-determination, de Gaulle clearly intended to keep Algeria in some kind of tight "association" with France, while he continued to pursue the elusive goal of constructing a "Eurafrican" federal ensemble with Paris at its core. In 1960 de Gaulle continued to try to get agreement to his "directorate," but shifted his emphasis from Anglo-Saxon cooperation to the effort to build a "Europe of states" on his own terms. He believed that with the Anglo-Americans at his side he could achieve the full integration of Algeria; failing that, with the less powerful but still impressive cooperation of Europe in French policies, he might still convince the Algerians of the advantages of association. Only when it became clear that he would achieve neither his big-three triumvirate nor his Europe of states, did he accept the reality of what he may have understood all along: that left to its own efforts, surrounded by a hostile world, France would be forced to grant Algeria independence.

All this goes ignored in the almost official orthodoxy that pervades contemporary French diplomatic historiography, according to which Charles de Gaulle was the founder of a new French independence and the creator of a virtual revolution in French diplomacy.[1] According to this view, de Gaulle's September 1958 memorandum reflected the return of stability in French political institutions, the achievement of economic equilibrium, and the consequent projection in world affairs of a new French assertiveness. The culmination of this policy, based on the creation of a French nuclear force, came in 1966 when France withdrew from NATO's integrated command. According to Frédéric Bozo, de Gaulle offered NATO a competing vision of how to organize the alliance, based on a concerted European policy and an independent European (French) deterrent in partnership with Washington, rather than the existing American-dominated "empire by invitation." Paradoxically, Bozo argues, the measured American response to de Gaulle's challenge, the refusal of polemic, the continuation of cordial relations despite disagreement, and increased consultation in the alliance actually strengthened NATO and made the Europeans more willing to accept American leadership. The "14 + 1" formula was thus an improvement over the integrated 15, even if de Gaulle was unable to win over the other Europeans to the rejection of American hegemony and the creation of an independent European policy.[2]

It is also claimed that de Gaulle's challenge went further than the declaration of French independence, and was ahead of its time, as became evident with the collapse of communism some thirty years later. For the French statesman saw beyond the bipolar world of his day to an independent world in which national states would once again assert themselves peacefully and in concert, allowing the construction of a Europe "from the Atlantic to the Urals." The definitive statement of this view is to be found in Maurice Vaïsse's *La Grandeur,* the title of which sets forth the message. Vaïsse, while paying due attention to elements of continuity in de Gaulle's policy with that of the Fourth Republic, nevertheless credits de Gaulle with a "Copernican revolution" in French diplomacy. The political and financial stability, prestige, authority, and determination with which de Gaulle endowed French policy constituted one element of this revolution, but more important was his way of pursuing French independence. Real self-determination for France in the postwar world required a change in the status quo and a new international equilibrium beyond Cold War politics. Once this was achieved, with France leading the way, an end of the bipolar world based on mutual assured destruction would become possible, and in time communism would be revealed as a superficial veneer masking the deeper reality of the national traditions of the countries in which it ruled, allowing them to join the West in a new world system of peace and equality.[3] De Gaulle was a prophet in advance of his time.

It is true that the idea of a Europe of nation-states reasserting itself was basic to the Gaullist vision. But Gaullist historians further argue that de Gaulle had first to deal with the messy Algerian situation before engaging in his policy of "grandeur." For Vaïsse, the policy of French independence could only be rhetorical from 1958 to 1962, but became real thereafter. So long as de Gaulle remained hampered by the Algerian albatross, France could not assume its normal role in world affairs. The general therefore is alleged to have proceeded carefully and methodically toward Algerian independence, understanding that it was in the best interests of France, but going only as quickly as the military situation and public opinion would permit. But the Algerian crisis brought de Gaulle back to power in May 1958, and the military rebels and colons who supported him did so with the understanding that he would preserve *Algérie française*, something, according to this view, that he had no intention of doing. For de Gaulle's historical vision allegedly extended to colonial affairs as well as to European and world politics. He understood that colonial empires were a thing of the past.[4] He had no intention of trying to integrate Algeria's nine million Muslims with the rest of the French nation.[5] Instead he systematically set about finding a way to separate Algeria from France while restoring the military to obedience to civil authority and preserving the rights of the one million colons of European origin. It took him four years to accomplish this, but once France granted Algeria its independence and rid itself of its legacy of the colonial past, he was finally free to embark upon his worldwide political design. Most treatments of de Gaulle's diplomatic policies grant Algeria and the whole subject of the decolonization of France in Africa a separate chapter if they deal with it at all, thus emphasizing its purportedly marginal, anachronistic character.[6] De Gaulle's policies are seen in conceptual and chronological sequence. First de Gaulle had to rid France of its colonial burden, strengthen the executive and restore political and financial stability, and establish the internal foundation of his external policy. Only then was he truly free to challenge American hegemony while transforming France into the spokesman for the aspirations of the nations of the so-called Third World for development and equality.[7] According to this view, 1962 was the turning point in de Gaulle's diplomacy, the point at which, Algeria behind him, he was able to chart an independent role for France in world affairs.

A corollary of this view sees French modernization and consumerism as a substitute for empire. The rapid economic takeoff France achieved in the 1960s tended in retrospect to validate the theory known as Cartierisme, for the editor of *Paris-Match* who popularized it: colonies in the long run cost more than they were worth and only by ridding itself of them could the nation achieve its full economic potential. Once free of Algeria and the empire, France could join the consumer society, modernize its army with nuclear weapons, and chart an independent course in world affairs. Algeria was an albatross, and de Gaulle once observed to Alain Peyrefitte that getting rid of it was perhaps the greatest service he had rendered France in his career.[8]

Some historians have argued, however, that the opposition between imperialism and modernization is artificial; in fact, the two were integrally related. It is not accidental that the years of the Algerian War were years of economic growth and prosperity in France. Kristin Ross has tried to integrate France's decolonization experience with its economic takeoff into consumerism. In *Fast Cars, Clean Bodies: Decolonization and the Reordering of French Culture,* she argues that French colonialism and Fordist modernization were linked; colonialism outlived its imperial history and was internalized by the development of consumer culture and modernization. Decolonization helped make the economic takeoff possible by bringing hundreds of thousands of low-wage immigrant workers to France, and then one million displaced colons from Algeria, in the process helping to create the conditions for the French economic boom of the 1960s and the contemporary problems of immigrant exclusion and racism. Ross is no doubt right about this, if wrong-headed in other respects; it is less obvious that consumer goods transformed women into household dependents analogous to the Algerian "native," or that the newly discovered very American concern for hygiene and cleanliness was related to the notion of France cleaning up its Algerian home. There was not necessarily a dialectical relationship between the accoutrements of modernization from electrical wires to the kitchen sink and their alternative use in electrical charges on genitals and the submerging of heads under water in the process of torture.[9] But no matter; Ross has posed the problem of the relationship between decolonization and French modernization and consumerism while Philip Dine has done a brilliant and sensitive job of demonstrating the relationship of the Algerian War to French fiction and film.[10]

If Algeria was at the basis of French economic development and culture, as these writers claim, how much more significant must it have been to a proper understanding of French diplomacy? My contention here is that the Algerian War is crucial to the interpretation of French diplomatic initiatives and their reception by the Anglo-Saxon powers and NATO before 1962 and after. This was understood by Edward Kolodziej in his very fine study, *French International Policy Under de Gaulle and Pompidou*. Barely hidden below de Gaulle's September 18, 1958, memorandum to Prime Minister Macmillan and President Eisenhower, Kolodziej says, were Algeria and the atomic bomb. De Gaulle wanted nuclear secrets from the United States and support for his Algerian policy from both Anglo-Saxon powers in exchange for French support of their policies in other parts of the world. "A common policy [of the big three] in North Africa would necessarily be a French policy," French diplomats never tired of repeating.[11] One can take Kolodziej's analysis much further, however. De Gaulle had more than just Algeria or the atomic bomb in mind, important as these were. If 1962 was a watershed, it was because it marked the collapse of a bold three-pronged effort by de Gaulle to reorder world affairs, with a new place for France in the whole, at the basis of which lay his vision of an Algeria closely associated with, indeed dominated by, France in a neocolonial relationship. In pursuing this policy de Gaulle adopted as his own the foreign policy of the Fourth Republic he despised. As had been true of Mollet, for de Gaulle France's transformed relationship with Algeria was to be the key to the French community, the basis for French leadership in Europe, and the foundation in turn of a new relationship of French equality with Britain and the United States. Far from a policy of "independence," this was a formula for the increased involvement of the "Anglo-Saxons" in French affairs and the ordering of relations among the big three on the basis of an ever greater interdependence.

De Gaulle's grandiose goals were also pragmatic and real. They were not "essentially symbolic" as Philip Cerny has argued, although they were also designed to play the simultaneous role of enhancing the legitimacy of the institutions of the Fifth Republic and endowing the French with a sense of common purpose.[12] De Gaulle did not suffer from an "inferiority complex," as so many American diplomats insisted was a national malady of the French after the war, nor was his nationalistic foreign policy aimed largely at consolidation rather than expansion. On the contrary, de Gaulle meant to expand French influence, prestige, and power by restructuring his nation's relations with Africa, Europe, and the world, much as the Fourth Republic had tried to do before him. If his vision was bold, however, its conceptualization and execution were fatally flawed. To make it work, de Gaulle needed the cooperation of the FLN, the agreement of the settlers to work with the Arab and black African populations in a spirit of equality, and the cooperation of the sub-Saharan African nations in the construction of a federal community. He also required the cooperation of his European partners in his particular vision of a loose confederation of independent European states and the assent of the United States and United Kingdom. For a wide variety of reasons, most of them attributable to de Gaulle himself, none of these were forthcoming.

De Gaulle himself helped conceptualize the link between decolonization and diplomacy, the basis of the present argument. He told Alain Peyrefitte that the Fourth Republic "constructed for us a foreign policy that was docile in the hands of the Americans and a colonial policy that was opposed by them." France was set against the Soviet bloc by the American alliance and against the Third World by its colonial policies; precisely because it pretended to subject its colonial possessions to its eternal protection, France in turn became the protectorate of the Americans, who did not hesitate to encourage the vassals of France to rebel against it even as they made of France their own vassal. This, for de Gaulle, was the fateful contradiction of French foreign policy which he intended to rectify, ensuring that what was good for the French was decided in Paris, just as what was good for the Senegalese would be decided in Dakar. Interestingly, Peyrefitte asked de Gaulle whether the policies of the Fourth Republic were not rather coherent than contradictory: did not the subjection of France to the United States enable France to maintain its colonial domination by bringing it large quantities of American aid? De Gaulle left this query unanswered. A significant silence, for Peyrefitte articulated the policy that de Gaulle not only inherited from the Fourth Republic but himself had sought to continue from 1958 to 1962. Under the terms of the "directorate" America would have remained the guarantor of the French empire.

This was the real sense of the September 16, 1958, memorandum. De Gaulle later told Peyrefitte that his proposal to the "Anglo-Saxons" was not meant seriously. "I asked for the moon," he said, knowing full well that his demand would not be granted, but providing the pretext for the progressive withdrawal of France from NATO's integrated command.[13] But de Gaulle was dissimulating: he offered his proposal in deadly seriousness, and not accidentally, at the height of his Algerian problem and immediately after his assumption of political power. France was not internally strengthened or politically stable from 1958 to 1962. On the contrary, de Gaulle faced renewed settler rebellion in January 1960 and a military rising in April 1961, a powerful antiwar movement at home, and a chaotic collapse of his hopes for an ordered Algerian solution in 1962 as one million colons fled their homeland to France amid a reign of terror unleashed by the Organisation de l'Armée Secrète (OAS). De Gaulle's regime at its outset did arguably worse than its immediate predecessors as bombs began to explode regularly in Paris, mass demonstrations against the war led to incidents of police brutality, and the president himself was subjected to an assassination attempt. Even the institutional disarray that so discouraged France's allies in dealing with the Fourth Republic reappeared in the double-headed executive that still plagues the Fifth Republic today, and that then revealed itself in the contradictory signals and policies put out by de Gaulle and his premier, Debré. De Gaulle did not take his NATO initiatives because he had achieved institutional stability and internal order, but rather to accomplish them with American and British help.[14]

Much has been written about de Gaulle's real motives with regard to Algeria when he came to power in 1958. As noted, there exist many examples of confidential remarks made by de Gaulle to selected individuals to the extent that France would not be able to keep Algeria, that it was too late, that Algeria was lost and its independence inevitable.[15] De Gaulle gave similar confidences to American and British officials. In his memoirs he said that he had concluded by May 1958 that there was no alternative left for Algeria except self-determination, and his biographer, Jean Lacouture, takes him at his word.[16] Benjamin Stora, certainly one of the most distinguished French historians of the Algerian War, says it was apparent from 1957 that de Gaulle intended to lead Algeria toward autonomy and self-determination.[17] But de Gaulle's remarks in this vein were always private and contradicted by his public posture and that of his followers. And they were phrased to convey the impression that Algeria was very likely already "lost," a regrettable but ineluctable state of affairs so long as France was governed by the ineffectual Fourth Republic. The implication was that he, de Gaulle, could have kept Algeria, and historians have not discovered a single example of a pre-1959 public statement by de Gaulle that refers to a necessary decolonization of Algeria or takes it as other than a disaster.[18] De Gaulle shared the French colonial consensus and he could conceive of no benefit to a France shorn of any of its colonies, least of all Algeria.[19]

De Gaulle was always very careful to maintain the impression among his closest associates that he favored *Algérie française*. To Jacques Foccart, for example, the most he ever said was that "This regime will never be able to maintain French sovereignty."[20] The regime was the key. As John Talbott has noted, de Gaulle attributed all French problems, not only imperial ones, to the decline of the state. His central aim when he came to power was to endow France with new institutions. If he could keep Algeria French he would do so; if it became an obstacle to his plans he would seek some other solution.[21] In this set of priorities, moreover, Pierre Miquel argues that de Gaulle was entirely in synchronization with the army in whose name he came to power in May 1958. The army wanted above all consolidation of authority in the French state and an end to the sense of growing estrangement between it and the nation.[22] His accession to power was a victory for the army and corresponded to its deepest aspirations: in Algeria it would follow his choice in the end, whether he led it to total victory or to negotiations. When de Gaulle addressed himself to France's role in the non-Western world during his years out of power, which he did infrequently, he almost always referred to France's colonial empire, ignoring the rest. And his travels during the period of traversing the "desert" from 1946 to 1958 were for the most part limited to France's imperial possessions.[23] These, for de Gaulle, represented the "world." De Gaulle never criticized the Indochina War, only the Fourth Republic for losing it.

To be sure, de Gaulle was not insensitive, after Dien Bien Phu, to the necessity for change in the colonial world. He supported Mendès France's bold grant of autonomy to Tunisia in 1954, and after the French bombardment of the Tunisian village of Sakiet, he held a private meeting with the ambassador of Tunisia, seemingly dissociating himself from that action, which, however, he did not condemn publicly. He told Louis Terrenoire in 1955 that "We are in the presence of a wave that is carrying all peoples toward emancipation. There are some imbeciles who do not want to understand this." But de Gaulle explained that he meant by emancipation that classic imperial ties must be replaced by new forms of association, which the Fourth Republic was incapable of carrying out. If he were to come to power he would try to accomplish such a transformation. Similarly, de Gaulle told British Ambassador Jebb in January 1957 that Algeria would become autonomous or independent one day, but in either case the evacuation of the French was "unthinkable." If de Gaulle came to power he would forge a new permanent relationship with Algeria, which the present regime was inca-

pable of achieving.[24] De Gaulle supported the colonialist goals of the
Suez operation in 1956, and he observed in 1957 that iron ore and oil
discoveries in Mauritania would be the basis of "a great [French] economic, cultural, and political ensemble," a diverse community in Africa
of which France would be the center and the pivot.[25] Moreover, de
Gaulle was bitterly impatient, even when in power and forced to grant
independence to France's former colonies, with the public statements of
African leaders critical of "imperialism." To the contrary, de Gaulle insisted always that indigenous peoples owed France their gratitude for its
efforts in the tradition of its *mission civilisatrice.*

The Challe plan and the Plan of Constantine, with their expenditures
in Algeria of both French blood and money in 1959 and 1960, defy explanation in terms other than the aim of keeping the territory French. It
was only as both plans revealed themselves as failures that de Gaulle
began to consider independence for Algeria as an option. General
Challe did win a kind of military victory. The Morice line held rebel incursions from Tunisia to a minimum, while the interior was "pacified."
But pacification could only be defined in terms of the number of terrorist incidents per month: what number was tolerable? De Gaulle once
ventured the figure of 200 per month, as opposed to the more than
1,500 that were occurring during the war's apogee. But in no respect did
it ever appear that Algeria would return to the halcyon days of what
was once considered normal. Nor could the Plan of Constantine be implemented in the time frame required; much of the private capital on
which its broader aims were based was not forthcoming. Private investors were more prescient than the state in anticipating that nothing
the French might do after 1958 was likely to prevent Algerian independence. By 1961, of 306 projects that comprised the industrial part of
the plan, only 43 were 95 percent completed; one-third of the planned
projects had not been begun by June 1961 and another third were less
than 50 percent complete, despite over 7 billion new francs, or $2 bil-
lion, of investment.[26] The evidence seems clear that for at least two and
a half years, from May 1958 until the end of 1960, de Gaulle tried,
while winning the confidence of the Muslim community through social
reforms and investment, to destroy by military means the entire infrastructure of the nationalist rebellion.[27] Only when it was clear that he
had failed did he entertain the idea of granting independence to Algeria.

Bernard Tricot, who was de Gaulle's secretary at the Elysée, finds de
Gaulle's key turn in the September 1959 declaration recognizing that
Algeria had the right to self-determination. But Tricot must admit that

this only inaugurated a new search for an alternative to FLN hegemony in Algeria, a search de Gaulle did not definitively abandon until March of 1961.[28] And even in 1961, after he had begun talks with the Algerian "Provisional Government," de Gaulle instructed his delegate general in Algeria, Jean Morin, to seek alternative Muslim leadership to the FLN from among elected Muslim moderates within Algeria who were willing to work with the French toward "association." And he entertained seriously the idea of partitioning Algeria between its European and Muslim populations should negotiations fail.[29]

This is not to say that de Gaulle was not dissimulating to the partisans of Algérie française in at least one respect. He did not interpret "Algérie française" in the sense of full assimilation of the Muslim population to the status of French people equal to all others: "These people are not like us," he often remarked of the Arab population, meaning that they were impossible to assimilate, and he did not want nine million Muslims voting in French elections for eighty representatives like themselves to sit in the French National Assembly. But the concept of integration was a recent invention and always more rhetorical than real. De Gaulle hoped to find another formula to keep Algeria French, one that would enable it to have its own "personality," as Guy Mollet had promised, yet take "a position of choice " in the construction of the French community outlined in the constitution.[30] Add to this the stubborn efforts of de Gaulle to hold on to North African military bases, in particular Bizerte, even after Algerian independence, and the location in the Sahara of deposits of oil and the sites of French nuclear testing, both regarded as essential for the recovery of French economic and political independence, and one can understand the depth of his commitment to keeping Algeria French after he came to power.

The French-African community as written into the constitution of 1958 and the Fouchet Plan for a European political community of states were companion policies to the proposal for a tripartite "directorate," the whole amounting to a coherent vision of a reordered world that would solve France's current problems and provide an enhanced place for France within it.[31] All three initiatives, moreover, had Algeria and North Africa at their core. The French-African community was to provide a model for the settlement of the Algerian problem and a pole of attraction for the return of Tunisia and Morocco to the fold; the European Economic Community was to provide the capital necessary for the construction of "Eurafrique," a European and African ensemble of which France would be the pivot and core. De Gaulle insisted on a federal community of African states headed by himself, with the key ministries of defense, foreign affairs, economics, and education occupied by French officials, as opposed to the loose confederation based on internal autonomy preferred by the Africans themselves. Had de Gaulle conceded on this point at the outset he might have avoided the collapse of the community in 1960. But de Gaulle would not allow the Africans to choose between confederation and federation; the choice they faced was the community as he wrote it or independence, which meant the loss of all French economic and technical aid. Not surprisingly, all of them except Guinea initially accepted the federation written into the constitution of the Fifth Republic.[32] To be sure, the problems involved in creating an African confederation tied to France might anyway have been insoluble. Economically, it might have been preferable to create two large federations, one in French West Africa and the other in Equatorial Africa, but this plan foundered in West Africa on the rivalry between Léopold Senghor of Senegal and Houphouet Boigny of the Ivory Coast. Senghor wanted the larger unit, but Houphouet Boigny feared that the Ivory Coast, as the richest African prize, would be plundered by the rest. Two large federations also would have had the same drawback as one federation headed by France in denying all the territories equal opportunity for democratic participation on the local level. De Gaulle, in any event, believed profoundly in the community created by the constitution of 1958, was affronted by Sekou Touré's demand for independence for Guinea, and was overcome with emotion at the collapse of the enterprise in 1960, when most of the others followed suit, telling Raymond Triboulet, allegedly with tears in his eyes, *"Ils s'en vont...ils s'en vont."*[33]

De Gaulle revealed the outline of his European plans in his September 14, 1958, meeting with Konrad Adenauer, whom he apparently charmed into accepting his contemplated status for Germany as France's privileged, if junior, partner in the construction of a "little Europe" of the six. This was days before the memorandum to the Anglo-Saxons; de Gaulle wanted France and Germany to be the core of a "Carolingian" Europe excluding England, with Germany to be the privileged partner of France in the construction of a new Europe of states. De Gaulle assured Adenauer that he recognized the German interest in reunification, even as he expected the Germans to understand France's "centrifugal" orientation toward Africa. Here he was again dissimulating, for he told the Americans and the British repeatedly that the division of Germany did not at all displease him. By agreeing to apply the Treaty of Rome, however, de Gaulle enlisted Adenauer's support in opposition to Great

Britain's preferred FTA, which would have absorbed the Common Market into a loose organization of all the members of the Organization for European Economic Cooperation (OEEC). This enabled de Gaulle to break off the desultory negotiations between Britain and the nascent EEC in November 1958; keeping Britain out of Europe was the key thread behind his pretensions to French domination of a "Europe of States." By standing firm against Moscow's threat to change the status of Berlin in November 1958, he further won Adenauer's support against the British desire to negotiate with the Russians. The chancellor, always grateful for de Gaulle's support, in turn remained steadfast behind France's policy in Algeria.

In 1960 de Gaulle went ahead with his proposals for his conception of a politically, culturally, and militarily organized Europe in what became known as the Fouchet Plan. But de Gaulle rejected the federalism preferred by his partners during the discussions over the Fouchet Plan and railed angrily against the proponents of supranationality in Europe, thus destroying his chances for a European Political Community, as he had done in the case of French Africa. De Gaulle expected to dominate Africa and tried to impose on the French Union as centralized a mechanism of power as possible. But in his European policy he rejected what he feared would be the submergence of France in a federalized entity among equals, holding out for a confederation of European states that France could more easily lead. In a "Europe of states," de Gaulle reasoned, Germany would follow France, and the others would necessarily follow the combined power of France and Germany acting together. An autonomous Europe, free of the American yoke, would be organized on the basis of cooperation among sovereign states; de Gaulle would accept no federalism or "supranationalist" schemes.[34]

De Gaulle's conceptions were embodied in the Fouchet Plan, which emerged from a committee set up by the six under the chairmanship of Christian Fouchet at the first meeting of heads of state of the six EEC nations on February 10, 1961. As proposed in October 1961, the Fouchet Plan would have created committees of inter-European cooperation in foreign affairs, defense, and culture, all to operate independently of the Brussels mechanism of the Common Market, which de Gaulle suspected of supranational ambitions. The Germans went along with the Fouchet Plan and the Italians appeared ready to sign on as well. De Gaulle's confederation and their hopes for a federal Europe were not contradictory; tactically, it was better to accept the French minimum program for cooperation than to get nothing. But Belgium and the Netherlands blocked the idea, holding out for a Europe of common institutions based on the existing Treaty of Rome as embodied in the Brussels Commission. The Belgians and the Dutch preferred to build a Europe of institutions that would then select European common policies; the cooperation offered by de Gaulle would have been based on existing French policy.[35] In the aftermath of the failure of the Fouchet Plan, de Gaulle went ahead with Adenauer in a joint effort to implement his scheme between France and Germany alone in the Franco-German treaty of January 1963. But de Gaulle had a way of undercutting his own victories by poor timing. In September 1958 he charmed Adenauer into accepting his ideas on Europe, only to offend the German chancellor by proposing three-power cooperation to the Anglo-Saxons, excluding Germany and NATO, a few days later. In July 1960 de Gaulle tried once again for his idea of tripartite hegemony, this time arousing Adenauer's suspicions as he prepared his proposals for the Fouchet Plan. And in January 1963 de Gaulle preceded the signing of the Franco-German treaty by his dramatic veto of British entry into the Common Market, again causing consternation in Germany. As a consequence, during the remainder of the 1960s, under Adenauer's successor Ludwig Erhard, the treaty, although ratified, never really got off the ground.[36] By seeking to impose a federalist system on French Africa, which preferred a confederation, while trying to force a confederation on a Europe that aspired to a dose of real federalism, de Gaulle got neither, consigning the notion of *Eurafrique* to failure.

Detailed examination of de Gaulle's policies from 1962 to 1968, when he presumably charted the course of a genuine French independence, falls outside the bounds of this study. There is no doubt that this policy had the consensus of the French behind it; it continued in one form or another under all his successors until the end of the Cold War, and elements of it, as previously noted, appear visionary for their time in retrospect. But other aspects of the policy appear, rather, to amount to so much posturing, without much effect. The withdrawal from NATO's integrated command only continued the policy of the Fourth Republic, which because of colonial wars supplied only a fraction of the forces promised, and the alliance did very nicely with French cooperation instead of integration. The independent nuclear force had logic on its side: could France really trust Washington to unleash a nuclear war solely for the purpose of defending Europe? But it unbalanced French military forces by slighting conventional arms in favor of nuclear expenditure, and squandered billions of francs that might better have been spent on its aging educational structure. The effects are visible today in France's inability to lead the kind of autonomous military force to which it aspires because conventional operations of NATO depend so heavily on American logistics. De Gaulle's opposition to America's pursuit of the Vietnam War was perhaps laudable and restored France's credit with the Third World. But as Fredrik Logevall has shown, de Gaulle seemed more interested in trumpeting his opposition to the Vietnam War in 1963 and 1964 than in seriously pressing upon Washington proposals that might have led to peace there.[37] France further lacked the power to make meaningful its policy of détente with the USSR, and it also failed thereby to displace West Germany as the Soviet Union's privileged economic partner. It was rather West Germany's policy of *Ostpolitik,* adopted as de Gaulle was leaving the scene, that brought the real change in the climate of the Cold War, for better or worse, currently being debated by historians. Nor did de Gaulle ever achieve the kind of privileged cooperation between France and Algeria for which he had hoped, as the Algerian revolution slid toward East bloc models of development.

The crude French shift from support of Israel to a pro-Arab policy in 1967 was certainly defensible from the standpoint of French interests, but it turned out to be very harmful to France in the way it was done, when de Gaulle followed it by accusing the Jews of being "an elite people, sure of themselves, and domineering." France lost a golden opportunity to play the role of honest broker in a Middle East peace, leaving that for the Americans. The most charitable interpretation it seems possible to offer of de Gaulle's gratuitous intervention in Canada's internal affairs—his proclamation of *"Vive le Québec libre"* from the balcony of the city hall of Québec City in 1967—is that de Gaulle got carried away in the emotion of the moment. Finally, one must note that de Gaulle sacrificed the economic and educational well-being of a generation of workers and students in his quest for "Grandeur," and they showed their gratitude by humiliating him in the May 1968 movement, eventually forcing his retirement from the scene in 1969. Not, however, before he suffered the ultimate affront of having to apply to Washington for support against a run on the franc: France's return to economic stability fell victim to the crisis.

France hardly projected an image of strength and stability between 1958 and 1962. The NSC report drawn up soon after the Eisenhower–de Gaulle talks of September 1959 demonstrated the continued concerns and evolution of American policy with regard to the Algerian War

since de Gaulle had come to power. The war remained "a divisive factor in the non-Communist world," weakening the military strength of
the alliance in Western Europe and the political influence of the West in
Africa and Asia. In more immediate terms, it contributed to pressures
for American troop evacuations in Morocco, Tunisia, and Libya. The
problem was most acute in Morocco, where the Americans were under
pressure to evacuate air bases that were critical to the credibility of the
Western nuclear deterrent. The war had a profound effect on French internal politics and military strength and was the major cause of the diminished French contribution to NATO. It continued the instability and
uncertainty in French political institutions. Nor was the war's end likely
to result in France's return to NATO's integrated command. Washington's dilemma remained: how to support a major ally and yet accommodate the nationalist tide in North Africa and develop satisfactory relations with the newly emerging states there. France had ceased its aid
to these states, which were safe havens for Algerian rebels; the United
States, in consequence, had been obliged to step in with arms and technical assistance.[38]

Most important, it was clear to the Americans that Algeria was going
to emerge in the end from all this with a considerable degree of autonomy, if not independence. The new offer of self-determination, made by
de Gaulle in September 1959, was, if implemented, "consistent with a
liberal and equitable solution that we could support." But it was not
enough: "some means of assuring the rebels that they can safely enter
the political arena is clearly a prerequisite to the cessation of hostilities
in Algeria." As yet France showed no willingness to recognize this fact.
There were signs that the Algerian provisional government (GPRA) was
ready for talks, but Paris would neither recognize nor negotiate with it.
This was a "grave handicap to U.S. policy," since the Arabs and Asians
regarded Washington as Paris's chief source of support, while the
French blamed Washington for their own failures in Algeria. Perhaps
the worst in all this was that the Americans enjoyed so little leeway in
trying to bring about a solution. They could do no more than discreetly
encourage French talks with the rebels, encourage "moderation" on
both sides, and try to facilitate continued French cooperation with
other North African states.[39]

France was vital to NATO; knowing this, de Gaulle demanded equality with the United States and United Kingdom and their support in Algeria. But while force objectives for France in NATO were 14 divisions,
France maintained 3.67 divisions in Germany and 16 in Algeria; until

the Algerian crisis was resolved France could not contribute more to NATO, and the Supreme Allied Command in Europe's ability to accomplish its defense mission was seriously reduced. A strong and resurgent France remained in the U.S. interest, and the NSC report recommended that "we should do all that we reasonably can to accommodate de Gaulle." Nuclear cooperation with France should be "studied," and tripartite talks continued. But it was equally clear that so long as the Algerian War continued the United States could go no further, and relations with France would consequently remain seriously compromised.[40]

The Americans tried to encourage a favorable evolution of the Algerian situation following the September 1959 de Gaulle statement. The State Department decided to work against any UN reconsideration of the question, although whether this was feasible would depend on whether French-FLN contacts, overt or covert, "have succeeded." It is not clear whether the Americans knew of such contacts, or were engaging in wishful thinking; there is no concrete reference to them in American sources. In December 1959 and again in February 1960, secret contacts between the French government and the rebels through an intermediary, Abderrahmane Farès, did take place, based on the idea of an Algerian republic becoming part of a reconstructed "French Commonwealth," but like previous efforts these came to nothing.[41] In the event, de Gaulle's September statement succeeded in convincing enough UN delegates to give France the benefit of the doubt. It was followed on November 10, 1959, by still another new offer to settle the Algerian problem on the basis of self-determination, and the general challenged the rebels to negotiate a cease-fire. Washington was briefly motivated to help Paris, and did what it could to prevent debate over Algeria in the UN; the General Assembly in consequence reported out only another anodyne resolution on Algeria in 1959. Washington even abstained on that, but de Gaulle took exception to any action at all by the world body. The State Department adopted the position that "the de Gaulle proposals represent a highly important substantive effort toward a resolution of the Algerian problem." The prestige and leadership of de Gaulle were now on the line, however. Close contact must be maintained with the French, and pressure on them avoided; the ball was now in the Algerian court.[42]

The rebels understood this. They recognized that from his offer of a "Peace of the Brave" in December 1958 to his current recognition of Algeria's right to self-determination, de Gaulle had shown a distinct positive evolution, even if he had pronounced the words "self-determination" only as a consequence of American pressure. But the French had often before given with one hand what they then took back with the other. The rebels continued to insist that any negotiations must be understood to be on the basis of full independence and the territorial integrity of Algeria, including the Sahara. The Army of National Liberation (ALN) must retain its arms and its positions while negotiations took place. The GPRA "took note" of de Gaulle's offer; on November 2 it formulated "counterpropositions" and designated five representatives to meet with the French should they agree to its terms. But de Gaulle refused, professing to be insulted by the designation of the imprisoned Ben Bella as one of the rebel negotiators. The FLN believed that the Challe plan and the Plan of Constantine were meant to achieve pacification and Muslim compliance with French rule, in short, continued colonialism. It is difficult to fault the rebels in this judgment. Predictably, after de Gaulle rejected the rebel terms, they in turn sought to intensify the war, mobilize the Arabs to the point of cobelligerence, and achieve another crisis on the scale of Suez or Sakiet. Only under such conditions, rebel leaders thought, would the French be brought to negotiate on acceptable terms.[43]

The stalemate, then, continued in Algeria. Nor were things much better in North Africa generally in terms of Franco-American relations. Friction between Washington and Paris continued over Tunisia. The Americans agreed to finance an agricultural bank, responded favorably to Bourguiba's requests for help in building a university, and sponsored a North African conference on cultural and technical cooperation. Paris protested; France alone was uniquely suited to provide agricultural aid to the Tunisians, its language and culture were dominant in the country, and it was uniquely suited to build a university there. Paris warned Washington that encouragement to "Arabization" in Tunisia would further close off North African countries to the West; only French institutions and schools could maintain necessary Western influence there.[44]

If the rebels thought the French gave with one hand what they took back with the other, the Americans had reason to think the same. In November 1959, a month after Eisenhower had visited France, de Gaulle gave one of his famous press conferences expressing his doubt about American determination to defend Western Europe with nuclear weapons in case of Soviet attack. De Gaulle was arguing for the necessity of a French deterrent and preparing the ground for the first French bomb test of February 1960. But Eisenhower professed to be insulted, and wrote the French president of his astonishment at French lack of faith in the United States and its government; he was disturbed that the French leader would put the United States on such a "low moral plane" as to be disregardful of commitments to its allies, and he objected to passages in de Gaulle's remarks implying the existence of a joint Soviet-American nuclear co-dominion of the world. Eisenhower was careful in the same letter, however, to congratulate the French leader on his further step in the Algerian matter, adding that "As you know I welcome your declaration of September 16 and continue to support your Algerian policy."[45]

De Gaulle replied courteously, but in the spirit of the debate and dialogue he was to continue with the Americans for the next ten years. He regretted that his remarks displeased Eisenhower and he meant no misgivings with regard to the present American government. But could he be equally sure of its successors? The evolution of world policy was impossible to predict; France must develop nuclear weapons, unfortunately with its own resources, "since its allies do not have sufficient trust in it to help it become such a power." After all, the United States had waited until 1917 to enter World War I, and entered World War II only after France had already endured eighteen months of military occupation.[46] France needed to look to its own defenses.

On December 10, 1959, General Twining, in a Joint Chiefs of Staff statement, warned that NATO was weakened by the refusal of any country to stockpile American nuclear weapons on its soil, and that would force the redeployment of NATO air strike forces. France risked jeopardizing the entire policy of collective security. Worse, it could encourage the return of Washington to a policy of "fortress America," as in the worst prewar days of American isolationism. Couve de Murville immediately protested Twining's statement: France was being "put in a box," he said, and it refused to be regarded as the "black sheep of NATO." The problem was not nuclear stockpiling in itself or the withdrawal of the French fleet from NATO's integrated command, but rather that "we are disunited on Africa and the Soviets know it." Once again, for France, every policy came back to Algeria. Twining was creating the appearance of a crisis where there was none, Couve de Murville said. But Paris had broader problems than the Americans themselves. Spaak warned of a "spirit of revolt" within NATO against French actions impeding the progress of the alliance. Herter defended the American abstention on Algeria in the UN and declared that the resolution in favor of peace in Algeria was in fact "identical with US views," and noted that six other NATO powers had also abstained.

Spaak warned that NATO was losing patience with de Gaulle's preoccupation with Algeria.[47]

Eisenhower was back in Paris for the NATO conference of December
1959, however, and the two presidents were able to overcome their fall
spat. De Gaulle said he hoped for a full settlement with Bourguiba and
he believed that the Algerian situation was much improved. There was
a brief discussion of the American abstention in the UN on Algeria,
which de Gaulle now said he "regretted, but understood." Eisenhower
said he meant no departure from American support of the policy declaration of September 16. Both men deplored the leak of General Twining's remarks, de Gaulle professed his support for the alliance, and he
promised that when the Algerian War was over French forces would return to NATO, although under a revised structure of command. In a
meeting with both Eisenhower and Prime Minister Macmillan, de
Gaulle once again raised the issue of the joint world responsibilities of
the big three requiring their cooperation. Eisenhower suggested the establishment of tripartite machinery to operate on "a clandestine basis"
to discuss common interests. Macmillan agreed, and de Gaulle said he
was satisfied with this idea. The next day de Gaulle met with Secretary
of State Herter and repeated some of the previous day's discussions,
adding that in March the French would explode their first atomic
bomb. De Gaulle appeared to assume that under the terms of the
McMahon Act American cooperation with the French nuclear program
would follow, France having demonstrated that it was now sufficiently
advanced to qualify. Herter guardedly said that this would be determined by existing legislation and the perception in Congress of the extent of French cooperation in NATO.[48]

All this provided sufficient basis for a noticeable détente in French-
American relations, which occurred in the spring of 1960. Three-power
talks began once again in London at the turn of the year. The shock of
the settler uprising in January in Algiers, coupled with the ambiguous reaction of the army, signaled rebellion against de Gaulle by the same
groups that had brought him to power, and it undoubtedly chastened
him with regard to the Americans, who were steadfast in their support
during the crisis. Eisenhower wrote de Gaulle that he had "the full support and confidence of the American Government and people in his policy toward Algeria," and the French president replied that he was
"deeply touched."[49] After the explosion of the French bomb in February,
Paris made another bid for American nuclear cooperation, and Norstad
seemed to favor accommodating the French, who were cooperating with

NATO in the air and in the Mediterranean despite withdrawal from the integrated fleet and air command. Now that they had exploded their own nuclear bomb it made sense to offer them help in the interest of avoiding duplication and unnecessary expense. In May 1960, Eisenhower further agreed to expanded tripartite strategic planning and regular consultations among the three governments at the highest level, with the foreign ministers to meet every two months. This was anyway becoming necessary as a result of the more serious turn in the Berlin crisis, the U2 spy plane episode, and the resulting collapse of the summit conference of May in Paris. France was now becoming amenable to American assistance on the Algerian question as well, with the government apparently evolving toward acceptance of negotiations with the FLN.

As Eisenhower showed himself more accommodating to de Gaulle's views in the spring of 1960, Paris showed itself to be more receptive toward possible peace overtures in Algeria. Washington showed that it could bring about movement on the Algerian question. Kohler and Satterthwaite of State's African desk suggested that the Americans might be able to bring the FLN to the negotiating table "through the various avenues of approach that we have." If France would agree, the department could approach Bourguiba and the Tunisian government to pressure the rebels; it would also call Mohammed Yazid to the State Department for consultation. This was put to the French, and, surprisingly, Alphand told Secretary of State Herter that France would be happy to receive U.S. assistance along the lines suggested.[50]

French receptivity to Washington's suggestions on Algeria was spurred by the Quai's careful noting of American movement toward accommodating France on the nuclear question; the Americans hinted that if France halted nuclear testing, Washington might decide after all that France had made "substantial progress" and qualify for assistance under the McMahon Act. The Quai wanted assurances, however, and insisted that no agreement could take hold until 1961, when the French would have finished their initial series of explosions.[51] De Gaulle visited Washington and held talks with President Eisenhower on April 22, 1960, in preparation for the forthcoming summit conference with the Russians to be held in Paris in May. French Foreign Minister Couve de Murville preceded the visit by renewing French requests for nuclear cooperation in Washington now that France had exploded a bomb, but Herter said "substantial progress" in the nuclear field, according to the McMahon Act, had to go beyond "a few explosions." Eisenhower told Herter that he wanted to put nuclear help to France before Congress;

Herter objected to doing so unless the French agreed to put their forces under NATO. But Eisenhower noted that all U.S. forces were not under NATO either, and he showed further willingness to accommodate the French on the nuclear question in tripartite discussions.[52]

At their Washington meeting de Gaulle and Eisenhower agreed that tripartite contacts were improving. Eisenhower passed on warnings from nine African nations, delivered in Washington, that French nuclear explosions in the Sahara were driving them into the Soviet camp. De Gaulle returned to the Algerian question. He made no mention of American attempts to push the GPRA into negotiations, but at Eisenhower's request reaffirmed his September 16, 1959, declaration of willingness to grant Algeria self-determination. He explained that he had asked the rebels to discuss a cease-fire, but they had refused unless the future status of Algeria was discussed in the negotiations, which de Gaulle could not do because it would imply prior recognition of the rebel government. This would violate the principle of self-determination. Following a cease-fire, there could be round-table talks with all representative groups of the Algerian population, including the FLN, and even a referendum, but no prior special position could be given the rebel "pseudo-government." De Gaulle then borrowed a tactic from Guy Mollet and Mendès France. Khrushchev had offered to help settle the Algerian question, the general said, remarking that France must remain in Algeria or the United States would move in and that would be worse. But de Gaulle had told the Russian leader to stay out of it. Eisenhower laughed, saying this was typical of the Soviet leader's efforts to divide the alliance. But once again the troubling subtext of a "planetary deal," involving peace in Algeria in exchange for a neutralist France, underlay the banter. The two presidents agreed that France's prior recognition of the Oder-Neisse line in Germany might improve the prospects for agreement on the Berlin crisis at the forthcoming summit. Before de Gaulle left on April 25, Eisenhower asked that the French president publicly reaffirm his September 16 statement so that Eisenhower could again publicly support it. De Gaulle did so twice during his public speeches in the United States, and he made a strong statement in San Francisco endorsing the rights of all peoples to self-determination.[53]

Evolution toward negotiations in Algeria moved ahead, but was interrupted by the failed Geneva summit conference of May 1960, at which Eisenhower accepted responsibility for the U2 spy-plane flights over the USSR that led to the Russian downing of a plane and capture of its pilot. De Gaulle used the occasion to offer Eisenhower his full sup-

Figure 3. President Charles de Gaulle of France posed on the steps of the
United States guest house, Blair House, with Mrs. de Gaulle and President
Eisenhower after his arrival in the capital on April 22, 1960, from Canada.
(Associated Press / WIDE WORLD PHOTOS)

port, which the American president deeply appreciated. With the conference in tatters, de Gaulle assured Khrushchev that Eisenhower was a
man of peace.[54] The common reaction of the three to the Khrushchev
display of anger in Paris gave a spur to their plans to pull together. On
May 24, Macmillan told Debré that the British were ready to go ahead
with tripartite talks as per the September 1958 memorandum and the
next day followed up with a letter to de Gaulle. On June 1, 1960, Secretary Herter hosted a meeting of the foreign ministers of the three. It
was agreed to keep the meetings secret, establish a secretariat to keep
records and prepare agendas, and appoint permanent representatives of
the three in Washington to keep up contacts. Some discussion took

place of the eventual deployment of medium-range American missiles in
Europe, the Congo crisis, and the situation in the Horn of Africa. On
June 11 de Gaulle wrote Eisenhower summarizing the arrangement:
there were to be regular meetings of the ministers of foreign affairs of
the big three, permanent representatives in Washington to prepare them,
and the whole to be supplemented by occasional meetings of the heads
of governments. De Gaulle further proposed that the talks be extended
to strategic and military cooperation around the world.[55] Superficially
at least, it seemed that the French aims had been realized.

Correspondingly, de Gaulle took another step toward Algerian negotiations. On June 14, 1960, he again reaffirmed his willingness to negotiate with the Algerian rebels, and he made what seemed a dramatic advance in his articulated policy by promising that there would eventually
be an "Algerian Algeria." The State Department immediately expressed
its pleasure, lauding the statement as a further evolution in French policy and a demonstration of de Gaulle's desire for peace. Washington
now advised the FLN through the Tunisian pipeline that it should seize
the opportunity for talks. On June 20 the FLN accepted de Gaulle's
offer to negotiate, and the first contacts between the French government
and the FLN began at Melun. They quickly went awry, however. The
French revealed at the outset that they were still not prepared to recognize the exclusive claim of the FLN to represent the Algerian people, or
even to acknowledge the existence of the GPRA as representative of Algeria.[56] Paris further encumbered the talks with restrictions, beginning
with the choice of the provincial city of Melun as the venue, where the
Algerian delegation was held incommunicado and forbidden to talk to
foreign governments or the press. The French delegate, Roger Moris,
was only an under-secretary for Algerian Affairs, not a member of the
government, which could not deal with "external emissaries of the rebellion." De Gaulle refused to receive Ferhat Abbas, the president of the
GPRA, nor were the delegates allowed to enter into contact with
Ahmed Ben Bella, whom the French insisted was not a minister but a
prisoner. The rebel delegates complained that they were being held prisoner in Melun as well.[57] The French would under no conditions discuss
a political settlement; the talks were to remain limited to the subject of
a cease-fire, after which the government would undertake to negotiate
with representatives of all segments of Algerian opinion, including the
colons. Moris was even forbidden to use the innocuous phrase "the
French government" in dealing with the rebel delegation; he was to say
only "the government," lest anyone get the impression that the French

thought any other government than their own was present at the talks. It is hard to see that the French position in reality had expanded beyond Mollet's 1956 position of a cease-fire, elections, and then negotiations with elected Muslim and French representatives in Algeria. The cease-fire, moreover, would be followed by a lengthy period of *apaisement*, during which the French authorities, and de Gaulle personally, would do what they could to win Muslim opinion over to France. Indeed, considerable evolution was as yet necessary in the French negotiating position before peace could be achieved.

A French summary report, written just before the Melun talks, defined French policy in terms of two essential objectives—a cease-fire with the FLN and self-determination, but within carefully circumscribed limits. Self-determination in Algeria was for France to manage through its own program of elections, which had begun in November 1958 with the legislative elections of that year, continued with municipal elections in Algeria in April 1959, senatorial elections in May 1959, and culminated with cantonal elections in May 1960. The French concluded that an infrastructure of local rule had now been put in place staffed by valid Muslim representatives. But all these elections were boycotted by the FLN, and most of the lists elected supported the Gaullists. This could hardly be expected to qualify as "self-determination" from any other vantage point than that of the French.[58] Yet the report characterized the French program in Algeria as a rather extraordinary success. Muslims and Europeans were cooperating on the same electoral lists. The departmental councils had all elected Muslim presidents. Some 200,000 "Frenchmen of North African ethnicity" served in the French armed or police forces.

The report admitted that there were, to be sure, about 23,000 "administrative internments" in Algeria, and "resettlements" of populations in fortified villages, sometimes military, sometimes spontaneous, which involved as many as 1,500,000 persons. This amounted to one-sixth of the Muslim population that had been displaced from their homes due to the war. One-third of these, the report said, continued to have access to their lands, but another third lived in "misery," and another one-third fell somewhere in between. But the French believed that many of the villages were becoming viable, providing schools, health services, and possibilities of "social promotion and human evolution" for their inhabitants. By 1961, 2,500,000 children, 235,747 of them girls, would be receiving education; some 149 hospitals had been built with 34,425 beds; the Guaranteed Minimum Salary (SMIG) was in effect in Algeria, and if salaries were 25 percent lower than in metropolitan France, they were 200 percent higher than those in Egypt. Over two billion new francs had been invested under the Plan of Constantine and land was being redistributed to Muslims.[59] None of this sounded as if the French planned as yet to leave Algeria. Nor did the French show any realization that these accomplishments, undertaken only after the rebellion had begun, rather demonstrated the bankruptcy of their Algerian policy prior to 1957 and the success of the revolution in forcing reform. The negotiations quickly terminated without result when it was clear that the French were not there to discuss a political settlement.[60]

The Quai d'Orsay trumpeted de Gaulle's offer of negotiations as a success for the French army and its program of pacification. The sealing off of Algerian borders, the constant pursuit of rebel forces, and the regrouping of peasants in controlled villages and settlements all represented the successful "noble work" of France's military. With recognition of the equality of the Muslim population in May 1958 and the promise of self-determination of September 1959, the basis for peace had been established. But a definitive settlement must be preceded by a long period of quiet (*apaisement*) such that "all the population understands...the necessity of union with France." There was no real evolution of French policy as yet. Algeria was to enjoy self-determination when it was ready to choose to remain with France, not before.[61] It is hardly surprising that the GPRA saw little more at Melun than a French demand that it surrender. It publicly protested the isolation of its delegation and condemned de Gaulle's refusal to meet Abbas before the talks. The French demands had not changed: a cease-fire at which the rebels surrendered their weapons, followed by a period of transition during which the French found or created Muslim collaborators independent of the FLN with whom to deal.[62]

GPRA President Ferhat Abbas drew the conclusions from the breakdown of negotiations in August 1960. American pressure was not the reason that the FLN had accepted de Gaulle's offer to negotiate; the problem was rather the military situation on the ground. It was more and more difficult to get supplies into Algeria owing to the effectiveness of the Morice line sealing off the Tunisian frontier; the French had indeed achieved important results economically, administratively, and socially, if this did not necessarily as yet translate into increased Muslim support for union with France. De Gaulle had set out to win over the Muslim population and there were signs that he was achieving some success. The Arab states used the Algerian struggle for propaganda purposes but did not really help it prevail; the Tunisians and Moroccans by their timidity harmed the revolution more than they helped. Melun had made it clear that France demanded rebel capitulation; no change would come until there was a modification in the unfavorable ratio of forces: oil, the Sahara, the large European population, and the rebelliousness of the French army made this a different case from classic colonialism.[63]

Abbas's conclusions from all this were chilling. Only the fuller insertion of the Algerian struggle into the context of the Cold War by the complete support of the socialist countries could bring the decisive element needed for a breakthrough. The current climate of détente in the Cold War, as exemplified by the summit conference in Geneva, meant only that the struggles of the underdeveloped nations would otherwise be forgotten. The Algerian leader called for a more vigorous diplomatic effort in the Soviet bloc, and an effort to warn Western investors of capital that their contracts with France for Algerian development were precarious, if not useless. Knowledge of the Algerian leader's conclusions was received with growing apprehension and concern in Washington, which was disappointed at the Melun failure. On July 2, Abbas visited Beijing, and received the promise of $80 million in arms aid from the Chinese, along with exhortations not to negotiate with the colonialists, who were doomed by history. Little concrete aid materialized in the short run, but Paris became increasingly fearful of increased American pressure to negotiate as a consequence of the Abbas trip, a fear that was shortly realized.[64]

Washington's unhappiness with the lack of progress toward a settlement was immediately reflected in the stalling of tripartite negotiations between France and the Anglo-Saxons. These had initially evolved favorably, and the French quickly suggested that they be extended to military talks and that these take place in NATO's existing Standing Group, with occasional meetings of the heads of state of the big three to be part of the mechanism as well. In letters to both Macmillan and de Gaulle, Eisenhower agreed to the consultations, and designated Livingston Merchant to prepare the agendas and serve as secretary for the Washington meetings, with counterparts to be appointed in London and Paris.

There were immediate reverberations among the other alliance members, however, particularly respecting the idea of military talks, which the French wanted to extend to Africa, and fears in the alliance of a French-British-American "directorate" once again surfaced. Herter consequently confronted Alphand on June 24 with the American desire to go slowly, particularly on military discussions in the Standing Group for which Alphand was pushing. Herter had to be aware of the opening of the Melun talks the next day. Did his sudden caution reflect a growing realization that Melun would lead to nothing, or did Paris use the blockage of the tripartite talks as an excuse to torpedo Melun? Both may be true. Did the French wish to discuss Algeria in the tripartite talks, Herter asked, "which appeared to us to be the single most important problem in Africa today?" Alphand parried this crack by raising once again the issue of nuclear cooperation and the obvious savings to France it would provide, observing "how greatly a solution to this problem could help the over-all NATO relationships."[65] But it is indeed remarkable how quickly the collapse of the negotiations at Melun was reflected in the slowing of American and British efforts to accommodate Paris on three-power collaboration.

The Americans felt truly caught now between the proverbial rock and a hard place. From Paris, reports made it clear that de Gaulle thought he had achieved joint decisions of the big three on a worldwide basis and steps toward shared nuclear strategic planning. In Washington, Eisenhower told Herter that "we had always refused to get into the tripartite thing but what we have now is wrecking NATO." The president wondered whether it was possible to have tripartite military discussions outside the alliance in exchange for de Gaulle cooperating in NATO. But Herter now said that it all boiled down to nuclear questions, and the law prohibited this because "under the law you can't claim that France has a nuclear capacity," this even though France had already exploded a bomb. But Eisenhower was personally loath to give up; in a letter to de Gaulle on August 2, he agreed to tripartite talks in preparation for the UN General Assembly meeting in the fall, and to separate military discussions outside the NATO Standing Group. But for the purposes of European cooperation, the president added, "we must perfect a viable NATO."[66]

On August 3, 1960, Eisenhower ordered study of weapons sharing with America's allies, expressed sympathy with de Gaulle's nuclear program, noting that the French leader was simply "trying to build his country," and protested that "we [the United States] too often treat them [the French] as second rate." Was there any reason, he asked General Norstad, why the United States could not help France build a nuclear submarine? The McMahon Act, the president protested, was a "terrible law" that could only harm America's relations with its allies. On August 25, Eisenhower pressed the National Security Council with his concerns, demanding a decision on nuclear sharing with France. The consensus, however, was that the law as written disqualified France from any exemption under the act and that Congress was unlikely to change it. The Atomic Energy Commission had too much power and it was resolutely against sharing with the French. The best the president could get was a directive for a report on the future of nuclear weapons sharing within NATO, and analysis of whether there could be such sharing and if so under what circumstances. Instead of a proposal to share with France, the report eventually came up with the ill-fated proposal for a multilateral nuclear force designed to prevent all Europe from building an independent nuclear deterrent; that proposal preoccupied the NATO alliance during the Kennedy and Johnson administrations and never came to fruition.[67]

De Gaulle meanwhile threw another monkey wrench of his own into any hopes for a meaningful tripartite arrangement. The Congo crisis had forced its way into the headlines, and in response to the virtual anarchy that broke out after the Belgian withdrawal, Washington opted to pursue a solution through the United Nations. This could hardly have been expected to sit well with de Gaulle, who deeply resented the world body for its numerous attempts to interfere with French policy in Algeria. The Congo was just another example of the consequences of the lack of harmony among the big three, de Gaulle wrote to Eisenhower on August 9. A tripartite approach would have produced reason; instead, there was anarchy, while not only in Algeria but now "all over the world France sees those whom it considers its allies behaving as if they were not." NATO had once again revealed its inefficacy in addressing world problems, and by integrating its forces with it France had deprived itself of responsibility for its own defense. Understandable in 1949, this was unacceptable in 1960. Once again the French president urged his Anglo-Saxon allies to seize the opportunity for organizing a common approach to world problems and reorganizing the alliance.[68]

The letter revealed de Gaulle's enigmatic self, open to the most divergent interpretations. Eisenhower told Herter the next day that the French president was demanding his "triumvirate" again. Herter thought that blaming the Congo on divergence among the Western powers "makes no sense"; de Gaulle could only be referring once again to Algeria. Eisenhower agreed that de Gaulle meant that the allies should support the Belgians, the former colonial power that had caused the problem, in the Congo, presumably as they should support France in Algeria. This was probably not far from the mark. The president also had a report that Adenauer was upset at de Gaulle's pursuit of tripartism, and de Gaulle had promised the chancellor not to pursue it further.

In fact, all this occurred during a low point in the recently cordial Franco-German relationship. The French were playing out a delicate balancing act in the summer of 1960 among the three poles of their *Weltpolitik,* Africa, Europe, and the Anglo-Saxons. In August the transformation of the French community into a grouping of independent states was consummated, as eight former colonies acceded to independence. On July 29–30, Adenauer came to France and held extensive talks with de Gaulle at the Chateau de Rambouillet. The chancellor was bitterly disappointed, if not angry. He complained first of Debré's insensitive remarks about Germany, which the French premier had characterized as a second-rate power in a recent speech extolling France's cooperation with the British and Americans. The German chancellor then denounced the reappearance of the three-power "directory" within NATO, complained about France's withdrawal from NATO's integrated command, and warned that France faced isolation in NATO, which spelled trouble for Franco-German cooperation and French plans for the reorganization of Europe. De Gaulle apologized for Debré, explaining that his premier's intemperate remarks often went beyond the true content of his thought. He then went on to defend the tripartite meetings, which were devoted to non-European, non-NATO problems, specifically of late Africa; how could the Germans take exception to this? As is, the French president said, NATO was a simple extension of American policy, and as such it was not acceptable to France, which demanded a greater voice in its councils. Adenauer now agreed; he had always warned, he said, that the Americans might not defend Europe in the last analysis if it meant running the danger of their own nuclear destruction. But could France maintain strength in both atomic and conventional forces, and if it chose atomic weapons, did not that mean less of a conventional shield for Germany?[69]

De Gaulle insisted that he wanted European cooperation among independent states anchored by the French-German partnership. He complained of the Brussels Commission's pretensions to supranationality; the French plan was for a political extension of the existing EEC through which the six would attempt to coordinate their foreign and defense policies, and further exchanges in culture and education. But the mechanism must be the Council of Ministers of the six, supplemented by occasional meetings of the heads of state, with a permanent body of representatives and a secretariat located in Paris. From this political Europe the Brussels Commission, which de Gaulle abhorred as "supranational," would be excluded from playing any role. This was the same mechanism de Gaulle sought for the tripartite arrangement with the British and Americans, and he later used it in the Franco-German treaty of January 1963 and even in the arrangements with the USSR in 1965.

As for NATO, de Gaulle said, each state had to have its own role in the alliance. But as it was, America arrogated to itself the right to declare war on Europe's behalf, while Europe could not even be sure that America would fight for it. As for the integration of forces in the alliance, it was of no interest to the peoples of Europe; in fact, it delegitimized their governments whose primary role was the defense of their populations. "The majesty, the nobility, the honor of military command," de Gaulle said, "is to be responsible to its government, responsible for the battles in which the destiny of the country is decided. Integration deprives it of that role." Adenauer was again charmed by the general, whom he could not help admiring. "God preserve us from a war under American command," he observed. NATO indeed required change, and Europe must ensure its own existence on the basis of the ideas of General de Gaulle. The two leaders resolved to cooperate in the reform of NATO and the construction of a political Europe built upon the bedrock of a confederation of independent states.[70]

De Gaulle assiduously set out to convince the other Common Market nations to fall in behind the French and the Germans. Initially, he had some success, not by vaunting his three-power cooperation but by demonstrating its limitations. American-British reliance on the United Nations in the Congo crisis irritated the Belgians and the Dutch. Both nations were firmly attached to NATO and fearful of the separation of England from the continent. But both aligned themselves with Paris against Washington on colonial issues. The Belgians objected to being everyone's whipping boy for their role in the Congo, and deeply appreciated the French rejection of the United Nations intervention and French sympathy for their continued assistance to the secessionist authority in Katanga. The Dutch were angry at Washington's earlier support of Indonesian independence and its arming of Indonesia, whose claim to New Guinea they were trying to resist. Both nations in turn gave de Gaulle full support in his efforts to maintain French control in Algeria. On that basis they were momentarily won over to the pursuit of de Gaulle's conceptions for political Europe, to which the Italians signed on as well.[71] De Gaulle won the assent of the six to a meeting of heads of state, originally scheduled for December 1960 but postponed to February 1961, during which the Fouchet committee, formally laying out the structure of the new Europe, was to be established.

Washington supported the Common Market as a step toward European integration. It could hardly take exception to de Gaulle's plans to cap the economic structure with a political one. The question was how this could be reconciled with a reformed NATO in which France would continue to play its assigned role, or with the tripartite proposals. Herter recognized that much of Franco-American contention came down to American nuclear help for France, to which Eisenhower was sympathetic. If that were accomplished, everything else could perhaps be negotiated. But the president did not see how he could satisfy de Gaulle on tripartism and throw out the Germans, Italians, Belgians, and Dutch, all of whom were already irritated. Herter said that in the end the problem was that de Gaulle never agreed with anyone else, but always expected everyone else to agree with him. Crude as it was, this analysis was not far from the mark. But was it not equally valid for the Americans? Eisenhower, in frustration, said the United States should tell de Gaulle that it did not want the command in Europe; we would be glad to see them take over and pull out our own troops. This was only partly rhetorical; Eisenhower continually expressed his frustration at having American troops defending Europe against the Soviets while the French were off fighting in Algeria.[72]

Livingston Merchant conveyed Eisenhower's concerns to Macmillan: a three-power meeting between heads of state would adversely affect NATO. Macmillan thought it was best to "play it soft," not to reject de Gaulle outright, but to point out the difficulties. But Merchant said that de Gaulle's views on NATO "strike at the basic US concept." Noting de Gaulle's nuclear ambitions, Macmillan advised seeking "clarification" from the French president while temporizing on a summit meeting and not closing the door. Eisenhower followed this advice, writing de Gaulle that he would like to meet, but that it would be difficult to arrange until later in the year. The alliance, he reminded the French president, was basic to U.S. policy, but if the European allies no longer shared a common purpose and desire, the United States would revert to isolationism and that would mean ending its troop commitment to Europe. The United States had world alliances with forty-three nations; not all of these involved France; small nations would no longer allow big ones to speak for them; and the big three could not develop "real political and military cooperation if it lessened relations with other nations and implied the reorganization of the alliance."

Integration in the alliance was necessary to Europe's defense, Eisenhower said. Its absence risked compromising military effectiveness and

would lead to the withdrawal of U.S. troops. French refusal to cooperate on naval matters, air defense, and nuclear stockpiling had weakened
the alliance, while the French had suggested no ways to reorganize it.
Expressing his frustration with de Gaulle's interpretation of the Congo
crisis, Eisenhower wrote: "I must confess, my dear General, that I cannot understand the basic philosophy of France today." The alliance and
tripartism simply appeared incompatible, and the role of France in the
three-power talks was unclear. Did France pretend to speak for Europe?
Did this imply lessened American relations with West Germany?[73]

The Eisenhower letter remained without a response, and three-power
talks on the foreign minister level continued without result. Eisenhower
continued to believe that cooperation with France would remain impossible until a settlement had been achieved in Algeria. While the
Melun contacts proceeded, the State Department remained silent, rejecting a suggestion from the Tunisians that it resume or establish
higher-level contacts with the GPRA. The department feared undermining the negotiations and creating political problems for de Gaulle in
France and it wanted to avoid the impression that it was intervening.[74]
But with the failure of the Melun talks to materialize into something
more serious, irritation once again grew in Washington at the French inability or unwillingness to find a solution. A confrontation took place at
a meeting of the three foreign ministers at the Waldorf Towers hotel on
September 23. British Secretary Home asked how Britain might help
France on Algeria, but Couve de Murville said France would once again
boycott the UN proceedings despite the favorable outcome the previous
year, counting on its allies to prevent a resolution calling for intervention by the world body. Herter asked if de Gaulle would make a new
statement on Algeria, but Couve said the September 16, 1959, offer
stood and had been repeated on several occasions, with the recent ad-
dendum by de Gaulle promising an "Algerian Algeria." That was sufficient. France was willing to accept a de facto truce, but the rebels remained opposed. The French position remained that following a
cease-fire, consultations must occur with everyone in Algeria—the FLN,
the unrepresented Muslim population, and the settlers. The FLN insisted on prior recognition of its power to speak for all Algeria, "something that the Government of France has no right to give." Herter asked
that the French argue their position in the UN; Home agreed, telling
Couve that "without you we can't win." Herter repeated the appeal:
"Couve, we want you back." But Couve said that the irresponsible delegations at the UN did not "give a damn" for the French position, and

the FLN saw its interest in the war's prolongation so long as it continued to receive subsidies from the outside. Couve denied that France still
regarded Algeria as part of France, but Herter said that it remained so
for NATO purposes by treaty; the allies could not pretend to be un-
involved. Moreover, the French army was still largely armed by the
United States and belonged on the Rhine, not in Africa.[75]

On September 27, 1960, Eisenhower told Herter that he still regarded the great problem of France to be Algeria. It remained a "running sore." Independence was the best and only solution there; it simply
was no longer possible for one nation to dominate another. An American intelligence report on "Problems and Prospects of the Fifth Republic" again noted that there would be no peace in Algeria without negotiations with the FLN; failure in Algeria "casts a long shadow on efforts
to strengthen France by reform at home or grandeur abroad." France
wanted nuclear weapons, independence, and leadership of both African
and European blocs of nations. But African nationalism, French instability, resistance within NATO, and Algeria blocked progress. French
differences with NATO were intensified by the use of NATO-earmarked
troops in Algeria, which irritated the rest of the alliance and diminished
French influence. The French community in Africa was a failure in the
form originally envisaged, and France's pretensions to lead a European
bloc remained vague and unreachable, reposing on the idea of political
cooperation with a dominant role for France and hostility to supra-
nationalism. Everyone resisted French claims to hegemony, leaving
France isolated in Europe if not the world.[76] Unstated in the report, but
a clear implication of it, was that under such conditions building anything like a tripartite leading organism of the alliance with France, or of
the "free world" for that matter, was impossible.

By October 1960 the failure to make progress on Algeria once again
appeared to present insuperable problems for Washington. It was now
apparent that the Algerian rebels had decided to rely on the Soviet bloc
for support. If they came to power under these conditions, Tunisia, Morocco, Libya, and Mali would be endangered, and even Bourguiba
might be tempted to throw his weight to the Soviets in a desperate effort
to survive. Bourguiba told Washington that American policies must
change or the Maghreb countries would not be able to escape the dangers of communist penetration.[77] The United States was losing friends
in the UN, the members of NATO were threatening to defect from the
French position, if they had not already done so, the Scandinavians,
Greece, and Turkey had long been antagonistic to French policy, but

now Italy and even Germany were in danger of giving way. The Americans would lose their last Libyan bases in North Africa while an independent Algeria became a "dynamic Soviet outpost" in the region. In a memorandum of October 20, Satterthwaite revived the Holmes proposal implemented during the Sakiet crisis: the United States should "make clear to de Gaulle that in the absence of progress [on Algeria] we will do what we can to prevent the collapse of Western-oriented policies of moderate leaders, especially in the North African states."[78] With de Gaulle in charge, the Americans were coming back full circle to where they had been with the Fourth Republic, once again threatening a serious rupture in French-American relations in the interests of forcing an Algerian peace. The problem was compounded by the possibility that the Algerian crisis could involve the NATO alliance in war, for the NSC noted that "in the event of intervention in Northern Algeria by organized identifiable units of armed forces of the USSR, the North Atlantic Treaty would be applicable."[79]

At virtually the same time the issue of nuclear cooperation with France came to a head in Washington. On September 12 a conference on the question was held in the president's office. Robert Bowie, director of the Center for International Studies, was fiercely hostile to nuclear aid for France, arguing that any proliferation would be a "catastrophe." General Norstad instead favored the creation of a multilateral nuclear force for NATO, but Eisenhower found the idea impracticable. De Gaulle had demonstrated, the president thought, that a sovereign nation would exercise its sovereignty on a unilateral basis, come what may. De Gaulle would never accept such a solution, he would go on to build his nuclear force, and he wanted the United States and the United Kingdom to work with France on a world basis. But Norstad insisted that this would destroy the alliance. On October 3 the American president capitulated to his advisors and his bureaucracy, accepting the idea of a multilateral nuclear force for NATO; the next day he outlined the idea to Paul-Henri Spaak, expressing the hope that the creation of such a force would overcome French isolation.[80]

The Americans were trying to extend to Paris the carrot and the stick. Washington accommodated Paris by continuing three-power discussions on the basis of the September 1958 memorandum, and these went through a second round, continuing through Eisenhower's term and ending only in 1961. Eisenhower seemed to hold out the possibility of a shift in American nuclear policy, or at least a scheme for sharing American weapons with NATO. But the Americans wanted movement in Algeria. If the French declined these inducements to act, there lurked in the background a return to the policy of Washington's taking North Africa in tow and risking a total rupture in French-American relations. It is impossible to say with certainty what role these potentialities played in de Gaulle's policy reversal. In Tunisia the rebels appeared to believe that, no matter who won the coming American election, support for de Gaulle in Algeria would continue unchanged.[81] But the danger of the election of John F. Kennedy, who as a senator in 1957 had introduced the infamous resolution critical of French Algerian policy, combined with the Eisenhower administration's newly discussed willingness again to intervene in the Algerian crisis were enough to bring about French action to seek peace. If under President Kennedy the United States openly championed the cause of the Algerian rebels, continuation of the war by France would obviously be untenable, and French isolation would become total, with nuclear cooperation impossible. Before such a catastrophe could take place, the Algerian conflict must be well on its way toward resolution.

In fact, worldwide diplomatic pressures were now converging on France with sufficient force to make continuation of the Algerian War impossible, despite the perceived favorable military balance and the claimed successful construction of an infrastructure of Muslim participation in a new Algeria tied to France. French relations with Tunisia and Morocco hit historic low points, and both countries threatened to accept Soviet bloc weapons on their soil for transit to the FLN. The Moroccans demanded a full French evacuation from military bases in their country, and brandished against the French an agreement secured from Washington to leave Morocco by the end of 1961. If Washington had agreed to leave Morocco, the French could do no less. Compounded by other issues such as frontier clashes with Algeria and the Moroccan claim to Mauritania, which the French rejected, the bases erupted into a full-scale crisis in Franco-Moroccan relations.[82] Bourguiba's continued toleration of the French presence was an embarrassment and he escalated his demands for French withdrawal to include the naval base at Bizerte, the one North African foothold outside of Algeria that the French were resolved to keep. French intelligence noted with increasing concern the FLN's willingness to align itself with the Soviet bloc in exchange for the hope of eventual material support. The Chinese had already given financial help and promised weapons. The Russians, not to be outbid, decided on de facto recognition of the FLN on October 8, and stepped up their anticolonial rhetoric, denouncing the Algerian War in brutal terms.[83] Fi-

nally, the war threatened the structure of the reformed African community; the newly independent French African states expressed their concern in the UN over the incompatibility of their ties to France and their
necessary alignment with the cause of Algerian independence.[84]

On November 2, 1960, in a lunch conversation with Charles Bohlen,
subsequently U.S. ambassador to France, Couve de Murville said that
de Gaulle had come to a firm decision to seek an Algerian settlement,
and offered French cooperation with Washington in the UN to head off
a resolution against France. On November 4, 1960, de Gaulle made yet
another of his rhetorical and elliptical advances on the Algerian question, declaring that "there will be an Algerian republic one day, which
will not be France." There seemed to be one of these statements per
year, each shortly before anticipated UN votes on Algeria; the timing of
this one was helped by the American presidential election, which
Kennedy won on November 8. Shortly thereafter de Gaulle dramatically announced a referendum on Algerian independence to be held on
January 8, 1961. De Gaulle had finally "grasped the nettle" of the Algerian problem, relieving Washington of the necessity of doing so.

On November 28, 1960, a Swiss economic official named Olivier
Long was approached by an Algerian, M. Boulharouf, who enjoyed the
confidence of Ferhat Abbas, about the possibility of Switzerland providing a pipeline for the reestablishment of French talks with the GPRA,
broken off since the failure at Melun in July. Long met with Boulharouf
on December 23 and, sufficiently impressed with what he heard,
arranged a meeting with de Gaulle's Special Assistant for Algeria Louis
Joxe, through a mutual friend, on January 10, 1961, after the referendum in which the French people massively endorsed de Gaulle's call for
Algerian self-determination, meaning independence if necessary. The
FLN had wanted to resume negotiations since Melun; its more moderate leaders feared and distrusted both Nasser and the Chinese, who
were the sole sources of their support. The Algerians rejected American
mediation or that of any other NATO power because they wished to
stay clear of the Cold War. The choice of the Swiss proved equally desirable to de Gaulle, who gave his go-ahead for the talks to continue,
designating Georges Pompidou as his personal negotiator. The FLN
agreed to meet with Pompidou on February 19, 1961, thus getting what
became the Evian negotiations under way.[85]

The Americans were pleased, but they knew the road ahead was still
encumbered with pitfalls. Herter told the NSC that de Gaulle's decision
to hold a plebiscite would finally bring the crisis to a head, and the army

and the colons were sure to oppose it. The FLN was equally suspicious of a referendum in France; the French people had no authority to legislate for Algerians in yet another version of the obsolete "framework law" for the territory. De Gaulle was playing the game of racial division, amputating the Sahara, and violating the principle of self-determination he had promised to respect. The GPRA alone was the guarantor of the national patrimony.[86] But the State Department had information that de Gaulle had "changed radically" and was now moving toward a realistic solution, although "he will not tell us what he plans." Eisenhower tried to avoid the embarrassment of a UN debate, but cooperation between France and the United States again broke down and the United States abstained on a resolution that clearly and unequivocally called for Algerian independence. But it was now of little moment. In November 1960, de Gaulle found himself faced with a call for civil disobedience in the manifesto of 121 intellectuals, led by Jean-Paul Sartre, in support of the Jeanson group, which was openly aiding the Algerian rebels. The atmosphere was heavy in Paris. On December 11, de Gaulle again visited Algeria, where he confronted massive Muslim demonstrations in favor of the FLN. The European population first took to the streets, but the Muslims confronted them angrily, and when the army took the side of the Europeans ninety Muslims and six Europeans were dead before order could be restored. De Gaulle himself was spat on and physically threatened by the angry *pieds noirs,* whom the general now accused of committing suicide and digging their own graves while they turned the French army against France.[87]

On December 22, 1960, Satterthwaite wrote that after the January 8 referendum de Gaulle would move toward real negotiations with the GPRA; the United States must renew high-level contacts with the Algerian rebels so as to be in a position to urge constructive reaction to the French initiative and to lay the groundwork for U.S. relations with the future Algeria.[88] It appeared that France would finally cut Algeria loose and Washington be free of the encumbrance that so hampered its policies in the Third World. On his last day in office, Eisenhower cabled de Gaulle that his "feeling of friendship [for France] never has been stronger than it is today."[89] But Eisenhower was premature: de Gaulle was still not ready to abandon Algeria, while by declining to help the French hold on there and by refusing France nuclear cooperation, Washington had perhaps already lost France as a safe and sure ally.

CHAPTER EIGHT

Peace

De Gaulle had hoped that peace in Algeria would leave France at the vortex of three concentric circles of power: a shared condominium over the West with Great Britain and the United States, a European political community of the six based on "cooperation" and devoid of any hint of supranationality, and a *Eurafrique* based primarily on France's former possessions, with Algeria in a "place of choice" by virtue of its bicultural characteristics acting as a bridge between European and African cultures. De Gaulle made a final desperate effort in all three directions in 1962, once again failing in all three in a final strikeout signaling the defeat of his vast ambitious enterprise. First, it proved virtually impossible to put relations on a satisfactory track with the Kennedy administration in Washington; the Americans could not accept the idea of a tripartite condominium with a France on the edge of chaos in Algeria, they were suspicious of de Gaulle's designs in Europe, and they distrusted his intentions in Africa. De Gaulle came closest to his aims with the Europeans, but there too he ran into problems, primarily with the Dutch, who resisted his efforts at cooperation among the six in that they excluded the existing mechanism constructed by the EEC treaty at Brussels, the British, and NATO. The sub-Saharan African countries of the former French Union, with some exceptions such as Guinea, were receptive to de Gaulle's ideas; but Algeria destroyed the larger enterprise of *Eurafrique*, of which it was expected to be the fulcrum. De Gaulle was defeated by the settlers, who tried to defend the anachronistic and colonialist *"Algérie de Papa"* with a campaign of terrorism and intimidation, and by the die-hard generals, whose rebellion in April 1961 undermined what otherwise seemed a successful struggle to pacify the country on the ground.

But in the final analysis de Gaulle defeated himself in Algeria, by holding out in his negotiations with the rebels for impossible demands while playing an elaborate double, or even triple, game, succeeding only in delaying peace for another year that gave the settlers time to react with a Secret Army Organization terrorist campaign of almost unparalleled viciousness and ferocity. On the one hand, the general attempted to detach the Sahara from Algeria in his negotiations with the FLN and threatened partition of Algeria proper if he did not get his way, and, on the other, he sought in a last desperate effort to construct a "third force" of moderate Muslims in Algeria that would bypass the FLN entirely. Neither tactic worked.

The Kennedy administration from the first showed a much less sympathetic appreciation of de Gaulle's foreign policy than had Eisenhower. This was in keeping with tradition; it had been the Democrats under Truman who distrusted de Gaulle as an authoritarian capable of taking procommunist turns and who had sought at all costs to keep him from power. Now he was back as the Democrats' problem. The tendency was to assimilate him to the once familiar: Assistant Secretary for Europe Foy Kohler wrote Dean Rusk, the new secretary of state, on January 24, 1961, that de Gaulle had simply accentuated positions taken under the Fourth Republic, and the French position was not likely to change when he left power either. The decision to make the atomic bomb had been taken in 1955–56 by the Fourth Republic and formally revealed to the United States early in 1958, although Washington had always been aware of French nuclear plans. The tripartite talks undertaken in response to de Gaulle's memorandum of September 1958 had not thus far been any more fruitful from the American point of view than the French. This should be communicated to the French ambassador with the suggestion that the talks be terminated. But Rusk quickly discovered that, rather than end the talks, the French wanted to widen them: Alphand proposed regular meetings of the heads of government and extending the talks to military matters. If the big three were in agreement on any given issue the French thought their allies in NATO and SEATO would have no choice but to go along. But Rusk would not agree to these suggestions.[1]

On February 15, Rusk interrogated Alphand on the Algerian question, asking whether a show of good will by the West toward the moderates in the FLN would help the negotiations under way. For the moment the Americans were satisfied that de Gaulle had consented to talk to the FLN. The feared pro-Algerian public posture that many had assumed would occur following Kennedy's assumption of power never materialized. Kennedy had been notably silent on Algeria since his statement of 1957; he did not even comment during the Sakiet crisis and he said nothing about Algeria during his campaign.[2] Once in power he seemed content to back de Gaulle in the latter's latest overture to the FLN. Rusk was not aware of the French negotiating position, however, which Michel Debré defined earlier, in January, and had he known he might have been alarmed. Debré wrote that the aim of the negotiations was to achieve an "Algerian Algeria united to France," secure for the European community, respectful of French interests, with France able to orient the direction of its internal political institutions "in the interest of western civilization." France must remain the dominant power in the Mediterranean and the Sahara, and Algeria remained the key to accomplishing this. This meant sovereignty over French bases in Algeria, control of the Sahara, and the union of Algeria itself with France economically, culturally, and in matters of defense. France would oversee economic aid, the Algerian army, and its universities, or the Americans would act in place of France, if not the Soviets.[3]

De Gaulle discussed his three-power directorate idea directly with Prime Minister Macmillan before approaching the new American administration, evidently trying to seduce the British leader to prior adoption of his views. British-French solidarity, de Gaulle told Macmillan, was the basis of three-power unity: France and Britain together would represent Europe to the United States. Macmillan deplored the impending split of Europe economically into groupings of six and seven, but de Gaulle said that if the Common Market had to absorb the Commonwealth it would split apart. The French leader was unhappy that Britain's special relationship with the United States on nuclear questions continued to exclude France, but Macmillan was not about to abandon it. De Gaulle also complained that there was no real integration in NATO, only American hegemony: the idea of a multilateral nuclear force was designed only to prevent the French from developing the *force de frappe* and would never escape Washington's control. The bomb for France was an independent means of protection and a gauge of its independence. The talks concluded without apparent result, and de Gaulle's unhappiness with Macmillan was apparent when Couve de Murville summarized them for the assembled foreign ministers of the

Common Market two weeks later. Macmillan, Couve reported, had wanted to focus the talks with de Gaulle on relations with the continent, but only succeeded in demonstrating that the English saw everything through the prism of their relationship with the United States.[4] Privately, to Adenauer, de Gaulle on several occasions confided his belief that the British were not ready to be a part of Europe, and the chancellor agreed.

On March 15, 1961, Alphand again put de Gaulle's proposals on three-power cooperation to Dean Rusk: the French wanted a permanent tripartite arrangement for global problems, while any nuclear weapons on French soil must be controlled by France and their use linked to worldwide strategic planning. It was up to the United States to decide when France had made "substantial progress" under the terms of the McMahon Act to qualify for U.S. assistance to its nuclear program. But France could only regret that "secrets" already held by the USSR were being denied to France by its major ally. Rusk replied that the United States opposed the spread of nuclear weapons, that it was difficult to assist France because of the McMahon Act unless it were in the context of NATO, and that Secretary Herter had developed a plan, in the multilateral force proposal, to end the French need to produce nuclear weapons of its own. Alphand for the moment ignored the multilateral force proposal, which was to be vigorously combated by Paris; he replied that France could not accept a test-ban treaty under present circumstances, that a three-nation nuclear monopoly by the Anglo-Saxon powers and the Soviet Union was unacceptable, and that France must become a fourth nuclear power before any lines were drawn against proliferation.[5]

The French experienced an arrogant dismissal of their three-power proposals when the Americans supported UN intervention in the Congo crisis. Couve de Murville wrote to all diplomatic posts that Kennedy's action was unacceptable to France because it was presented as a fait accompli; the U.S. government again had failed to consult with its allies in its quest for the goodwill of the neutrals. On February 6, Alphand delivered a personal message from de Gaulle to Kennedy: the Congo was a test of what the three could do together in the world and the Americans had already failed it. The three should have concerted their efforts to force Belgium and the Congolese government to implement their independence treaty and given assistance to the central government of President Kasavubu. No good could come of involving the UN, which could not act in a concerted or disinterested way; the UN secretary-general was proposing to use the forces of "pro-Soviet" countries for his international force of intervention and that would encourage the secession of the resources-rich province of Katanga.[6]

Adenauer was in Paris on February 9; he immediately imparted to de Gaulle his own impression that the new American administration was full of male "prima donnas," an observation with which de Gaulle could only agree; the United States was drifting away from Europe as it became increasingly preoccupied with the rest of the world. Adenauer proposed a new initiative toward integration of the six, but de Gaulle objected to any "supranationality." Instead he proposed that regular meetings between the heads of government of the six and their respective ministers of foreign affairs, education, culture, and communications take place to discuss cooperation in their respective domains.[7] The German chancellor agreed to proceed along these lines. On April 12, Adenauer went on to Washington, where he showed the effects of de Gaulle's seduction. Complaining to his American hosts that NATO was devoid of life and "diseased," he blamed U.S. policies in the UN for causing a setback for France in its relations with Algeria, and remarked that he could not forgive Washington for this. The rebels had been ready two years earlier to sign a peace agreement with France and would have done so had they not been supported by the United States; Adenauer said he had raised this at the time with Eisenhower, who replied that Americans once had been a colonial people too, and could not leave Algeria in the lurch. The chancellor said he could not understand this or go along, adding that the president had then authorized him to tell de Gaulle that the United States would not oppose France in the UN, which Adenauer did, only to see the United States later vote against France anyway. De Gaulle had never forgotten this.[8] Nor apparently had the chancellor.

Kennedy tried to make things up with de Gaulle. He told Alphand that he sincerely wanted harmonious relations with France, and he apologized for the hasty American action in the Congo, admitting that his administration was as yet a bit out of control. But why did de Gaulle continue to support a so-called neutralist regime under Savanna Phouma in Laos that had the backing of Moscow? Kennedy said he would study further de Gaulle's ideas on three-power cooperation, and then asked about Algeria. Alphand pointed to the success of de Gaulle's referendum and asked that the United States do nothing to hinder the secret and delicate negotiations then under way. Kennedy expressed his belief that only de Gaulle was capable of accomplishing peace in Algeria. He repeated that he wanted the best possible relations with France, and said that a gauge of this was his choice of General Gavin, his close personal friend who always had his ear, as the new American ambassador to France.[9] In his February 15 conversation with Alphand, Rusk said he admired the orderly way in which France had decolonized in Africa and retained the friendship of its former colonies. Any American aid to them would be complementary to that of France, and the United States had no desire to substitute the use of the English language for French in Africa.

Rusk then asked about Algeria. Alphand said there were two tendencies in the GPRA, one fanatic and pro-Moscow, the other disposed to reasonable discussion. De Gaulle's policy at its present stage required absolute secrecy and the full confidence of its allies. Rusk said that if in any way the Americans could be useful, Alphand had only to ask. Alphand remarked that the best help the United States could offer was confidence in the French government's sincerity and desire for peace. Rusk, however, noted that a moment of "pregnant opportunity" existed, and warned the ambassador that the United States was under great internal and external pressure to intervene.[10] Washington played no role in the actual peace negotiations, as it turned out, but the French were to feel its presence at every step along the way.[11]

Rusk continued to express Kennedy's desire for the best possible relations with France at every turn, but a subtext of tension underlay each interchange, occasionally bursting to the surface when one or the other nation could not avoid doing something to annoy or antagonize the other. Thus on February 23, Alphand found himself explaining to Rusk that de Gaulle's recent speech emphasizing France's historic "role" in Latin America was not meant to undermine American interests there. Was it, however, tit for tat for perceived American intervention in Africa? De Gaulle wanted to accelerate the economic unification of Europe and give it a *"prolongement politique"* devoid of supranationality and based on the cooperation of states; France meant no harm thereby to NATO, Alphand promised, and it was not interested in creating any rumored "third force" between East and West. Rusk saw a contradiction, however, between de Gaulle's political Europe of the six and Atlantic cooperation in NATO; were there not too many dispersed consultations of various groupings within NATO already? France wanted to add the big three and the six to the existing council of 15, complicating the problems the United States had with the UN, the Commonwealth, and in terms of its own domestic politics. Alphand said, on the contrary, France wanted to strengthen NATO, and that the economic unification of Europe needed a political extension to better integrate Germany with the West. However, the powers with world responsibilities needed to consult among themselves *à trois*. Rusk reiterated Washington's support for the great enterprise of European unification.[12]

De Gaulle rejected external intervention in the Algerian problem whether it came from Washington or Moscow. With Soviet Ambassador Vinogradov he refused to discuss Algeria; it was a private matter that concerned France exclusively, and Soviet public declarations on the subject were "intolerable." Vinogradov said France had implicitly recognized the GPRA by holding talks with it at Melun; therefore, Paris could hardly complain that the USSR did the same by de facto recognition of the GPRA now. Soviet statements on Algeria, moreover, were not aimed at France but at the general evils of colonialism, which the Soviets opposed throughout the world. De Gaulle retorted that this was absurd coming from the most colonialist of countries, and he cautioned the Russians against delivering arms to the FLN.[13] On the other hand, in contrast to his dismissal of Moscow, de Gaulle did try to mollify Washington on Algeria, occasionally even providing privileged confidences. When Averell Harriman came to Paris to prepare Kennedy's visit, de Gaulle told him to inform Kennedy that France was now prepared to negotiate with the FLN without preconditions. Harriman was obviously pleased, and said Kennedy had the greatest admiration for the way that de Gaulle was handling the problem.[14] But within days, Jacques Chaban-Delmas was dispatched to Washington to complain that no satisfactory method of tripartite cooperation had yet been found and that France resented continuously being confronted with American faits accomplis in the Congo, Laos, and China.

On March 16, Alphand again told Rusk that NATO must be revised to meet the changed circumstances in Europe, and that three-power cooperation was necessary. Rusk now said that the United States wanted the greatest possible consultation with Britain and France but could not "institute" any such cooperation beyond the existing NATO Council; the Standing Group, as it existed, must suffice. Moreover, the United States expected mutuality in its relations with its allies: as it put NATO first, so must others. Portugal, like France, demanded solidarity from its allies on Africa without putting into effect genuine reforms there, causing problems in the alliance. France must stop protecting Portugal from criticism of its colonial policies. Rusk repeated that the United States opposed nuclear proliferation and could not help France with its nuclear program. It proposed instead to place medium-range missiles in the hands of the alliance in order to make the building of national nuclear forces unnecessary. Alphand replied that the French nuclear program was irrevocable, and he doubted that any American president would ever delegate his power of decision on nuclear use to NATO or anyone else.[15]

Divisions with France's allies over NATO affected French efforts to secure peace in Algeria. De Gaulle had ample evidence in the preparations for the Melun talks of American ability to mediate in relations with the Algerian rebels; he could also have turned to Tunisia and Morocco, whose offers of good offices dated back to 1956. He rejected all these alternatives as unwanted interference in French internal affairs, preferring to use a pipeline established by the FLN through the Swiss; the confidence the latter enjoyed with the GPRA was not regarded as threatening to French interests. On January 23, 1961, de Gaulle agreed to hold conversations with the GPRA on the future status of Algeria without the prior requirement of a cease-fire.[16] But he would still not recognize the exclusive right of the GPRA to speak for the Algerian people. Consequently the preliminary talks, which began on February 19, 1961, in Lucerne between Georges Pompidou and Ahmed Boumanjel, quickly reached an impasse. Early in March de Gaulle agreed to limit the talks to the GPRA without preconditions, as noted, confiding his decision to Averell Harriman.[17] This concession opened the way for the French government and the FLN to agree on the peace talks themselves, which began at Evian in May. As a gesture of goodwill, de Gaulle amnestied rebel prisoners held in Algeria.

But de Gaulle was by no means optimistic with regard to the outcome of the talks, nor had he abandoned several illusions about the possibilities in Algeria. Discussing the talks with Debré on March 23, de Gaulle observed that if the negotiations failed and Algeria seceded from France, "there will be a regrouping [of populations] and a partition." Not now or later could France renounce this possibility. In effect, France began a none too subtle double, or even triple, game, menacing partition while searching for Muslim moderates in Algeria with whom it could work to create the independent but associated Algeria of its dreams, even as it dealt with the GPRA. De Gaulle and Debré agreed that there could be no sharing of sovereignty with the FLN or anyone else in Algeria until the institutions of self-determination authorized by the referendum of January 8, 1961, were in place. If independence occurred, it would be voted on by all the Algerian people and not "pro-

Figure 4. A group of Algerian rebels shown leaving their camp at Medjana, Constantinois area, where they had been held prisoner. The Algerian "fellaghas" were freed in May 1961 in accordance with the wishes of the French government and its "goodwill" campaign marking the opening of the first talks between France and the FLN in Evian. (Associated Press / WIDE WORLD PHOTOS)

claimed" by the FLN. The Sahara would remain separate from Algeria; when an Algerian state existed, France would negotiate its status with all the other interested states that surrounded it. The Sahara was too important to France's independence, harboring both its projected oil supplies and its terrain of nuclear experimentation. The French army would remain in Algeria after independence to guarantee the rights of the European minority and to prevent a possible dictatorship by the FLN. France would, after a suitable interval, train and equip an Algerian army, but French bases in Algeria and the Sahara would remain under French sovereignty.[18] In the event, de Gaulle got very little of this imposing list a year later when the Evian accords were signed.

On April 4 the French chargé in Tunis reported that American Ambassador Walter Walmsley and Mohammed Boussouf and Mohammed Yazid of the FLN had met: Walmsley reported that the GPRA was ready to negotiate within the framework agreed on between it and the French on March 30 if the French government showed goodwill and "clarified" its position. Walmsley could get nothing more specific but he believed that "clarification" meant that the FLN wanted the release of Ben Bella, for which Sultan Mohammed V of Morocco had also been pressuring. The Americans were not seeking to intervene in the impending negotiations, of course, but they had asked their representative to contact the GPRA to show Washington's support for the peace process.[19] Paris reacted to this with controlled fury. Couve de Murville called in U.S. Ambassador Gavin to express his "shock" at this new American initiative; whatever Washington's motives, Algeria remained a French problem that Paris would deal with itself without intermediaries. Washington knew the French position on recognition; the French had only recently warned the Russians that official recognition of the GPRA on their part would cause France to break off diplomatic relations with Moscow. This incident was somewhat different, but changed nothing in terms of France's objection to what the Americans had done. Already the FLN was taking propaganda advantage of the gesture. In a follow-up message to all French diplomatic representatives abroad, Couve de Murville noted the tendency of allied governments to treat the FLN with new consideration because of the impending peace talks; he defined this as an obstacle to French policy that conferred undeserved prestige on the rebels. France did not recognize the FLN as a government; it had no claim to be one, and nobody could predict that the Algerian people would select it to rule as the outcome of Algerian self-determination. Failing agreement with the FLN, France would implement self-determination in Algeria by itself, bypassing the GPRA in the process.[20]

It is difficult to understand what the French hoped to gain by this attempt to exclude Washington from the peace process. The Americans could pressure the rebels to accept French terms; they were intimately involved with Tunisia and Morocco and would seek ties to an independent Algeria anyway, extending arms and economic aid to all North Africa. Both Tunisia and Morocco had ambitions to be brokers of peace in Algeria and should also have been brought into the final status negotiations in the interest of constructing a pro-French North Africa within which French cooperation with Algeria could take place. Instead de Gaulle rigidly froze both countries out of the negotiations, pushing both further toward Washington. The sultan wanted Ben Bella released to his custody as a French gesture of goodwill to jump-start the negotiations. Bourguiba had been promised negotiations on the final status of Bizerte as part of the settlement of the Sakiet affair, but the French had been dilatory about proceeding with these. The sultan's success in ridding Morocco of both American and French bases caused Bourguiba to conclude that it was an affair of honor for him to do no less. On an amiable visit with de Gaulle in February 1961 at the Chateau de Rambouillet, Bourguiba firmly demanded final status negotiations on Bizerte leading to eventual French withdrawal, but de Gaulle continued to refuse.[21]

The referendum on the creation of an autonomous Algeria on January 8, 1961, was meant to be a show of popular support for de Gaulle: it carried by 15 million yes votes to 5 million no votes in metropolitan France, while 1,749,969 persons cast yes votes as against 767,566 who voted no in Algeria. The results clearly reflected the contrasting views of the Europeans and Muslims, and resulted in the second revolt against de Gaulle in Algiers on April 20, 1961, this time spearheaded by dissatisfied elements of the army rather than the settlers, who took to the streets in support. The army had not openly supported the settler rebellion of January 1960, but it had permitted it to take place; de Gaulle was then able to master the uprising with a rousing television speech. But General Challe, whose military planning had seemingly put Algeria on the road to pacification in 1960, lost de Gaulle's confidence as a result of his attitude during the earlier insurrection and was replaced by General Crépin. Challe resigned from the army altogether on March 1, 1961, disturbed to learn that de Gaulle's policies in Algeria had become part of a grand design to break with the United States, construct an independent nuclear force, and weaken the NATO alliance. Generals Zeller, Salan, and Jouhaud apparently shared Challe's illusion that the United States would help France to keep Algeria if France gave up its nuclear weapons and accepted integration with NATO; the four generals justified their seizure of power in Algiers by claiming that they had prevented Mers-el-Kébir from becoming a Soviet base.[22] Joseph Alsop wrote that Challe believed he could get U.S. support by playing the anticommunist card, given de Gaulle's hostility to NATO. Another reason was thus handed de Gaulle for blaming the Americans: the generals' revolt was the consequence of the American refusal to accept French plans for the reform of NATO.

There was a flurry of rumors at the time affirming that the CIA was in some way involved in the generals' coup. Paris appeared to take them seriously. Gavin was called in by Alexandre Sanguinetti of the Interior Ministry and warned of the anger of the highest French authorities at the suggestion that American "special services" had encouraged General Challe. When Alphand went to see Rusk in Washington, the secretary categorically denied the rumors, terming them "preposterous." He had verified with Allen Dulles that at no level could any agent of the CIA have had authorization to act in such a way. It was true that the rebellious generals had promised Washington that they would make France more cooperative with regard to NATO. However, the American government fully supported General de Gaulle, who represented legality in France against the uprising, and Rusk wanted to quash any rumors and avoid giving the appearance of intervening in French affairs.[23] The French should have understood that the rumors were inherently implausible and almost certainly false. Perhaps, indeed, they did: the CIA in fact had one or more agents active alongside the FLN, providing an alternative form of contact with the rebels in the absence of State Department links since early 1960. Thomas Powers speculates that the French charges of CIA complicity with the generals' revolt in fact reflected de Gaulle's irritation with its actual contacts with the rebels. In a goodwill gesture to the rebels of which the French had to be aware, the CIA arranged in 1961 for Frantz Fanon, the black theorist of colonialism and ideological voice of the FLN, to be treated in Washington for cancer. After his death a CIA officer accompanied his body to Tunisia, from which the FLN carried it to Algeria for burial.[24]

C. L. Sulzberger wrote that the rumors were spread by Moscow with the assistance of certain anti-American milieus in France; alleged in *Izvestia,* they were even given some credence by *Le Monde,* which reported that American agents were involved in Algiers behind General Challe.[25] Such rumors were to be expected given the agency's reputation, and it was not impossible that the plotters had made contact with CIA representatives in Algiers or Paris. General Challe was linked to certain American officers who disliked de Gaulle, and he regarded the defense of Algeria as the key to an overall successful Atlantic strategy. But nobody in Washington wanted the coup to succeed, and Kennedy was known to be in favor of Algerian independence, which was certainly not the position of the rebellious officers.[26] Redha Malek claimed that the rumors arose because two American military attachés were seen using the studios of Radio France, which was under the control of the insurgents in Algiers, to transmit their dispatches; the Quai was alleged to have protested, but then to have withdrawn the protest with apologies.[27] Allen Dulles issued a blanket public denial of all such rumors, blaming them on the French political right, and State Department spokesmen stressed that American policy during the coup was fully to support France. The Americans noted that it was unusual for the CIA to concern itself with public rumors, but this case was regarded as exceptional.

American policy was quite the opposite of what the rumors charged: General Gavin was authorized by Kennedy to put American naval units at the disposition of France to help suppress the rising, and his visit to de Gaulle on April 23 was clearly meant as a demonstration of official American support. Although de Gaulle's personal authority and prestige were recognized, the U.S. press trumpeted the American action as producing the turnaround in de Gaulle's fortunes the next day. The American consul in Algiers warned Challe that U.S. forces would be used to prevent the rebellion from spreading to France; the U.S. fleet in the Mediterranean was ready to intercept any rebel planes headed for Paris. Jeffrey Lefebvre quotes American officials as rejecting Challe's offers because if he succeeded, "the US would inevitably take a violently opposite line to his Algerian policy and by definition we would be opposed to him."[28] Alphand saw claims of an American role in mastering the crisis as a gross exaggeration: the victory in the crisis was de Gaulle's alone, whose dramatic televised call to conscripts not to heed their rebellious leaders was heard. But in the event, neither the rumored American support for the rebels nor the actual American offer of assistance against them were welcome in Paris. This was again a case in which Washington was damned if it did and damned if it didn't, which had been typical of the Algerian crisis from its inception.

It had apparently occurred to nobody in Washington that no French government worthy of the name would have called on foreign troops to restore order at home. Alphand thought the United States was seeking a foreign policy success at the expense of France in the face of its recent failures; Kennedy had suffered a humiliation only a month earlier when the CIA-sponsored invasion of Cuba came to disaster at the Bay of Pigs. But Alphand thought the crisis salutary in one respect; it had given the Americans renewed appreciation of the importance of de Gaulle to the stability of France. The way was now open to peace in Algeria, moreover; with the opposition of the army and the settlers neutralized, all now depended on the attitude of the FLN.[29] In the event, this analysis was far too simple and optimistic: it takes two to negotiate and as much or more depended on de Gaulle. Nor did Alphand realize that the coup was a disturbing example of continued political instability in France and militated in Washington against those who thought cooperation with, or nuclear aid to, France desirable. Kennedy was so irritated at continued French charges of CIA complicity with the insurrection that he considered calling off his June 1961 trip to Paris.[30]

De Gaulle never indicated that he expected anything from the Americans for his policy change in Algeria, but it was reasonable to suppose that with the Algerian problem removed as an irritant in relations he might expect that they would show some give on other questions. This had been the case with Eisenhower and Herter. But if de Gaulle believed this, he was badly mistaken: U.S. policy seemed bent on a collision course with France notwithstanding. The French took no solace from the fact that the United States was causing problems with the British too by its determination that both Britain and France be phased out of the nuclear business while the United States responded to the deterrent needs of both countries through NATO.[31] This, together with the looming Berlin crisis, was the background to the de Gaulle-Kennedy meeting of June 1, 1961. On Berlin, de Gaulle repeated to Kennedy the hard line that Paris had been following from the beginning. The Russians were bluffing and did not want war; the West should give them nothing. De Gaulle would not associate himself with any Anglo-American attempt to negotiate an altered status for Berlin. This was all very admirable and it made de Gaulle the hero he wished to be in the eyes of Chancellor Adenauer.[32] But it was also unrealistic and was taken by the Americans as so much bombast coming from the French. There existed a tripartite plan of the big three, dubbed "Live Oak," for opening access to Berlin by force if the Russians or East Germans blockaded the city, and the French were expected to contribute a division to it. But with French forces still tied up in Algeria, France could not supply more than a battalion. The Quai was aware that the Anglo-Americans took de Gaulle's policy of firmness as "more apparent than real."[33]

De Gaulle again demanded of Kennedy that the organization of the alliance be changed. Europe and France were no longer weak and the American nuclear monopoly was gone. France had regained its ambition and must have its own defense. Kennedy asked what would happen if the Germans demanded nuclear weapons too, but de Gaulle did not reply. Integration of French forces in NATO was unacceptable to France: the generals' revolt of April, de Gaulle said, had been a consequence of the "denationalization" of French defenses which left the military lacking in a sense of national responsibility. The insurrection was the fault of NATO's system of integrated command rather than of France's being embroiled in Algeria. Kennedy promised to transfer nuclear weapons to NATO's command, making the French deterrent unnecessary, but de Gaulle doubted that the Americans would ever surrender veto power over their use, in which reasoning he turned out to be on the mark once the American multilateral force proposals were formulated.[34] In February 1961 de Gaulle had put it bluntly to Gavin: "Unless the US will relinquish veto control over launch of a nuclear weapon, France will not seriously consider a NATO nuclear force."[35] The United States could not and did not do so.

There were limited areas of agreement between the two leaders: a firm policy on Berlin, but not negotiations, and, finally, Algerian self-determination, at least insofar as the Americans understood what the French were up to there. But there was disagreement on Cuba, the Congo crisis, and Laos, about which de Gaulle prophetically warned the young president not to become caught up in "entanglement without end" in Indochina; the problem, de Gaulle said, was that Indochina lacked states but was rather made up of "*nébuleuses*," invertebrate organisms that could not be defended. Indochina was unmanageable and peripheral to broader Western security concerns anyway.[36] Wise words that the Americans were to ignore at their peril. It is extraordinary how clairvoyant each leader could be about the problems of the other. But then it was a pity de Gaulle had not himself thought of neutralization or withdrawal when France was embroiled in Indochina from 1947 to 1954. Not to mention the applicability of these words to Algeria.

The military revolt of April weakened France's negotiating position with the Americans and limited French ability to make concessions at the Evian negotiations as well. Agreement to discuss political questions in the absence of a cease-fire was of little use without some willingness to compromise on these questions. The instructions given the French delegates specified that Algerian self-determination was dependent on the January 8, 1961, referendum, which was now law; it provided for a free vote of the Algerian people to determine their future until which time France remained sovereign. In the event of separation, France would protect the European population through a policy of regrouping. It remained ambiguous as to whether regrouping meant permanent partition, but French negotiators assumed so. If association were the choice, as expected, it would involve ties between the two countries in matters of the economy, finance, culture, and defense. France would under these circumstances continue the Constantine Plan, preserve the French language and culture, and maintain its army and bases under French sovereignty.[37]

De Gaulle had spoken of an "Algerian Algeria" and said that an "Algerian Republic" would exist one day. What did he mean by these elliptical statements? Did he have a specific settlement in mind? Jean Morin was appointed his delegate general in Algeria in January 1961 in place of Paul Delouvrier. Morin defined an "Algerian Algeria" to mean a political entity with its own "personality," in association with France, and based on a domestic structure of shared power, with institutions representing both Europeans and moderate Muslims that would provide an alternative to the FLN. Morin's task was to put in place departmental assemblies, a majority of which would be Muslim, and to find competent moderate Muslim prefects to run ten of Algeria's thirteen departments. By the terms of decrees of January 21, 1961, regional consultative economic and social councils were to be put in place to advise the prefects, increased powers were granted to the departmental councils, councils were instituted in *arrondissements*, and Muslim prefects and prefects of police were empowered to take office. Morin began an extensive program to prepare Muslims to enter the existing bureaucratic structure in the country at the lower levels. The idea was to confront the FLN with a fait accompli: a moderate structure of Muslim power, in cooperation with France, that the FLN could not dismantle and which it would eventually enter with the aim of taking advantage of its democratic features. The FLN would become one party among others and accommodate itself democratically to the existing reality.[38]

Why did this plan fail? There were many reasons. The generals' revolt of April dealt it an early blow, and it was followed by the proliferation of ultra groups who joined forces behind the terrorist Organisation de l'Armée Secrète (OAS), which carried out a campaign of intimidation and violence that opened an unbridgeable gulf between the Muslim and European communities such that, faced with the reality of Muslim power in the end, the Europeans felt that they had no alternative but to emigrate. Just as important was the continued FLN campaign of "compliance terrorism" among the Muslim population that threatened to punish any suspected collaboration with death and mutilation. Morin found it virtually impossible to find competent Muslims to collaborate in the setting up of the projected institutions of Muslim power; he tried to create a national consultative assembly and a provisional executive composed of Muslims and Europeans, but he could not entice a sufficient number of moderate Muslims to work with him. Morin blamed Louis Joxe, de Gaulle's minister for Algeria and chief negotiator, who put more faith in his ability to negotiate a satisfactory settlement with the FLN than in any projected structure of French-created Muslim power. De Gaulle later blamed himself for failing to oversee directly what was taking place in Algeria. He allegedly left implementation of his decrees to Joxe, who did not carry them out, although it is hard to take this claim seriously. More likely, after the generals' revolt, he concluded that it had become more important to disengage from Algeria rapidly than to have alternative institutions in place.[39] France was isolated in the UN and alienated from its allies, and time was working against it.

Already right-wing groups in the army and among the settler population were organizing to prevent independence coming to Algeria violently through the OAS. This created an objective alliance between de Gaulle and the rebels against the OAS that was to play itself out in an orgy of violence. At Evian, Joxe demanded guarantees for the European population in the form of dual nationality, which he also wanted extended to Algeria's Jews, who enjoyed French citizenship. The paradox here is evident: France, the uniform homogeneous state par excellence, was advocating or proposing a binational or multicultural state in Algeria. Nor would France consider surrendering the Sahara, whose oil reserves appeared essential to the pursuit of *la grandeur* and which had only been integrated with Algeria since 1947. The GPRA made no concessions on any of this. Taking its cue from the historic French notion of *la nation*, it insisted that all its future population must have Algerian nationality exclusively. The Europeans would enjoy full democratic rights within an independent Algeria, but as Algerians. If they chose to remain French, they would have to apply to be foreign residents. The Sahara, moreover, was an integral part of the Algerian national territory.

The Evian talks quickly threatened, like those at Melun, to become a dialogue of the deaf. Joxe insisted that France was sovereign in Algeria until it voted under French auspices; Belkacem Krim replied that Algeria was sovereign and had been so since de Gaulle on September 16, 1959, declared that self-determination was to be applied there. Under these conditions it is hardly surprising that the negotiations at Evian, held from May 20 to June 13, 1961, once again broke down.[40] Neither side showed any willingness to compromise. Taking stock of the three weeks of talks, the GPRA concluded that the French had offered nothing beyond the September 1959 declaration of de Gaulle. The French position removed all positive content from decolonization; the Algerians had made all the "constructive proposals," which the French turned down.[41] The French expressed frustration that the FLN responded to a cessation of military operations by augmenting their own. Other than the vague principle of self-determination, there had been disagreement on virtually everything else. The FLN said Algeria existed as a state; the French said it was only a state "in formation." The FLN refused to discuss the internal organization of an independent Algeria or to guarantee its European population its rights because that would "predetermine" Algeria's constitution. Algerian Jews, the FLN said, were "simple autochthonous residents" who required no special rights. The Sahara was a province and, most ominously, the property rights of European citizens were in some cases "revocable." The French thought no peace was possible under such circumstances.[42]

There was another attempt at agreement in Lugrin from July 20 to 28, but it was no more successful, and the GPRA broke off negotiations. In the interval the idea of partitioning Algeria between the European and the Muslim populations was floated publicly in Paris, possibly as a ruse to pressure the FLN into moderating its negotiating position, but more likely as a trial balloon. De Gaulle had given every indication of meaning it seriously. If it was meant to pressure the rebels, it was a failure; the FLN did not change its demands. Alain Peyrefitte says that de Gaulle asked him to float the idea by writing newspaper articles and a short book proposing a kind of "French Israel" in the coastal region in which the European population would be in the majority. The Sahara would be tied to the French part of Algeria, thus solving the two problems of the colons and the Sahara independently of the GPRA.[43] De Gaulle's real aim for Peyrefitte was to pressure the GPRA into a more accommodating negotiating posture. But in discussions with Debré, de Gaulle indicated his seriousness about the idea and Joxe warned Krim at Evian that failing the establishment of "organic" relations between an independent Algeria and France, the FLN ran the risk of partition. Krim remained unmoved: Algeria would determine the nature and extent of its relations with France after it was independent, he said. Joxe noted the example of India and Pakistan and said France would protect the Europeans in Algeria who chose to remain there. Krim remained impassive.[44]

The idea caused a flurry of discussion in France and was taken seriously by the rebels. A national day of protest against partition was held in Algeria on July 5, 1961, accompanied by a general strike in Algiers, which the French tried to break. Over 100 people died in confrontations between French authorities and demonstrators around the country as a direct consequence.[45] There were also demonstrations in Tunisia, where the GPRA denounced the idea as a threat to negotiations and the negation of the principle of self-determination: it was an invitation to permanent war between the European and Muslim populations, and presented the greatest danger to the Europeans.[46] On November 19 de Gaulle told Peyrefitte to squelch further discussion of the issue; it had grown too big too quickly, and the general feared he would be obliged to deal with an impractical idea as he had had to do with *Algérie française*. The problem was the colons; Ben-Gurion had pushed the idea on him, de Gaulle later said, but the Israeli model was inapplicable in Algeria. The Israelis had defended themselves, but the colons depended entirely on France.

It was in this context of failed negotiations, the threat of partition of Algeria, and rising OAS terror that the Bizerte crisis erupted. Bourguiba lost patience with the French refusal to negotiate or withdraw from the base and ordered his troops to attack on July 27. It was a rash and ill-considered move born of frustration. De Gaulle fortified the base and ordered his troops to hold firm, and the attacking Tunisians, who were outmatched and outgunned, took hundreds of casualties before calling off their effort. Washington was infuriated, and an acerbic exchange took place between Rusk and Couve de Murville. Rusk observed that forty-seven out of forty-eight countries in the UN now wished to reprimand France; the United States would not again offer its good offices, but Franco-Tunisian relations must be restored. There was a link for Rusk between Bizerte and Berlin: mesmerized by Tunisia, the Afro-Asian bloc had lost sight of Soviet aggression. They cared only that the USSR supported an African state against a NATO ally that was supported by the United States. Couve said France could not reward aggression, but Rusk demanded to know why Paris refused to talk to the Tunisians about the base. What was the legal basis for the French claim? What plans did the French have for it in the long term? Rusk demanded a French gesture of goodwill toward the Tunisians. It was impossible to preserve bases against the will of the country in which they were situated. Couve pointed to Guantanamo in Cuba, where the American presence was not welcome either. But Rusk demanded that France begin talks with the Tunisians, and warned that the UN debate would damage U.S. relations with France.[47]

As the Berlin crisis reached a climax in August 1961, France clashed with the Americans and British over the correct approach to Moscow. De Gaulle, to placate Adenauer, would make no concessions to Moscow.

If the Soviet Union tried shifting control of access to the East Germans, de Gaulle warned Vinogradov, then France would resign itself to nuclear war. Rusk wanted a firm posture toward Moscow but thought negotiations essential to win over Third World opinion and the neutrals, for whom the French continued to show only contempt. Yet when it came to military measures to back up the tough Western stance, Couve de Murville could point to only one French division recalled from Algeria to Lorraine, with a second to follow, "conditions permitting." Algeria was not discussed, but there was no question of where the rest of the French army was deployed.[48] Rusk saw de Gaulle personally on August 8; the French president said that the existing three-power consultations on Berlin did not meet his criteria for organized cooperation of the big three, while Rusk pointedly refused to reject negotiations with the Russians. France had best go along since it could not fight the Russians alone. But de Gaulle was as uncompromising on Berlin as on Bizerte: Tunisia had attacked, France had defended itself. If the Tunisians wanted to talk now, fine, if the Americans had influence with them, so much the better. But de Gaulle was telling Rusk this "*pour lui faire plaisir,*" just as the Americans had done with France in the case of Cuba, implying that Bizerte was really none of Rusk's business.[49]

The sealing of Berlin by the East Germans and the building of the wall tempered the French approach to the Anglo-Americans. Couve de Murville still saw no point to negotiations with the Russians, but agreed that the West had to reinforce itself militarily. De Gaulle wrote a conciliatory message to Kennedy, but Rusk could not understand the French position. American opinion demanded a diplomatic initiative to Moscow. This did not imply weakness; on the contrary, it was the French-created disunity of the West that caused it to be weak. The U.S. government failed to understand why it was so difficult to come to agreement with France. Whether it was the test-ban treaty, disarmament, Laos, the Congo, the United Nations, or Berlin, the two countries could not seem to work in harmony. Couve de Murville thought Rusk spoke too "hastily"; despite differences, he reminded the American, the long-term goals of the two nations and their values remained the same. But it was clear that relations had come to a critical point.[50]

De Gaulle, however, was forced to come to terms with the weakness of the French army, which was in crisis as a result of the revolt of April and the unwelcome task of having to confront the violence of the OAS along with that of the FLN. An intelligence mission to Algeria by Chief of Staff General Olié found the army's morale devastated by its politicization and involvement in tasks for which it was not suited. Since April there had been a degradation of discipline, political "intoxication," and "denationalization." After a month of the unilateral French cease-fire, the rebel bands had been reconstituted and their logistics and infrastructure once again put in place. Their hold on the Muslim population appeared firm. The army had done everything possible to win over the Muslim population to French rule, but the colons had done nothing, and now the army's heart was no longer in the struggle. The situation was dangerous: the French state now lacked a functioning system of intelligence, an efficient and loyal police, and an exemplary system of justice; it could not afford to lose its army as well. Whether the consequence in Algeria was to be association or divorce, whether it was accomplished in order or disorder, the imperative was to get out.[51]

In the absence of further negotiations with the French, a power shift occurred within the FLN; at a meeting of the rebel national council on September 1, Abbas was replaced as president by Youssef Ben Khedda in a victory for the hard-liners. Krim moved from the Ministry of the Interior to Foreign Affairs, which oriented the GPRA closer to the Chinese in its foreign policy. Five top ministers now were all hardened revolutionaries, and Ben Khedda was an avowed Marxist. The new government said it remained committed to negotiations. But its formation was the final straw in the collapse of de Gaulle's policy. There was clearly nothing to be got now from the FLN except continued warfare under increasingly adverse conditions in Algeria, with a demoralized French army fighting on two fronts, against the FLN and the settlers, who overwhelmingly appeared to back the OAS.

De Gaulle now made the inevitable deduction. His policy, he told U.S. Ambassador General Gavin on September 2, was one of disengagement. The creation of a satisfactory Algerian government, under the FLN or another group, would result in self-determination. If no such government emerged, France would leave Algeria to itself, regrouping the European population around Algiers and Oran. There would be chaos in the rest. Gavin said that the United States feared chaos and wanted to avoid it. The Americans were in periodic contact with the FLN; Washington could press the rebels to put into place an orderly transitional government for Algeria. Should it not do so, keeping France informed? De Gaulle no longer objected. France did not need association with Algeria anyway, he said, resigning himself to the worst: Algeria had become burdensome and unprofitable, and whether it was under Abbas or Ben Khedda was now a matter of indifference to him. If

France were approached, it would come to an agreement, if not, Algeria could go the way of Guinea. Pre-informing Gavin of his all-important policy shift, de Gaulle said he understood that the Sahara must revert to Algeria. French interests there were in gas and oil; if there were agreement on common exploitation, France would remain there, if not it would leave. Gavin said UN Ambassador Adlai Stevenson was working with the Tunisians for détente over Bizerte. De Gaulle said there could be no evacuation of the base, which was all the more necessary to the West in view of the crisis over Berlin. France had no objection to Stevenson trying to calm Tunisia down, but the United States, when it intervened, should ask as much of the Tunisians as it did habitually of France. For his part, de Gaulle would write once again to Kennedy. The Americans should know that in case of catastrophe, France remained with the United States.[52]

De Gaulle now faced stalemate in Algeria and a crisis with the Americans, frozen relations with both Tunisia and Morocco, and the hostility of the world over Tunisia and the continued war in Algeria, not to mention the demoralization of the French army. He announced the crucial decision to recognize the GPRA's claim to the Sahara on September 5, 1961. This opened the way for the resumption of negotiations with the FLN. Pressures were overwhelming, making it clear that much of what France hoped to salvage in North Africa was threatened by further continuation of the war. Washington had been given the green light by Paris; on September 13, Ambassador Walmsley met with Krim and Saad Dahlab in Tunis, while Chanderli talked to UN representatives in New York. The United States sought to encourage negotiations and assured the FLN of its goodwill while urging it to cooperate with France. The rebels said they were ready for further negotiations despite the dispiriting results of Evian and Lugrin; they were interested in de Gaulle's change of policy on the Sahara, and they could promise the Americans that once independent, their policy would be nonaligned. In October France came under renewed attack in the UN; few of those addressing the Algerian situation expressed confidence any longer in de Gaulle's policies. The French were also caught between their support of Adenauer's refusal to negotiate with the USSR over its demands on Berlin and the British-American resolve to do so. On October 30, Gavin read de Gaulle a blunt Kennedy message. The American people were deceived and disappointed by de Gaulle's position on Berlin. Public opinion in a democracy required that all peaceful means be explored before a decision could be made to go to war. The French position was prejudicial to American policy and harmful to the West. The United States had called up its reserves, had more troops ready for combat over Berlin than all the other NATO powers combined, and was negotiating from strength. Kennedy was mystified by the refusal of the French to do the same.[53]

De Gaulle's hopes for European political cooperation on his own terms also met with disappointment. Opposition came from the Dutch, who saw de Gaulle abandoning the Atlantic alliance, maneuvering himself into a privileged place alongside the Anglo-Americans, and seeking to make of Paris the capital of a European "third force" whose policies would be largely made in France. The Belgians backed the Dutch in insisting that talks on European political cooperation include the British and reaffirm the alliance with the Americans. Rejecting de Gaulle's scheme as "minimalist," the two smaller powers held out for real integration or nothing. Ironically, the French negotiator Christian Fouchet noted at the time that admitting England to the talks would actually have furthered de Gaulle's project, since the British were also opposed to the integration of Europe and favored something more akin to de Gaulle's Europe of states. But having the British as part of Europe would have foiled de Gaulle's plans for a European third force, independent of Washington and headed by France alone.[54]

Secret talks with the FLN in Basle, Switzerland, produced agreement on the terms of a reprise of the negotiations on November 19. Washington now continued regular contacts with the FLN, which informed it of the status of its negotiations with the French; the Americans informed Paris of these contacts in turn. The French protest in Washington now was feeble. But problems remained: the Sahara was to be Algerian, but how its self-determination was to be carried out still had to be determined along with the terms of Algerian-French cooperation in exploiting it.[55] There also remained the issue of the rights of the colons. The French demanded a separate justice system for the Europeans and guarantees of their political representation. They should enjoy dual nationality and have their property rights guaranteed, or the French thought too many of them would leave and Algeria would become an Arab state. But this was precisely the aim of the extremist group now in power in the GPRA, which feared the creation of a settler state within a state. It was revealing of France's negotiating weakness that all these issues were settled on the GPRA's terms during nine tense days of negotiations, February 11 to 20, 1962. The signing of the accords came on March 19.

The agreements brought little satisfaction to the main protagonists. The right in France saw in the accords a shameful capitulation, centrists deplored the wholesale violation of the agreements shortly after they were signed, and leftists condemned what they saw as the construction of a neocolonialist system. But the Americans and the world were relieved. Perhaps this confusion was the necessary result of the strange way the war ended; France was never defeated on the ground, but was obliged to give in because it could neither end the war satisfactorily—by establishing a level of pacification such that normal life could continue—nor deal with the international consequences of the war's continuation. Nor could it prevent the explosion of violence against the peace accords initiated by the OAS, whose campaign of terror killed 2,500 persons, while the climate of semi-anarchy and civil war created by Algerian reprisals convinced the overwhelming majority of the European population in Algeria that it had to choose between "the valise or the coffin." On the other hand, the failure of the GPRA to achieve a clear-cut victory meant that it had to accept what it regarded as infringements on its sovereignty, which it would repudiate later when conditions permitted.[56]

Scholars have tended to praise de Gaulle for extricating France from Algeria, but it seems hard to avoid the conclusion that his stubbornness up to the last phase of the negotiations, idle threats to carry out partition, and vain efforts to construct a third force of moderate Muslims contributed to the chaos that accompanied the peace accords. By July 1962, the bulk of the European population had fled in disorder. De Gaulle was in large part responsible for this worst of all possible outcomes. His untenable promises to the army and the settlers when he took power, followed by the elliptical nature of his policy statements that elude clear interpretation today, helped produce the disillusionment and vicious extremism that followed. The same policies helped ensure the victory of the extremists in the FLN, who succeeded in ousting the moderate Ferhat Abbas before the final phase of negotiations, determining that the French would get fewer of their demands than would have been the case otherwise. The refusal to negotiate French withdrawal from Bizerte caused a futile and stupid war with Tunisia that alienated Bourguiba from further cooperation with France for many years and brought down the opprobrium of the world, while de Gaulle's insistence on keeping Ben Bella in prison to the last, against the advice of his own ambassador in Morocco, alienated the sultan and further strengthened the hand of the extremists in the FLN. The chaotic French withdrawal resulted in the slaughter of many thousands of *harkis*, Muslims who had fought on the French side, who inexplicably were denied

Figure 5.   French armored vehicles replaced civilian traffic in the heart of
Algiers on March 24, 1962, after French troops' bloody battle with die-hard
Europeans opposing the move to make Algeria free. These battle-ready
army cars took up their stations in Guillermin Square behind a barbed-wire
barricade in downtown Algiers following the outbreak of full-scale fighting in
the city's Bab el Oued district. (Associated Press / WIDE WORLD PHOTOS)

refuge in France as recompense for their having fought for it. It is hard
to conceive of a worse outcome than the one de Gaulle managed to produce short of an actual French civil war. His policy resembled that of
Nixon in Vietnam, who pursued the Vietnam War longer than Johnson
did, and escalated it by bombing Cambodia before bringing it to an end.
Similarly, de Gaulle, whom Nixon so much admired, fought longer in
Algeria than had the Fourth Republic and escalated the war in a vain attempt to win it before negotiating peace.[57]

Could the actual signing of the agreements produce a thaw in French-
American relations? Kennedy's new ambassador to France, General
James Gavin, appeared to think so. Noting existing tensions with France,
he nevertheless argued that the French leader stood with the West on fun-

damental questions, and pleaded for an understanding of de Gaulle's policies and for greater willingness in Washington to listen to his counsel.[58] In
a conversation with former Premier Edgar Faure on February 28, 1962,
President Kennedy regretted that relations with France were less good
than they had once been. With Algeria settled, there remained as points of
contention NATO, nuclear weapons, and Berlin.[59] Maxwell Taylor also
now pleaded with the president for a change in policy toward France. The
depressed state of American relations with France was almost entirely
due to American opposition to the French atomic program. If the United
States changed its policy, Taylor thought, it would secure loyal French cooperation in NATO and the normalization of relations with a France free
of colonial conflicts. The French were bitter over their exclusion from
U.S. aid on projects so basic that "it strains the imagination to find justification in the McMahon act." No European officials believed that
France would not carry out its program in spite of the cost of having to
rediscover what the United States and the Soviets already knew. The U.S.
insistence that it not do so was self-defeating and harmful to NATO itself.[60] But Rusk opposed Taylor on the grounds that assisting France
would mean that Germany in turn would want its own nuclear program.

Rusk's resentment of de Gaulle was not limited to the nuclear question, however. De Gaulle, he said, wanted consultation only on matters
of interest to others but accepted no advice himself, whether on Bizerte
or Algeria. All American proffers of aid and advice respecting North
Africa had been systematically rejected right through the peace negotiations of 1962. France was not de Gaulle, despite the pretensions of the
French leader personally to embody his nation, and under de Gaulle's
rule it did not deserve the same trust and confidence the United States
was able to place in the United Kingdom. Robert McNamara argued
that France would have an aircraft strike capability for its nuclear force
by 1965 and missiles by 1970 anyway, and this robbed its conventional
force strength and thus limited its participation in NATO. It was worth
finding out what it would take to change this. But the president supported Rusk; he feared the reaction of Germany to such a policy, as well
as that of the United Kingdom. Rusk said the United States should reduce aid to the British and not increase it to the French, calling the 1958
agreement to aid Britain under the terms of the revised McMahon Act a
mistake. The multilateral force, on which Washington pinned its hopes
that all the NATO powers would forgo the construction of independent
nuclear forces, was formally proposed to NATO on May 9, 1962, in

Athens, in what Washington thought one of the most successful meetings in the history of the alliance.

Gavin tried again in a letter to President Kennedy on March 9, 1962. Noting the refusal of nuclear help to France, even extending to the sale of enriched uranium, the ambassador observed that the United States was asking France to buy more in America for balance of payments reasons while refusing to sell France what it wanted. The criterion of "substantial progress" in terms of the McMahon Act needed reevaluation; there was an acute danger of this question affecting other areas at issue between the two countries. As if it had not already done so. But Under Secretary of State George Ball replied to Gavin that there was an impasse with France on nuclear questions, and it was best to cease discussing the issue, which could only become worse.[61]

The Americans were also irritated by their inability to get the Israelis to agree to an inspection of their French-built nuclear reactor at Dimona. When access was finally granted, inspectors found no evidence of a weapons program but were bothered by the strong evidence of close French scientific collaboration and support to be seen. An analysis for the Joint Chiefs noted that France had supplied the plans, material, equipment, uranium, and technical assistance necessary to make the manufacture of nuclear weapons possible, and it was also training Israeli personnel. Covert French support for Israeli nuclear programs, the Americans feared, would touch off a wave of criticism of France in the Arab world and have an impact on U.S. policies in the Middle East. Moreover, if France gained too strong an influence over Israeli policy, differences in NATO might be projected into the Middle East. The United States must try to convince France and Israel that an Israeli nuclear capability was against the best interests of France, the United States, Israel, and the Middle East.[62] But it was no more possible to deter the Israelis from producing nuclear weapons than it was the British or the French.

While proposing the multilateral force in Athens in May 1962, Rusk laid out the problems with regard to nuclear sharing with France for the benefit of the Germans and Canadians. He also went on to vent all his other grievances against the French: their policies inhibited European integration, their views on the alliance favored a narrow nationalism rather than collective defense, they vigorously and inflexibly pushed for their three-power directorate of NATO but otherwise showed "contempt" for NATO and the UN, the pillars of U.S. policy, and they were not pulling their weight with regard to Berlin and NATO's forward defense in Germany. Most strongly of all, Rusk rejected the idea that France had regained its strength and stability. It was, rather, paralyzed by the danger of a right-wing coup, and it still contained a powerful Communist party and extreme left as candidates for a successor government should de Gaulle fail. Unmentioned were the OAS terrorist outrages, the bombs constantly being exploded in Paris, the flight of refugees from newly independent Algeria, and the danger of assassination of de Gaulle himself, all of which made France appear a poor candidate for nuclear assistance. Despite the conclusion of the Evian agreements, the Algerian problem would not so quickly go away. France needed years beyond the troubled picture it continued to present to the world in 1962, and indeed for the duration of de Gaulle's hold on power, before Washington would trust it as a suitable custodian of nuclear weapons. If the purpose of creating a French deterrent was de Gaulle's pursuit of independence and not cooperation with NATO, which is what Rusk suspected, then cooperation was really impossible.[63]

Kennedy's agreement with Rusk became clear in a conversation with the visiting André Malraux, then de Gaulle's minister of culture, on May 11, 1962. The president told Malraux that he disliked the French idea of a Europe without the United Kingdom and independent of the United States, a powerful third force that France pretended to speak for. The United States would be glad to leave Europe if the Europeans wished it, but it had called up 160,000 men during the Berlin crisis while France had moved only two divisions. Malraux said that for France to master its army, it must have a truly national defense. He would have done better to omit this argument; it could not have done the French any good to admit tacitly that their army was still disobedient to civilian authority. But passing this issue by, President Kennedy said he found it hard to understand the latent, "almost female" hostility in Germany and France lying behind the sentiment that the United States might not be reliable in keeping its engagements. Kennedy thus continued a long tradition of Washington stereotyping alleged French inferiority in terms of then-prevailing views of gender.[64] Why was there such strong opposition to NATO in France? Kennedy asked. If there was a Franco-German axis, let it handle Berlin; the Americans were willing to get out. The alliance was in disarray and the president was "getting tired of it." There was no cooperation to be had from de Gaulle, who was working to expel the United States from Europe.[65] A few days later, Gavin found de Gaulle in possession of Malraux's report of the conversation; he had "never seen de Gaulle in a more unfriendly and tense state of mind." The French president was tired himself of excessive American claims to "leadership." The Americans had opened negotiations with the Russians on Berlin without consulting with their allies and decided that France should not have an atomic force. Well, France was responsible for itself, thank you; if the United States persisted, everyone in Europe would discover that they needed to look out for themselves. Gavin thought the gap between the two countries worse than it had been in a long time.

On his European trip in June 1962, Rusk got a cold reception from Couve de Murville. The French foreign minister saw nothing new accomplished at Athens. Nobody knew what a multilateral European weapon might mean, Couve complained. France was a world power: it had non-NATO interests to consider and its own nuclear force was a "fact of life." Rusk asked whether the end of the Algerian War meant that more French forces would now be available to NATO. Couve was evasive and would not say where or in what strength the army would be deployed outside France. The French nuclear weapons program had begun in 1954, and China, India, Sweden, and Israel, in addition to France, were all now capable of building nuclear weapons. It was inconceivable that France not have its own nuclear arms as well. After seeing the French president, Rusk moderated his views. He now thought de Gaulle's motive for building a nuclear force "psychological and subjective" and based on a simple desire for equality that must be understood if not acquiesced to. De Gaulle had contempt for smaller and weaker countries, and he wanted the status that the Americans and British could help confer upon him, failing to understand that the United States could not do so without injury to the Italians and Germans. He was basically friendly to the United States and had been favorably impressed by Kennedy, and those under him remained eager to work with the United States. He could be educated to the indivisibility of nuclear warfare and would eventually accept European integration.[66]

By the terms of the Nassau agreement of January 1963, the British abandoned their effort to purchase the air-to-air missile, Skybolt, which Washington cancelled, and accepted the offer of Polaris missile-launching submarines instead, with the proviso that they would be integrated with the NATO multilateral force. After the agreement, Rusk still vainly hoped that de Gaulle would not reject cooperation with NATO and he offered Polaris submarines to France on the same terms as Britain. But de Gaulle reacted angrily, feeling that Britain had abandoned its deterrent and its claims to be a world power and demonstrated that it preferred its relationship to the United States to the construction of Europe. He responded by rejecting Britain's candidacy for the Common Market along with the Nassau agreement. Kennedy panicked. He now feared "heavy going" with de Gaulle, who might turn to Moscow. Having locked the British out of Europe, he might try to lock the Americans out as well. At present "de Gaulle is cooperating with us in none of our policies" and would try to "run us out of Europe by means of a deal with the Russians." There was a danger that the Germans might even follow him in this. He was prepared to break up NATO and neutralize Europe.[67] McNamara was depressed about the remaining American options, saying that the United States must perhaps "disengage entirely from Europe" and tie itself to powers other than France. McGeorge Bundy of the NSC more realistically thought NATO headquarters might be moved out of Paris; the Americans were prepared to propose this three years before de Gaulle demanded that it happen. Robert Kennedy agreed with McNamara that the United States might be better off getting out of Europe altogether.

Ambassador to France Charles Bohlen tried to tone down the apocalyptic thinking about France to which Washington seemed to be leaning. De Gaulle was simply in bad humor, the ambassador said, and suspicious of everyone. He had no "deal" in the works with the USSR, although he was certainly contemplating some kind of move in that direction. His ministers were kept in ignorance of his policies, however, and even Couve de Murville knew nothing. De Gaulle was not, however, a Machiavellian plotter; rather his purposes were clear. He was constructing a conservative, hierarchical, religious, and military France. He was ignorant of the United States, believed ideologies to be transitory and the national state the reality, and he looked forward to the reemergence of a Russian state in Europe that would be devoid of communist ideology. The Americans continued to regard these ideas as absurd. But Bohlen noted that de Gaulle's nuclear force was intended to deal with the reemergence of Germany as much as anything else. Nassau had convinced de Gaulle that Britain was not ripe for Europe, and the United Kingdom would not compromise on the fundamental Common Market issues involving French agriculture. Bohlen thought frankly, however, that although the situation was not catastrophic, there was very little at this point that could be done to improve relations. He had full access to de Gaulle but very little to say to him. Perhaps a dialogue by means of letter would be better than conversation.[68]

The Europeans in any case, especially the Germans, fell into line with Washington. At the NSC meeting of April 2, 1963, Ball said that de Gaulle was isolated and had no "grand design." He could only oppose others but had nothing positive to offer Europe himself. On May 28, 1963, the president told Paul-Henri Spaak that "we have no assurance that if we help France become stronger it will be our ally." Having studied de Gaulle's policy, he did not consider de Gaulle a good risk. Neither did Lyndon Johnson, whose negative beliefs about France were confirmed by the events of May 1968, when he concluded that the country was caught up in a vast plot of communist subversion. Nor were many politicians in Washington at any point during the 1960s fully confident about what the future in France, after de Gaulle, might bring. He had come to power semi-illegally in 1958, presided over four more years of a colonial war that had ended amid chaos and confusion, and despite a period of unprecedented growth and expansion in his country's economy from 1963 to 1967, managed to provoke a massive explosion of economic and social discontent in May 1968 that once again brought his nation to the brink of total anarchy and revolution. In the interval of relative stability during which he pursued his policies of national "grandeur" from 1963 to 1968, he excluded the British from Europe, took France out of NATO's integrated command, pursued a lonely détente with Moscow that aroused American suspicions, and opposed the Vietnam War. He wrought havoc with the American balance of payments and the international monetary system. He vainly sought to undercut American influence in Latin America, gratuitously tried to destabilize Canada, and slapped an arms embargo on Israel that obliged the Americans to step in to save it, to the long-term harm of their own interests in the Middle East and the Third World. De Gaulle had initially been thought an improvement over the Fourth Republic, and there is little evidence of regret in Washington over the role the Americans had played in bringing him to power. But he was not and never would be close to becoming the plaster saint that a recent semi-official French historiography has made of him.

Conclusion

The Algerian War has in recent years reclaimed its place in popular memory in France; it has receded as a subject of polemic in some circles and become a dispassionate matter of historical analysis. Its interpreters, however, have continued to see it as a national drama, its outcome explicable by internal causes. Many accounts exist of the role of French intellectuals, of the positions of the various political parties toward the war, in particular the Socialists and Communists who invite accusations of betraying their anticolonial heritages, of the policies of the various governments, and of the evolution of French public opinion during the war. Various pressure groups, the settlers, the army, the colonial lobby in France, the political right have all claimed their share of historical study. De Gaulle has taken his place as a second-time savior of the French nation, elevating both his place in history and his claim to political sainthood. The man of June 18, 1940, who saved the national honor against the treasonous policies of Vichy, also is said to have had the wisdom and foresight to end French participation in a ruinous and anachronistic colonial war. In only one respect has the Algerian War not been extensively studied: in terms of international relations, the role of which in the war's outcome has largely been discounted by historians.

This study has attempted to rectify that omission. There are two ways of approaching foreign policy in dealing with the Algerian War. One focuses on the world and the United Nations, the other on the United States and NATO. It is my contention here that the world and the United

Nations, although never absent in French consideration, played a secondary role in French perception; there was only one international actor of importance, the French understood from the outset, and that was the United States.[1] The United States during the Fourth Republic was in effect the guarantor of the French empire. This had been understood in Washington, where during the Second World War President Roosevelt had freely indulged the notion of not permitting France at all to return to its colonial possessions. In the end, however, the Americans concluded that world stability would be better achieved if the French empire and the British Commonwealth were left intact. The French accommodated to the new order by converting their empire into a "French Union," with ostensible gradations of their territories and member states in terms of their readiness for eventual independence.

Algeria, however, was exempt from this adjustment to the new postwar world. From the inception of the French expansion there, which dated to 1830, well before the beginnings of the "new imperialism" of the 1880s, it had been domesticated by the army, brought under the control of the Ministry of the Interior, and made a part of metropolitan France. Its three northern departments were departments of the metropole to which the Sahara was later attached. Alone among French possessions overseas, Algeria had attracted extensive European colonization; in 1954, when the war began, there were almost one million persons of European descent there, a privileged minority over a largely dispossessed and impoverished mass of nine million Muslims. The demographic tide, however, had long since been reversed; the European population was increasing slowly while the Muslim population was expanding dramatically by the time the war began.

The United States enabled France to restore its imperial position and create the French Union by assisting the French return to their colonies after the war and by helping restore French economic strength so that the French could reaffirm their political authority. In Indochina, where the French early ran into resistance to their return, the Americans aided France militarily, guided by new perceptions determined by the Cold War. France entered NATO and became an American ally; Washington correspondingly looked with more benevolence upon French efforts to hold on to their imperial possessions. Washington pressured for internal reform in the French colonies in the belief that accommodation to the aspirations of local populations was the best way to maintain Western influence. Many French politicians did not disagree, but for internal reasons they found reform difficult to achieve. But realities on the ground forced the French to come to terms with the rising tide of Third World aspirations for national independence. Despite billions of dollars in American aid for its Indochina War, more in the end than the Americans expended on the Marshall Plan, France was defeated. The combination of American pressure and French inability to maintain internal stability in its North African protectorates of Tunisia and Morocco led to a gradual and grudging French acceptance of autonomy and eventual independence there as well. Mendès France, after terminating the Indochina War, dramatically announced autonomy in Tunisia, and it was clear before the Algerian War ever reached a truly dangerous stage that the Sultan of Morocco, who had been deposed in 1953 for nationalist opposition to the French, would have to be restored as well. The two protectorates were launched down the road toward political independence in 1955, and it appears safe to say that they would have accomplished it even without the Algerian conflict, although the war there made clear French limitations in trying to hold on. Likewise, the growing aspirations of the African peoples for self-determination would have to be met; Paris moved, with American applause, to grant partial autonomy to its Black African possessions in 1956, coming ultimately to accept the American premise that gradual concessions offered the best means of maintaining eventual influence in the former colonies.

Algeria, however, remained impervious to these general trends. As a settler colony with an internal system of apartheid, administered under the fiction that it was part of metropolitan France, and endowed with a powerful colonial lobby that virtually determined the course of French politics with respect to its internal affairs, it experienced insurrection in 1954 on the part of its Muslim population. And unlike neighboring Morocco and Tunisia, where moderate Arab leaders emerged with whom France could initially negotiate new arrangements short of full independence, the Algerian rebels were radicals who made total demands. Algeria, moreover, loomed in French thinking as the key to its position as an African power and the basis of its hopes to lead a conglomerate of nations that would blend the emerging European Economic Community and the French African possessions in a combined concept of "Eurafrica." For these reasons the French could find no alternative to repression in dealing with the Algerian rebellion.

Unfortunately, these distinctions were largely lost on France's partners, and to an even greater extent on the world community of nations, which tended to interpret the war in classic colonial terms. Even President Eisenhower, a longtime friend of France, who understood the

dilemma of the French in Algeria and repeatedly expressed his sympathies for the settler population there, ultimately regarded the fiction that
Algeria was part of France as "nonsense." The American reaction to the
Algerian War was to press France all the harder for internal reform and
negotiations, while officially maintaining a policy of support for its embattled ally. That support was hesitant, tepid, and occasionally lapsed
into neutrality as Washington tried to balance its concern to maintain
France in NATO with its desire not to alienate the emerging nations of
the African and Asian continents, for whom the French struggle in Algeria became a central symbolic issue around which to mobilize their
newfound strength in the United Nations.

As the war continued the American dilemma grew. Washington initially rallied around the Guy Mollet government in 1956, lured into
stronger support by the belief that it had been elected under a platform
of negotiations and promised reforms. And indeed, Mollet undertook to
open secret negotiations with the rebels. Ambassador Dillon made the
strongest statement of American support for France during the war in
March 1956, and Washington approved the use of French troops earmarked for NATO in Algeria while agreeing to the sale of increased arms
and helicopters. But quite aside from his personal humiliation at the
hands of the settler population early in his premiership, Mollet's government proved no match for the *Algérie française* lobby. Moreover the premier himself seems to have become traumatized by the Egyptian role in
support of the Algerian rebels and Nasser's putative plans for Pan-Arab,
Pan-Islamic, and Pan-African movements, with Egypt at their center.
When Nasser nationalized the Suez Canal, Mollet was galvanized into
action, engineering a joint invasion of Egypt by Israel, Great Britain, and
France. Despite the Israeli military success and the strong showing of
French paratroops, the firm opposition of Washington brought the ex-
peditions to a quick end, their objectives unrealized. The French lost
their British ally and whatever goodwill they had enjoyed in Washington, and more seriously, the prestige of the Fourth Republic suffered an
irreparable blow when French intelligence services brought down a Moroccan plane carrying five leaders of the Algerian insurrection, including
Ahmed Ben Bella, who were immediately placed under arrest for the duration of the war. It was at once clear to American diplomatic sources
that the operation had not been authorized by Mollet, who felt obliged
to cover for it. The virtual autonomy of French bureaucratic services in
pursuit of often divergent policies became increasingly clear. And as
Paris demonstrated repeatedly its inability to bring the problem under

control, suspicion grew in Washington that its obsessive concern for a
precarious French political stability, in large part generated by the postwar strength of a menacing Communist party in France, was now
anachronistic and misplaced. The French Communist party seemed no
longer a threat; divided about the Algerian War, it had even given its support to Mollet. Rather, a chaotic French administrative structure, with
civil servants and ministers occasionally determining their own policies
in Algeria, the colonies in general, and even foreign policy in the case of
the Franco-Israeli alliance, convinced Washington that the Fourth Republic was a dysfunctional regime in terms of fulfilling its international
obligations. France was too important to the Americans, indeed the key
to much of what happened in Europe, Africa, and Asia from the American perspective, to be allowed to run amok.

The clincher was the Sakiet episode. Curiously, the bombardment of
the Tunisian village appears to have been part of fully authorized retaliatory policies on the Tunisian border, where the Bourguiba regime
stood accused of maintaining sanctuaries for the Algerian rebels. But in
the face of virtually universal world condemnation of an indefensible
act, French leaders took refuge in what appeared to be their least effective line of defense, claiming that the bombardment was initiated by
local commanders on the spot without authorization. Washington had
long been aware of dissident feeling within the French army in Algeria,
which increasingly came to sympathize with the colons; rumors of possible insurrection, should France attempt a policy of peace, had long
since been reported by its consuls and intelligence services. But the
United States was not prepared for the tissue of lies and evasion with
which the French now bombarded it; in particular, Premier Gaillard
confidentially assured the Americans that he would never have authorized a rogue operation so obviously fraught with danger, while publicly
he affirmed his full support for an embattled military and covered the
operation, as had his predecessor, Mollet, during the Ben Bella arrest. In
exasperation, Dulles and Eisenhower now ceded to what elements in
the State Department had long been insisting upon: a firm American
policy of diplomatic intervention to end the Algerian War. Through the
guise of providing its "good offices" in the negotiation of a Franco-
Tunisian settlement of the issues raised by the Sakiet bombardment,
Washington tried clumsily to force a settlement of the war, risking in the
process the undermining of the Fourth Republic and the coming to
power of de Gaulle. Long anathema in Washington, the general now appeared as France's last resort; and although he was known to be an ad-

vocate of NATO reform and of a larger role for France in the councils of the alliance, he was clearly preferable to the Fourth Republic, which gave the alliance lip service but whose policies in effect weakened it and threatened its destruction. For his part, the general showered Washington with assurances of his benevolent intent in order to prepare his way to power. Janus-faced, he promised a liberal policy in Algeria up to and including independence if necessary, such that Washington's faith in his intent to finish the war persisted through his seizure of power with the support of forces firmly committed to *Algérie française*. He repeatedly told his British and American interlocutors that he would maintain France in NATO and do nothing to sabotage the construction of the European Community, while he made France a valued and worthwhile ally by restoring its internal institutions and strength. During the May 1958 crisis his emissaries were almost daily at the American Embassy with further assurances. If some, such as Henri Tournet, appeared of doubtful value, others, like Michel Debré and Edmond Michelet, were known to enjoy his full confidence. And all brought the same comforting message. Far from opposing him, Washington looked with benevolence upon his return.

Whatever his intentions with regard to Algeria when he came to power, de Gaulle faced the same problems as his predecessors. Realities in the territory would ultimately force him to acknowledge its independence, despite heroic efforts to the contrary. De Gaulle gave the army free rein in Algeria and in a manner of speaking, in 1959–60, it "won" the war. Such astute observers as Benjamin Stora have been motivated to pose as one of the unanswered questions surrounding the war why the French military success should have led to Algerian independence. But the question really answers itself. The war was lost even as military victory was won in terms of the permanent alienation of the Muslim population, 25 percent of whom were forced into strategically defensible villages, becoming virtual refugees in their own country. "Victory" was defined as a reduction in the number of violent rebel incidents per month, which was in fact reduced from a high of 1,500 in 1956–57 to no more than 200 in 1960. But with one million French in a demographically exploding sea of ten times as many Muslims, was the total ever likely to decrease to acceptable or tolerable levels? Moreover, French public opinion had long since sickened of the war; France's intellectuals had rallied under the banner of dissidence, and it was clear that the torture and other abuses routinely tolerated in order to vanquish the terror in Algeria were unacceptable at home. But just as important as these was the relentless American pressure in the vanguard of virtual universal world hostility, isolating France internationally not only from the newly emergent Asian and African nations other than those in its own French Union but also from its NATO allies.

De Gaulle realized from the outset that even as he "won" the war on the ground, he would have to devise a settlement in Algeria acceptable to Washington. From his return to power he laid out what must have appeared to him an appealing strategy. In his famous memorandum he asked that Washington grant Paris parity with Great Britain as one of the big three in the making of world policy, in recognition of France's new status as a nuclear power. Nuclear weapons were prepared under the Fourth Republic; de Gaulle was to reap the fruit of their existence for his foreign policy. In exchange, France would cooperate fully with American goals, be a loyal NATO ally, and offer unwavering support in areas of Washington's unique concerns, whether Japan, China, or Cuba. France would moreover coordinate and lead a Eurafrican assemblage of nations, including the EEC and the French Union, in firm commitment to the free world. Washington and Britain would proffer their support for France in Africa and the Mediterranean, just as France supported them in their own worldwide commitments. And Washington's firm support in Algeria would inevitably force the Algerian rebels to come to terms, for France would be invincible with American power behind it, while the Eurafrican community would offer Algeria an irresistible pole of attraction.

In all this it is hard to see the multipolar model of international affairs with which scholars are wont to credit de Gaulle. The Americans had only to accept him as a member of a "directorate" of the West to keep him from straying and the West intact in what would always be, simply because of the reality of American power, a bipolar world. In understanding de Gaulle one must also always wonder whether the manner of his making proposals and policies was not the greatest impediment to their successful implementation. His posture was one of arrogance; he did not request, he demanded, nay insisted that France be given what was its due as a world power. This tactic, curiously, had worked during the Second World War; the aggressiveness of de Gaulle's behavior seemed to be in inverse proportion to France's real strength. Perhaps de Gaulle expected it to work the same way in 1958, for France was once again very weak. Its burgeoning economy was racked by chronic financial crises, its political institutions were in disarray, and its empire in dissolution while it pursued an unwinnable war from which it could not extricate itself. The proposal to the Americans and the British was a desperate appeal for help in overcoming France's intractable problems. De Gaulle meant in return to integrate France into the American bloc so long as it played a consultative role alongside the British commensurate with what he saw as his nation's due. But neither the Americans nor the British could see it that way. Precisely because of France's disarray, it still was not deemed a worthy partner. Rather than offer their support as a solution to the Algerian problem, the Americans insisted that it be solved before they dealt with France on other matters. They were unimpressed with France's nuclear prowess and thought it a dangerous step toward the world proliferation they had decided to oppose. Just as de Gaulle saw France's control of Algeria as the ultimate key to its proper world role, the Americans saw France's relinquishing of the territory as the prerequisite for the maintenance of Western influence in the Third World. De Gaulle's initiatives were rejected. Algeria was lost, and every further step de Gaulle took toward relinquishing French control in the territory was made to coincide with forthcoming UN debates in which France counted on the United States to save it from isolation, or in anticipation of American developments that boded ill for its future in Algeria—the major development perhaps being the election of John F. Kennedy in 1960, which led directly to French acceptance of direct negotiations with the National Liberation Front without preconditions, the key to an Algerian settlement. Faced with the collapse of his policies during the Kennedy administration, de Gaulle petulantly embarked on a policy of putative "independence," to the satisfaction of future French historians, many of whom bought his subsequent claims that he had always intended to give Algeria its independence and to withdraw France from NATO's integrated command while initiating a policy of détente with the USSR and the construction of Europe "from the Atlantic to the Urals."

If there is an ultimate lesson in all this, it is to illuminate how the actions of its European allies were constrained by the realities of American power, even to the point, in the case of France, of forcing a change in its internal institutions. Much of the effort that the Americans had expended in France in the interest of preserving the Fourth Republic's internal stability had been rewarded by 1954, when the regime appeared to have reached internal equilibrium—sufficient, in fact, for Mendès France to have done with the Indochina War despite Washington's wish that he continue it. But Mendès himself was similarly unable to deal with Algeria, and as the crisis there deepened France lapsed once again into weakness and greater dependence on Washington, whose loyalty emerged, in its eyes, as the key to its victory. In exchange the Americans resolved to end their investment in French institutional stability. The Fourth Republic was allowed to collapse because its maintenance was no longer consistent with the proper functioning of the NATO alliance and the broader interest of American policy in the Third World.

De Gaulle recognized this by making a last-ditch bid for American cooperation. Only with the support of the United States, he understood, could France hold on to Algeria and its world role. But so long as he meant to continue the war in Algeria, the Americans would not give him what he wished, in recognition of which he finally let it go. By then, however, it was too late; Eisenhower, in the absence of the Algerian problem, would perhaps have given him some of what he wanted, but Kennedy would not. The general embarked upon a policy of "independence," which, however dramatic, collapsed ignominiously in 1968 in the face of the events of May 1968 in Paris and August in Prague. Just before he resigned he was obliged, despite everything, to negotiate again American financial help in maintaining his regime. Even today, after the collapse of communism and the construction of the Euro, neither France nor Europe has achieved the foreign policy independence that eluded de Gaulle. Whether in Iraq or Bosnia or Kosovo, the United States has taken the lead; when it abdicates, despite numerous French efforts, there is no European policy to fill the vacuum. France has not been up to the measure of its foreign policy ambitions.

Notes

1. THE UNITED STATES AND THE ALGERIAN WAR

1. On U.S.-French relations during the early Cold War, see Irwin M. Wall, *The United States and the Making of Postwar France, 1945–1954* (New York: Cambridge University Press, 1991). For an overall view of American-French relations, see Frank Costigliola, *France and the United States: The Cold Alliance since World War II* (New York: Twayne Publishers, 1992). Edgar S. Furniss, Jr., *France, Troubled Ally: De Gaulle's Heritage and Prospects* (New York: Harper, 1960), pp. 276–77, 293, is still useful for these points. See also Edward Fursdon, *The European Defense Community: A History* (New York: St. Martin's Press, 1980).

2. Charles-Robert Ageron, *Modern Algeria: A History from 1830 to the Present,* trans. Michael Brett (London: Hurst & Co., 1991), pp. 82–87. See also John Ruedy, *Modern Algeria: The Origins and Development of a Nation* (Bloomington: University of Indiana Press, 1992), pp. 114–26.

3. Martin Thomas, *The French North African Crisis: Colonial Breakdown and Anglo-French Relations, 1945–62* (London: Macmillan, 2001). I am grateful to Professor Thomas for letting me see an advance copy.

4. Georgette Elgey, *Histoire de la IVe République: La république des tourmentes,* tome 2, *1954–1959, Malentendu et passion* (Paris: Fayard, 1997), p. 432; Pierre Miquel, *La Guerre d'Algérie* (Paris: Fayard, 1993), pp. 39–47.

5. Samya El Machat, *Les Etats-Unis et l'Algérie: De la méconnaissance à la reconnaissance, 1945–1962* (Paris: L'Harmattan, 1996), p. 18.

6. Irwin M. Wall's *L'influence américaine sur la politique française* (Paris: André Balland, 1989) contains a brief chapter on American policy toward North Africa that was left out of the American edition (see note 1). A more detailed study by Annie Lacroix-Riz, *Les Protectorats d'Afrique du Nord entre la*

France et Washington (Paris: L'Harmattan, 1988), accuses the United States of trying to replace French influence in North Africa through its military bases and pressures for reform. Memorandom of Conversation, Paris, Schuman, Pinay, Acheson, James Dunn, et al., 28 May 1952, U.S. Department of State, *Foreign Relations of the United States, 1952–1954,* 11, Part 1:767–69 (hereinafter *FRUS,* with years and volume number).

7. El Machat, *Les Etats-Unis et l'Algérie,* pp. 30–31.

8. "Current Developments in North Africa," 12 September 1952, Harry S. Truman Library, Independence, Mo., President's Secretary's File, CIA Reports. Cited in Wall, *L'Influence américaine,* p. 393.

9. Herman Lebovics, *True France: The Wars over Cultural Identity, 1900–1945* (Ithaca, N.Y.: Cornell University Press, 1991).

10. John Talbott, *The War Without a Name: France in Algeria, 1954–1962* (New York: Knopf, 1980), p. 48; Alistair Horne, *A Savage War of Peace: Algeria 1954–1962* (New York: Viking Press, 1977), pp. 85–122.

11. The quotation is from Robert J. McMahon, "Eisenhower and Third World Nationalism: A Critique of the Revisionists," *Political Science Quarterly* 101, 3 (1986):453–75. H. W. Brands, *The Specter of Neutralism: The United States and the Emergence of the Third World, 1947–1960* (New York: Columbia University Press, 1989), pp. 5, 308; Peter L. Hahn, *The United States, Great Britain, and Egypt 1945–1956: Strategy and Diplomacy in the Early Cold War* (Chapel Hill: University of North Carolina Press, 1991); Irene L. Gendzier, *Notes from the Minefield: U.S. Intervention in Lebanon and the Middle East, 1945–1958* (New York: Columbia University Press, 1997), p. 23.

12. When General Cutler said that perhaps others were doing the Soviets' work for them in these areas, President Eisenhower took "vigorous exception" to Cutler's assertion. Dulles to the National Security Council, 20 March 1958, Anne Whitman File, National Security Council Series, NSC 359, Eisenhower Library, Abilene, Kansas. All these crises involved the Islamic world, giving Dulles's remark an even more contemporary resonance.

13. Sylvia K. Crosbie, *A Tacit Alliance: France and Israel from Suez to the Six-Day War* (Princeton, N.J.: Princeton University Press, 1974), p. 32.

14. For an example of growing interest in de Gaulle, see U.S. Embassy, Paris, to State Department, 21 June 1957, *FRUS, 1955–57, 27:* 127–29.

15. American Embassy, Paris, to State Department, January 19, 1955, 611.51/1–1955, RG 59, NA.

16. El Machat, *Les Etats-Unis et l'Algérie,* p. 31.

17. Letter, Douglas Dillon to Livingston Merchant, April 4, 1955, 611.51/4–1955, RG 59, NA.

18. American Embassy, Paris, to State Department, May 9, 1955, 611.51/5–1955, RG 59, NA.

19. Thomas, *The French North African Crisis,* p. 79.

20. Matthew Connelly, "The Algerian War for Independence: An International History" (Ph.D. dissertation, Yale University, 1997), pp. 175–76.

21. Memorandum, Livingston Merchant to the Secretary, September 23, 1955, 611.51/9–2355, RG 59, NA.

22. Rapport sur les travaux de la XVème session du Conseil du Tutelle (25 janvier-28 mars 1955), C2225, Dossier 2, Archives d'Histoire d'Outre-Mer, Aix-en-Provence (hereinafter AOM). Report on Franco-Belgian meeting, Brussels, May 25, 1956, D 3A.

23. Memorandum of Conversation, Paul Reynaud, Maurice Couve de Murville, Robert Murphy, Washington, October 20, 1955, 611.51/10–2055, RG 59, NA.

24. Quoted in El Machat, *Les Etats-Unis et l'Algérie,* pp. 111–14.

25. American Consul-General, Algiers, to Department of State, July 1, 1955, 611.51S/7–155, RG 59, NA.

26. Cited in Connelly, "The Algerian War for Independence," p. 171.

27. Thomas, *The French North African Crisis,* p. 191.

28. Ibid., passim.

29. Parodi, Representative of France to NATO, to Pineau, Minister of Foreign Affairs, March 7, 1956, *Documents Diplomatiques Français* (hereinafter *DDF*), 1956, tome I (1 January-30 June 1956), pp. 329–30; Couve de Murville, French Ambassador in Washington, to Pineau, February 29, 1956, *DDF,* tome I, pp. 429–31. Pineau to French Representatives abroad, March 28, 1956, *DDF,* 1956, I, pp. 496–97.

30. El Machat, *Les Etats-Unis et l'Algérie,* quotes François Mitterrand in September 1957: "The Mediterranean, not the Rhine, is the axis of our security and our foreign policy," pp 93–100.

31. Frédéric Bozo, *Deux stratégies pour l'Europe: De Gaulle, les Etats-Unis, et l'Alliance Atlantique, 1958–1959* (Paris: Plon, 1996), pp. 22–25.

32. NSC 284, May 10, 1956, Secretary Dulles, Memorandum, July 13, 1956; Eden to Eisenhower, July 18, 1956. *FRUS,* 1955–57, 4, West European Security and Integration, pp. 85–91.

33. Dulles-Lloyd Memorandum of Conversation, *FRUS,* 1955–57, 4:127–29.

34. Parodi to NATO Council, March 7, 1956, *DDF,* I, Jan.-June 1956, pp. 329–30; Pineau to Lloyd and Dulles, Karachi, March 7, 1956, pp. 335–36; General Valluy to NATO Standing Group, March 11, 1956, pp. 429–31; Pineau to All French Diplomatic Representatives Abroad, March 28, 1956, p. 496.

35. State Department to U.S. Embassy, Paris, 17 March 1956, *FRUS,* 1955–1957, 27:46. U.S. Embassy, Paris, to State Department, 25 July 1956, *FRUS,* 1955–1957, 27:50. Memorandum from General Valluy to General Lawton Collins, 12 March 1956, Eisenhower Library, Whitman File, International Series, 12. State Department to U.S. Embassy, Paris, 27 May 1955, *FRUS,* 1955–1957, 18:219.

36. Memorandum from Le Directeur des Industries Mécanique et Eléctrique, January 12, 1956, in Programme 1955, juillet à décembre, MA 695, AOM. Secrétaire d'Etat aux Affaires Economiques, July 24, 1956, Folder marked "Dodge Trucks," PR 95, MA 695.

37. U.S. Consulate, Algiers, to State Department, 21 November 1956, *FRUS,* 1955–57, 18:250; U.S. Consulate, Algiers, to State Department, ibid., 262. Frank Costigliola quotes a State Department official as likening U.S. policy to "trying to sit on a fence which is not there" (*France and the United States,* p. 111). Eisenhower to the NSC, 31 January 1957, Whitman File, NSC Series, NSC 311.

38. "Ingérences Américaines, Notes," September 15, 1955, MA 28, AOM.

39. "Le Gouverneur-Général de l'Algérie à M. le Ministre de l'Intérieur," Folder, "Ingérences Américaines, Notes," MA 28, AOM.

40. Maurice Vaisse, "La guerre perdue à l'ONU?" in Jean-Pierre Rioux, ed., *La Guerre d'Algérie et les Français* (Paris: Fayard, 1990), pp. 451–63.

41. See Pierre Melandri, "La France et le 'jeu double' des Etats-Unis," in Rioux, ed., *La Guerre d'Algérie et les Français;* and Hervé Alphand, *L'étonnement d'être: Journal 1939–1973* (Paris: Fayard, 1977), p. 277.

42. "Note sur la politique américaine en Afrique du Nord," 20 November 19₌6; "Note sur l'evolution de l'opinion américaine," 11 December 1956. Both in Ministère des Affaires Etrangères, Quai d'Orsay, Paris, France (hereinafter MAE), Amérique, 1952–1960, Etats Unis, Box 15.

43. Tony Smith, *The French Stake in Algeria* (Ithaca, N.Y.: Cornell University Press, 1978); Irwin Wall, *French Communism in the Era of Stalin: The Quest for Unity and Integration, 1945–1962* (Westport, Conn.: Greenwood Press, 1983), pp. 181–201. Smith places the Communists outside the consensus, however, while I argued that they belonged inside it.

44. Denis Lefebvre, *Guy Mollet: Le mal aimé* (Paris: Plon, 1992), pp. 180–96.

45. Memorandum, Herbert Hoover, Jr. to President Eisenhower, commenting on a memorandum from Robert Murphy to the Secretary of State, March 3, 1956, 611.51/3–356, RG 59, NA.

46. Dulles to U.S. Embassy, Paris, and Mideast Posts, 4 February 1956, RG 59, 751S.oo/2–456. This was considerably more than the French as yet were willing to promise. U.S. Embassy, Paris, to the State Department, 10 February 1956, RG 59, 751S.oo/2–1056. U.S. Embassy, Paris, to State Department, 12 March 1956, in Eisenhower Library, Whitman File, International Series, Box 12. U.S. Embassy, Paris, to State Department, 2 March 1956, RG 59, 751.oo/3–256. Auriol was further quoted as asking whether France "can count on the solidarity established by the [NATO] pact."

47. Dejean (Moscow) to Paris, January 13, 1956, *DDF,* I, Jan.-June 1956, p. 33; Auriol to Molotov, Paris, March 10, 1956, p. 366; Franco-Soviet Conversations, May 16–19, 1956, pp. 823–30.

48. Diane Kunz, *The Economic Diplomacy of the Suez Crisis* (Chapel Hill: University of North Carolina Press, 1991), pp. 62–66.

49. Paris to State Department, March 19, 1956, 651.72/3–756, RG 59, NA. Public Record Office (London), FO 371, 131590 (hereinafter PRO).

50. American Embassy, Paris, to State Department, March 13, 1959, 611.51/3–1356, RG 59, NA.

51. Text of Dillon speech to the Ango-American press luncheon, March 20, 1956, 611.51/3–2056, RG 59, NA.

52. U.S. Consulate, Algiers, to State Department, 9 February 1956, RG 59, 751S.oo/2–956. U.S. Embassy, Paris, to State Department, 21 February 1956, RG 59, 751S.oo/2–2156. State Department (Dulles) to U.S. Embassy, Paris, 24 February 1956, RG 59, 751.oo/2–2456. Memorandum, Herber Hoover, Jr. to the President, 2 March 1956, RG 59, 751.oo/3–256. Henry Cabot Lodge to State Department, 7 March 1956, RG 59, 751.oo/3–756. U.S. Embassy, Paris, to State Department, 17 March 1956, RG 59, 751.oo/3–1756. U.S. Embassy, Paris, to

State Department, 20 March 1956, RG 59, 751.00/3–2056. *Le Monde,* 21 March 1956.

53. Président du Conseil, SDECE Report, "Les Activités du FLN et du Groupe Afro-Asiatique aux Etats-Unis," May 14, 1956. MA 28, Conférences Internationales, AOM.

54. M. Couve de Murville, Ambassadeur de France aux Etats Unis, à M. Christian Pineau, Ministre des Affaires Etrangères, April 27, 1956, "Evolution des esprits à l'égard du problème colonial," July 27, 1956, MA 28, AOM, Aix. Couve du Murville's report can be found in *DDF,* 1956, I, pp. 670–77.

55. Acting Secretary of State Herbert Hoover, Jr. to the American Embassy in Paris, March 17, 1956, 611.51/3–1756, RG 59, NA.

56. American Consulate, Lyon, to Department of State, May 15, 1956, 611.51/5–1556, RG 59, NA.

57. American Consulate, Algiers, to Department of State, March 20, 1956, 611.51S/3–2056. American Embassy, Paris, to Department of State, July 9, 1956, 611.51S/7–956, RG 59, NA.

58. General Cabell to the NSC, 27 September 1956, Eisenhower Library, Whitman File, NSC Series, NSC 298. U.S. Consulate, Algiers, to State Department, 12 July 1956, RG 59, 751S.00/7–1256.

59. Michael Kettle, *De Gaulle and Algeria 1940–1960: From Mers El Kébir to the Algiers Barricades* (London: Quartet Books, 1993), pp. 58–59. On Brown's earlier operations in France, see Irwin Wall, *The United States and the Making of Postwar France.*

60. American Embassy, Paris, to Department of State, July 12, 1956, 611.51S/7–1256, RG 59, NA.

61. "Attitude des Représentants Consulaires Américains en Algérie," November 1956, Folder, "Ingérences: Position de Consul Général des USA à Alger," MA 28, AOM.

2. THE SUEZ CRISIS

1. See the contributions of Georgette Elgey and Charles-Robert Ageron in Maurice Vaïsse, ed., *La France et l'operation de Suez de 1956* (Paris: Centre d'Etudes d'Histoire de la Défense, 1997), pp. 23–60.

2. Abel Thomas, *Comment Israel fut sauvée: Les secrets de l'expédition de Suez* (Paris: Albin Michel, 1978), p. 32.

3. Keith Kyle, *Suez* (London: Weidenfeld and Nicholson, 1991), pp. 110–15.

4. Connelly, "The Algerian War for Independence," p. 222.

5. Horne, *A Savage War of Peace,* pp. 108–9.

6. Miquel, *La Guerre d'Algérie,* pp. 230–50.

7. *DDF,* Mollet to Ministry of Foreign Affairs from Chequers, March 11, 1956, pp. 380–84. See also Martin Thomas, *The French North African Crisis,* p. 226.

8. *DDF,* II, 1956, French-American Conversations of June 18–19, 1956, pp. 1022; Ambassador Dejean, Moscow, to Ministry of Foreign Affairs, June 23, 1956, pp. 1046–49, June 30, 1956, pp. 1073–75.

9. Thomas, *The French North African Crisis,* p. 79.

10. David Carleton, *Britain and the Suez Crisis* (Oxford: Blackwell, 1988), pp. 28–36.

11. *DDF*, II, 1956, Cairo to Paris, July 27, 1956, p. 164. Chauvel, London, to Pineau, Paris, July 27, 1956, pp. 166–67.

12. *FRUS*, 1955–57, 16, *The Suez Crisis*, July 26–December 31, 1956 (hereinafter *FRUS, Suez*), Murphy, London, to Washington, July 31, 1956, pp. 61–62.

13. *DDF*, II, 1956, Chauvel, London, to Pineau, Ministry of Foreign Affairs, July 30, 1956, pp. 187–88.

14. Jacques Georges-Picot, *The Real Suez Crisis: The End of a Great Nineteenth-Century Work* (New York: Harcourt Brace, 1975), pp. 91–107.

15. *FRUS, Suez*, Conference with the President, July 28, 1956, p. 28; Conference with the President, July 31, 1956, Eisenhower to Eden, July 31, 1956, pp. 61–70.

16. *FRUS, Suez*, Dillon, Paris, to State Department, Washington, July 31, 1956, p. 77.

17. Keith Kyle, *Suez,* pp. 174–75.

18. *DDF*, II, 1956, Pineau, from London, to Ministry of Foreign Affairs, August 1, 1956; Dulles-Pineau Conversations, August 1, 1956; Pineau, from London, to MFA, August 2, 1956. Pp. 201–24.

19. *FRUS, Suez*, Eden-Dulles Conversations, August 1, 1956; Murphy, Dillon, and Pineau Conversations, August 2, 1956; Three Power Conference, August 3, 1956, pp. 100–124.

20. *DDF*, II, 1956, Du Chayla, Cairo, to Pineau, MFA, p. 353.

21. Moshe Dayan, *The Story of My Life* (London: Weidenfeld and Nicolson, 1976), pp. 153–55.

22. *FRUS, Suez*, Watch Committee Report, September 5, 1956, pp. 358–59; National Intelligence Estimate, pp. 385–88.

23. *FRUS, Suez*, Dulles to Eisenhower, August 20, 1956, p. 210; Joint Chiefs of Staff, "Conclusions," August 22, 1956, p. 248; Eden to Dulles, August 28, 1956, pp. 312–13; Dulles to Eisenhower, August 29, Lloyd to Dulles, August 28, 1956, pp. 314–15.

24. Dulles to the NSC, 31 August 1956, Eisenhower Library, Whitman File, NSC Series, NSC 295; *FRUS, Suez*, Dulles-Eisenhower Conversation, p. 334; State Department to Certain Diplomatic Missions, September 2, 1956, p. 352.

25. *DDF*, II, 1956, Franco-British Conversations of September 10, 1956, at 10 Downing Street, p. 360.

26. *FRUS, Suez*, Dillon, Paris, to State Department, September 10, 1956, p. 461; Pineau-Dulles Conversation, Washington, September 19, 1956, p. 510.

27. On this question, see the essay by Charles Cogan in Vaïsse, ed., *La France et l'opération de Suez de 1956,* pp. 121–43.

28. *DDF*, II, 1956, Dejean, Moscow, to Pineau, MFA, September 11, 1956, pp. 354–67; Alphand, Washington, to Pineau, MFA, September 21, 1956, pp. 423–24.

29. *DDF*, II, 1956, Ambassador Dubois, Rabat, to Savary, Secretary of State for Moroccan and Tunisan Affairs, September 24, 1956, pp. 439–40.

30. *FRUS, Suez*, Memorandum of Conversation, Alphand and Dulles, September 25, 1956, pp. 574–77.

31. *FRUS, Suez*, Memorandum of Conversation, Department of State, September 25, 1956, Dulles, Makins, and Macmillan, pp. 578–81.

32. Abel Thomas, *Comment Israel fut sauvée*, pp. 149–53.

33. Dayan, *The Story of My Life*, pp. 155–73; Général d'Armée Paul Ely, *Mémoires: Suez...le 13 mai* (Paris: Plon, 1969), pp. 111–49.

34. Dayan, pp. 178–83.

35. *FRUS, Suez*, Dulles-Alphand Conversation, September 27, 1956, p. 599; Dulles-Eisenhower Conversation, October 2, 1956, p. 627; NSC 299, October 4, 1956, pp. 632–33.

36. Alan S. Milward, *The European Rescue of the Nation State* (Berkeley: University of California Press, 1992), pp. 212–15; Frances M. B. Lynch, *France and the International Economy: From Vichy to the Treaty of Rome* (London: Routledge, 1997), pp. 178–83.

37. *FRUS, Suez*, Telegram from the Department of State to the American Embassy in France, October 4, 1956, pp. 635–36.

38. *FRUS, Suez*, Memorandum of Conversation, Secretary Dulles's Suite, Waldorf Astoria, October 5, 1956, pp. 640–43.

39. *FRUS, Suez*, Message from the Secretary of State to the President, October 5, 1956, p. 648; Telegram from the Embassy in France to the Department of State, October 6, 1956, p. 655.

40. Keith Kyle, *Suez*, pp. 288–89.

41. Anthony Nutting, *No End of a Lesson: The Story of Suez* (New York: Clarkson N. Potter, 1967), pp. 72–77. Nutting was the British Minister of State for Foreign Affairs and resigned over the Suez invasion.

42. *FRUS, Suez*, Editorial Note; Letter from Foreign Secretary Lloyd to Secretary of State Dulles, October 15, 1956, p. 740.

43. See the oral histories provided by Douglas Dillon, Allen Dulles, and Christian Pineau in the John Foster Dulles Papers, Oral History Project, Seely Mudd Library, Princeton University. Allen Dulles was later embarrassed by John Foster Dulles's implication that the United States had been caught flat-footed by the British-French-Israeli action. The Americans also could guess it was coming from the increased volume of radio communications among the participants and the meetings held in Paris of which they had word, but they were ignorant of the specific agreements concluded at Sèvres and they were unable to read the coded radio messages.

44. Elgey, *Histoire de la IVe République*, tome 2, p. 178.

45. See Patrick Facon, "Suez et l'Emploi de la puissance aérienne," in *La France et l'opération de Suez*, pp. 228–39; also Charles Cogan, "De la politique du mensonge à la farce de Suez: Appréhensions et réactions américains," pp. 121–37.

46. Connelly, "The Algerian War for Independence," p. 235.

47. John Talbott, *The War Without a Name*, p. 105. Alistair Horne, *A Savage War of Peace*, pp. 185–91.

48. Philippe Bourdrel, *La dernière chance de l'Algérie Française: Du gouvernement socialiste au retour de De Gaulle, 1956–1958* (Paris: Albin Michel, 1996), p. 78.

49. Lalouette, Chargé d'Affaires in Rabat, to Savary, Secretary of State for Moroccan and Tunisian Affairs, October 16, October 18, October 21, 1956, *DDF*, II, July-October 1956, pp. 636–37, 655–57.

50. El Machat, *Les Etats-Unis et l'Algérie,* pp. 60–65. Denis Lefebvre, *Guy Mollet,* p. 229, has the most complete account. Also excellent is Bourdrel, *La dernière chance de l'Algérie Française,* pp. 79–85.

51. Lalouette to Savary, October 23, 1956, *DDF*, II, July-October 1956, p. 664.

52. Acting Secretary of State Hoover to American Embassy, Paris, November 16, 1956, 651.71/11–1056, RG 59, NA.

53. Memorandum of Conversation, Ambassador Slim, Habib Bourguiba, Jr., and Under Secretary Robert Murphy, November 8, 1956, 651.72/11–856, RG 59, NA.

54. American Embassy, Paris, to Department of State, October 26, 1956, 651.71/10–2656, RG 59, NA.

55. American Embassy, Paris, to Department of State, October 26, 1956, 651.71/10–2656, October 31, 1956, 10–3156, RG 59, NA.

56. J.Y. Goeau-Brissonnière, *Mission secrète pour la paix en Algérie 1957* (Paris: Lieu Commun, 1992), pp. 37–39. Goeau worked in the Ministry for Morroccan and Tunisian Affairs, for Commin and Alain Savary, and then in the Foreign Ministry for Pineau in 1957. See also Denis Lefebvre, *Guy Mollet,* pp. 203–5.

57. Cornut-Gentile, Head of the French Mission to the United Nations, to Pineau, October 23, 1956, *DDF*, II, July-October 1956, pp. 670–71.

58. Memorandum of Conversation Between the President and the Secretary of State, October 24, 1956, *FRUS, Suez,* 370, p. 774.

59. Telegram from the American Embassy in the UK to the Department of State, Oct. 26, 1956, *FRUS, Suez,* p. 792.

60. U.S. Embassy, Tunis, to State Department, 22 October 1956, 751S.oo/10–2256, RG 59, NA. U.S. Embassy, Rabat, to State Department, 22 October 1956, 751S.oo/10–2256, RG59; Dulles to European and Mid-East Posts, 24 October 1956, 751S.oo/10–2456, RG 59, NA.

61. *DDF*, III, 1956, Secretary of State for Tunisian and Moroccan Affairs Alain Savary to French Diplomatic Representatives Abroad, October 25, 1956, p. 27.

62. Paul Marie de la Gorce, *Apogée et mort de la IVe République, 1952–1958* (Paris: B. Grasset, 1979), p. 444; Yves Courière, *La Guerre d'Algérie, 1954–1957* (Paris: Fayard, 1990), I:755–57. Alistair Horne presents a more nuanced version, allowing for some mystery as to the French government's complicity. Mollet and Lacoste both denied prior knowledge of the hijacking when interviewed by him personally, however. Horne, *A Savage War of Peace,* p. 159. Memorandum, Wilkins to Rountree, 26 October 1956, 751S.oo/10–2656, RG 59, NA, has Mollet previously uninformed; Savary's version appears in U.S. Embassy, Paris, to State Department, 24 October 1956, 751S.oo/10–2456, RG 59, NA. Another telegram of the same date cites "sources" insisting that Lacoste knew at least twenty-four hours in advance. French Foreign Minister Christian Pineau, who was apparently not pre-informed of the operation, reports in his memoir that in the cabinet meeting following the incident, Mollet asked who had ordered the plane downed "sans

l'accord du gouvernement" (without the agreement of the government): this would seem to indicate that Mollet knew of the plans and had not approved them. See Christian Pineau, *1956/Suez* (Paris, 1976), p. 142. Goeau-Brissonnière also says the incident was carried out against the will of Mollet: see note 33.

63. American Embassy, Paris, to Department of State, October 31, 1956, 651.71/10–3156, RG 59, NA.

64. Memoranda, Robert McBride to Matthew Looram, Paris, February 25, 1957; Matthew Looram to McBride, March 27, 1957, Lot 61, D30, Box 2, Algeria-Aramco, N.A.

65. Buron, *Les dernières années de la IVe République,* p. 196.

66. *FRUS, Suez,* 1956, Dulles to American Embassy, Paris, October 29, 1956; American Embassy, Paris, to State Department, October 29, 1956, pp. 824–30.

67. *FRUS, Suez,* 1956, Dulles to Eisenhower, October 30, 1956, Dulles-Alphand Conversation, Washington, October 30, 1956, pp. 854–67.

68. Keith Kyle, *Suez,* p. 365.

69. See Maurice Vaïsse, "Post-Suez France," in William Roger Louis and Roger Owen, eds., *Suez 1956: The Crisis and Its Consequences* (Oxford: Clarendon, 1989), pp. 335–41. Dulles to the NSC, 1 November 1956, Whitman File, NSC Series, NSC 302. Yet when British Foreign Minister Selwyn Lloyd and Christian Pineau visited Dulles in the hospital in the aftermath of Suez, he is reported to have asked why they had not finished the job and gone on to bring Nasser down. William Roger Louis, "Dulles, Suez, and the British," in Immerman, ed., *John Foster Dulles and the Cold War.*

70. *FRUS, Suez,* 1956, NSC 302, October 30, 1956, p. 904.

71. Dillon Oral History, J. F. Dulles Papers, Oral History Project, Mudd Library, Princeton University, p. 25.

72. *FRUS, Suez,* 1956, Note, November 2, 1956, p. 933; Memorandum of Telephone Conversation between the Secretary of State and UN Ambassador Lodge, November 2, 1956, p. 938; Memorandum of Conversation at the Department of State, p. 949; Telegram from the U.S. Mission at the United Nations to the Department of State, November 3, 1956, pp. 958–59. Memorandum of Conversation, Department of State, Alphand and Murphy, November 5, 1956, pp. 1003–5. Memorandum of Conversation, Department of State, November 6, 1956, p. 1024.

73. *DDF,* III, 1956, Note, November 10, 1956, pp. 271–75.

74. Stephen Ambrose, *Eisenhower.* Vol. 2, *The President* (New York: Simon & Schuster, 1984), p. 538.

75. Dillon Oral History, p. 21. These observations were made with reference to Murphy and Merchant and Douglas MacArthur, Jr., regarding the European Defense Community treaty ratification struggle of 1954, but seem equally applicable to the Suez crisis.

76. Renseignement, January 8, 1957, Service de Securité de la Défense Nationale, 1H 1754, D5, Archives de l'Armée, Vincennes.

77. "Note pour le secrétaire," 28 February 1957, MAE, Amérique, 1952–1960, Etats Unis, Box 15. An accompanying document labeled simply "Note" appears to assume the falsehood of the charge that American oil com-

panies were implicated by materials in Ben Bella's possession at the time of his arrest.

78. American Embassy, Paris, to the Department of State, November 11, 1956, 651.51S/11–756, RG 59, NA.

79. American Embassy, Paris, to the Secretary of State, November 30, 1956, 611.51/11–2956, RG 59, NA.

80. American Embassy, Paris, to the Department of State, November 27, 28, 29, 1956, 751.00/11–2756, 11–2856, 11–2956, RG 59, NA.

81. See the fascinating piece "De soldat à soldat: Juin, Eisenhower et les leçons de Suez (Novembre–Décembre 1956)" by Philippe Vial and Nicolas Vaicbourdt in Vaïsse, ed., *La France et l'opération de Suez de 1956*, pp. 267–300. The authors believe that the letter was in fact approved by de Gaulle and Mollet, but it is difficult to see why either would have wanted to be associated with the name of General Weygand, who had administered North Africa under Vichy following his forceful role in encouraging the armistice of 1940.

82. Dillon to State Department, December 19, 1956, 751.00/12–1956; Dillon to State Department, December 20, 1956, 751.00/12–2056; Dillon to State Department, January 16, 1957, 751.00/1–1657, RG 59, NA.

83. "Action Psychologique aux Etats-Unis," C 2259, D6, Affaires Politiques, March 14, 1957, AOM.

84. Pierre Guillen, "La France et la négociation des Traités de Rome: L'Euratom," in Enrico Serra, ed., *Il relancio dell'Europa et i Trattati di Roma* (Brussels and Milan: A. Giufré, 1989), pp. 513–29. Robert Marjolin, *Architect of European Unity: Memoirs, 1911–1986* (London: Wiedenfeld and Nicolson, 1989), supports Guillen's interpretation, pp. 297–300. Marjolin at the time held the position of Pineau's advisor for European affairs.

85. Lynch, *France and the International Economy*, pp. 173–80. An excellent and detailed study of this debate is in Paul Marsh Pitman III, "France's European Choices: The Political Economy of European Integration in the 1950s" (Ph.D. dissertation, Columbia University, 1997), especially pp. 330–64.

86. Lynch, *France and the International Economy*, pp. 186–205; also see her chapter "Restoring France: The Road to Integration," in Alan S. Milward et al., eds., *The Frontier of National Sovereignty: History and Theory 1945–1992* (London: Routledge, 1993), pp. 59–87.

87. Daniel Lefeuvre, *Chère Algérie 1930–1962: Comptes et mécomptes de la tutelle coloniale* (Paris: Société Française d'Histoire d'Outre-Mer, 1997), pp. 271–72.

88. René Girault, "La France entre l'Europe et l'Afrique," in Enrico Serra, ed., *Il relancio dell'Europa*, pp. 351–77.

89. Pascaline Winand, *Eisenhower, Kennedy, and the United States of Europe* (New York: St. Martin's Press, 1993), pp. 89–94; Marc Trachtenberg, *A Constructed Peace: The Making of the European Settlement, 1945–1963* (Princeton, N.J.: Princeton University Press, 1999), pp. 147–56.

90. Ennio Di Nolfo, "Gli Stati Uniti e le origini della Comunità Economica Europea," in Enrico Serra, ed., *Il relancio dell'Europa*, pp. 339–51; Winand, *Eisenhower, Kennedy and the United States of Europe*, pp. 89–94.

91. *DDF*, III, Mollet-Adenauer Talks, November 6, 1956, pp. 236–38.

92. American Embassy, Paris, to Department of State, November 30, 1956, 751.00/11–3056, RG 59, NA.

93. U.S. Embassy, Paris, to Secretary of State, November 27, 1956, 740.00/11–2756, RG 59, NA.

94. *FRUS,* 1956, 3, Note, November 16, 1956.

95. U.S. Embassy, Paris, to Secretary of State, November 29, 1956, 611.51/11–2956, RG 59, NA.

96. American Embassy in Bonn to Department of State, January 8, 1957, 740.00/1–857, NA, RG 59.

97. Keith Kyle, *Suez,* pp. 259–300, 548.

98. Memorandum of Telephone Call, 27 November 1956, Eisenhower Library, Dulles-Herter Series, Telephone Logs. Costigliola, *France and the United States,* p. 116. Maurice Vaïsse, "France and the Suez Crisis," in Louis and Owen, eds., *Suez 1956,* pp. 131–43. This is not to say, of course, that Mollet would not have followed these policies in any case. U.S. Embassy, Paris, to State Department, 28 November 1956, *FRUS,* 1955–1957, 27:89–91.

3. THE DEGENERATION OF THE REGIME

1. Connelly, "The Algerian War for Independence," p. 252.

2. Pierre Miquel, *La Guerre d'Algérie,* p. 269. See David Schalk's excellent comparison of opposition to the Algerian and Vietnam wars in France and the United States, *War and the Ivory Tower: Algeria and Vietnam* (New York: Oxford University Press, 1991).

3. UN Ambassador Lodge, New York, to the Secretary of State, January 10, 1957, 751.00/1–1057, RG 59, NA.

4. Miquel, *La Guerre d'Algérie,* p. 331.

5. On February 3, 1956, Julius Holmes, then American consul in Tangiers, cabled Washington that the French approach to negotiations was liberal and should be encouraged by the United States. American Consulate in Tangiers to Department of State, February 3, 1956, 651.71/1–2656, RG 59, NA.

6. Président du Conseil, Information, "La semaine tunisienne," October 24, 1955, Affaires Politiques, C 2259, AOM.

7. American Embassy, Paris, to Department of State, February 21, 1956, 651.71/2–2156, RG 59, NA.

8. This is very well covered in Samya El Machat, *Les Etats-Unis et la Tunisie: De l'ambiguité à l'entente, 1945–1949* (Paris: L'Harmattan, 1996), pp. 88–96.

9. See, for example, "Comptes rendus des négociations Franco-Tunisiennes relatives à l'ordre public," Paris, 4–7 April 1956, *DDF,* 1956, I, pp. 540–49; Pineau to Diplomatic Representatives of France Abroad, April 28, 1956, *DDF,* 1956, I, pp. 676–77.

10. Memorandum, Robert Murphy to Gordon Grey, Assistant Secretary of Defense, March 30, 1956; American Embassy, Paris, to Department of State, March 3, 1956, 651.71/3–356, RG 59, NA. See also Note du Secrétaire Général, July 12, 1956, and Note de la Direction Générale des Affaires Marocaines et Tunisiennes, July 13, 1956, *DDF,* 1956, II, pp. 87, 98.

11. "Note du Secrétariat d'Etat aux Affaires Marocaines et Tunisiennes, Politique des Etats-Unis au Maroc et en Tunisie," *DDF,* 1956, I, pp. 912–16.

12. American Embassy, Paris, to Department of State, February 15, 1957, 651.84a/2–1557, RG 59, NA. The Americans had it about right as to how the policy worked: see Abel Thomas, *Comment Israel fut sauvée*, pp. 73–76.

13. American Embassy, Paris, to Department of State, April 24, 1957, 651.84a/4–2457, RG 59, NA.

14. American Embassy, Paris, to Department of State, "French Problems for 1957," December 10, 1956, 611.51/12–1056, RG 59, NA.

15. Frédéric Bozo, *Deux stratégies pour l'Europe: De Gaulle, les Etats-Unis, et l'Alliance Atlantique, 1958–1969* (Paris: Plon, 1996), pp. 27–30.

16. Gérard Bossuat, *L'Europe des Français, 1943–1959: La IVe République aux sources de l'Europe communautaire* (Paris: Publications de la Sorbonne, 1996), pp. 303–12. Bertrand Goldschmidt, *The Atomic Complex: A Worldwide Political History of Nuclear Energy* (La Grange Park, Ill.: American Nuclear Society, 1982), pp. 129–37.

17. *FRUS*, 1954–57, 4, West European Security and Integration, January 25, 1956, State-AEC, pp. 394–95; February 3, 1956, Dillon to State, p. 412; February 10, 1956, Memo of Conversation, p, 407; December 3, 1956, Elbrick to Dulles, pp. 492–95.

18. Pineau to NAC, December 11, 1956, *FRUS*, 1955–57, 4:110.

19. *DDF*, I, 1957, 135, Note du Secrétariat général (Coordination des questions atomiques), "Problème de la quatrième puissance et proposition américaine sur le désarmement," pp. 245–46.

20. Jean-Baptiste Duroselle, "La relance européenne 1954–57," and Ennio Di Nolfo, "Gli Stati Uniti e le origini della Communità Economica Europea," in Enrico Serra, ed., *Il relancio dell'Europa et i Trattati di Roma* (Brussels and Milan: A. Giufré, 1989), pp. 45–55, 344–49. Pierre Melandri argues that the success of the Common Market as opposed to Euratom subsequently was actually due to the policies of the United States: in *Les Etats-Unis et le défi européen, 1955–1958* (Paris: Presses Universitaires de France, 1975). Also Pascaline Winand, *Eisenhower, Kennedy, and the United States of Europe* (New York: St. Martin's Press, 1993) on the Eisenhower decision, pp. 94–97.

21. See Marc Trachtenberg, *History and Strategy* (Princeton, N.J.: Princeton University Press, 1991), especially chapter 4, pp. 153–69. Trachtenberg traces a direct line from the Korean War to the New Look to the projected nuclear arming of the Bundeswehr, which became the immediate cause of the Berlin crisis of 1961.

22. Memorandum of Conversation, Secretary Dulles and Premier Guy Mollet, May 6, 1957, 611.51/5–657; Memorandum, C. Burke Elbrick to Secretary of State Dulles on the forthcoming Radford-Ely talks, June 26, 1957, 611.51/6–2657, RG 59, NA.

23. Minute on the "French Political Situation," October 3, 1957, Public Record Office (PRO), London, FO 371, 130629.

24. Bossuat, *L'Europe des Français*, p. 259. See also Denis Lefebvre, *Guy Mollet: Le mal aimé*, pp. 175–210, and Georgette Elgey, *Histoire de la IVe République, tome 3*, pp. 406–620. Elgey has the most sympathetic portrait of Mollet of the three.

25. Daniel Lefeuvre, *Chère Algérie 1930–1962: Comptes et mécomptes de la tutelle coloniale* (Paris: Société Française d'Histoire d'Outre-Mer, 1997), pp. 271–72.

26. Georges-Henri Soutou, "Les Accords de 1957 et 1958: Vers une communauté stratégique et nucléaire entre la France, l'Allemagne et l'Italie,"
Matériaux pour l'histoire de notre temps 31 (Avril-Juin 1993): 1–12.

27. Soutou, "Les Accords de 1957 et 1958"; Bossuat, *L'Europe des
Français,* pp. 334–65.

28. American Embassy, Paris, to Secretary of State, November 27, 1956,
740.00/11–2756, RG 59, NA.

29. Memorandum, Richard Service to C. Burke Elbrick, January 16, 158,
Records of the Office of West European Affairs, Subject File relating to France,
1944–1960, Box 1, Lot 61, D30, NA.

30. Memorandum of Conversation, State Department and Algerian Leaders, 29 November 1956, *FRUS, 1955–57,* 18:255–58. Editorial Note, Algeria,
FRUS, 1958–60, 13:643–44.

31. "Texte d'une note envoyée par M. M'Hammed Yazid auprès du 1er
Comité de la 12ième session de l'Assemblée Générale des Nations Unis," October 1, 1957, 1H 1751, D1, AA, Vincennes.

32. "Documents Présentés par le FLN devant l'ONU," December 10, 1957,
"Le FLN et la Communauté Juive en Alger," 1 H 1751, D1, AA, Vincennes.

33. Report of April 29, 1957, Ministre de la Défense Nationale; SDECE,
Président du Conseil, May 2, 1957, "Rapport du MNA sur 'les crimes de la
France en Algérie,' " May 2, 1957; Notice d'Information, "Documentation du
MNA addressée au President Eisenhower," July 4, 1957, 1 H 1751, D1, AA,
Vincennes.

34. Memorandum of Conversation, Secretary Dulles and Amory Houghton,
April 1, 1957, 611.51/4–157, RG 59, NA.

35. Memorandum of Conversation, Secretary Dulles, Amory Houghton, et.
al., Prime Minister Guy Mollet, Christian Pineau, etc., May 6, 1957,
611.51/5–657, RG 59, NA.

36. American Embassy, Paris, to Department of State, December 19, 1956,
December 21, 1956, 751.00/12–1956, 12–2156, RG 59, NA.

37. American Embassy, Paris, to Department of State, May 2, 1956, *FRUS,
1955–57,* 27:50. Jean Lacouture, *De Gaulle.* Vol. 2, *The Ruler, 1945–1971*
(New York, 1992), pp. 185–92. U.S. Embassy, Paris, to State Department, 21
June 1957, *FRUS, 1955–57,* 27:127.

38. Kettle, *De Gaulle and Algeria,* p. 73.

39. Paris (Jebb) to Foreign Office, June 25, 1957, Public Record Office
(PRO), FO 371, 130628.

40. American Embassy, Paris, to Department of State, February 15, 1957,
751.00/2–1557, RG 59, NA. British Embassy, Paris, to Foreign Office, Jebb to
Selwyn Lloyd, September 25, 1957, PRO, FO 371, 130629.

41. Acting Secretary Herter to American Embassy, Paris, April 9, 1957,
751.00/4–957, RG 59, NA.

42. American Embassy, Paris, to Department of State, June 11, 1957,
751.00/6–1157, RG 59, NA.

43. Memorandum, Richard Elbrick to the Secretary, July 1, 1957,
611.51/7–157, RG 59, NA.

44. Goeau-Brissonnière, *Mission secrète pour la paix en Algérie 1957,* p. 113.

45. Dulles to American Embassy, Paris, July 10, 1957, American Embassy, Paris, to Department of State, July 10, 15, 17, 18, 1957, 751.00/7–1057, 7–1557, 7–1757, 7–1857, RG 59, NA.

46. British Embassy in Paris to Foreign Office, G.P. Young to A. Rumbold, October 3, 1957, PRO, FO 371, 120630.

47. Memorandum of Conversation, Louis Joxe, Secretary-General of the French Ministry of Foreign Affairs, Francis Wilcox and Matthew Looram, July 10, 1957, 611.51/7–1057; Memorandum of Conversation, Hervé Alphand and Richard Elbrick, September 5, 1957, 611.51/9–557, RG 59, NA.

48. Minute by C.M. Anderson, October 8, 1957, PRO, FO 371, 120630.

49. Jacob J. Kaplan and Günther Schleiminger, *The European Payments Union* (Oxford: Clarendon Press, 1989), p. 266.

50. Memorandum of Conversation, Louis Joxe and Robert Murphy, July 8, 1957, 751.00/7–557, RG 59, NA.

51. Hubert Bonin, *Histoire économique de la IVe République* (Paris: Economica, 1987), pp. 245–53; Jacques Marseille, "La guerre a-t-elle eu lieu? Mythes et réalités du fardeau algérien," in Jean-Pierre Rioux, ed., *La Guerre d'Algérie et les Français,* pp. 289–304.

52. Bonin, *Histoire économique,* pp. 256–59.

53. American Embassy, Paris, to Department of State, October 29, 1957, 751.00/10–2957, October 31, 1957, 10–3157, RG 59, NA.

54. Dulles to the NSC, 2 October 1957, DDE Library, Whitman File, NSC Series, NSC 338; Humphrey to the NSC, 7 February 1957, NSC 312.

55. Paris to Foreign Office, November 25, 1957, PRO, FO 371, 130631.

56. Matthew Connelly, in his dissertation and in his article "The French-American Conflict over North Africa and the Fall of the French Republic," *Revue Française de l'Histoire d'Outre-Mer* (1997), pp. 9–27, argues that the question of extending a loan to the French was used to pressure the French to bring an end to the war. Jean Monnet, negotiating the loan package in Washington, in fact promised that France would withdraw 175,000 troops from Algeria, but he did not say when this would happen: DDE Library, AW File, International Series, Reel 7/793–98. I am grateful to Matthew Connelly for calling my attention to this document and allowing me to see his revised dissertation and projected book. In it, Connelly does agree that in the end there was no quid pro quo for the aid package: no troops were withdrawn, and the French went right ahead escalating the war. Dulles later regretted that the aid package had been given.

57. U.S. Embassy, Paris, to State Department, January 25, 1958, 840.00/1–2558; Under secretary Herter to American Embassy in Paris, January 29, 1958, 840.00/1–2958; Memorandum, Near East Affairs, 840.00/2–558; RG 59, NA.

58. DDE Library, Anne Whitman File, NSC Series, NSC 340, October 18, 1957. Dulles noted to Paul-Henri Spaak in October 1957 that in 1954 France had envisioned contributing fourteen divisions to NATO and the Germans twelve. Instead, the breakdown in Germany in 1957 was five German divisions to less than four for France. *FRUS,* 1954–57, 4, West European Security and Integration, Dulles-Spaak Note of Conversation, October 24, 1957, pp. 176–77.

See also Philip H. Gordon, *A Certain Idea of France: French Security Policy and the Gaullist Legacy* (Princeton, N.J.: Princeton University Press, 1993).

59. Dulles-Spaak Memorandum of Conversation, October 24, 1957, *FRUS,* 1955–57, 4:176–77.

60. French Embassy, Washington, to MAE, March 11, 1957, AM 1952–1963, Etats-Unis, 46, Tunisie, MAE.

61. American Embassy in Paris to State Department, May 24, 1957, 651.72/5–2457, and May 29, 1957, 651.72/5–2957, RG 59, NA. French Embassy in Washington to MAE, May 23, 1957, May 24, 1957, AM 1952–1963, Etats-Unis, 46, Tunisie, MAE.

62. American Embassy, Rabat, to Department of State, June 15, 1957, 651.71/6–1457, RG 59, NA.

63. MAE to Washington, May 29, 1957; French Embassy in Washington to MAE, May 31, 1957, AM 1952–1963, Etats-Unis, 46, Tunisie, MAE.

64. *DDF,* 1957, I, Jan.–June, 415, Gorse to Faure, May 18, 1957, p. 815, in which Tunis is notified of the suspension of French aid; 424, Alphand to Pineau, May 24, 1957, pp. 847–49, reports that Washington will step in to aid Tunisia if France persists in its refusal. Vol. II, July–December, 8, "Note de la Direction des affaires Marocaines et Tunisiennes," July 2, 1957, p. 23.

65. MAE to French Embassy in Washington, July 6, 1957; French Embassy in Washington to MAE, September 14, 1957, AM 1952–1963, Etats-Unis, 46, Tunisie, MAE.

66. American Consulate in Tunis to State Department, September 4, 1957, 651.72/9–457, September 9, 1957, 651.72/9–957, RG 59, NA.

67. Secretary of State Dulles to Tunis, September 11, 1957, and September 22, 1957, 651.72/9–957, 551.72/9–1157; Tunisia to Department of State, September 13, 1957, 651.72/9–1357, RG 59, NA.

68. The crisis is very well covered in El Machat, *Les Etats-Unis et la Tunisie,* pp. 126–45.

69. Secretary of State Dulles to Tunis, October 5, 1957, 651.72/10–457, RG 59, NA.

70. Tunis to State Department, October 7, 1957, 651.72/10–757, Tunis to State Department, October 14, 1957, 651.72/10–1457, RG 59, NA.

71. Foreign Office to Washington, Selwyn Lloyd to Sir Harold Caccia, October 31, 1957, PRO, FO 371, 125872.

72. Dulles to American Embassy, Paris, and North African Posts, November 5, 1957, 651.51S/11–557, RG 59, NA.

73. Talbott, *The War Without a Name,* p. 115.

74. "Fourniture d'Armes à l'Armée Tunisienne," undated, MAE, Nations Unis, 567. Foreign Office to Paris, November 3, 1957, November 5, 1957, PRO, FO 371, 125872.

75. Paris to Foreign Office, November 6, 1957, PRO, FO 3711, 125873.

76. Washington to Foreign Office, November 8, 1957; Foreign Office to Washington, November 9, 1957; Paris to Foreign Office, November 9, 1957, PRO, FO 371, 125873.

77. Message from Secretary Dulles to Selwyn Lloyd, November 11, 1957, PRO, FO 371, 125873.

78. French Embassy in Washington to MAE, Alphand-Elbrick Conversation, AM 1952–1963, Etats-Unis, 46, Tunisie, MAE.

79. Paris to Foreign Office, November 12, 1957, Foreign Office to Tunis, November 13, 1957, Paris to Foreign Office, November 13, 1957, Paris to Foreign Office, November 14, 1957. PRO, FO 371, 125874.

80. Eisenhower's reaction is in DDE Library, Anne Whitman File, DDE Diary, November 14, 1957, and letter to Premier Gaillard, November 13, 1957.

81. Paris to Foreign Office, November 15, 1957, PRO, FO 371, 125874. The lone rational voice was *Le Monde,* which said that France should have provided arms to Tunisia.

82. MAE Circular to all diplomatic posts of Gaillard speech, November 16, 1957, AM 1952–1963, Etats-Unis, 46, Tunisie, MAE. The crisis over arms to Tunisia may be followed from the French point of view in *DDF,* 1957, II, July-December, in particular 193, Alphand to Pineau, September 14, 1957, pp. 399–400; 252, Note de la Direction des Affaires Marocaines et Tunisiennes, October 8, 1957, pp. 514–21; 324, Alphand to MAE, November 11, 1957, pp. 650–53; 329, Premier Gaillard to President Eisenhower, November 12, 1957, pp. 662–63; and 331, Alphand to Pineau, November 13, 1957, p. 665.

83. Michael Kettle, *De Gaulle and Algeria,* p. 167. Paris to London, November 16, 1957, PRO, FO 371, 125874.

84. British Embassy in Washington to Foreign Office, November 19, 1957, PRO, PREM 11 2560. Paris to Foreign Office, November 22, 1957, PRO, PREM 11 2560.

85. Memorandum of Conversation, Ambassador Alphand and Under Secretary of State Matthew Looram, January 16, 1958, Lot 61, D30, Box 1, NA.

86. Dulles to State Department from Paris, December 13, 1957, 651.51S/12–1357, RG 59, NA.

87. National Intelligence Estimate, 13 August 1957, *FRUS,* 1955–57, 27:139–65. The contrary State Department view from Algiers is in U.S. Consulate, Algiers, to State Department, 10 January 1957, RG 59, 751S.00/1–1057. It is impossible to judge how influential the CIA analysis was, but the superiority of State Department understanding to that of the CIA is worthy of note.

4. THE UNITED STATES, GREAT BRITAIN,
    AND THE SAKIET CRISIS

1. The American Secretary of State referred to this scenario many times, but the most dramatic moment was just after the Sakiet bombardment to French Ambassador Hervé Alphand in Washington: see *DDF,* 1958, I, Alphand to Pineau, February 9, 1958, p. 149. Dulles told Alphand that France could not settle the Algerian problem by military force; eventually it would quit and communism triumph as in Indochina: *DDF,* 1958, I, Alphand to Ministère des Affaires Etrangères, March 5, 1958, p. 277.

2. Report of September 27, 1957, 1H1589, D1, Archives des Armées, Vincennes. The report cites an "informer."

3. American Consul in Tunis, Jones, to State Department, June 1, 1957, 611.72/6–157, Secretary of State Dulles to Paris and Tunis, June 8, 1957,

651.72/6–857, American Embassy in Paris to State Department, June 11, 1957, 651.72/6–1157, RG 59, NA.

4. MAE, Paris, à Ambafrance, Tunis, September 6, 1957. MAE, Nations Unis, 567.

5. MAE, Paris, au Représentant de la France aux Nations Unis, New York, September 14, 1958. MAE, Nations Unis, 568. American Embassy in Paris to State Department, June 27, 1957, 651.72/6–2757, RG 59, NA.

6. MAE à New York, September 30, 1957, October 2, 1957, MAE, Nations Unis, 568.

7. "Position du Gouvernement Tunisien vis à vis du problème algérien," French Embassy, Tunis, to MAE, Paris, August 23, 1957. MAE, Nations Unis, 567, D2.

8. "Tableau des incidents de frontière algéro-tunisienne," July 1–February 10, 1958, MAE, Nations Unis, 567.

9. Report of January 18, 1957, 1H1587, D1, AA, Vincennes.

10. Report of February 28, 1957, 1H1587, D1, AA, Vincennes.

11. Note, "Du 'droit de suite' qu'aurait la France de poursuivre les rebelles algériennes en territoire tunisien ou marocain: L'inexistence et l'inutilité de ce droite." MAE, Nations Unis, 568.

12. Report of August 9, 1957, and accompanying map, Reports of August 29, 1957, September 4, 1957, September 11, 1957, and September 17, 1957, 1H1587, D1, AA, Vincennes.

13. Reports of November 8, 1957, December 7, 1957, December 8, 1957, December 12, 1957, and December 20, 1957, 1H1587, D1, AA, Vincennes.

14. Tunis to State Department, January 3, 1958, 651.72/1–358, RG 59, NA.

15. Fiche, envoyé par le Ministre Résident en Alger aux Affaires Etrangères, January 14, 1958, Fiche de Renseignements, January 15, 1958, Commandant Supérieur Interarmées, 10ième Région Militaire, "Incident du Frontière, Sakiet Sidi Youssef, January 25, 1958, 1H 1965, D1, Sakiet Sidi Youssef, AA, Vincennes.

16. American Embassy, Tunis, to Department of State, January 17, 1958, 651.51S/1–1758, RG 59, NA.

17. American Embassy, Tunis, to Department of State, January 28, 1958, 651.51S/1–2858, RG 59, NA.

18. American Embassy, Tunis, to Department of State, January 15, 1958, 651.72/1–1558, Secretary of State Dulles to Paris and Tunis Embassies, January 15, 1958, 651.72/1–1558, RG 59, NA.

19. El Machat, Les Etats-Unis et la Tunisie, pp. 158–60.

20. The Tunisians thought the French were seeking a border incident that would provide them with an excuse to reoccupy Tunisia on a permanent basis. Paris to State Department, January 18, 1958, Paris and Tunis to State Department, January 18, 1958, Tunis to State Department, January 18, 1957, 651.72/1–1858, RG 59, NA.

21. Report of December 31, 1957, with accompanying map; Reports of January 5, 1958, January 10, 1958, January 16, 1958, January 17, 1958, through January 27, 1958, 1H1587 D1, 1958, AA, Vincennes.

22. Report number 141, February 7, 1958, with accompanying aerial maps of Tunisian border villages (Sakiet not included), 1H1587, 1958, D1, AA, Vin-

cennes. See reports for the remainder of the month of February and continuing thereafter which detail continued border clashes with French forces.

23. MAE à New York, February 2, 1958. MAE, Nations Unies, 567. The telegram quotes the minister for Algeria.

24. "Instruction Personnelle pour le Général Commandant la Zone Est Constantine," September 14, 1957, 1 H 2961, AA, Vincennes.

25. Le Général de Corps de l'Armée Loth, Commandant de Corps d'Armée de Constantine à M. le Général d'Armée, Cdt Supérieure Interarmées, Alger, September 24, 1957, 1H 2961, D1, AA, Vincennes.

26. Général Salan à M. le Ministre de la Défense Nationale, October 30, 1957, 1 H 2961, D1, AA, Vincennes.

27. Plan "Dozer" destiné à assurer la protection et la sauvegarde des troupes françaises en Tunisie, January 19, 1958, 1H 2961, D1, AA, Vincennes.

28. Algiers to Foreign Office, February 11, 1958, PRO, PREM 2561. Samya El Machat asserts that the French cabinet as a whole bore responsibility for the Sakiet raid consequent to a decision made on January 29, 1958, but she offers no source. *Les Etats-Unis et la Tunisie*, p. 161. Jacques Chaban-Delmas, in his memoirs, attributes responsibility for the raid to the local commander, who acted with the approval of General Salan, but admits that he accepted full responsibility for it thereafter. Jacques Chaban-Delmas, *Mémoires pour demain* (Paris: Flammarion, 1997), pp. 303–5.

29. Secretary of State Dulles to Embassies in Paris and Tunis, February 1, 1958, 651.72/2-158, RG 59, NA.

30. British Embassy, Paris, to Foreign Office, January 27, 1958; Paris to Foreign Office February 3, 1958, PRO, FO Tunisia 131576.

31. Embassy in Paris to State Department, February 4, 1958, 651.72/2-458; Secretary of State Dulles to Tunis, February 6, 1958, 651.72/2-458, RG 59, NA.

32. "Appuis Feux" specified for "Plan Dozer" included a group of 16 B 26 bombers and an unspecified number of F 47 Corsairs of American manufacture as well as Mistrals, precisely the matériel used in the Sakiet raid. See note 10 above.

33. Chaban-Delmas, *Mémoires pour demain*, pp. 294–95.

34. *L'Express,* February 13, 1958, 1H 1966, D4, AA, Vincennes.

35. Ibid.

36. Michael Kettle, *De Gaulle and Algeria,* p. 171.

37. Memorandum of Conversation, 9 February 1958, Washington, D.C., Ambassador Alphand and the Secretary of State, 751S.00/2–958, RG 59, NA.

38. Memorandum of Conversation, 11 February 1958, Washington, Ambassador Alphand and Assistant Secretary of State Elbrick, 751S.00/2–1158, RG 59, NA.

39. Message of 17 February 1958, "Dossier Sakiet," 1H 1759, D1, AA Vincennes.

40. "Fiche de Renseignement," Commandant Supérieur Interarmées, February 17, 1958, 1H 1965, D1, Sakiet Sidi Youssef, AA, Vincennes.

41. "Fiche sur Sakiet Sidi Youssef," February 22, 1958, MAE, Nations Unies, 567.

42. Le Général de Corps de l'Armée Loth à M. Le Général d'Armée Salan, Alger, February 11, 1958, 1H 1965, D1, Sakiet Sidi Youssef, AA, Vincennes. A

lengthy "Synthèse de l'Action Contre Sakiet" by the Military Command of the 10th Region, submitted February 13, 1958, repeated several times that the attack was within the framework of received orders and not the result of any unauthorized local initiative by the military command.

43. Le Général de Corps Aérien Jouhaud à M. le Général d'Armée Salan, February 13, 1958, 1H 1965, D1, Sakiet Sidi Youssef, AA, Vincennes.

44. Lettre du Général Salan au Ministre de la Défense Nationale, February 13, 1958, 1H 1965, D1, Sakiet Sidi Youssef, AA, Vincennes.

45. Securité d'Air, Message de Tunis, February 12, 1958, Message du 10 Régiment Militaire Algérien, February 9, 1958, Dossier "Affaire de Sakiet," 1H 1759, D1, AA Vincennes.

46. "Note Politique, L'Affaire de Sakiet et le Malaise de l'Armée Française," February 12, 1958, 1H 1965, D1, Sakiet Sidi Youssef, AA, Vincennes.

47. Secretary of State Dulles to Paris Embassy, February 8, 1958, Ambassador Jones, Tunis, to State Department, February 8, 1958, 651.72/2–858, RG 59, NA.

48. French Embassy in Washington to MAE, February 10, 1957, February 11, 1957, AM 1952–1963, Etats-Unis, 46, Tunisie, MAE.

49. American Consulate, Algiers, to Department of State, February 11, 1958, 751S.00/2–1158, Consulate, Algiers, to Department of State, February 14, 1958, 751S.00/2–1458, RG 59, NA.

50. Algiers to State Department, February 9, 1958, 651.72/2–958, Secretary of State Dulles to Paris Embassy, February 10, 1958, Paris to State Department, February 10, 1958, Ambassador Houghton to State Department, February 10, 1958, 651.72–2–1058, RG 59, NA.

51. Memorandum of Conversation, Ambassador Slim and Secretary Dulles, Washington, February 10, 1958, 651.72–2–1058; Paris Embassy to State Department, February 12, 1958, 651.72/2–1258, RG 59, NA.

52. Tunisian Embassy to State Department, February 12, 1958, 651.72/2–1258, RG 59, NA. *DDF,* I, 1958, Alphand (Washington) to Pineau, February 13, 1958, pp. 166–69.

53. Under Secretary of State Herter to Paris and Tunis, February 13, 1958, 651.72/2–1358, RG 59, NA.

54. Memoranda of Conversations, C. Burke Elbrick and Hervé Alphand, February 16, 1958, 772.00/2–1658, February 17, 1958, 772.00/2–1758, RG 59, NA. See also El Machat, *Les Etats-Unis et la Tunisie,* pp. 168–70.

55. French Embassy, Washington, to MAE, February 18, 1958; MAE to French Embassy, Washington, February 18, 1958, MAE, Tunisie, 1958, 312.

56. American Embassy, Tunis, to Department of State, February 19, 1958, 651.51S/2–1958, RG 59, NA.

57. *FRUS,* 1958–60, 13, North Africa, Algeria, Holmes to the Secretary of State, February 20, 1958, p. 627.

58. Foreign Office to Washington, April 7, 1958: "If the Americans decide they must grasp the Algerian nettle, it is important that they do so in terms likely to influence the French in the right direction." PRO, FO 371, 131589.

59. French Embassy in Washington to MAE, February 28, 1957, AM 1952–1963, Etats-Unis, 46, Tunisie, MAE.

60. Tunis to Foreign Office, March 13, 1958, PRO, PREM file 11, 2561. The telegram, in the Prime Minister's personal file, is marked in pencil "this is very serious."

61. Paris to Foreign Office, March 13, 1958; Foreign Office to Tunis, March 13, 1958, PRO, PREM 11, 2561. Paris to Foreign Office, March 15, 1958, PRO, FO 131656.

62. Minute by W. Hayter, March 17, 1958, PRO, FO 131656. Hayter thought Jebb could give his opinion to the French about adopting an "imaginative policy," but in yet another reply in the margins A. Rumbold wrote that "Nobody can help the French in this matter."

63. Confidential Minute, February 24, 1958, PRO, FO 371, 131578.

64. Memorandum of Conversation between the German Ambassador and the Secretary, January 21, 1958, 840.00/1–2158; Secretary Dulles to Paris and All European Posts, February 20, 1958, 840.00/2–1958; American Embassy, Paris, to Department of State, March 13, 1958, 840.00/3–1258. RG 59, NA. Could the French raid on Sakiet and the evident instability in Paris have suddenly made British reluctance to join the six comprehensible in Washington?

65. Memorandum of Conversation on European Integration, Secretary Dulles, Ambassador Alphand, Robert Schuman, and Matthew Looram, March 29, 1958, 840.00/3–2958, RG 59, NA.

66. Memoranda of Conversations, Alphand, Acting Secretary Herter, et al., February 13, 1958, 651.72/2–1358; Alphand, Wilcox, Looram, et al., February 14, 1958, 651.72/2–1458, RG 59, NA.

67. RG 59, Herter to Tunis, 651.72/2–1258, February 12, 1958; Herter to New York, 651.72/2–1258, February 12, 1958; Memorandum of Conversation, French Ambassador Alphand and the Acting Secretary, 651.72/2–1358, February 13, 1958; Jones to State Department, 651.72/2–1458, February 14, 1958. RG 59, NA.

68. RG 59, Houghton to State Department, 651.72/2–1558, February 15, 1958; Herter to Tunis, 651.72/2–1558, February 15, 1958; Memorandum of Conversation, Alphand and Herter, Washington, 651.72/2–1558, February 15, 1958. RG 59, NA.

69. For an account of Murphy's relations with France, see Irwin Wall, L'influence américaine sur la politique française, 1945–1954, and "The United States, Algeria, and the Fall of the Fourth French Republic," Diplomatic History 18, 4 (Fall 1994): 489–511; and Robert Murphy, Diplomat Among Warriors (New York: Doubleday, 1964), p. 382.

70. On Murphy, see Martin Weil, A Pretty Good Club: The Founding Fathers of the U.S. Foreign Service (New York: Norton, 1978), p. 123, and Wall, The United States and the Making of Postwar France, pp. 26–29. Michel Debré, Trois Républiques pour une France (Paris, 1986), p. 293; Ely, Mémoires, p. 229; Robert Murphy, Diplomat Among Warriors, p. 382.

71. Memorandum of Conversation, Alphand and Murphy, February 19, 1958, 651.72/2–1958, RG 59, NA.

72. Dulles to Tunis and Paris, February 19, 1958, 651.72/2–1958, RG 59, NA.

73. Paris to State Department from Murphy, February 24, 1958, 651.72/2–2458, RG 59, NA.

74. Tunis to Foreign Office, February 25, 1958; Tunis to Foreign Office, February 26, 1958. PRO, FO 371, 131585. Murphy from Tunis to State Department, 651.72/2–2858, February 28, 1958. On FLN contacts with Washington, see Tunis to Secretary of State, 751.00S/3–458, March 4, 1958, RG 59, NA. The British reports have Abbas in Tunisia instead of Krim; the American reports, more complete, make clear that it was Krim.

75. RG 59, Murphy to State Department, 651.72/2–2858, February 28, 1958, RG 59, NA.

76. Paris to State Department, March 5, 1958, 651.72/3–558, RG 59, NA.

77. Robert Murphy, Paris, to Department of State, March 3, 1958, 651.72/3–358; March 5, 1958, 651.72/3–558; Acting Secretary of State Herter to Murphy in Paris, March 8, 1958, 651.72/3–858 and 651.51S/3–858, RG 59, NA.

78. Telegram, Washington to Paris, March 14, 1958, MAE, Tunisie 1958, 314.

79. Murphy to State Department from Tunis, March 12, 1958, 651.72/3–1258, RG 59, NA.

80. RG 59, NA. Murphy to State Department, 651.72/3–1558, March 15, 1958. Washington to Paris, April 5, 1958, RG 59, NA. Tunis to Paris telegram, April 8, 1958, MAE, Tunisie 1958, 314. An English text of the agreement is in PRO, FO 371, 131587, March 16, 1958.

81. Tunis to Foreign Office, March 13, 1958; Foreign Office to Tunis, March 14, 1958; Tunis to Foreign Office, March 15, 1958, PRO, FO 371, 131587.

82. Murphy to State Department, 651.72/3–1358, March 13, 1958, RG 59, NA.

83. Secretary Dulles to U.S. UN delegation, New York, March 20, 1958, 772.00/3–2058, RG 59, NA. Dulles summarized Murphy's assurances to Bourguiba on March 13 in terms of the United States being fully conscious of the need for an Algerian settlement.

84. Paris to Foreign Office, March 19, 1958; March 21, 1958. PRO, FO 371, 131587. Murphy to State Department, 651.72/3–2558, March 25, 1958; Jones to State Department, 651.72/3–2658, March 26, 1958. RG 59, NA.

85. MAE telegram to Washington, April 3, 1958, MAE, Tunisie 1958, 314.

86. Dulles to Murphy in Paris, March 22, 1958, 651.72/3–2258, RG 59, NA.

87. Herter to Good Offices, 652.72/3–1458, March 14, 1958. RG 59, NA.

88. Minute on "Algeria" by H. Beeley, March 31, 1958. PRO, FO 371, 131588.

89. Tunis to State Department, March 17, 1958, 751.00S/3–1758, RG 59, NA.

90. Dulles to Good Offices for Murphy, 651.72/3–3158, March 31, 1958. RG 59, NA.

91. American Embassy, Paris, to Department of State, April 3, 1958, 611.51S/4–358, RG 59, NA.

92. Dulles to Good Offices for Murphy, 651.72/4–358, April 3, 1958; Tunis to State Department, 651.72/4–458, 4–658, April 4 and April 6, 1958. RG 59, NA.

93. Interestingly, drafts and the final version of Eisenhower's letter to Gaillard are to be found in the Public Record Office in London; in contrast, I have not been able to find even the final draft in Paris or Washington, which still is withholding its texts in the interests of "national security." The missing document notice is dated April 10, 1958, 651.51S/4–1058, RG 59, NA. The actual

drafts are in Washington to Foreign Office, April 5, 1958, Washington to Foreign Office, April 10, 1958, for the final draft, PRO, FO 371, 131590. It is also reproduced in French in François Le Douarec, *Felix Gaillard, 1919–1970: Un destin inachevé* (Paris: Economica, 1991).

94. Foreign Office to Washington, April 7, 1958, PRO, FO 371, 131590.

95. Murphy from Paris to Department of State, April 7, 1958, Secretary of State Dulles to Murphy in Paris, April 8, 1958, 651.51S/4–758, RG 59, NA.

96. Paris to Foreign Office, April 9, 1958, PRO, FO 371, 131589.

97. "Rencontre Murphy-Beeley-Gaillard à Barbézieux," April 9, 1958, MAE, Tunisie 1958, 314.

98. Paris to Foreign Office, April 10, 1958, PRO, FO 371, 131590.

99. Telegram, London to Paris, April 11, 1958, MAE, Tunisie 1958, 314.

100. Telegram, Washington to Paris, April 10, 1958, MAE, Tunisie 1958, 314.

101. Murphy, Paris, to Department of State, April 10, 1958, Dulles to Murphy in Paris, April 10, 1958, 651.51S/4–1058, RG 59, NA.

102. Murphy, Paris, to Department of State, April 11, 1958, 651.51S/4–1158, RG 59, NA.

103. Washington to Foreign Office, April 11, 1958, PRO, FO 371, 131590; Foreign Office to Paris, April 11, 1958; Paris to Foreign Office, April 11, 1958.

104. American Embassy, Paris, to Department of State, April 14, 1958, 651.51S/4–1458, RG 59, NA.

105. Memorandum of Conversation, Alphand and the Secretary, Washington, April 14, 1958, 651.51S/4–1458, RG 59, NA.

106. Minute, April 22, 1958, PRO, FO 371, 131590. The Foreign Office concurred: "It looks very much like the Americans were responsible in both capitals [Paris and Washington]."

107. Letter, Livingston Merchant to Secretary of State Dulles, June 6, 1958; Secretary Dulles to Merchant, June 10, 1958, 611.51/6–658, RG 59, NA.

108. Memoranda of Conversations, Joseph Luns and Douglas Dillon, April 23, 1958, Luns and Secretary Dulles, April 24, 1958, 651.51/4–2358, 4–2458, RG 59, NA.

109. American Embassy, Paris, to Secretary of State, April 18, 1958, 611.51/4–1858, RG 59, NA.

110. Memorandum of Conversation, Alphand and the Assistant Secretary, 18 April 1958, 751.00S/4–1858, RG 59, NA. *Le Monde*, 19–20 May 1958. Also Secretary of State to U.S. Embassy, Paris, 18 April 1958, *FRUS*, 1958–60, 13:632–33.

111. Michael Harrison in Denis Lacorne, Jacques Rupnik, and Marie-France Toinet, *The Rise and Fall of Anti-Americanism: A Century of French Perception* (New York: St. Martin's Press, 1990), p. 174.

112. American Consulate in Algiers to State Department, April 19, 1958, *FRUS*, 1958–60, 13, Algeria, p. 634.

113. Paris to Foreign Office, March 24, 1958, PRO, PREM 11, 2338.

114. Paris to Foreign Office, June 5, June 17, 1958, PRO, FO 371, 131591.

115. Dwight David Eisenhower Library (Abilene, Kansas), National Security Council Series, NSC 369, June 19, 1958.

5. THE FALL OF THE REPUBLIC AND THE COMING OF DE GAULLE

1. Président du Conseil, SDECE Reports of February 6, 1958, and April 4, 1958, Conférences Internationales, MA 28, Archives d'Outre-Mer, Aix-en-Provence.

2. Président du Conseil, SDECE Report of April 29, 1958, "Conférences Internationales," MA 28, AOM.

3. Paris to State Department, April 16, 1958, 651.72/4–1658, RG 59, NA.

4. "Algerian Situation," FY 1958 MSP for Europe, Presidential Report to Congressional Committees, April 28, 1958, Lot 61, D30, Box 1, NA.

5. De la Gorce, *Apogée et mort,* p. 517; Odile Rudelle, *Mai 1958: De Gaulle et la République* (Paris: Plon, 1988), pp. 148–55, 157; U.S. Embassy, Paris, to State Department, 1 May 1958, 751.00/5–158, RG 59, NA.

6. U.S. Embassy, Paris, to Department of State, May 1, 1958, 751.00/5–158, RG 59, NA.

7. U.S. Embassy, Paris, to Department of State, May 12, 13, 1958, 751.00/5–1258, 5–1358, RG 59, NA.

8. Memoranda, F.W. Jandrey and Richard Service to Secretary of State, May 13, 1958, F.W. Jandrey to Secretary, May 14, 1958, Lot 61, D30, Box 1, Folder 1.7, NA.

9. "Ambassador Jebb record of conversation with de Gaulle," March 20, 1958, PRO, PREM 11, 2338.

10. Michel Poniatowski, *Mémoires,* tome I (Paris: Plon, 1997), pp. 291–326.

11. Paris to Foreign Office, May 15, 1958, Algiers to Foreign Office, May 16, 1958, PRO, FO 137241.

12. U.S. Embassy, Paris, to Department of State, May 14, 1958, 751.00/5–1458, RG 59, NA.

13. U.S. Embassy, Paris, to Department of State, May 15, 1958, 751.00/5–1558, RG 59, NA.

14. Ambassade de France à Washington au Ministère des Affaires Etrangères, Paris, 16 May 1958, 21 May 1958, both in MAE, Amérique, Etats-Unis, Box 16. Secretary of State to U.S. Embassy, Tunis, and U.S. Embassy, Paris, 14 May 1958, 751S.00/5–1458, RG 59, NA. Memorandum of Conversation, 16 May 1958, Washington, Secretary of State Dulles and the Ambassadors of Morocco and Tunisia, 751S.00/5–1658, RG 59, NA.

15. American Embassy, Paris, to Department of State, May 18, 1958, 651.51S/5–1558, RG 59, NA.

16. American Embassy in Tunis to Department of State, May 22, 1958, 772.00/2–2258, RG 59, NA.

17. American Embassy, Rabat, to Department of State, May 16, 1958, 651.71/5–1658, May 23, 1958, 5–2358, RG 59, NA.

18. U.S. Embassy, Paris, to State Department, 16 May 1958, 751.00/5–1658, RG 59, NA. Secretary of State to U.S. Embassy, Paris, 18 May 1958, 751.00/5–1858. U.S. Embassy, Paris, to State Department, 24 May 1958, 751/00/5–2458, RG 59, NA. Foccart, in his memoirs, denies that Tournet spoke

for de Gaulle: *Foccart Parle. Entretiens avec Philippe Gaillard* (Paris: Fayard/Jeune Afrique, 1995), pp. 139–40.

19. U.S. Embassy, Paris to State Department, 18 May 1958, 751.00/5–1858, RG 59, NA. Michel Debré, *Trois Républiques pour une France,* I, 308. Even more interesting, Debré, incapacitated by a swollen foot at this time, was being shepherded around Paris by an American graduate student, Nicholas Wahl, who was doing a study of the Gaullist party.

20. U.S. Embassy, Paris, to Department of State, May 19, 1958, 751.00/5–1958, RG 59, NA.

21. Secretary of State Dulles to U.S. Embassy, Paris, May 19, 1959, 751.00/5–1958, RG 59, NA.

22. Buron, *Les dernières années de la IVe République,* pp. 244–45.

23. U.S. Embassy, Paris, to Secretary of State, May 20, 1958, 751.00/5–2058, RG 59, NA.

24. Memorandum of Conversation, Alphand, Dulles, Elbrick, and Looram, Washington, May 21, 1958, 611.51/5–2758, RG 59, NA.

25. U.S. Embassy, Paris, to Department of State, May 20, 1958, 751.00/5–2058, RG 59, NA.

26. U.S. Embassy, Paris, to State Department, 20 May 1958, 751.00/5–2058. Secretary of State Dulles to U.S. Embassy, Paris, 21 May 1958, 751.00/5–2158. U.S. Embassy, Paris, to State Department, 18 May 1958, 751.00/5–1858. RG 59, NA. Allen Dulles to the NSC, 22 May 1958, Eisenhower Library, Whitman File, NSC Series, NSC 366.

27. U.S. Embassy, Paris, to Department of State, May 22, 1958, 751.00/5–2258, RG 59, NA.

28. Jeffrey A. Lefebvre, "Kennedy's Algerian Dilemma: Containment, Alliance Politics, and the 'Rebel Dialogue,'" *Middle Eastern Studies* 35, 2 (April 1999): 61.

29. U.S. Embassy, Tunis, to State Department, 20 May 1958, 751.00S/5–2058. U.S. Embassy, Paris, to State Department, 22 May 1958, 751.00/5–2258. RG 59, NA.

30. Fiche, Commandant Supérieure Interarmées, 10ème Région Militaire, Etat Major, 2e Bureau, May 23, 1958, 1H 1759, D1, AA, Vincennes.

31. Secretary of State Dulles to U.S. Embassies, Tunis and Rabat, and U.S. Embassy, Paris, 22 May 1958, 751.00S/5–2258. U.S. Embassy, Tunis, to State Department, 23 May 1958, 751.00S/5–2358. U.S. Embassy, Tunis, to State Department, 24 May 1958, 751.00S/5–2458. RG 59, NA.

32. UN Delegation in New York to Department of State, May 26, 1958, 751.00/5–2658, RG 59, NA.

33. American Consulate, Algiers, to Department of State, July 7, 1958, 651.51S/7–358, RG 59, NA. The message was received in Algiers on May 19, dated May 16, but forwarded to Washington on July 7.

34. Algiers to Foreign Office, May 19, 1958, May 20, 1958, PRO, FO 131657.

35. "Note, pour Alger," Pleven to Salan, May 22, 1958, MAE, Tunisie, 306.

36. U.S. Embassy, Paris, to Department of State, May 24, 25, 1958, 751.00/5–2458, 5–2558, RG 59, NA.

37. Memorandum of Conversation, Ambassador Slim and Robert Murphy, Washington, May 26, 1958, 772.00/5–2658, RG 59, NA.

38. Secretary of State Dulles to U.S. Consulate, Algiers, 18 May 1958, 751.00S/5–1858. U.S. Embassy, Paris, to State Department, 19 May 1958, 751.00S/5–1958. U.S. Consulate, Algiers, to State Department, 23 May 1958, 751.00S/5–2358. U.S. Consulate, Algiers, to State Department, 25 May 1958, 751.00S/5–2558. Memorandum of Conversation, Ambassador Alphand and Secretary Dulles, Washington, 21 May 1958, 751.00/5–2158. U.S. Embassy, Paris, to State Department, 27 May 1958, 751.00/5–2758. RG 59, NA.

39. Kettle, *De Gaulle and Algeria*, p. 222.

40. U.S. Embassy, Paris, to Department of State, May 28, 1958, 751.00/5–2858, RG 59, NA.

41. U.S. Embassy, Paris, to State Department, 19 May 1958, 751.00/5–1958, RG 59, NA. Dulles to the NSC, 22 May 1958, Eisenhower Library, Whitman File, NSC Series, NSC 366.

42. U.S. Embassy, Paris, to Department of State, May 27, 1958, 751.00/5–2758, RG 59, NA.

43. Memorandum, C. Burke Elbrick to the Acting Secretary, May 27, 1958, 751.00/5–2758, RG 59, NA.

44. Memorandum, Stanley Cleveland to Mr. Timmons, for Brentano and Macmillan Talks, May 27, 1958; Memorandum, Timmons to Elbrick, June 2, 1958, Lot 60, D30, Box 2, 1.12, De Gaulle Government, NA.

45. American Embassy, Paris, to Department of State, May 29, 1958, 611.51/5–2958, RG 59, NA.

46. Minute, "The Future Relationship between the US, France, and the UK," June 2, 1958, PRO, FO 137259.

47. Without being sure of de Gaulle's future policies, Dulles, whose impatience with the cabinet instability of the Fourth Republic had become extreme, remarked that whatever the general did, "in the long run a strong ally is better than a weak one." See Richard Challener, "Dulles and de Gaulle," in Robert Paxton and Nicholas Wahl, eds., *De Gaulle and the United States: A Centennial Reappraisal* (Oxford: Berg Publishers, 1994), p. 143.

48. U.S. Embassy, Luxembourg, to Secretary of State, June 14, 1958, 840.00/6–1458, RG 59, NA.

49. Ambassade de France à Washington au Ministère des Affaires Etrangères, 2 June 1958, 3 June 1958, 12 June 1958, 29 October 1958, MAE, Amérique 52–60, Etats Unis-Algérie 1959, Box 22. See also Pierre Melandri, "La France devant l'opinion américaine: Le retour de De Gaulle, début 1958–printemps 1959," *Relations Internationales* 58 (Été 1989): 195–215.

50. André Dulac, *Nos guerres perdues* (Paris: Fayard, 1969), p. 72.

51. Kettle, *De Gaulle and Algeria*, p. 231.

52. U.S. Embassy, Paris, to State Department, 29 May 1958, 751.00/5–2958, RG 59, NA. Dwight D. Eisenhower, *The White House Years: Waging Peace, 1956–1961* (New York, 1965), p. 430.

6. THE UNITED STATES, ALGERIA,
    AND DE GAULLE'S DIPLOMACY

1. Note du Secrétariat des Conférences, May 3, 1957, Mollet-Dulles talks, *DDF*, 1957, I, Jan.-June, p. 362. Pleven to Alphand, May 26, 1958, *DDF*, 1958, I, Jan.-June, p. 670.

2. Goldschmidt, *The Atomic Complex*, pp. 137–42.

3. Eisenhower realized this and continuously expressed his unhappiness with U.S. legislative restrictions on the sharing of nuclear information. On August 25, 1960, he ordered the National Security Council to study "whether and under what circumstances it might be in the security interests of the United States to enhance the nuclear capability of France." But the prior consensus of the Council, despite the will of the president, and the fact that France had by then already exploded its first bomb, was that the law still disqualified France from such help and Congress was unlikely to change it. *FRUS*, 1958–60, 7, West European Integration and Security, NATO, NSC 457, August 25, 1960, p. 627.

4. G. de Wailly, "Esquisse pour une politique de l'Afrique du Nord," April 16, 1958, MAE, Tunisie 1958, 313.

5. Alfred Grosser, *French Foreign Policy under de Gaulle* (Boston, 1967), pp. 52–58.

6. See Jouhaud's *Serons-nous enfin compris?* (Paris: Albin Michel, 1984). Interestingly, memoirs by Jacques Foccart, *Foccart Parle. Entretiens avec Philippe Gaillard* (Paris: Fayard, 1995), Pierre Lefranc, *Avec qui vous savez* (Paris: Plon, 1979), and Raymond Triboulet, *Un ministre du Général* (Paris: Plon, 1985), all concur in their absolute belief in 1958 that de Gaulle fully intended to keep Algeria French. Foccart admits that if de Gaulle did confide to strangers his belief that Algeria would become independent, he never admitted it to partisans of *Algérie française* among his collaborators (p. 154).

7. Michele Cointet, *De Gaulle et l'Algérie française, 1958–1962* (Paris: Librairie Académique Perrin, 1995), pp. 21–25. Cointet sees signs of early doubt, however, in the appointment of Paul Delouvrier as delegate general in December 1958 and the restoration of civil authority; Delouvrier later said he was in favor of independence in 1958.

8. Miquel, *La Guerre d'Algérie*, pp. 352–55. De Gaulle's rhetoric, for Miquel, was entirely in the spirit of integration through the remainder of 1958 and early 1959. Only by midsummer 1959 does there begin to appear a change in emphasis from full integration with France toward "association," which became his mantra for the remainder of the war through the peace agreements of Evian in 1962.

9. Alistair Horne, *A Savage War of Peace*, p. 338. The Challe plan as a whole is discussed on pp. 330–40.

10. Benjamin Stora, *La gangrène et l'oubli: La mémoire de la guerre d'Algérie* (Paris: La Découverte, 1991).

11. Persuasively argued by Michele Cointet, *De Gaulle et l'Algérie française*, pp. 18–21. Lacouture also admits that de Gaulle's first priority in Algeria was winning the war: *De Gaulle*, vol. 2, *The Ruler*, pp. 240–46.

12. Daniel Lefeuvre, *Chère Algérie 1930–1962: Comptes et mécomptes de la tutelle coloniale*, pp. 281–93.

13. "French Situation, Brentano Talks," Washington, June 5, 1958; "Memorandum on de Gaulle's Prospective Foreign Policy and the United States," by Arnold Wolfers, June 6, 1958, Lot 61, D30, Box 1, NA.

14. Memorandum of Conversation, Raymond Aron, Under Secretary Herter, Allen Dulles, Frederick Jandrey, June 13, 1958, Lot 61, D30, Box 2, 1.12, De Gaulle Government, NA.

15. American Embassy, Rabat, to Department of State, June 4, 1958, 651.71/6–458, RG 59, NA.

16. "Chronologie des Evènements de Tunisie depuis le 13 mai, 1958," May 28, 1958, MAE, Tunisie, 306.

17. "Principaux évènements survenus au cours du mois de juin 1958," June 17, 1958, MAE, Tunisie 1958, 306.

18. Position Paper, "U.S. Policy Toward Tunisia," Briefing Papers, Dulles visit to Paris, July 3–6, 1958, Lot 61, D30, Box 1, 1.A.4, NA.

19. Position Papers, "U.S. Policy Toward Morocco," "Arms for Morocco and Tunisia," and "U.S. Policy Toward Algeria," Briefing Papers, Dulles visit to Paris, July 3–6, 1958, Lot 61, D30, Box 1, 1.A.4, NA.

20. Jacques Chevallier, the moderate mayor of Algiers, told Houghton that Farès, a moderate Algerian, was the middleman between de Gaulle and the Algerian leaders, American Embassy, Paris, to Department of State, September 15, 1958, 651.51S/9–1558. Jones reported the FLN position, American Embassy, Tunis, to Department of State, October 14, 1958, 651.51S/10–1458, RG 59, NA.

21. Minute by Consul Sarell, June 12, 1958; Minute by Ambassador Jebb, June 17, 1958, PRO, FO 371, 131659.

22. Prime Minister to Foreign Minister Lloyd, June 6, 1958, PRO, PREM 2339; Michael Kettle, De Gaulle and Algeria, pp. 246–48.

23. Kettle, pp. 258–66.

24. American Embassy, Paris (Dulles), to Department of State, July 5, 1958, 611.51/7–558, RG 59, NA.

25. Bozo, Deux stratégies pour l'Europe, p. 34.

26. Memorandum of Conversation, Secretary Dulles and Premier de Gaulle, July 5, 1958, FRUS, 1958–60, 7, West European Integration and Security: NATO, p. 320.

27. Memorandum of Private Lunch Conversation between Secretary Dulles and Premier de Gaulle, July 5, 1958, 611.51/7–558, RG 59, NA.

28. Couve de Murville to Gorse, July 18, 1958; Alphand to Couve de Murville, August 5, 1958; Couve de Murville to Alphand, September 9, 1958. DDF, 1958, tome II, July-December, pp. 107, 223–25, 322–24.

29. "Algérie-Tunisie-RAU," SDECE Report, December 15, 1958, 1H1162, D3, AA, Vincennes.

30. American Embassy in Tunis to Department of State, October 3, 1958, 611.51/10–358, RG 59, NA.

31. "Algérie-Etats-Unis," SDECE Report, November 26, 1958; "Algérie-Etats-Unis-Egypte," Président du Conseil, SDECE, November 25, 1958, in 1H1162, D3, AA, Vincennes.

32. "Note pour la Direction des Affaires Marocaines et Tunisiennes," September 19, 1958, MAE, Tunisie 1958, 313.

33. "Compte rendu détaillé de la réunion sur l'Algérie organisée par l'American Committee on Africa, le 1 Décembre, 1958," SDECE Report, 1H1164, D1, AA, Vincennes.

34. Président du Conseil, SDECE Reports of August 25, 1958, August 17, 1959, September 30, 1959, folder marked Ingérences, USA, MA 30, AOM.

35. Dulles to the American Embassy in Tunis, October 31, 1958, 651.51S/10–3158, RG 59, NA.

36. SDECE Report, November 28, 158, 1H1162, D3, AA, Vincennes.

37. "Note sur les Représentants du FLN à l'Etranger," MAE, Directeur Général des Affaires Politiques, Mission de Liaison avec l'Algérie, in 1H 1164, D1, AA, Vincennes.

38. Alphand to Couve de Murville, July 29, 1958; Couve de Murville to Alphand, September 26, 1958, DDF, 1958, tome II, July-December 1958, pp. 181–84, 431–42. Dulles to African Desk, September 22, 1958; Dulles-Alphand Conversation, October 17, 1968, FRUS, 1958–60, 13, North Africa, pp. 643–44.

39. Maurice Couve de Murville, Une politique étrangère, 1958–1969 (Paris: Plon, 1971), pp. 38–42.

40. With the notable exception of Edward Kolodziej, French International Policy Under de Gaulle and Pompidou (Ithaca, N.Y.: Cornell University Press, 1974), pp. 75–76.

41. See Philip Gordon, A Certain Idea of France. In October 1957, Secretary of State John Foster Dulles noted to Paul-Henri Spaak, Secretary General of NATO, that France had envisioned contributing 14 divisions to NATO and the Germans 12; instead, the breakdown in Germany in 1957 was 5 German divisions and 4 understrength French divisions: Memorandum of Conversation, Department of State, Secretary Dulles and Paul-Henri Spaak, October 24, 1957, FRUS, 1955–57, 4, West European Security and Integration, pp. 176–77.

42. Frank Costigliola, "Kennedy, De Gaulle, and the Challenge of Consultation," in Paxton and Wahl, eds., De Gaulle and the United States, A Centennial Appraisal, pp. 169–94.

43. Bozo, Deux stratégies, pp. 38–39.

44. Irwin M. Wall, The United States and the Making of Postwar France, 1945–1954, p. 193.

45. Memorandum, Richard Elbrick to Secretary of State Dulles, October 16, 1958, Lot 61, D30, Box 2, 1.12, De Gaulle Government, NA.

46. An extraordinary secret summary of the American response to the de Gaulle proposals appears in the George Ball papers, Series 8, General, Box 153, Briefing Book for President Kennedy's Visit to de Gaulle, Paris, May 31–June 2, 1961, NA. This will be noted hereinafter as George Ball, Briefing Book.

47. Caccia to Lloyd, PRO, PREM, File 11, 2339.

48. Memorandum of Conversation, Secretary Dulles and Paul-Henri Spaak, September 27, 1958, FRUS, 1958–60, 7, NATO, p. 359.

49. George Ball, Briefing Book.

50. Paris to the Foreign Office, March 13, 1958, PRO, PREM File 11, 2561.

51. George Ball, Briefing Book.

52. The text of de Gaulle's memorandum is in President de Gaulle to Prime Minister Macmillan (and President Eisenhower), *DDF,* 1958, II, September 17, 1958, p. 377. See also Couve de Murville to French Diplomatic Representatives, September 20, 1958, pp. 396–97. France rejected American explanations of FLN activity in the United States on September 26, and reluctantly accepted Washington's decision to arm Tunisia on October 13. The text of Eisenhower's reply to the de Gaulle memorandum is in President Eisenhower to Charles de Gaulle, October 20, 1958, *FRUS,* 1958–60, 7, Part 2, France, p. 108. Macmillan's reply is in Prime Minister Macmillan to Charles de Gaulle, *DDF,* 1958, II, 272, October 20, 1958, pp. 558–59.

53. Jandrey to Secretary, October 9, 1958, p. 97. Dulles-Alphand Conversation, *FRUS,* 1958, 7, Part 2, October 17, 1958, p. 104.

54. Memorandum to the Secretary from Gerard C. Smith regarding the de Gaulle Letter to the President, October 15, 1958, 611.51/10–1758, RG 59, NA.

55. Dulles to the American Embassy, Paris, October 17, 1958, 611.51/10–1758, RG 59, NA.

56. Memorandum, "France, Internal Political Scene," November 13, 1958, Lot 61, D30, Box 1, NA.

57. Couve de Murville to Alphand, November 3, 1958, *DDF,* II, 1958, pp. 620–621.

58. Bozo, *Deux stratégies,* pp. 46–49.

59. Couve de Murville, *Une politique étrangère,* p. 43.

60. Alphand to Couve de Murville, December 4, 1958, *DDF,* II, 1958, pp. 802–808.

61. Note de la Délégation française aux Nations Unies, December 13, 1958, pp. 858–66, *DDF,* 1958, II, 412.

62. Telegram from the Department of State to the American Embassy in France, December 14, 1958, *FRUS,* 1958–60, 13, North Africa, pp. 646–47.

63. Memorandum, Alfred Boegner to Mr. Merchant, December 16, 1958, 611.51/12–1658, RG 59, NA.

64. Under Secretary Herter to Secretary Dulles at the American Embassy, Paris, December 16, 1958, 611.51/12–1658, RG 59, NA.

65. Bernard Ledwidge, *De Gaulle et les Américains: Conversations avec Dulles, Eisenhower, Kennedy, Rusk, 1958–1964* (Paris: Flammarion, 1984), pp. 50–60.

66. American Embassy, Paris, to Department of State, April 7, 1957, 611.51/4–457, RG 59, NA.

67. Memorandum, Livingston Merchant to Mr. Murphy, December 23, 1958, Lot 61, D30, Box 1, 1.10, "Debré Government 1959," NA.

68. Memorandum, William Whitman to Vaughan Ferguson, American Embassy, Paris, February 10, 1959, Memorandum of Conversation, Randolph Kidder and Gérard Amanrich, March 6, 1959, Lot 61, D30, Box 1, 1.10, Debré Government, NA.

69. Ambassador Jebb to Prime Minister Macmillan, September 23, 1958, PRO, FO 371, 131667.

70. Kettle, *De Gaulle and Algeria,* pp. 316–26.

71. Couve de Murville to Alphand, January 18, 1959, *DDF,* 1959, Tome I, Jan.-June 1959, p. 68. Memoranda, March 2, March 3, 1959, *FRUS,* 1958–1960, 7, NATO, pp. 413–16.

72. Memorandum of Conversation, Alphand and Murphy, January 27, 1959, *FRUS,* 1958–60, 7, Part 2, pp. 167–68. Alphand to Couve de Murville, *DDF,* 1959, I, 125, March 9, 1959, pp. 260–61.

73. Telegram from the Department of State to the Embassy in France, March 6, 1959, *FRUS,* 1958–60, 13, North Africa, p. 650.

74. Memorandum of Conversation, Ambassador Houghton and President de Gaulle, March 16, 1959, Eisenhower to de Gaulle, March 19, 1959, Memorandum, March 22, 1959, *FRUS,* 1958–60, 7, NATO, pp. 433–39.

75. Directives du Département pour ses conversations de Washington, March 25, 1959, *DDF,* 1959, I, 198, pp. 439–43.

76. Comptes rendus des conversations sur l'Afrique, April 16–21, 1959, *DDF,* 1959, I, 235, pp. 534–35.

77. George Ball, Briefing Book.

78. Memorandum, Livingston Merchant to Secretary Herter, April 27, 1959, 611.51/4–2759, RG 59, NA.

79. Memorandum of Conversation, Herter and Debré, Paris, May 1, 1959, *FRUS,* 1958–60, 7, Part 2, pp. 198–201.

80. Memorandum of Conference with President Eisenhower, Gettysburg, May 2, 1959, *FRUS,* 1958–60, 7, Part 2, pp. 205–6.

81. Memorandum, Livingston Merchant to the Secretary, May 5, 1959, 611.51/5–559, RG 59, NA.

82. Telegram from the Department of State to the Embassy in France, March 30, 1959, *FRUS,* 1958–60, 13, North Africa, p. 651.

83. French Embassy in Tunisia to MAE, May 27, 1959, AM 1952–1963, Etats-Unis, 46, Tunisie, MAE. The French ambassador to Tunisia carried the title of "Envoyé Exceptionnel."

84. Letter from Prime Minister Debré to the Ambassador in France (Houghton), April 28, 1959, *FRUS,* 1958–60, 13, Algeria, pp. 652–53.

85. Memorandum, Foy Kohler to Robert Murphy, June 15, 1959, Lot 61, D30, Folder marked Visas 1957–1959, Lot 61, D30, 1–D.2, NA.

86. Memoranda, J. C. Satterthwaite to Secretary of State, November 3, 1959, J.W. Haines to Secretary, November 3, 1959, Foy Kohler to Secretary, November 2, 1959, in folder marked Visas, 1957–1959, Lot 61, D30, Box 1, 1.D.2, NA.

87. Memorandum, Cameron to Livingston Merchant, May 6, 1959, 611.51/5–659, RG 59, NA.

88. Livingston Merchant to Secretary Dulles, May 5, 1959; Memorandum of Conversation, Merchant and Cameron, Consultation with the UK Embassy on France, May 4, 1959; Memorandum of Conversation, John Tuthill and Jean Villechaise, American Embassy, Paris, May 21, 1959, Lot 60, D30, 1.10, Debré Government, NA.

89. Letter from President de Gaulle to President Eisenhower, May 25, 1959, *FRUS,* 1958–60, 7, Part 2, pp. 229–31.

90. Memoranda of Conversations, Lebel, Winckler, and Leprette of the French Embassy, McBride and Looram, Washington, June 16, 1959, June 23, 1959, 611.51/6-1659, 6-2359, RG 59, NA.

91. Memoranda of Conversations, Lebel and State Department, June 30, 1959, July 7, 14, 28, 1959, 611.51/6-3059, 7-759, 7-1459, 7-2859, RG 59, NA.

92. Merchant to Herter, July 10, 1959; Satterthwaite to Herter, August 13, 1959; Memorandum by President Eisenhower, August 21, 1959, FRUS, 1958-60, 13, Algeria, pp. 664-68.

93. MAE to French Embassy in Washington, August 4, 1959, AM 1952-1963, Etats-Unis, 46, Tunisie, MAE.

94. Memorandum of Conversation, Lebel and McBride, Washington, August 18, 1959, 611.51/8-1859, RG 59, NA. Memorandum of Conversation, Gerard Amanrich and Cecil Lyon, French Foreign Ministry, Paris, August 27, 1959, Lot 60, D30, Box 1, 1.10, Debré Government, NA.

95. Memorandum of Conversation, General Norstad and President Eisenhower, August 24, 1959, FRUS, 1958-60, 7, NATO, p. 478.

96. NSC 417, August 18, 1959, FRUS, 1958-60, 7, Part 2, pp. 243-48.

97. Lacouture, De Gaulle, Vol. 2; cited in Connelly, "The Algerian War for Independence," p. 432.

98. Edmond Jouhaud, Serons-nous enfin compris? p. 86.

99. Redha Malek quotes Vincent Labouret, the chef du cabinet of Louis Joxe, as citing three reasons for de Gaulle's change of policy: the refusal of Sekou Touré of Guinea to enter the community, meaning that Algeria would not do so; the maturing of de Gaulle's thought while out of power; and the fear of U.S. intervention if the crisis were prolonged. American abstention in the UN in December 1958, after de Gaulle's personal appeal to Eisenhower, aggravated this fear. Malek, L'Algérie à Evian: Histoire des négociations secrètes, 1956-1962 (Paris: Seuil, 1995), p. 47.

100. Memorandum of Conversation, President Eisenhower and President de Gaulle, September 2, 1959, Paris, FRUS, 1958-60, 7, Part 2, pp. 256-61.

101. Memorandum of Conversation, Eisenhower, de Gaulle, Walters, September 2, 1959, FRUS, 1958-60, 7, Part 2, pp. 268-71, September 3, 1959, Rambouillet, p. 271.

102. Letter, President Eisenhower to Prime Minister Macmillan, September 11, 1959, FRUS, 1958-60, 7, Part 2, p. 277; American Embassy, Paris, to Department of State, September 15, 1959, FRUS, 1958-60, 7, Part 2, p. 281.

7. DE GAULLE RECONSIDERED

1. Maurice Vaïsse in La France et l'OTAN, Actes du colloque tenu à l'Ecole militaire, 8,9, et 10 février 1996, sous la direction de Maurice Vaïsse, Pierre Melandri, et Frédéric Bozo (Brussels: Editions Complexe, 1996), pp. 219-45.

2. Frédéric Bozo, Deux stratégies pour l'Europe: De Gaulle, les Etats-Unis, et l'Alliance Atlantique, 1958-1969 (Paris: Plon, 1996), pp. 16-31.

3. Maurice Vaïsse, La grandeur: Politique étrangère du général de Gaulle 1958-1959 (Paris: Fayard, 1998), pp. 35-61. See also Vaïsse's contribution to

the colloquium *La France et l'OTAN 1949–1966*, pp. 219–46. I recall Vaïsse using the term "Copernican revolution" in the oral version delivered at the colloquium in Paris on February 9, 1996, but I have not seen it in the written versions. It is nevertheless apt. These views of de Gaulle, somewhat nuanced, also characterized Stanley and Inge Hoffmann's essay "De Gaulle as Political Artist: The Will to Grandeur," in Stanley Hoffmann, *Decline or Renewal? France Since the 1930s* (New York: Viking, 1974), pp. 202–53. Hoffmann wrote without benefit of diplomatic documents, however, whereas Vaïsse is one of the editors of their recent publication in France.

4. Louis Terrenoire quoted de Gaulle to this effect in 1955; see his *De Gaulle et l'Algérie: Témoignage pour l'histoire* (Paris: Fayard, 1964), pp. 29–30.

5. This point is reinforced repeatedly in Alain Peyrefitte, *C'était de Gaulle* (Paris: Fayard, 1994).

6. Indeed, Maurice Couve de Murville's memoir, *Une politique étrangère, 1958–1959*, does not even deal with Algeria, implying that it can be safely ignored in any effort to explain the success or failure of French diplomatic policies or their formulation.

7. The theme of de Gaulle as the decolonizer and emancipator of colonial peoples underlay many of the contributions to the volumes of *De Gaulle en son siècle: Actes des Journées internationales tenue à l'Unesco, Paris, 19–24 novembre 1990* [organisées par l'] Institut Charles de Gaulle. 5 vols. (Paris: La Documentation française; Plon, 1991–92).

8. Peyrefitte, *C'était de Gaulle*, pp. 56, 74, 89, and passim.

9. Kristin Ross, *Fast Cars, Clean Bodies: Decolonization and the Reordering of French Culture* (Cambridge, Mass.: MIT Press, 1995).

10. Philip Dine, *Images of the Algerian War: French Fiction and Film, 1954–1992* (Oxford: Clarendon Press, 1994).

11. Edward Kolodziej, *French International Policy Under de Gaulle and Pompidou* (Ithaca, N.Y.: Cornell University Press, 1974), cited on p. 73. See the totality of the argument, pp. 69–100.

12. Philip Cerny, *The Politics of Grandeur: Ideological Aspects of de Gaulle's Foreign Policy* (Cambridge: Cambridge University Press, 1980), pp. 5–29.

13. The relevant quotations are in *C'était de Gaulle*, pp. 293–94 and 352.

14. Bozo, *Deux stratégies pour l'Europe*, concludes that the memo was real enough, although de Gaulle had no illusions about its ultimate acceptance. He did hope it would have an effect, however, or he would not have continued discussions for so long about its implementation. Pp. 40–41.

15. A representative sample of contradictory statements by de Gaulle to various interlocutors may be found in John Talbott, *The War Without a Name*, pp. 137–41. See also Terrenoire, *De Gaulle et l'Algérie*, pp. 29–30; Jean Lacouture, "Revision dans le désert," and Paul Isoart, "Le Général de Gaulle et le Tiers Monde," both in *De Gaulle et le Tiers Monde: Actes du Colloque organisé par la Faculté de Droit et des Sciences Economiques et l'Institut du Droit de la Paix et du Développement de l'Université de Nice et l'Institut Charles de Gaulle*, Nice, 25–26 février, 1983 (Paris, 1983). Also Alain Ruscio, *La décolonisation tragique: Une histoire de la décolonisation française, 1945–1962* (Paris: Editions Sociales, 1987), and Charles-Robert Ageron, *La décolonisation française* (Paris:

Armand Colin, 1994). Ruscio argues that de Gaulle initially intended to keep Algeria, Ageron that he hoped for an Algeria associated with France that would play a key role in the newly organized French community. Stanley Hoffmann also wrote that de Gaulle, while in exile before 1958, "fully absorbed the lessons of decolonization." Hoffmann, *Decline or Renewal?* p. 102.

16. Charles de Gaulle, *Memoirs of Hope: Renewal and Endeavor* (New York: Simon and Schuster, 1971), p. 46; Jean Lacouture, *De Gaulle*. Vol. 2, *The Ruler* (New York: Norton, 1992), p. 181.

17. Stora notes a comment to Christian Pineau in October 1957: "there is only one solution: independence. I will make this known at the opportune moment." But de Gaulle's actions were always much more important than his ambiguous and contradictory words. *La gangrène et l'oubli: La mémoire de la Guerre d'Algérie* (Paris: La Découverte, 1991), p. 81.

18. Alan Ruscio, *La décolonisation tragique,* p. 149.

19. Tony Smith, *The French Stake in Algeria* (Ithaca, N.Y.: Cornell University Press, 1978).

20. *Foccart Parle. Entretiens avec Philippe Gaillard* (Paris: Fayard/Jeune Afrique, 1995), pp. 148–54.

21. Talbott, *The War Without a Name,* p. 141. See also the very fine analysis by Matthew Connelly in the chapter "Decoding de Gaulle" of his "The Algerian War for Independence," pp. 346–60. Connelly and I are in basic agreement.

22. Pierre Miquel, *La Guerre d'Algérie* (Paris: Fayard, 1993), p. 347. Miquel is very close to the analysis of Jean-Jacques Becker, who wrote that de Gaulle initially favored integration, taking the November 1958 referendum result as an endorsement by the Muslim population. By September 1959 he had abandoned the idea for "association," still excluding the idea of negotiations with the FLN. Only in November–December 1960 did he finally understand the need to negotiate with the FLN on Algeria's political future before a cease-fire. "La Solution De Gaulle," in L. Gervereau, Jean-Pierre Rioux, and B. Stora, eds., *La France en Guerre d'Algérie, Novembre 1954–Juillet 1962* (Paris: BDIC, 1992), pp. 138–45.

23. William Cohen informs me that as a schoolboy at the French lycée in Addis Ababa in 1951, he shook hands with de Gaulle, who was on a visit there. However, de Gaulle did not mention this encounter in his memoirs.

24. Michael Kettle, *De Gaulle and Algeria,* p. 59.

25. Terrenoire, p. 41, quoted in Jean Lacouture, "Revision," in *Actes du Colloque,* pp. 119–21. Isoart, "Le General de Gaulle et le Tiers Monde," notes that de Gaulle had a geopolitical vision of France as "un puissance africaine et oceanique," and the term "tiers monde" was not in his vocabulary until 1965. *Actes du Colloque,* pp. 123–25.

26. Lefeuvre, *Chère Algérie,* pp. 310–17.

27. See Constantin Melnik, *Mille jours à Matignon: Raisons d'état sous de Gaulle, Guerre d'Algérie 1959–1962* (Paris: Bernard Grasset, 1988), p. 211. Melnik, who worked closely with Debré, says that "La thèse de l'abandon volontaire de l'Algérie par le général de Gaulle ne résiste pas à l'examin."

28. Bernard Tricot, *Mémoires* (Paris: Quai Voltaire, 1994), pp. 110–22. Tricot was a high official in the group charged with Algerian policy in 1959 and later became de Gaulle's secretary-general of the Elysée.

29. Jean Morin, *De Gaulle et l'Algérie: Mon témoignage,* 1960–1962 (Paris: Albin Michel, 1999), pp. 185–93. Michel Debré reported a conversation with General de Gaulle on March 23, 1961, in which the general told him that if a part of Algeria no longer wanted France in Algeria, there would be a regrouping of populations and a partition. Michel Debré, *Entretiens avec le Général de Gaulle* (Paris: Albin Michel, 1993), p. 30. Morin, however, believes that de Gaulle intended a regrouping of the population only as a preparation for its embarkation.

30. Ageron, *La décolonisation française,* pp. 158–59.

31. On this see Pierre Maillard, *De Gaulle et l'Europe: Entre la nation et Maastricht* (Paris: Tallandier, 1995), pp. 191–201.

32. Edward Mortimer, *France and the Africans, 1944–1960: A Political History* (New York: Walker and Company, 1969), pp. 310–11.

33. Raymond Triboulet, "Les Moyens d'Action du Général de Gaulle," in *Actes du Colloque,* pp. 143–46. See also his *Un ministre du Général* (Paris: Plon, 1985). Triboulet was one of those whom, like Foccart, de Gaulle assured that he would never permit the abandonment of Algeria by France.

34. Pierre Maillard, *De Gaulle et l'Europe,* pp. 145–56.

35. Ibid., pp. 200–213.

36. See Pierre Maillard, *De Gaulle et l'Allemagne* (Paris: Plon, 1990).

37. Fredrik Logevall, *Choosing War: The Lost Chance for Peace and the Escalation of War in Vietnam* (Berkeley: University of California Press, 1999).

38. Policy Statement, NSC Report, November 4, 1959, *FRUS,* 1958–60, 13, North Africa, pp. 619–23.

39. NSC Report, November 4, 1959, *FRUS,* 1958–60, 13, pp. 619–23.

40. NSC Report, U.S. Policy on France, November 4, 1959, *FRUS,* 1958–60, 7, Part 2, France, pp. 298–310.

41. Note de M. Moris, Discussions avec l'émissaire des dirigeants de l'Organisation extérieure de la rebellion, Conclusions sur les entretiens de Melun, *DDF,* 1960, II, July 5, 1960, editor's note, annex, p. 23. The note cites Bernard Tricot, *Les sentiers de la paix: Algérie 1958–1962* (Paris: Plon, 1972), pp. 119–20, among other sources.

42. Telegram from the Department of State to the Mission at the United Nations, November 19, 1959, *FRUS,* 1958–60, 13, North Africa, p. 676.

43. Rapport du Dr. Lamine Debaghine au GPRA, Cairo, November 17, 1959, Note of Belkacem Krim, March 7, 1960, Mohammed Harbi, *Les archives de la révolution algérienne* (Paris: Jeune Afrique, 1980), pp. 272–73, 384. Cointet, pp. 58–70.

44. MAE to Washington, November 18, 1959, AM 1952–1963, 46, Tunisie, MAE.

45. Letter from President Eisenhower to President de Gaulle, November 17, 1959, *FRUS,* 1958–60, 7, Western Europe, pp. 311–12.

46. Letter from President de Gaulle to President Eisenhower, November 24, 1959, *FRUS,* 1958–60, 7, Western Europe, pp. 313–14.

47. Statement by General Twining, December 10, 1959; Memorandum of Conversation, Foreign Minister Couve de Murville and Secretary Herter, December 14, 1959; Memorandum of Conversation, Secretary General Spaak and Secretary Herter, December 15, 1959. *FRUS,* 1958–60, 7, NATO, pp. 525–30.

48. Telegram from Secretary Herter to Department of State, Interpretive Summary of Eisenhower-de Gaulle Conversation at the Elysée, December 19, 1959; Record of Meeting at Chateau Rambouillet, de Gaulle, Macmillan, Eisenhower, Debré, et al., December 20, 1959; Memo of Conversation, President de Gaulle and Secretary Herter, *FRUS*, 1958–60, 7, Western Europe, pp. 318–21.

49. Letter from Secretary Herter to Foreign Minister Couve de Murville, December 30, 1959; Editorial Note regarding February 2 letter from President Eisenhower to de Gaulle, *FRUS*, 1958–60, 7, Western Europe, pp. 322–27.

50. Anthony Clayton, *The Wars of French Decolonization* (London: Longman, 1994), p. 164.

51. Note de la Direction Politique: Arrêt des explosions nucleaires, 8 avril 1960, *DDF,* 1960, I, pp. 442–43.

52. Memorandum of Conversation, Secretary Herter, Foreign Minister Couve de Murville, and Ambassador Alphand, April 15, 1959; Memorandum of Conference with President Eisenhower, April 22, 1959, *FRUS*, 1958–60, 7, Western Europe, pp. 336–37, 341–42.

53. Memorandum of Conversation, Eisenhower-de Gaulle, April 22, 1960; Memorandum of Conversations at Camp David, April 24 and 25, 1960; Memorandum from Acting Secretary of State Dillon to President Eisenhower, May 2, 1960, *FRUS,* 1958–60, 7, Western Europe, pp. 343–59. Also Entretiens du Général de Gaulle et de M. Khrouchtchev, 23 mars, 1–2 avril 1960; Entretiens de Gaulle-Eisenhower aux Etats-Unis, 22–25 avril 1960, *DDF,* 1960, I, pp. 356–75, 514–17.

54. Conférence au Sommet de Paris, Entretien entre le Général de Gaulle et M. Khrouchtchev le 15 mai, Réunion occidentale à trois le 15 mai à l'Elysée, Entretien entre le Général de Gaulle et M. Khrouchtchev le 18 mai, *DDF,* 1960, I, pp. 638–44, 646, 680.

55. Entretien de M. Macmillan et du Premier Ministre à l'Hotel Matignon, 24 mai 1960; M. Macmillan, Premier Ministre de Grande Bretagne, au Général de Gaulle, Président de la République Française, 25 mai 1960; Entretien des Trois Ministres des Affaires Etrangères chez M. Herter à Washington, 1 juin 1960; M. Couve de Murville to French Embassy in Washington, including letter from de Gaulle to Eisenhower, June 11, 1960, *DDF,* 1960, I, pp. 721–23, 724, 746–51, 804–5.

56. Raymond Triboulet, *Un ministre du Général*, p. 73.

57. Premier Debré message to French Embassy in Tunis, June 30, 1960, *DDF,* 1960, I, pp. 926–27. Foreign Minister Couve de Murville to French Diplomatic Representatives Abroad, July 3, 1960, *DDF,* 1960, II, pp. 6–8; Note de M. Moris, Discussions avec l'emissaire des dirigeants de l'Organisation Extérieure de la rébellion, Conclusions sur les entretiens de Melun, July 5, 1960, pp. 14–19. In the Annex, titled "Consignes du Premier Ministre," of June 18, 1960, it is explained that political talks were to follow a long period of peace during which France would do all it could to convince the Algerian population of the benefits of union with France.

58. "ONU, Algérie 1960, Le FLN et les elections cantonales dans les départements algériens le 29 mai 1960," bound folder "Affaires Politiques," MA 16, AOM.

59. "Affaires Politiques," MA 16, AOM.

60. Memorandum, Kohler and Satterthwaite to Department, February 10, 1960; Memorandum of Conversation, Alphand and Herter, March 11, 1960; Department to Tunis Consulate, June 16, 1960, *FRUS, 1958–60,* 13, Algeria, pp. 687–91.

61. MAE to All Diplomatic Posts Abroad, June 19, 1960, MAE, Tunisie, 301.

62. Embassy in Tunis to Ministry of Foreign Affairs, Paris, July 11, 1960, MAE, 301, Tunisie.

63. Rapport de Politique générale pour le GPRA par Ferhat Abbas, August 1960, in Harbi, *Archives de la révolution algérienne,* pp. 303–5.

64. M. Soulié, French Consul in Hong Kong, to Couve de Murville, July 2, 1960, *DDF,* 1960, II, p. 5. Also "Note de la Direction Politique, Mission de liaison pour les Affaires Algériennes au sujet de l'aide chinoise au 'GPRA,'" p. 124.

65. Memo of Conversation, Herter and Alphand, May 20, 1960; Memo of Conversation, Foreign Ministers Lloyd, Couve de Murville, and Secretary Herter, June 1, 1960; Letters from President Eisenhower to Prime Minister Macmillan and President de Gaulle, June 10, 1960; Telegram from Department of State to Embassy in France, June 17, 1960; Memorandum of Conversation, Secretary Herter and Ambassador Alphand, June 24, 1960, *FRUS, 1958–60,* 7, Western Europe, pp. 368–91.

66. Telegram from Embassy in Paris to Department of State, June 24, 1960; Memorandum of Conversation between President Eisenhower and Secretary Herter, July 1, 1960; Letter from President Eisenhower to President de Gaulle, August 2, 1960, *FRUS, 1958–60,* 7, Western Europe, pp. 393–98.

67. General Norstad to President Eisenhower, April 20, 1960; Conference in the President's Office, August 3, 1960; NSC 457, August 25, 1960. *FRUS, 1958–60,* 7, NATO, pp. 580–81, 615–20.

68. Letter from President de Gaulle to President Eisenhower, August 9, 1960, *FRUS, 1958–60,* 7, Western Europe, pp. 400–401.

69. Entretiens Franco-Allemands de Rambouillet (29–30 juillet 1960), *DDF,* 1960, II, pp. 163–78.

70. Rambouillet meetings, *DDF,* 1960, II, pp. 175–78.

71. "Réunion Restreinte des Ministres des Affaires Etrangères tenu à Bruxelles pour le Conseil de l'UEO," November 17, 1960, *DDF,* 1960, II, pp. 599–601.

72. Memorandum of Telephone Conversation between President Eisenhower and Secretary Herter, August 10, 1960, *FRUS, 1958–60,* 7, Western Europe, pp. 402–6.

73. Letter from President Eisenhower to President de Gaulle, August 30, 1960, *FRUS, 1958–60,* 7, Western Europe, pp. 414–17. Marc Trachtenberg argues that Eisenhower had lost effective control of policy in 1960 and allowed Herter to sabotage his desire for nuclear cooperation with France. I can find no evidence of this. Trachtenberg ignores Algeria and all the other questions at issue between the two countries: *A Constructed Peace: The Making of the European Settlement 1945–1963,* pp. 228–45.

74. Telegram from the Department of State to the Embassy in Tunis, June 19, 1960, *FRUS, 1958–60,* 13, North Africa, pp. 692–94.

75. Memorandum of Meeting, Waldorf Towers Hotel, New York, September 23, 1959, *FRUS, 1958–60,* 13, North Africa, pp. 695–97. See the somewhat

different version in "Entretiens tripartites au rang des Ministres," September 23, 1960, *DDF,* 1960, II, pp. 390–95.

76. Eisenhower-Herter Conversation, September 27, 1960; Intelligence Report, Problems and Prospects of the Fifth Republic, *FRUS,* 1958–60, 7, Part 2.

77. French Embassy in Tunis to Ministry of Foreign Affairs, Paris, November 7, 1960, MAE, 301, Tunisie.

78. Memorandum from Assistant Secretary of State for African Affairs Satterthwaite to the Undersecretary of State for Political Affairs, Merchant, October 20, 1960, *FRUS,* 1958–60, 13, North Africa, p. 701.

79. NSC 466, November 7, 1960, *FRUS,* 1958–60, 13, Algeria, p. 707.

80. Conference in the Office of the President, September 12, 1960; Memorandum, October 3, 1960; Memorandum of Conversation, Eisenhower and Paul-Henri Spaak, October 4, 1958, *FRUS,* 1958–60, 7, NATO, pp. 627–40.

81. French Embassy in Tunis to Ministry of Foreign Affairs, Paris, November 6, 1960, MAE, 301, Tunisie.

82. M. Roger Seydoux, French Ambassador in Rabat, to Couve de Murville, November 29, 1960, *DDF,* 1960, II, pp. 656–59.

83. "Note d'Informations de l'Etat-Major de la Défense Nationale: Développement des relations entre le FLN et communisme," October 14, 1960, *DDF,* 1960, II, pp. 501–4.

84. "Note de la Délégation Française auprès du Conseil de Sécurité des Nations Unies," November 24, 1960, *DDF,* 1960, II, pp. 632–34.

85. Olivier Long, *Le dossier secret des Accords d'Evian: Une mission suisse pour la paix en Algérie* (Lausanne: Editions 24 heures, 1988), pp. 3–30.

86. French Embassy in Tunis to Ministry of Foreign Affairs, Paris, November 18, 1960, MAE, 301, Tunisie.

87. Alain Peyrefitte, *C'était de Gaulle* (Paris: Fayard, 1994), pp. 69–74.

88. Message from Secretary of State Herter to Foreign Minister Couve de Murville, November 2, 1960; Letter from French Foreign Minister Couve de Murville to Herter, November 5, 1960; NSC 467, Note; Memorandum, Satterthwaite to Assistant Secretary of State for Political Affairs Hare, December 22, 1960, *FRUS,* 1958–60, 7, pp. 703–20.

89. George Ball, Briefing Book.

8. PEACE

1. Memorandum from Assistant Secretary of State for European Affairs (Kohler) to Secretary of State Rusk, January 24, 1961; Memorandum of Conversation, Secretary Rusk and Ambassador Alphand, February 24, 1961, *FRUS,* 1961–63, 13, Western Europe, pp. 641–44, 645–48.

2. See Miloud Barkaoui, "Kennedy and the Cold War Imbroglio: The Case of Algerian Independence," *Arab Studies Quarterly* 21, 2 (Spring 1999), and Jeffrey A. Lefebvre, "Kennedy's Algerian Dilemma: Containment, Alliance Politics and the 'Rebel Dialogue,'" *Middle Eastern Studies* 35, 2 (April 1999): 61.

3. "Note du Premier Ministre au sujet de 'l'Algérie algérienne' et de son union avec la France," January 15, 1961, *DDF,* 1961, I (January-June), pp. 42–47.

4. "Compte Rendu: Entretien du Général de Gaulle et de M. Macmillan au chateau de Rambouillet, le 28 janvier 1961," *DDF*, 1961, I, pp. 104–14; "Compte Rendu: Réunion de consultation politique des Ministres des Affaires Etrangères des Six," January 31, 1961, *DDF*, 1961, I, p. 137.

5. Memorandum of Conversation between Secretary Rusk and the French Ambassador, March 15, 1961, *FRUS*, 1961–63, 13, Western Europe and Canada, pp. 266–68.

6. Alphand to Couve de Murville, February 5, 1961, *DDF*, 1961, I, pp. 154–60.

7. Entretiens de Gaulle-Adenauer, February 9, 1961, *DDF*, 1961, I, pp. 168–75.

8. Memorandum of Conversation, Adenauer, President Kennedy, April 12, 1961, *FRUS*, 1961–63, 13, Western Europe and Canada, pp. 272–79.

9. Alphand to Couve de Murville, February 10, 1961, *DDF*, 1961, I, pp. 180–82.

10. French Embassy, Washington, to Ministry of Foreign Affairs, Paris, February 15, 1961, MAE, Etats-Unis, 46d.

11. Alphand to Couve de Murville, two separate telegrams of February 15, 1961, *DDF*, 1961, I, pp. 200–202, 206–7.

12. Alphand to Couve de Murville, February 23, 1961, *DDF*, 1961, I, pp. 245–46.

13. Entretien du Général de Gaulle et de M. Vinogradov, February 23, 1961, *DDF*, 1961, I, pp. 252–53.

14. Entretien entre le Général de Gaulle et M. Averell Harriman, March 4, 1961, *DDF*, 1961, I, pp. 291–302.

15. Alphand to Couve de Murville, two separate telegrams of March 16, 1961, *DDF*, 1961, I, pp. 356–60.

16. Cointet, *De Gaulle et l'Algérie française, 1958–1962*, p. 202.

17. Olivier Long, *Le dossier secret des Accords d'Evian: Une mission suisse pour la paix en Algérie* (Lausanne: Editions 24 heures, 1988), p. 41.

18. Note du Premier Ministre à propos de l'Algérie, March 23, 1961, *DDF*, 1961, I, pp. 390–93.

19. Chargé Raoul-Duval, Tunis, to Couve de Murville, April 4, 1961, *DDF*, 1961, I, pp. 423–24.

20. Couve de Murville to Alphand, April 6, 1961, *DDF*, 1961, I, pp. 428–29; Couve de Murville to French Diplomatic Representatives Abroad, April 12, 1961, *DDF*, 1961, I, pp. 454–55.

21. Chargé in Tunis Raoul-Duval to Couve de Murville, March 15, 1961, *DDF*, 1961, I, pp. 346–50, pleaded for both the Ben Bella release and movement on Bizerte, which both the sultan and Bourguiba felt to be critical to their own prestige.

22. Cointet, *De Gaulle et l'Algérie française, 1958–1962*, pp. 141–67; see also Maurice Vaisse, *Alger: Le Putsch* (Brussels: Editions Complexe, 1983), pp. 93, 124–25.

23. Alphand to Couve de Murville, April 23, 1961, *DDF*, 1961, I, pp. 513–15.

24. Thomas Powers, *The Man Who Kept the Secrets: Richard Helms and the CIA* (New York: Alfred A. Knopf, 1979), p. 337, note 2. On Fanon and his Washington treatment, see Peter Geismar, *Fanon* (New York: Dial Press, 1971), p. 182; also John Ranelagh, *The Agency: The Decline and Fall of the CIA* (London: Weidenfeld and Nicolson, 1986), p. 20.

25. C.L. Sulzberger, *The Test: De Gaulle and Algeria* (New York: Harcourt Brace and World, 1962), pp. 127–35.

26. Vaïsse, *Alger: Le Putsch,* 124–25.

27. Redha Malek, *L'Algérie à Evian,* p. 115.

28. Lefebvre, "Kennedy's Algerian Dilemma," based on documents in the Kennedy Library, Boston.

29. Hervé Alphand, French Ambassador in Washington, to M. Couve de Murville, Minister of Foreign Affairs, Paris, April 28, 1961, MAE, Etats-Unis, 46d, Algérie, 1960–63.

30. Lefebvre, "Kennedy's Algerian Dilemma," p. 61.

31. Policy Directive, NATO and the Atlantic Nations, April 20, 1961, *FRUS,* 1961–63, 13, Western Europe, pp. 285–89.

32. Comptes rendus des entretiens de Gaulle-Kennedy, May 31–June 2, 1961, *DDF,* 1961, I, pp. 669–70.

33. Note de la Direction de l'Europe, June 1, 1961, *DDF,* 1961, I, pp. 664–66.

34. Memorandum of Conversation, Kennedy-de Gaulle, Paris, June 1, 1961, *FRUS,* 1961–63, 13, Western Europe, pp. 309–14.

35. Telegram from the Embassy in France to the Department of State, February 21, 1962, *FRUS,* 1961–63, 13, Western Europe, pp. 364–65.

36. Memorandum of Conversation, de Gaulle and Kennedy, June 2, 1961, Paris, *FRUS,* 1961–63, 13, France, pp. 663–66. *DDF,* 1961, I, p. 675. See also Fredrik Logevall, *Choosing War: The Lost Chance for Peace and the Escalation of War in Vietnam* (Berkeley: University of California Press, 1999), p. 25.

37. Instructions de la Délégation Française aux pourparlers d'Evian, May 2, 1961, *DDF,* 1961, I, pp. 558–63.

38. Jean Morin, *De Gaulle et l'Algérie: Mon témoignage, 1960–62* (Paris: Albin Michel, 1999), pp. 332–40.

39. Morin, *De Gaulle et l'Algérie,* pp. 182–93.

40. Procès-verbaux de la Conférence d'Evian, May 21–June 13, 1961, *DDF,* 1961, I, pp. 772–95. Cointet, *De Gaulle et l'Algérie française,* pp. 202–42.

41. French Embassy in Tunis to Ministry of Foreign Affairs, Paris, June 18, 1961, MAE, 303, Tunisie, 1961.

42. Couve de Murville to Diplomatic Representatives of France Abroad, June 16, 1961, *DDF,* 1961, I, p. 909.

43. Alain Peyrefitte, *C'était de Gaulle* (Paris: Fayard, 1994), pp. 77–89.

44. Procès-verbaux de la Conférence d'Evian, May 21–June 13, 1961, *DDF,* 1961, I, pp. 772–95.

45. Georges Fleury, *La Guerre en Algérie* (Paris: Plon, 1993), pp. 539–40.

46. French Embassy in Tunis to Ministry of Foreign Affairs, July 1, 1961, July 6, 1961, MAE, 303, Tunisie, 1961.

47. Compte rendu, Entretien entre M. Couve de Murville et M. Dean Rusk, Paris, August 4, 1961, *DDF,* 1961, II, pp. 226–30.

48. Réunion des Ministres des Affaires Etrangères Occidentaux à Paris (5–7 August, 1961), *DDF,* 1961, II, pp. 236–49.

49. Entretien du Général de Gaulle et de M. Dean Rusk, August 8, 1961, *DDF,* 1961, II, pp. 280–86.

50. Couve de Murville to Alphand, August 18, 1961, *DDF,* 1961, II, pp. 314–17; Alphand to Couve de Murville, August 24, 1961, *DDF,* 1961, II, pp. 325–26; Couve de Murville to Alphand, August 26, 1961, *DDF,* 1961, II, pp. 331–32. De Gaulle wrote twice to Kennedy, on August 18 and August 26.

51. Compte rendu du Chef d'Etat-Major Général de la Défense Nationale sur sa mission en Algérie du 18 au 23 juin 1961, *DDF,* 1961, I, pp. 953–60.

52. Couve de Murville to Diplomatic Representatives of France Abroad, September 1, 1961, *DDF,* 1961, II, pp. 342–43; Entretien du Général de Gaulle et du Général Gavin, Ambassadeur des Etats Unis, September 2, 1961, *DDF,* 1961, II, pp. 353–58.

53. Compte rendu, Audience du Général Gavin, October 23 and 30, 1961, *DDF,* 1961, II, pp. 542–43 and 559–60.

54. Couve de Murville to Common Market Capitals, London, and Washington, November 14, 1961, *DDF,* 1961, II, pp. 587–88; Compte rendu, audience of M. Hallstein, Président de la Commission de la CEE, November 16, 1961, *DDF,* 1961, II, pp. 599–600.

55. Note du Ministère d'Etat Chargé des Affaires Algériennes; Projet de propositions en vue de la reprise des négociations, November 21, 1961, *DDF,* 1961, II, pp. 607–15.

56. For a good summary of the issues, see Charles-Robert Ageron, "Les Accords d'Evian (1962)," *Vingtième Siècle* 35 (July-September 1992): 3–16.

57. The parallel was suggested to me by Marilyn Young. See her *The Vietnam Wars, 1945–1990* (New York: HarperCollins, 1991).

58. Telegram from the Embassy in France to the Department of State, November 6, 1961, *FRUS,* 1961–63, 13, France, pp. 674–75.

59. Memorandum of Conversation, February 28, 1962, President Kennedy and Edgar Faure, *FRUS,* 1961–63, 13, France, p. 682.

60. Letter from the President's Military Representative to President Kennedy, April 3, 1962, *FRUS,* 1961–63, 13, Western Europe, pp. 369–73.

61. Letter from the Ambassador in France (Gavin) to President Kennedy, March 9, 1962; Telegram from the Department of State to the Embassy in France, March 14, 1962, *FRUS,* 1961–63, 13, France, pp. 683–90.

62. Memorandum from Executive Secretary of the Department of State (Battle) to the Special Assistant for National Security Affairs (Bundy), May 26, 1961; Paper prepared by the Joint Chiefs of Staff, Washington, undated, *FRUS,* 1961–63, 17, Near East, pp. 125, 254.

63. Telegram from Secretary of State Rusk from Athens to the Department of State, May 4, 1962, *FRUS,* 1961–63, 13, France, pp. 690–91.

64. Frank Costigliola, "The Nuclear Family: Tropes of Gender and Pathology in the Western Alliance," *Diplomatic History* 21, 2 (Spring 1997): 163–84.

65. Memorandum of Meeting, President Kennedy, André Malraux, Ambassador Alphand, McGeorge Bundy, May 11, 1962, *FRUS,* 1961–63, 13, France, pp. 696–700.

66. Telegram from Secretary of State Rusk to the Department of State, June 21, 1962, *FRUS,* 1961–63, 13, France, pp. 725–26.

67. Summary Record of NSC Executive Meeting, No. 38, Part II, January 25, 1963, *FRUS,* 1961–63, 13, Western Europe, pp. 487–91.

68. Letter from the Ambassador to France (Bohlen) to the President's Special Assistant for National Security Affairs (Bundy), March 2, 1963, *FRUS,* 1961–63, 13, France, pp. 762–75.

CONCLUSION

1. For a fine analysis of how the world situation affected American leaders and the Algerian War, see Matthew Connelly, "Taking Off the Cold War Lens: Visions of North-South Conflict During the Algerian War for Independence," *American Historical Review* 105, 3 (June 2000): 739–69.

Bibliography

The following list makes no pretense of being exhaustive; it is simply a summary of the archives and published sources I have used and the published books and articles that I have found most useful in writing this book.

PRIMARY SOURCES

Archives de l'Histoire des Armées, Ministère de la Défense Nationale, Chateau de Vincennes, Paris (AA)
Archives d'Histoire d'Outre-Mer, Aix-en-Provence, France (AOM)
Archives du Ministère des Affaires Extérieures, Quai d'Orsay, Paris, France (MAE)
Archives Nationales, Paris, France (AN)
Dwight D. Eisenhower Library, Abilene, Kansas (DDE)
John Foster Dulles Papers, Mudd Library, Princeton University
National Archives and Records Service, Washington, D.C. (NA)
Oral History Project, Columbia University
Public Record Office, London (PRO)

PUBLISHED DIPLOMATIC SOURCES

Documents Diplomatiques Français, 1954–1962 (DDF)
Foreign Relations of the United States, 1954–1962 (FRUS)

MEMOIRS AND SECONDARY SOURCES

Abbas, Ferhat. *Autopsie d'une guerre: L'Aurore.* Paris: Garnier Frères, 1980.
Ageron, Charles-Robert. "Les Accords d'Evian (1962)." *Vingtième Siècle* 35 (Juillet-Septembre 1992): 3–16.

———. *La décolonisation française.* Paris: Armand Colin, 1994.

———. *Modern Algeria: A History from 1830 to the Present.* Translated by Michael Brett. London: Hurst and Co., 1991.

Alphand, Hervé. *L'étonnement d'être: Journal 1939–1973.* Paris: Fayard, 1977.

Alwan, Mohamed. *Algeria Before the United Nations.* New York: Robert Speller & Sons, 1959.

Ambler, John Steward. *The French Army in Politics, 1945–1962.* Columbus: Ohio State University Press, 1966.

Andereggen, Anton. *France's Relationship with Sub-Saharan Africa.* Westport, Conn.: Greenwood Press, 1994.

Andrews, William G. *French Politics and Algeria.* New York: Appleton-Century-Crofts, 1962.

Aron, Raymond. *Mémoires.* Paris: Julliard, 1983.

Barkaoui, Miloud. "Kennedy and the Cold War Imbroglio: The Case of Algerian Independence." *Arab Studies Quarterly* 21, 2 (Spring 1999): 31–45.

Barnavi, Elie, and Saul Friedlander, editors. *La politique étrangère du Général de Gaulle.* Paris: Presses Universitaires de France, 1985.

Betts, Raymond. *France and Decolonization, 1900–1960.* New York: St. Martin's Press, 1991.

Bonin, Hubert. *Histoire économique de la IVe République.* Paris: Economica, 1987.

Bossuat, Gérard. *L'Europe des Français, 1943–1959: La IVe République aux sources de l'Europe communautaire.* Paris: Publications de la Sorbonne, 1996.

Bourdrel, Philippe. *La dernière chance de l'Algérie française: Du gouvernement socialiste au retour de De Gaulle, 1956–1958.* Paris: Albin Michel, 1996.

Bozo, Frédéric. *Deux stratégies pour l'Europe: De Gaulle, les Etats-Unis, et l'Alliance Atlantique, 1958–1969.* Paris: Plon, 1996.

Brands, H. W. *The Specter of Neutralism: The United States and the Emergence of the Third World, 1947–1960.* New York: Columbia University Press, 1989.

Bromberger, Merry and Serge. *Les 13 complots du 13 mai ou la délivrance de Gulliver.* Paris: Fayard, 1959.

Brown, L. Carl. "The United States and the Maghreb." *Middle East Journal* 30, 3 (Summer 1976): 273–90.

Burin des Roziers, Etienne. *Retour aux Sources: 1962, l'année décisive.* Paris: Plon, 1986.

Buron, Robert. *Les dernières années de la IVe République: Carnets politiques.* Paris: Plon, 1968.

Carleton, David. *Britain and the Suez Crisis.* Oxford: Blackwell, 1988.

Cerny, Philip. *The Politics of Grandeur: Ideological Aspects of de Gaulle's Foreign Policy.* New York: Cambridge University Press, 1980.

Chaban-Delmas, Jacques. *Mémoires pour demain.* Paris: Flammarion, 1997.

Clayton, Anthony. *The Wars of French Decolonization.* London: Longman, 1994.

Cogan, Charles C. *Oldest Allies, Guarded Friends: The U.S. and France since 1940.* Westport, Conn.: Praeger, 1994.

Cointet, Michele. *De Gaulle et l'Algérie française, 1958–1962*. Paris: Librairie Académique Perrin, 1995.

Connelly, Matthew. "The Algerian War for Independence: An International History." Ph.D. dissertation, Yale University, 1997.

———. "French-American Conflict over North Africa and the Fall of the Fourth Republic." *Revue française d'histoire d'Outre-Mer* (1997): 9–27.

———. "Taking Off the Cold War Lens: Visions of North-South Conflict During the Algerian War for Independence." *American Historical Review* 105, 3 (2000):739–69.

Costigliola, Frank. *France and the United States: The Cold Alliance since World War II*. New York: Twayne Publishers, 1992.

———. "The Nuclear Family: Tropes of Gender and Pathology in the Western Alliance." *Diplomatic History* 21, 2 (Spring 1997):163–84.

Courière, Yves. *La Guerre d'Algérie, 1954–1957*. Paris: Fayard, 1990.

Couve de Murville, Maurice. *Une politique étrangère, 1958–1969*. Paris: Plon, 1971.

Crosbie, Sylvia K. *A Tacit Alliance: France and Israel from Suez to the Six-Day War*. Princeton, N.J.: Princeton University Press, 1974.

Daniel, Jean. *De Gaulle et l'Algérie*. Paris: Seuil, 1986.

Dayan, Moshe. *Story of My Life*. London: Weidenfeld and Nicolson, 1976.

Debré, Michel. *Gouverner: Mémoires, 1958–1962*. Paris: Albin Michel, 1988.

———. *Trois républiques pour une France: Mémoires, II, 1946–1958, Agir*. Paris: Albin Michel, 1988.

De Gaulle, Charles. *Memoirs of Hope: Renewal and Endeavor*. New York: Simon and Schuster, 1971.

De Gaulle en son siècle: Actes des Journées internationales tenue à l'Unesco, Paris, 19–24 novembre 1990. 5 vols. Institut Charles de Gaulle. Paris: La Documentation française, Plon, 1991–92.

De Gaulle et le Tiers Monde: Actes du Colloque organisé par la Faculté de Droit et des Sciences Economiques et l'Institut du Droit de la Paix et du Développement de l'Université de Nice et l'Institut Charles de Gaulle, Nice, 25–26 Février, 1983. Paris: A. Pedone, 1983.

De la Gorce, Paul-Marie. *Apogée et mort de la IVe République, 1952–1958*. Paris: Bernard Grasset, 1979.

———. *La guerre et l'atome*. Paris: Plon, 1985.

Dine, Philip. *Images of the Algerian War: French Fiction and Film, 1954–1962*. Oxford: Clarendon Press, 1994.

Droz, Bernard, and Evelyn Lever. *Histoire de la Guerre d'Algérie*. Paris: Seuil, 1982.

Dulac, André. *Nos guerres perdues*. Paris: Fayard, 1969.

Elgey, Georgette. *Histoire de la IVe République: La république des tourments*, tomes 1 et 2, *1954–1959*.

El Machat, Samya. *Les Etats-Unis et l'Algérie: De la Méconnaissance à la reconnaissance, 1945–1962*. Paris: L'Harmattan, 1996.

———. *Les Etats-Unis et le Maroc: Le choix stratégique, 1945–1959*. Paris: L'Harmattan, 1996.

———. *Les Etats-Unis et la Tunisie: De l'ambiguité à l'entente, 1945–1959*. Paris: L'Harmattan, 1996.

———. *Tunisie: Les chemins vers l'indépendance (1945–1956)*. Paris : L'Harmattan, 1992.

Ely, Général d'Armée Paul. *Mémories: Suez...le 13 mai*. Paris: Plon, 1969.

Evans, Martin. *The Memory of Resistance: French Opposition to the Algerian War, 1954–1962*. Oxford: Berg Publishers, 1997.

Fleury, Georges. *La Guerre en Algérie*. Paris: Plon, 1993.

Foccart, Jacques. *Foccart parle. Entretiens avec Philippe Gaillard*. Paris: Fayard/Jeune Afrique, 1995.

La France et l'OTAN, Actes du colloque tenu à l'Ecole militaire, 8,9, et 10 février 1996. Sous la direction de Vaïsse, Maurice, Melandri, Pierre, et Bozo, Frédéric. Centre de l'Histoire de la Défense Nationale. Brussels: Editions Complexe, 1996.

Furniss, Edgar S., Jr. *France, Troubled Ally: De Gaulle's Heritage and Prospects*. New York: Harper, 1960.

Fursdon, Edward. *The European Defense Community: A History*. New York: St. Martin's Press, 1980.

Geismar, Peter. *Fanon*. New York: Dial Press, 1971.

Gendzier, Irene L. *Notes from the Minefield: US Intervention in Lebanon and the Middle East 1945–1958*. New York: Columbia University Press, 1997.

Georges-Picot, Jacques. *The Real Suez Crisis: The End of a Great Nineteenth-Century Work*. New York: Harcourt, Brace & Jovanovich, 1975.

Gervereau, L., Jean-Pierre Rioux, and Benjamin Stora, editors. *La France en Guerre d'Algérie, Novembre 1954–Juillet 1962*. Paris: Bibliothèque de la Documentation Internationale et Contemporaine, 1992.

Gildea, Robert. *The Past in French History*. New Haven: Yale University Press, 1994.

Giles, Frank. *The Locust Years: The Story of the Fourth French Republic, 1946–1958*. New York: Carroll & Graf, 1991.

Goeau-Brissonnière, J. Y. *Mission secrète pour la paix en Algérie 1957*. Paris: Lieu Commin, 1992.

Goldschmidt, Bernard. *The Atomic Complex: A Worldwide Political History of Nuclear Energy*. La Grange Park, Ill.: American Nuclear Society, 1982.

Gordon, H. Philip. *A Certain Idea of France: French Security Policy and the Gaullist Legacy*. Princeton, N.J.: Princeton University Press, 1993.

Grimaud, Nicole. *La Tunisie à la recherche de sa sécurité*. Paris: Presses Universitaires de France, 1995.

Grosser, Alfred. *Affaires extérieures: La politique de la France 1944–1989*. Paris: Flammarion, 1989.

———. *French Foreign Policy under de Gaulle*. Translated by Lois Ames Pattison. Boston: Little Brown, 1967.

———. *The Western Alliance*. Translated by Michael Shaw. New York: Continuum, 1980.

Hahn, Peter L. *The United States, Great Britain, and Egypt 1945–1956: Strategy and Diplomacy in the Early Cold War*. Chapel Hill: University of North Carolina Press, 1991.

Harbi, Mohammed. *Les archives de la révolution algérienne*. Paris: Jeune Afrique, 1980.

Harrison, Alexander. *Challenging de Gaulle: The OAS and the Counterrevolution in Algeria, 1954–1962.* New York: Praeger, 1989.

Harrison, Michael M. *The Reluctant Ally: France and Atlantic Security.* Baltimore: Johns Hopkins University Press, 1981.

Hélie, Jerome. *Les Accords d'Evian: Histoire de la paix ratée en Algérie.* Paris: Olivier Orban, 1992.

Hoffmann, Stanley. *Decline or Renewal? France since the 1930s.* New York: Viking, 1974.

Hoopes, Townsend. *The Devil and John Foster Dulles.* Boston: Little Brown, 1973.

Horne, Alistair. *A Savage War of Peace: Algeria, 1954–1962.* New York: Viking Press, 1977.

Immerman, Richard H. "Confessions of an Eisenhower Revisionist: An Agonizing Reappraisal." *Diplomatic History* 14, 3 (Summer 1990):319–42.

———. *John Foster Dulles and the Diplomacy of the Cold War.* Princeton, N.J.: Princeton University Press, 1990.

Jebb, Lord Gladwyn. *De Gaulle's Europe or Why the General Says No.* London: Secker & Warburg, 1969.

Jouhaud, Edmond. *Ce que je n'ait pas dit: Sakiet, O.A.S., Evian.* Paris: Fayard, 1977.

———. *Serons-nous enfin compris?* Paris: Albin Michel, 1984.

Kahler, Miles. *Decolonization in Britain and France: The Domestic Consequences of International Relations.* Princeton, N.J.: Princeton University Press, 1984.

Kaplan, Jacob J., and Günther Schleininger. *The European Payments Union.* Oxford: Clarendon Press, 1989.

Kettle, Michael. *De Gaulle and Algeria, 1940–1960: From Mers El-Kébir to the Algiers Barricades.* London: Quartet Books, 1993.

Kissinger, Henry. *Diplomacy.* New York: Simon & Schuster, 1994.

Kolodziej, Edward. *French International Policy under de Gaulle and Pompidou.* Ithaca, N.Y.: Cornell University Press, 1974.

Kunz, Diane. *The Economic Diplomacy of the Suez Crisis.* Chapel Hill: University of North Carolina Press, 1991.

Kyle, Keith. *Suez.* London: Weidenfeld & Nicolson, 1991.

Lacorne, Denis, Jacques Rupnik, and Marie-France Toinet. *The Rise and Fall of Anti-Americanism: A Century of French Perception.* New York: St. Martin's Press, 1990.

Lacouture, Jean. *De Gaulle.* Vol. 2, *The Ruler, 1945–1970.* Translated by Alan Sheridan. New York: Norton, 1992.

Lacroix-Riz, Annie. *Les protectorats d'Afrique du Nord entre la France et Washington.* Paris: L'Harmattan, 1988.

Lebovics, Herman. *True France: The Wars over Cultural Identity, 1900–1945.* Ithaca, N.Y.: Cornell University Press, 1992.

Le Douarec, François. *Felix Gaillard, 1919–1970: Un destin inachevé.* Paris: Economica, 1991.

Ledwidge, Bernard. *De Gaulle et les Américains: Conversations avec Dulles, Eisenhower, Kennedy, Rusk, 1958–1964.* Paris: Flammarion, 1984.

Lefebvre, Denis. *Guy Mollet: Le mal aimé*. Paris: Plon, 1992.

Lefebvre, Jeffrey A. "Kennedy's Algerian Dilemma: Containment, Alliance Politics and the 'Rebel Dialogue.'" *Middle Eastern Studies* 35, 2 (April 1999): 61–90.

Lefeuvre, Daniel. *Chère Algérie 1930–1962: Comptes et mécomptes de la tutelle coloniale*. Paris: Société Française d'Histoire d'Outre-Mer, 1997.

Lefranc, Pierre. ... *Avec qui vous savez: Vingt-cinq ans avec de Gaulle*. Paris: Plon, 1979; London: Routledge, 1997.

Logevall, Fredrik. *Choosing War: The Lost Chance for Peace and the Escalation of War in Vietnam*. Berkeley: University of California Press, 1999.

Long, Olivier. *Le dossier secret des Accords d'Evian: Une mission suisse pour la paix en Algérie*. Lausanne: Editions 24 heures, 1988.

Louis, William Roger, and Roger Owen, editors. *Suez 1956: The Crisis and Its Consequences*. Oxford: Clarendon Press, 1989.

Luethy, Herbert. *France Against Herself*. New York: Praeger, 1955.

Lynch, Frances M. B. *France and the International Economy: From Vichy to the Treaty of Rome*. London, New York: Routledge, 1997.

Mahoney, Daniel J. *De Gaulle: Statesmanship, Grandeur, and Modern Democracy*. Westport, Conn.: Praeger, 1996.

Maillard, Pierre. *De Gaulle et l'Allemagne: Le rêve inachevé*. Paris: Plon, 1990.

———. *De Gaulle et l'Europe: Entre la nation et Maastricht*. Paris: Tallandier, 1995.

Malek, Redha. *L'Algérie à Evian: Histoire des négociations secrètes, 1956–1962*. Paris: Seuil, 1995.

Maran, Rita. *Torture: The Role of Ideology in the French-Algerian War*. New York: Praeger, 1989.

Marseille, Jacques. *Empire colonial et capitalisme français: Histoire d'un divorce*. Paris: Albin Michel, 1984.

McMahon, Robert J. "Eisenhower and Third World Nationalism: A Critique of the Revisionists." *Political Science Quarterly* 101, 3 (1986): 453–75.

Melandri, Pierre. *Les Etats-Unis et le défi européen, 1955–1958*. Paris: Presses Universitaires de France, 1975.

———. "La France devant l'opinion américaine: Le retour de De Gaulle, début 1958–printemps 1959." *Relations Internationales* 58 (Eté 1989): 195–215.

Melanson, Richard, and David Mayers, editors. *Reevaluating Eisenhower: American Foreign Policy in the 1950s*. Urbana: University of Illinois Press, 1987.

Melnik, Constantin. *Mille jours à Matignon: Raisons d'état sous de Gaulle, Guerre d'Algérie 1959–1962*. Paris: Bernard Grasset, 1988.

Ménager, B., editor. *Guy Mollet: Un camarade en république*. Lille: Presses Universitaires de Lille, 1987.

Menard, Orville. *The Army and the Fifth Republic*. Lincoln: University of Nebraska Press, 1967.

Merrill, Dennis. "America Encounters the Third World," *Diplomatic History* 16 (Spring 1992): 325–31.

Milward, Alan S. *The European Rescue of the Nation State*. Berkeley: University of California Press, 1992.

Miquel, Pierre. *La Guerre d'Algérie*. Paris: Fayard, 1993.

Morin, Jean. *De Gaulle et l'Algérie: Mon témoignage, 1960–1962*. Paris: Albin Michel, 1999; New York: Norton, 1990.

Mortimer, Edward. *France and the Africans, 1944–1960: A Political History*. New York: Walker and Company, 1969.

Murphy, Robert. *Diplomat among Warriors*. New York: Doubleday & Co., 1964.

Nutting, Anthony. *No End of a Lesson: The Story of Suez*. New York: Clarkson N. Potter, 1967.

Paxton, Robert O., and Nicholas Wahl, editors. *De Gaulle and the United States: A Centennial Reappraisal*. Oxford: Berg Publishers, 1994.

Peyrefitte, Alain. *C'était de Gaulle*. Paris: Fayard, 1994.

Pickles, Dorothy. *Algeria and France: From Colonialism to Cooperation*. New York: Praeger, 1963.

Pineau, Christian. *1956/Suez*. Paris: R. Laffont, 1976.

Pitman, Paul Marsh III. "France's European Choices: The Political Economy of European Integration in the 1950s." Ph.D. thesis, Columbia University, 1997.

Poniatowski, Michel. *Mémoires*. Tome I. Paris: Plon, 1997.

Powers, Thomas. *The Man Who Kept the Secrets: Richard Helms and the CIA*. New York: Alfred A. Knopf, 1979.

Rabe, Stephen G. "Eisenhower Revisionism." *Diplomatic History* 17 (Winter 1993): 97–115.

Rioux, Jean-Pierre. *The Fourth Republic, 1944–1958*. New York: Cambridge University Press, 1987.

———, editor. *La Guerre d'Algérie et les Français*. Paris: Fayard, 1990.

Rioux, Jean-Pierre, and J. F. Sirinelli, editors. *La Guerre d'Algérie et les intellectuals français*. Paris: Editions Complexe, 1991.

Ross, Kristin. *Fast Cars, Clean Bodies: Decolonization and the Reordering of French Culture*. Cambridge, Mass.: MIT Press, 1995.

Roy, Jules. *Mémoires barbares*. Paris: Albin Michel, 1989.

Rudelle, Odile. *Mai 1958: De Gaulle et la République*. Paris: Plon, 1988.

Ruedy, John. Pp. 114–26 of *Modern Algeria: The Origins and Development of a Nation*. Bloomington: University of Indiana Press, 1992.

Ruscio, Alain. *La décolonisation tragique: Une histoire de la décolonisation française, 1945–1962*. Paris: Editions Sociales, 1987.

Sampson, Anthony. *The Seven Sisters: The Great Oil Companies and the World They Made*. New York: Viking Press, 1975.

Schalk, David L. "Has France's Marrying Her Century Cured the Algerian Syndrome?" *Historical Reflections* 25, 1 (1999): 149–64.

———. *War and the Ivory Tower: Algeria and Vietnam*. New York: Oxford University Press, 1991.

Scheinman, Lawrence. *Atomic Energy in France under the Fourth Republic*. Princeton, N.J.: Princeton University Press, 1965.

Schoenbrun, David. *As France Goes*. New York: Harper & Bros., 1957.

Serra, Enrico, editor. *Il relancio dell'Europa et i Trattati di Roma*. Brussels and Milan: A. Giufré, 1989.

Silj, Alessandro. *Europe's Political Puzzle: A Study of the Fouchet Negotiations and the 1963 Veto.* Occasional Papers in International Affairs no. 17, Center for International Affairs. Harvard University, 1967.

Smith, Tony. *The French Stake in Algeria.* Ithaca, N.Y.: Cornell University Press, 1978.

Soustelle, Jacques. *A New Road for France.* Translated by Benjamin Protter. New York: Robert Speller & Sons, 1965.

Soutou, Georges-Henri. "Les accords de 1957 et 1958: Vers une communauté stratégique et nucléaire entre la France, l'Allemagne et l'Italie." *Matériaux pour l'histoire de notre temps* 31 (Avril-Juin 1993): 1–12.

Stora, Benjamin. *La gangrène et l'oubli: La mémoire de la Guerre d'Algérie.* Paris: La Découverte, 1991.

———. *Histoire de la Guerre d'Algérie, 1954–1962.* Paris: La Découverte, 1993.

Sulzberger, C. L. *The Test: De Gaulle and Algeria.* New York: Harcourt, Brace & World, 1962.

Talbott, John. *The War Without a Name: France in Algeria, 1954–1962.* New York: Knopf, 1980.

Terrenoire, Louis. *De Gaulle et l'Algérie: Témoignage pour l'histoire.* Paris: Fayard, 1964.

Thomas, Abel. *Comment Israel fut sauvée: Les secrets de l'expédition de Suez.* Paris: Albin Michel, 1978.

Thomas, Martin. "The Dilemmas of an Ally of France: Britain's Policy towards the Algerian Rebellion, 1954–1962." *Journal of Imperial and Commonwealth History* 23, 1 (January 1955): 129–54.

———. *The French North African Crisis: Colonial Breakdown and Anglo-French Relations, 1945–1962.* London: Macmillan, 2000.

Trachtenberg, Marc. *A Constructed Peace: The Making of the European Settlement, 1945–1963.* Princeton, N.J.: Princeton University Press, 1999.

———. *History and Strategy.* Princeton, N.J.: Princeton University Press, 1991.

Triboulet, Raymond. *Un ministre du Général.* Paris: Plon, 1985.

Tricot, Bernard. *Mémoires.* Paris: Quai Voltaire, 1994.

———. *Les sentiers de la paix: Algérie 1958–1962.* Paris: Plon, 1962.

Troen, S. I., and Moshe Shemesh. *The Suez-Sinai Crisis 1956: Retrospective and Reappraisal.* New York: Columbia University Press, 1990.

Vaïsse, Maurice. *Alger: Le putsch.* Brussels: Editions Complexe, 1983.

———. *La grandeur: Politique étrangère du général de Gaulle 1958–1959.* Paris: Fayard, 1998.

———. "Aux origines du memorandum de septembre 1958." *Relations Internationales* 58 (Eté 1989): 253–68.

———, editor. *La France et l'opération de Suez de 1956.* Paris: Centre d'Études d'Histoire de la Defense, 1997.

Vidal-Naquet, Pierre. *Face à la raison d'état: Un historien dans la Guerre d'Algérie.* Paris: La Découverte, 1989.

Wall, Irwin M. *L'influence américaine sur la politique française, 1945–1954.* Paris: André Balland, 1989.

———. "The United States, Algeria, and the Fall of the Fourth French Republic." *Diplomatic History* 18, 4 (Fall 1994): 489–512.

———. *The United States and the Making of Postwar France, 1945–1954.* New York: Cambridge University Press, 1991.

Weil, Martin. *A Pretty Good Club: The Founding Fathers of the U.S. Foreign Service.* New York: Norton, 1978.

Williams, Philip M. *Wars, Plots and Scandals in Postwar France.* New York: Cambridge University Press, 1970.

Willis, F. Roy. *France, Germany, and the New Europe.* Stanford, Calif.: Stanford University Press, 1965.

Winand, Pascaline. *Eisenhower, Kennedy, and the United States of Europe.* New York: St. Martin's Press, 1993.

Winock, Michel. *La République se meurt: Chronique 1956–1958.* Paris: Seuil, 1978.

Young, Marilyn. *The Vietnam Wars, 1945–1990.* New York: Harper Collins, 1991.

Zingg, Paul J. "The Cold War in North Africa: American Foreign Policy and Postwar Muslim Nationalism, 1945–1963." *The Historian* 39, 1 (November 1976): 40–61.

Index

Text:	10/13 Sabon
Display:	Sabon
Composition:	Impressions Book and Journal Services, Inc.
Printing and binding:	Sheridan Books, Inc.